■ Reward and Punishment in S

Series in Human Cooperation

PAUL VAN LANGE Series Editor

BOOKS IN THE SERIES

Reward and Punishment in Social Dilemmas
Edited by Paul Van Lange, Bettina Rockenbach, and Toshio Yamagishi

Reward and Punishment in Social Dilemmas

EDITED BY
Paul A. M. Van Lange
Bettina Rockenbach
Toshio Yamagishi

OXFORD
UNIVERSITY PRESS

Oxford University Press is a department of the University of Oxford.
It furthers the University's objective of excellence in research, scholarship,
and education by publishing worldwide.

Oxford   New York
Auckland   Cape Town   Dar es Salaam   Hong Kong   Karachi
Kuala Lumpur   Madrid   Melbourne   Mexico City   Nairobi
New Delhi   Shanghai   Taipei   Toronto

With offices in
Argentina   Austria   Brazil   Chile   Czech Republic   France   Greece
Guatemala   Hungary   Italy   Japan   Poland   Portugal   Singapore
South Korea   Switzerland   Thailand   Turkey   Ukraine   Vietnam

Oxford is a registered trademark of Oxford University Press
in the UK and certain other countries.

Published in the United States of America by
Oxford University Press
198 Madison Avenue, New York, NY 10016

© Oxford University Press 2014

All rights reserved. No part of this publication may be reproduced, stored in a
retrieval system, or transmitted, in any form or by any means, without the prior
permission in writing of Oxford University Press, or as expressly permitted by law,
by license, or under terms agreed with the appropriate reproduction rights organization.
Inquiries concerning reproduction outside the scope of the above should be sent to the
Rights Department, Oxford University Press, at the address above.

You must not circulate this work in any other form
and you must impose this same condition on any acquirer.

Library of Congress Cataloging-in-Publication Data
Reward and punishment in social dilemmas / edited by Paul A.M. Van Lange,
Bettina Rockenbach, Toshio Yamagishi.
   pages cm
Includes bibliographical references and index.
ISBN 978-0-19-930073-0 (hardback)—ISBN 978-0-19-930074-7 (paperback)
1. Cooperativeness. 2. Reward (Psychology) 3. Punishment. 4. Incentive (Psychology)
5. Social interaction. I. Lange, Paul A. M. Van. II. Rockenbach, Bettina.
III. Yamagishi, Toshio, 1948–
HM716.R49 2014
302—dc23
2013039355

9 8 7 6 5 4 3 2 1
Printed in the United States of America
on acid-free paper

CONTENTS

Preface	*vii*
Contributors	*xi*

1. Reward and Punishment in Social Dilemmas: An Introduction — 1
   PAUL A. M. VAN LANGE, BETTINA ROCKENBACH, AND TOSHIO YAMAGISHI

PART ONE The Workings of Reward and Punishment

2. When Punishment Supports Cooperation: Insights from Voluntary Contribution Experiments — 17
   LOUIS PUTTERMAN

3. How (and When) Reward and Punishment Promote Cooperation: An Interdependence Theoretical Perspective — 34
   DANIEL BALLIET AND PAUL A. M. VAN LANGE

4. Regulating the Regulation: Norms about Punishment — 52
   PONTUS STRIMLING AND KIMMO ERIKSSON

5. For the Common Good? The Use of Sanctions in Social Dilemmas — 70
   ERIC VAN DIJK, LAETITIA B. MULDER, AND ERIK W. DE KWAADSTENIET

PART TWO The Organization of Reward and Punishment

6. Promoting Cooperation: The Distribution of Reward and Punishment Power — 87
   DANIELE NOSENZO AND MARTIN R. SEFTON

7. Broadening the Motivation to Cooperate: Revisiting the Role of Sanctions in Social Dilemmas — 115
   XIAO-PING CHEN, CAROLYN T. DANG, AND FONG KENG-HIGHBERGER

8. Leadership, Reward and Punishment in Sequential Public Goods Experiments — 133
   MATTHIAS SUTTER AND M. FERNANDA RIVAS

PART THREE ■ **The Functions of Reward and Punishment In Society**

9. Social Decision-making in Childhood and Adolescence 161
EVELINE A. CRONE, GEERT-JAN WILL, SANDY OVERGAAUW, AND BERNA GÜROĞLU

10. Why Sanction? Functional Causes of Punishment and Reward 182
PAT BARCLAY AND TOKO KIYONARI

11. Self-governance Through Altruistic Punishment? 197
NIKOS NIKIFORAKIS

12. Beyond Kin: Cooperation in a Tribal Society 214
PIERRE LIENARD

Index *235*

PREFACE

Social dilemmas pose a key challenge to human society. Conflicts between self-interest and collective interests are not easy. Whether we want to admit it or not, making choices that serve the self rather than the collective are tempting, sometimes even when we think that many other people will make a choice serving the collective. And, in fact, many social dilemmas pose an even greater challenge, in that it is self-interest that materializes immediately or in the short-term, whereas collective interests materialize in the longer term. Scarce fish might be enjoyed in the here and now, but if we all do, that fish might over time be depleted. We need to contribute to important public goods, such as high quality libraries, public television, and safe and clean environments, but the individuals' costs often precede the enjoyment of these public goods.

Many people may have their implicit theories as how to approach social dilemmas from an individual perspective or "manage" social dilemmas from a collective perspective. Scientists, professionals, and laypeople alike are likely to agree that some form of reward (for collectively desirable behavior) and punishment (for collectively undesired behavior) should be effective. After all, reward and punishment are general tools that the many authorities use to promote behavior that is expected to enhance collective interests. Governments use subsidies and taxes as tools to promote cooperation, and management in organizations may use positive evaluations along with additional pay raises to promote various citizenship behaviors and negative evaluations along perhaps with no pay raise when employees fail to meet criteria for productivity. Likewise, the topic of reward and punishment has also received much attention in the scientific literature. Broad concepts such as reinforcement, conditioning, and incentives are closely linked to rewards and punishment. The literature is even broader in that reward and punishment are also topics important to learning, parenting, or teaching. It is important to note the obvious: Our scope is not that broad. Rather, our focus is on reward and punishment in *social dilemmas*, a topic that is already sufficiently broad. And as one can witness in the literature, and in this book, this topic is addressed by scientists working in a variety of disciplines, including anthropologists, biologists, economists, evolutionary scientists, neuroscientists, psychologists, political scientists, and sociologists.

While the social dilemma literature has addressed reward and punishment (or sanctioning) for several decades, we have witnessed an enormous growth in research on reward and punishment in social dilemmas in the past 10 to 15 years. Many intriguing questions were asked and addressed by researchers working in various disciplines. For example, researchers seek to understand the effectiveness of reward and punishment as tools for promoting cooperation, thereby also addressing the efficiency of these incentives. Also, there is research focusing on emotions and the neurobiological processes that might help explain why people punish others in the absence of any tangible benefit for themselves. Such questions are getting at the workings of reward and punishment. Another emerging theme is how reward and punishment are organized? Do we need all people, only some people, or perhaps only one person, to administer incentives such as rewards and punishments? Again, questions regarding effectiveness and efficiency become important. A final emerging theme is how rewards and punishment are used in society, what form they might take, how these acts might in turn be rewarded, and whether reward and punishment may be accompanied or preceded by other tools, such as gossip. Such questions are getting at the functions of reward and punishment in society.

We have used three broad themes as an organizing framework for the chapters on reward and punishment: The workings of reward and punishment, the organization of reward and punishment, and the functions of reward and punishment in society. This book benefits from contributions of scientists that are all active researchers on the topic of reward and punishment in social dilemmas, often public good dilemmas. Because the contributors differ in their scientific backgrounds, be it anthropology, economics, neuroscience, or psychology, the chapters complement each other in various ways. Indeed, this book series was inspired by two general ideas. First, we wanted a topic, within the social dilemma literature, that is key to understanding human cooperation and that has generated considerable research. Second, we believe that for many broad topics in social dilemmas, it takes the expertise from scientists working in different fields and disciplines to make scientific progress in understanding how exactly cooperation can be promoted. For such reasons, we invited researchers working from different perspectives and backgrounds, but who all seek to answer the question how reward or punishment can promote cooperation, to contribute to this book project. And we were fortunate that nearly all of the scientists that we invited were happy to contribute to this book project, and did so in time.

We hope to reach a broad audience of scientists in various fields and disciplines, as well as the interested reader or practitioner who is committed to managing and resolving social dilemmas in various domains of social life. We should add that this book is primarily aimed at the scientific community of researchers interested in the question of human cooperation. After all, the book provides an up-to-date overview of many of the key issues in reward and punishment in social dilemmas. As such, the book should be especially informative to students and faculty working in these areas. At the same time, our view, perhaps slightly biased, is also that the book should also be relevant to scientists and practitioners in areas such as conflict resolution, management, morality, fairness, negotiation, and public policy. Reward and punishment in social dilemmas are at heart of these issues, as one could also infer from the programs of research that are covered in this book. As such, we hope the book will be helpful to a relatively broader field of students, faculty, and professionals working in areas that are importantly linked to social dilemmas.

We would like to extend our gratitude to a number of people for making valuable contributions to this book project. To begin with, we wish to thank the community of all social dilemma researchers who collectively have contributed to this interesting, and important, theme. Moreover, this book grew out of the bi-annual international conferences on social dilemmas. The first conference was held in Groningen, the Netherlands, in 1984, and the most recent conference, was held in Zurich, in 2013. In between there were conferences in the United States, Netherlands, Japan, Australia, Germany, Israel, Poland, and Sweden, a period during which the community of social dilemma researchers that attends these conferences grew from around 15 in 1984 to about 150 scientists. And these scientists work in various disciplines, adopt diverse theoretical perspectives, address complementary topics in social dilemmas—and they work in different parts of the world. It was not only the topic as such, but also the increasing popularity and breadth of social dilemma research, that our Publisher seems to appreciate. Indeed, we want to thank Abby Gross who has expressed her genuine enthusiasm and commitment from the very beginning at a meeting of the *Society of Personality and Social Psychology*, and throughout the three years after that meeting while we edited the book.

Finally, we hope that you will enjoy reading this book—as a student, a fellow academic, teacher, and perhaps practitioner, or member of the general public—and that it makes a meaningful difference, even if only a small difference, in how you think about your next step in research on human cooperation, in your theoretical work on social dilemmas, or in the ways in which you effectively promote cooperation in your everyday lives and society at large.

The Editors, June 2013

CONTRIBUTORS

Daniel Balliet
Department of Social Psychology
VU University
Amsterdam, The Netherlands

Pat Barclay
Department of Psychology
University of Guelph
Guelph, Canada

Xiao-Ping Chen
Department of Management and Organization, Michael G. Foster School of Business
University of Washington
Seattle, Washington

Eveline A. Crone
Department of Developmental and Educational Psychology
Leiden University
Leiden, The Netherlands

Carolyn T. Dang
Department of Management and Organization, Michael G. Foster School of Business
University of Washington
Seattle, Washington

Eric van Dijk
Department of Social and Organizational Psychology
Leiden University
Leiden, The Netherlands

Kimmo Eriksson
Department of Mathematics
Mälardalen University
Västerås, Sweden

Berna Güroğlu
Department of Developmental and Educational Psychology
Leiden University
Leiden, The Netherlands

Fong Keng-Highberger
Department of Management and Organization, Michael G. Foster School of Business
University of Washington
Seattle, Washington

Toko Kiyonari
School of Social Informatics
Aoyama Gakuin University
Kanagawa, Japan

Erik W. de Kwaadsteniet
Department of Social and Organizational Psychology
Leiden University
Leiden, The Netherlands

Pierre Lienard
Department of Anthropology
University of Nevada
Las Vegas, Nevada

Laetitia B. Mulder
Department of Business and Economics
Groningen University
Groningen, The Netherlands

Nikos Nikiforakis
Department of Economics
New York University
Abu Dhabi, United Arab Emirates

Daniele Nosenzo
School of Economics
University of Nottingham
Nottingham, United Kingdom

Sandy Overgaauw
Department of Developmental and Educational Psychology
Leiden University
Leiden, The Netherlands

Louis Putterman
Department of Economics
Brown University
Providence, Rhode Island

M. Fernanda Rivas
Economics Program
Middle East Technical University
Northern Cyprus Campus

Bettina Rockenbach
Economic and Social Sciences Department
University of Cologne
Cologne, Germany

Martin R. Sefton
School of Economics
University of Nottingham
Nottingham, United Kingdom

Pontus Strimling
Center for Studies of Cultural Evolution
Stockholm University
Stockholm, Sweden

Matthias Sutter
Department of Economics, European University Institute
 and University of Cologne
Florence, Italy

Paul A. M. Van Lange
Department of Social Psychology
VU University
Amsterdam, The Netherlands

Geert-Jan Will
Department of Developmental and Educational Psychology
Leiden University
Leiden, The Netherlands

Toshio Yamagishi
Department of Behavioral Science
The University of Tokyo
Tokyo, Japan

1 Reward and Punishment in Social Dilemmas: An Introduction

■ PAUL A. M. VAN LANGE,
BETTINA ROCKENBACH,
AND TOSHIO YAMAGISHI

Abstract
While the social dilemma literature has addressed reward and punishment (or sanctioning) for several decades, we have witnessed an enormous growth in research on reward and punishment in social dilemmas in the past 10 to 15 years. Many intriguing questions were asked and addressed by researchers working in various disciplines. A final emerging theme is how rewards and punishment are used in society, what form they might take, how these acts might in turn be rewarded, and whether reward and punishment may be accompanied or preceded by other tools such as gossip. Such questions are getting at the functions of reward and punishment in society.

Social dilemmas pose real challenges to humankind. They did so in the past, they do so now, and they will do so in the future: Social dilemmas cross "the borders of time." Our ancestors must have faced many social dilemmas in their small groups and societies. The sharing or gathering of scarce resources, such as food or shelter, often must have been accompanied by conflicts between self-interest and collective interest. Likewise, in our contemporary society, we often face social dilemmas at home, at work, or at many other places where we are interdependent with other people. Who is going to do the labor that serves the collective but that most people do not prefer to do themselves, such as doing the dishes at home? Newspapers are filled with articles about societal problems that frequently are rooted in conflicts between self-interest and collective interest, such as littering in parks, free-riding on public transportation, evading taxes, or exploiting natural resources. And social dilemmas may involve many people who do not know each other, may include different countries, and for some issues, such as global change, may concern the entire world. In many respects, social dilemmas also cross "the borders of space."

In his *Annual Review of Psychology* article, Robyn Dawes (1980) was one of the first who formally coined the term *social dilemma*, which he defined as a situation in which (a) each decision maker has a dominant strategy dictating non-cooperation (i.e., an option that produces the highest outcome, regardless of others' choices), and (b) if all choose this dominant strategy, all end up worse off than if all had cooperated (i.e., an inefficient equilibrium). Since that seminal paper, several definitions have been advanced. For example, some theorists suggest that social dilemmas capture not only the well-known prisoner's dilemma, but also games that are quite similar in structure (such as Assurance and Chicken). Yet others have emphasized the temporal dimension, whereby self-interest is often satisfied (or not) in the short term, whereas collective interests often stretch over longer periods of time. As such, social dilemmas may be defined as situations in which a non-cooperative course of action is (at times) tempting for each individual in that it yields superior (often short-term) outcomes for self, and if all pursue this non-cooperative course of action, they are (often in the longer-term) worse off than if they had cooperated (see Van Lange, Joireman, Parks, & Van Dijk, 2013; p. 126).

REWARD AND PUNISHMENT

General solutions to social dilemmas may easily come to mind: When one wants to encourage cooperation, make it more attractive. When one wants to discourage noncooperation, make it less attractive, or more unattractive. Both truisms already seem to underline the relevance of reward and punishment, respectively. While these interventions seem straightforward at the general level, at the level of implementation the issues become increasingly complex. Questions such as "Who is able to reward?," "Who is able to punish?," and "What behavior constitutes such sanctions?" may well be some of the key issues that render the science of rewards and punishment more complex than one might initially imagine. Issues that make it even more challenging are those revolving around the time horizon (or simply duration of the interaction), availability of information regarding one another's actions, or information regarding others' provision of rewards and punishments. The complexity of reward and punishment is also conveyed by the variety of constructs that scientists have used in reference to reward and punishment. Indeed, concepts such as reinforcement, incentives, payoffs, sanctions, temptation, the sucker's payoff, and instrumental cooperation are all linked to the broad notion of reward and punishment.

Clearly, the concepts of reward and punishment go back some time in the history of research on social dilemmas. But the scientific meaning of reward and punishment has been subject to some conceptual development, continuity *and* change, over the years. Up until the early eighties, reward and punishment were linked to the outcome matrix, and indicated how good or "rewarding" the outcomes are following from mutual cooperation, and how bad or "costly" the outcomes are following from mutual noncooperation. With tools such as taxing noncooperation, or rewarding cooperation, authorities were often in the position to reward massive cooperation and to punish massive noncooperation by altering the outcome matrix. For example, in an effort to promote commuting with public transportation rather than cars (to reduce congestion and polluted air) the government could seek to make public transportation cheaper, more comfortable, and more reliable, along with perhaps taxing gasoline, especially when many tend to use the car. In doing so, authorities can affect the outcome matrix in important ways. Later, reward and punishment were linked to reward and sanctioning systems—to actions that changed the outcomes for particular individuals. In particular, this line of research focuses on people's willingness to contribute to the installment or maintenance of, for example, a system that would punish free-riders. And more recently, the attention has shifted toward the possibility of individual members involved in the social dilemma itself to reward or punish each other. We discuss these developments in the following sections in greater detail.

Reward and Punishment as Part of the Outcome Structure

In some earlier research in psychology, the constructs of reward and punishment were used in reference to the outcomes (payoffs) obtained after mutual cooperation (Reward) or the outcomes (payoffs) obtained after mutual non-cooperation (Punishment). The outcomes of Reward and Punishment were distinguished from each other, as well as from the highest possible outcome (Temptation) that would be obtained if an individual is the only one making a noncooperative choice, and the lowest possible outcome (Sucker's outcome) that would be obtained if one is the only one making a cooperative choice. This also provided the definition of the outcome structure underlying a prisoner's dilemma: *Temptation > Reward > Punishment > Sucker*.

Rapoport (1967) used these parameters to calculate an index of cooperation. The difference between outcomes for Reward and Punishment emphasize how much mutual cooperation should be preferred to mutual noncooperation (this is sometimes called collective rationality). The difference between the outcomes for Temptation and the Sucker is the difference between the best possible outcome through noncooperation and worst possible outcome through cooperation. The index of cooperation is then formally expressed as:

$$Index\ of\ Cooperation = \frac{R - P}{T - S}$$

The outcomes must conform to the structure of outcomes that define a prisoner's dilemma (T > R > P > S). Capturing a broader range of extreme outcome structures, the index of cooperation can vary from 0 to 1, but prisoner's dilemmas often yield indices with intermediate values. The important point to be made is that in "older" research of social dilemmas, reward and punishment were part of the outcome structure. They defined how good the outcomes following from mutual cooperation are, and how poor the outcomes following from mutual noncooperation are. And people do respond to these variations in Reward and Punishment.

Several studies have subsequently examined the impact of the index of cooperation on behavior in social dilemmas. For example, cooperation can be enhanced by both decreasing the outcome associated with noncooperative behavior, and increasing the incentive associated with cooperative behavior (e.g., Kelley & Grzelak, 1972; Marwell & Ames, 1979; Oliver, 1980). Research has also demonstrated that people are much more likely to cooperate to the extent that interdependent others can benefit more from it (Komorita et al., 1980). There is also some evidence suggesting that the effects of knowing that others might be able to reward cooperation or punish noncooperation can promote cooperation (Komorita & Barth, 1985). Of course, in dyads, similar mechanisms might be at work in accounting for the strong effects of direct reciprocity, and variants of Tit-For-Tat, that promote cooperation (Axelrod, 1984; see also Parks & Rumble, 2001; Sattler & Kerr, 1991; Van Lange, Ouwerkerk, & Tazelaar, 2002). Generally, the influence of payoff structure has been shown to be strong not only in experimental work on social dilemmas, but also in field studies. Early research by Maki, Hoffman and Berk (1978), for example, found that monetary reward for electricity conservation was one of the most effective means to attaining electricity conservation. Other work has also revealed that "subsidizing" cooperative behavior, and taxing noncooperative behavior are indeed effective tools for promoting cooperation. Although they sometimes can have negative side effects, such as undermining intrinsic motivation for cooperation or undermining needs for autonomy, the effects of rewards and punishments presumably are effective because they weaken the conflict between self-interest and collective interest.

Reward and Punishment as (Collective) Sanctioning Systems

In the mid-eighties, a new approach to the effects of incentives was introduced. In particular, Yamagishi (1986a, b) outlined two theoretical challenges in theorizing at the time. He noted that forms of rewards and punishment that people might implement in the context of dyadic interaction could not be readily applied to groups larger than dyads, especially large groups. In particular, he noted that several rational choice approaches would prescribe free-riding in the context of public goods that involve many members. Yamagishi noted that from a rational choice perspective, people need to be able to contribute to structural changes to the public good. One such structural change would be the possibility to contribute to a sanctioning system that would punish (or reward) free-riding (or cooperative behavior). Second, Yamagishi argued that allowing a contribution to an effective sanctioning system should remove one important barrier for cooperation: If the sanctioning system functions well, those who are interested in achieving mutual cooperation in groups should less strongly fear free-riding. That is, even people with low trust are likely to think that most people will not free-ride on the efforts of others if they realize the system will punish them for doing so.

In one of his initial studies, Yamagishi (1986a) examined contributions to public goods dilemmas in four-person groups, and compared three conditions: a public good without a sanctioning system, and a public good with a weak or a strong sanctioning system. If there was a sanctioning system, participants were enabled to contribute to a "punishment fund" which was the system that would punish the least contributing member in the four-person group by the amount that was collected in the punishment fund (weak sanctioning) or twice that amount (strong sanctioning). One of the key findings was that levels of cooperation were higher in the public goods that included a sanctioning system than those that did not. The level of cooperation was particularly high in the strong sanctioning condition (on average, 74% of their endowment), compared to weak sanctioning (52%) and no sanctioning (44%) conditions. It was also striking to see that, unlike the no or weak sanctioning systems, participants with low trust increase their level of cooperation over time in the public goods with a strong sanctioning system. And finally, participants did not really contribute much of their endowment to the punishment fund, suggesting that the mere threat of punishment was strong enough to promote cooperation in a sustainable manner.

Subsequent studies replicated many of the patterns described previously, across samples in Japan and the United States (Yamagishi, 1998b). Moreover, there is interesting evidence suggesting that when social dilemmas or public goods are seriously challenged, participants are more likely to contribute to the punishment fund to promote cooperation (Yamagishi, 1988a). Such findings are consistent with other evidence indicating that people are more likely to endorse and contribute to structural changes, such as privatization (Cass & Edney, 1978) or leadership (Messick et al., 1983), when many members do not cooperate or contribute to the public good. The studies by Yamagishi also contributed to the realization that many social dilemmas may pose a second challenge to participants—whether or not to contribute to the sanctioning system.

Scientists increasingly recognized that social dilemmas also may include a second-order social dilemma (or *second order public good*, Oliver, 1980), in that it is tempting to free-ride on others to contribute to the punishment fund to sanction free-riders. Similarly, one might argue that voting, and other forms of political action, may be characterized as a second-order social dilemma, in that people contribute resources (such as time and effort) to a particular form of government (and governance) that they believe should help resolve various social dilemmas, including the free-rider problem (even literally, in public transportation). It does seem to be the case that individuals, and nations as well, differ in their ideology and political views as to how much a higher authority should "regulate" individuals with sanctioning.

In the history of social dilemma research, it is especially Gerret Hardin (1968), who drew attention to the idea that societies are often unable to regulate themselves in such a manner as to maintain shared resources that are threatened by individual overconsumption. In particular, by describing the "tragedy of the commons," Hardin (1968) provides anecdotal evidence showing how shared resources may become depleted or even destroyed when people can continue to consume (or harvest) from that shared resource. In particular, he described why shepherds want to add sheep to the commons (shared pasture, in this case), and how such individually beneficial actions might lead to detrimental outcomes for the collective: the depletion of the commons from which they harvest. By adding sheep, the individual shepherd could receive benefits, but such actions undermine the quality or vitality of commons that is shared by all. The solution he proposed for similar social dilemmas, or resource dilemmas, is not to rely on "conscience" or an individual's self-control to exercise restraint on their consumption. Rather, he proposed a system of collective control, phrased as "mutual coercion, mutually agreed upon," by which individuals agree to the restriction of individual freedom to preserve shared resources. In his influential writings, Hardin did not express much optimism for collective success when individuals or local communities act in systems with considerable freedom (Hardin & Baden, 1977).

But since then, there is evidence that groups and local communities are quite able to organize themselves and "manage" themselves the social dilemmas as they appear—and as they pose a challenge. In particular, Ostrom (1990) developed views as to how social dilemmas, in this particular case ensuring the maintenance of natural resources and minimizing the risk of ecosystem collapses, can be best regulated. In essence, she argued that local communities are in a superior position to regulate themselves without much interference from global authorities. A later experiment indeed provided evidence for some of this reasoning (Ostrom, Walker, & Gardner, 1992). They designed a common pool resource game in which participants in small groups could punish one another at a cost to themselves. Also, as in many local communities, this experiment involved repeated interaction and the group did not change in composition. One of the main findings was that people did punish, and they did so selectively: They punished especially those members who tended to gain a reputation as a free-rider. So, over time, they were able to self-organize through punishment so that cooperation was promoted and sustained. Moreover, it need not always be a global or national authority, or even institute, to promote cooperation through sanctioning. Individuals themselves, or the "peers," also seem quite willing to enact sanctions, thereby promoting cooperation (Ostrom, Burger, Field, Norgaard, & Policansky, 1999).

Costly Punishment and Reward Among Group Members

Over a decade ago, two experimental economists developed a public good dilemma in which peer punishment was the primary focus of their attention (Fehr & Gächter, 2000, 2002). In doing so, they were also inspired by the strong emotions that participants expressed, in particular after hearing that (some) others had not cooperated, or had contributed very little to the public good. They designed a public good dilemma in which it was possible to punish others, and in doing so, they were particularly interested in examining whether people were willing to punish at a cost to self, and with no material gain for themselves. So, after each trial in which the individuals in the four-person groups had made a decision how much to contribute to the public good, they were informed about one another's contributions. Great care was taken that participants did not know each other, and that they did not meet repeatedly with the same person; also, they received no information about others' past behaviors, and so participants were not responding to information about the others' reputation. The goal was to examine people's willingness to punish in the absence of reputational concerns by which they themselves could benefit from their own punishment. Note that this design was different from the earlier-discussed study by Ostrom et al. (1992), whose goal was to explore the benefits of punishment through reputational concerns in small groups.

The complete absence of both repeated interaction and reputation information ensured that direct reciprocity or indirect reciprocity were excluded as mechanisms underlying cooperation, which allowed Fehr and Gächter to study punishment in the absence of material gain for self. Only (unknown) others in next interactions could benefit from such punishment, and in this sense, punishment was labelled altruistic. Under these controlled conditions, Fehr and Gächter showed that people were quite willing to punish—and to do so at a material cost to themselves. It was also evident that most punishments were directed at defectors or free-riders who contributed below average, and most of the punishment was executed by cooperators who contributed above average: In fact, this pattern was observed in 74% of all punishment acts. They also provided some evidence that free-riding causes strong negative emotions, and that people expect such emotional reactions from other people as well. Moreover, people were more prepared to punish if the free-rider deviated more strongly from the average contribution by the other members. Perhaps the most important conclusion from this research is that the introduction of option for punishment leads to strong increases in contributions to the public good, while the elimination of the option for punishment leads to strong decreases in contributions to the public good. Thus, the inspiring finding was that people are quite willing to punish, even when such punishment could not be explained in terms of material or reputational gain, and that such punishment promoted cooperation in an effective manner in non-repeated social dilemmas.

We discuss the experimental set-up by Fehr and Gächter in great detail because it has inspired numerous studies. In fact, especially since their 2002 paper in *Nature*, hundreds of published and unpublished studies have been conducted. Some of these studies have sought to replicate the findings, and the patterns are indeed quite replicable. A recent meta-analysis revealed that the effect of punishments has been replicated in numerous studies, and seems to generalize across a number of variables, such as group size, cost-to-fine ratio, and whether the dilemma involved actual or hypothetical pay (Balliet, Mulder, & Van Lange, 2011). Moreover, the effects were observed in the Public Good dilemma, as well as in the Resource Dilemma and the Prisoner's Dilemma. And, not surprisingly, the effects were not only observed in non-repeated social dilemmas, but also in iterated social dilemmas.

However, two "moderators" were found to be important. First, the effect of punishment was more pronounced when the incentives are costly (versus free) to administer. Presumably, the administration of costly punishment might signal a strong commitment to the goal of promoting cooperation, rather than pursuing self-interest or competition (spite) (Balliet et al., 2011). Second, cross-societal studies on punishment have found much variation across societies in the degree to which punishment promotes cooperation (Henrich et al., 2006; Herrmann, Thoni, & Gächter, 2008; Marlow et al., 2008). In fact, in the paradigm used by Fehr and Gächter (2000, 2002), punishment is effectively directed toward free-riders and promotes cooperation in several societies, but not in all societies. In some societies, the effectiveness of punishment to promote contributions to public goods is weak or even absent (Herrmann et al., 2008). Recently, a meta-analysis uncovered what it might be about culture that helps explain the variation in the effectiveness of punishment (Balliet & Van Lange, 2013). Specifically, they found that the effectiveness of punishment in promoting cooperation in a public goods experiment is greater in societies with high trust (such as Denmark, China, or Switzerland), rather than low trust (such as Turkey, Greece, or South Africa). It is possible that a history of political systems underlies such differences in trust, especially in strangers (Gintis, 2008), with the more proximal explanation being that those who punish must feel part of a network where such norm-enforcement is appreciated and supported (Balliet & Van Lange, 2013).

As noted earlier, several interesting theoretical analyses and experiments have been conducted to explore the further potential (and limits) of punishment. For example, one study showed that people are initially reluctant to interact in a sanctioning regime when they have the choice to avoid it. Over time, however, the entire population opted for having the sanctioning possibility and this enabled them to achieve almost full cooperation even in a relatively large group (Gürerk, Irlenbusch & Rockenbach, 2006). Another study suggested that it is important to realize that punishment brings about costs, and that sometimes this combines well with influences on reputation—because undermining another's reputation is also quite effective, but is less expensive for the punisher (Rockenbach & Milinksi, 2006). Clearly, reputational concerns are very important to people, and strategies are also aimed at maintaining a "profitable" reputation. For example, a recent study explored the option by which people could pay to hide information and demonstrated that people tend to reveal their cooperativeness but tend to hide their punishment (Rockenbach & Milinksi, 2011).

EMERGING THEMES AND PUZZLES

The literature on reward and punishment has been inspiring from various perspectives, and has generated several new theoretical issues and puzzles. One issue is related to the economics and psychology of rewards versus punishment. While this is a classic theme in the literature on motivation, parenting, and behavioral modification, the issue of reward and punishment has also received some attention in the literature on social dilemmas. Some of the earlier findings—when reward and punishment were examined as part of the outcome structure—suggested that they are both effective motivators of cooperation. This conclusion has also been reinforced in research using the Fehr and Gächter (2002) paradigm, the broad conclusion being that reward and punishment are about equally effective in promoting cooperation (Balliet et al., 2011). Still, many issues are not clear. One important issue is the motives and emotions that might trigger reward and especially punishment—this is an issue that needs to be unpacked since the original study by Fehr and Gächter (2002) where they highlight the importance of negative emotions and fairness (see also Fischbacher, & Gächter, 2004; Fowler, Johnson, & Smirnov, 2005).

This reasoning was also complemented by neuroscientific evidence showing that people derive satisfaction from punishing other individuals who violate a norm of fairness by taking advantage of another's cooperation (De Quervain et al., 2004; Singer et al., 2006). Moreover, such patterns may well combine with some rational decision making processes, in which people at some level weigh the costs of punishment against the impact it has on the person punished (Egas & Riedl, 2008). Also, it is not really clear whether the punisher benefits at all from punishing. The collective is likely to benefit at least somewhat from punishment in most social dilemmas. But it is indeed especially those that have not punished who benefit, as they free-ride on the efforts of the punishers (Dreber, Rand, Fudenberg, & Nowak, 2008). So, the question remains if and how punishers are rewarded (Milinski & Rockenbach, 2008).

These, and other findings, have also been discussed from broader theoretical perspectives. For example, several researchers have conceptualized such findings in terms of *strong reciprocity*, proposing that a human propensity to cooperate with others similarly disposed, even at personal cost, and to punish those who violate cooperative norms, even when punishing, is personally costly (see Gintis, Bowles, Boyd, & Fehr, 2003). The ultimate, evolutionary account for such other-regarding motives might be rooted in group selection supported by gene-culture co-evolution. For example, cooperative groups might have been more successful in creating and sustaining cultural and social institutions that overall support the fitness of other-regarding behavior, such as tendencies to strong reciprocity (Bowles & Gintis, 2011). Thus, the issue of reward and punishment has elicited new theoretical developments in accounting for the evolution of cooperation. It is also true that the theorizing of strong reciprocity has also elicited debate, because these new concepts and ideas are critically discussed and have not received consensus across disciplines. The point to be made is that literature on reward and punishment has inspired theorizing that is essential to understanding the evolution of cooperation, especially among strangers.

Several other intriguing issues remain. For example, how do reward and punishment function as systems over longer periods of time (Gächter, Renner, & Sefton, 2008)? Do these systems communicate different expectations and norms? For example, might a punishment system communicate the badness of free-riding (but not necessarily the goodness of cooperation), while a reward system largely communicates the goodness of cooperation (and not necessarily the badness of free-riding)? Are people more willing to reward than to punish? And how about second-order punishment, punishing those who fail to punish noncooperators, and how about second-order reward, rewarding those who rewarded cooperators?

A second emerging theme is focused on power and leadership. By far, most studies have focused on decentralized forms of sanctioning. In most paradigms, all participants in a group are equipped with the option to sanction (reward or punish) others. However, in many situations in everyday life, groups tend to organize themselves in ways such that punishment is administered by some but not all members. Informal and formal groups tend to have emerging or appointed leaders who are the ones who tend to reward and punish. A further analysis of these issues may make the dilemma somewhat more complex yet more realistic. Scientifically, numerous topics suggest themselves. For example, are leaders more likely to reward than punish? Who are the leaders who volunteer to lead? Are they the cooperators? And related to the topic of leadership and power is the broader issue of the role of social institutions, and the debate about the effectiveness versus efficiency of sanctioning systems. Sometimes a sanctioning system is quite effective in terms of promoting cooperation, but not efficient because it is too expensive to maintain. Also, sometimes there may be less expensive solutions to enforce norms and promote cooperation.

A final emerging topic emphasizes the translation of findings of the public good paradigm to the ongoing cultures. In particular, these lab-based research findings have been challenged in a provocative article by Guala (2012), who reviews evidence from anthropology to reach the conclusion that people may not engage in costly punishment to encourage cooperation outside the laboratory. It is possible that in the real world people might often consider other options than punishment. For example, perhaps people start to evaluate and discuss the behavior of free-riders among each other before they might consider punishment. Also, formal and informal communities always are able to threaten free-riders in various ways. Gossip might already be a threat, in that it may entail reputational costs. Related to this issue is whether the mere threat—which seems almost always present in everyday life—already provides a strong incentive to cooperate in the real world, at least when one another's actions are not completely private.

OVERVIEW OF THE BOOK

The major themes and puzzles discussed previously are central to the contemporary research on reward and punishment in social dilemmas—although there are several other puzzles that can be addressed as well. The themes we highlighted here cut across scientific fields and disciplines, and together, they should provide the bigger picture on the workings, the organization, and functions of reward and punishments. Although many chapters can be categorized in a variety of ways, we have decided to organize the book around three complementary topics: (a) the workings of reward and punishment (Section 1), (b) the organizational structure of reward and punishment (Section 2), and (c) the functions of reward and punishment in society (Section 3).

The first section of this book, entitled "*The workings of reward and punishment*" addresses the key questions about the how and why of reward and punishment. In Chapter 2, economist Louis Putterman discusses the role of norms, communication, and information in shaping cooperation and punishment in social dilemmas. In doing so, he also draws attention to the idea that punishment invites counter-punishment, which is relevant not only to cooperation, but also to the important difference between effectiveness and efficiency of punishment. In Chapter 3, psychologists Daniel Balliet and Paul Van Lange discuss how understanding the specific incentive structure of interdependent social interactions may lead to greater insight into both the use and the effectiveness of reward and punishment in promoting cooperation. In doing so, they draw attention to conflict of interest, information, and the role of communicating other-regarding motives. In Chapter 4, evolutionary scientists Pontus Strimling and Kimmo Eriksson seek to understand people's views about punishment in several countries, demonstrating a fair amount of consensus about norms across cultures and different scenarios of social dilemmas. Such evidence suggests that general principles underlie the construal of norm violations in social dilemmas. In Chapter 5, psychologists Eric van Dijk, Laetitia Mulder and Erik de Kwaadsteniet discuss the pros and cons of sanctions in social dilemmas. They outline that although sanctions may make cooperation more attractive, sanctions may also undermine the importance people assign to furthering the collective interest. By undermining people's internal motivation to cooperate (i.e., by reducing the weight they put on the collective interest), they suggest that sanctions may sometimes change things for the worse.

The second section is entitled *"The organization of reward and punishment"* and addresses leadership and power in social dilemmas, especially in relation to (the administration of) reward and punishment. In Chapter 6, economists Daniele Nosenzo and Martin Sefton address the distribution of power to administer rewards and punishment. They outline that many self-organizing groups and societies concentrate the power to reward or punish in the hands of a subset of group members ('central monitors'), and show important differences between reward and punishment. For punishment, decentralized sanctioning systems tend to outperform centralized sanctioning systems, while a tendency for the opposite was observed for reward. In Chapter 7, psychologists Xiao-Ping Chen, Carolyn Dang, and Fong Keng-Highberger emphasize the role of time-horizon, and note that most research has focused on monetary, short-term, and individual-based ways to promote cooperation. They propose a further exploration of long-term cooperation through the usage of sanctions that is non-monetary, group-based, decentralized, and not focused on immediate reinforcement strategies. In Chapter 8, economists Matthias Sutter and Fernanda Rivas examine, among other issues, the effectiveness of leadership with the power to reward or the power to sanction through exclusion, finding that leaders who sanction through exclusion were more effective and leaders who sanction through reward were more effective than no leaders at all. The advantage of sanctioning is that the mere threat upholds high levels of cooperation.

The third section, entitled *"The functions of reward and punishment in society,"* emphasizes neuroscientific correlates of cooperation, the functional value of reward or punishment, and the translation from lab-based research to actual societies. In Chapter 9, psychologist and neuroscientist Eveline Crone and colleagues review a relatively new literature on human development across adolescents' tendencies to cooperate. Their review reveals a consistent pattern of both increasing strategic motivations and other-oriented concerns in social decision-making across development. The combination of brain and behavior measures has the advantage of allowing for a deeper understanding of the separable processes involved in the emergence of advanced forms of social decision-making, which seems clearly relevant to (natural) tendencies to reward and punishment in social dilemmas. In Chapter 10, evolutionary scientists, Pat Barclay and Toko Kiyonari, provide an analysis of second-order punishment, and show that people do not tend to punish others who fail to punish free-riders. In contrast, there may be merit in second-order reward, in that people are much more likely to reward those who rewarded cooperators. They also suggest that punishment may be better when cooperation is common and needs to be unanimous, whereas reward may be better when cooperation is less common or does not need to be. In Chapter 11, economist Nikos Nikiforakis, argues that while there can be little doubt that many individuals are willing to enforce cooperation at a personal cost, the conditions required for altruistic punishment to promote efficiency by itself appear to be rare in daily life. He also draws attention to the role of other options that people might use in everyday life, including talking to the target and gossip, as well as the evolution of social institutes and other sanctioning systems. Finally, in Chapter 12, anthropologist Pierre Lienard actually provides some evidence for the importance of communication, and especially the role of emerging informal structures, as way of dealing with free-riders in tribal societies. In particular, he studies Turkana pastoralist groups of northwest Kenya, a tribal society without central institutions. He found that such communities tend to develop generation and age-sets systems that regulate norm violations (especially among the younger people) through coordination of autonomous groups, collective sanctioning, and reinforcement of mutual monitoring.

SUMMARY AND CONCLUSION

Reward and punishment in social dilemmas represents a classic theme in research on social dilemmas. Historically, reward and punishment were conceptualized as parameters of the outcome structure, such that reward stands for a reinforcing mutual cooperation by increasing the outcomes following from it while punishment stands for a penalizing for mutual noncooperation by decreasing the outcomes following from it (Rapoport, 1967). Reward and punishment were already included in the social dilemma structure, as if they were "externally provided." In the next phase, by examining elementary and instrument cooperation, participants were given a choice to contribute to a sanctioning system, a collective unit that would punish (or reward) noncooperators (or cooperators; Yamagishi, 1986b). The literature then moved to individual-level sanctioning, where each member could decide to reward or punish other members in a social dilemma task, often a public goods dilemma (Fehr & Gächter, 2000, 2002).

After an explosion of research on reward and punishment during the past decade, scientists are now "en route" to examining basic issues revolving around the workings, the organization, and the functions of reward and punishment in social dilemmas. These are exciting times because the topic of reward and punishment is very fundamental, and there is little doubt that reward and punishment are effective tools to promote cooperation. At the same time, the last decade has also increasingly revealed emerging themes, new theoretical developments, intriguing questions, and a challenging debate revolving around the evolution, as well as strengths and limitations, of reward and punishment. One of the next challenges is to examine the workings of reward and punishment, how best to organize a system that monitors reward and punishment and to explore the functions of reward and punishment in contemporary society. We hope this book provides a state-of-the-art of this literature, and that the themes discussed in this book will indeed turn out to be prominent ones in future research on reward and punishment in social dilemmas.

REFERENCES

Axelrod, R. (1984). *The evolution of cooperation*. New York: Basic Books.
Balliet, D., Mulder, L. B., & Van Lange, P. A. M. (2011b). Reward, punishment, and cooperation: A meta-analysis. *Psychological Bulletin, 137*, 594–614.
Balliet, D., & Van Lange, P. A. M. (2013, in press). Trust, punishment, and cooperation across 18 societies: A meta-analysis. *Perspectives on Psychological Science*.
Bowles, S., & Gintis, H. (2011). *A cooperative species: Human reciprocity and its evolution*, Princeton, NJ: Princeton University Press.
Cass, R. D., & Edney, J. J. (1978). The commons dilemma: A simulation testing the effect of resource visibility and territorial division. *Human Ecology, 6*, 371–386.
Dawes, R. M. (1980). Social dilemmas. *Annual Review of Psychology, 31*, 169–193.
De Quervain, D. J. F., Fischbacher, U., Treyer, V., Schellhammer, M., Schnyder, U., Buck, A., & Fehr, E. (2004). The neural basis of altruistic punishment. *Science, 305*, 1254–1258.
Dreber, A., Rand, D. G., Fudenberg, D., & Nowak, M. A. (2008). *Nature, 452*, 348–351.
Egas, M., & Riedl, A. (2008). The economics of altruistic punishment and the maintenance of cooperation. *Proceedings of the Royal Society Biological Sciences, 275*, 871–878.
Fehr, E., & Gächter, S. (2000). Cooperation and punishment in public goods experiments. *American Economic Review, 90*, 980–994.
Fehr, E., & Gächter, S. (2002). Altruistic punishment in humans. *Nature, 415*, 137–140.
Fischbacher, U., & Gächter, S. (2010). Social preferences, beliefs, and the dynamics of free riding in public goods experiments. *American Economic Review, 100*, 541–556.
Fowler, J. H., Johnson, T., & Smirnov, O. (2005). Egalitarian motives and altruistic punishment. *Nature, 433*, 1038.
Gächter, S., Renner, E., & Sefton, M. (2008). The long-run benefits of punishment. *Science, 322*, 1510.
Gintis, H. (2008). Punishment and cooperation. *Science, 319*, 1345–1346.
Gintis, H., Bowles, S., Boyd, R., & Fehr, E. (2003). Explaining altruistic behavior in humans. *Evolution and Behavior, 24*, 153–172.
Guala, F. (2012). Reciprocity: Weak or strong? What punishment experiments do (and do not) demonstrate. *Behavioral and Brain Sciences, 35*, 1–15.
Gürerk, Ö., Irlenbusch, B., & Rockenbach, B. (2006). The competitive advantage of sanctioning institutions. *Science, 312*, 108–111.
Hardin, G. (1968). The tragedy of the commons. *Science, 162*, 1243–1248.
Hardin, G., & Baden, J. (Eds.). (1977). *Managing the commons*. San Francisco: W. H. Freeman.
Henrich, N., & Henrich, J. (2007). *Why humans cooperate*. Oxford: Oxford University Press.
Henrich, J., et al. (2006). Costly punishment across human societies. *Science, 312*, 1767–1770.
Herrmann, B., Thöni, C., & Gächter, S. (2008). Antisocial punishment across societies. *Science, 319*, 1362–1367.
Kelley, H. H., & Grzelak, J. L. (1972). Conflict between individual and common interests in an N-person relationship. *Journal of Personality and Social Psychology, 21*, 190–197.
Kelley, H. H., & Grzelak, J. L. (1972). Conflict between individual and common interests in an N-person relationship. *Journal of Personality and Social Psychology, 21*, 190–197.
Komorita, S. S., & Barth, J. M. (1985). Components of reward in social dilemmas. *Journal of Personality and Social Psychology, 48*, 364–373.
Komorita, S. S., Sweeney, J., & Kravitz, D. A. (1980). Cooperative choice in the N-person dilemma situation. *Journal of Personality and Social Psychology, 38*, 504–516.

Maki, J. E., Hoffman, D. M., & Berk, R. A. (1978). A time series analysis of the impact of a water conservation campaign. *Evaluation Quarterly, 2,* 107–118.

Marwell, G., & Ames, R. E. (1979). Experiments on the provision of public goods I: Resources, interest, group size, and the free rider problem. *American Journal of Sociology, 84,* 1335–1360.

Messick, D. M., Wilke, H., Brewer, M. B., Kramer, R. M., Zemke, P. E., & Lui, L. (1983). Individual adaptions and structural change as solutions to social dilemmas. *Journal of Personality and Social Psychology, 44,* 294–309.

Milinksi, M., & Rockenbach, B. (2008). Punisher pays. *Nature, 452,* 297–298.

Oliver, P. (1980). Rewards and punishments as selective incentives for collective action: Theoretical investigations. *American Journal of Sociology, 85,* 1356–1375.

Ostrom, E. (1990). *Governing the commons: The evolution of institutions for collective action.* Cambridge: Cambridge University Press.

Ostrom E., Burger J., Field, C. B., Norgaard, R. B., & Policansky, D. (1999). Revisiting the commons: Local lessons, global challenges. *Science, 284,* 278–282.

Ostrom, E., Walker, J., & Gardner, R. (1992). Covenants with and without a sword: Self-governance is possible. *American Political Science Review, 86,* 404–417.

Parks, C. D., & Rumble, A. C. (2001). Elements of reciprocity and social value orientation. *Personality and Social Psychology Bulletin, 27,* 1301–1309.

Rapoport, An. (1967). A note on the "index of cooperation" for prisoner's dilemma. *Journal of Conflict Resolution, 11,* 100–103.

Rockenbach, B., & Milinski, M. (2006). The efficient interaction of indirect reciprocity and costly punishment. *Nature, 444,* 718–723.

Rockenbach, B., & Milinski, M. (2011). To qualify as a social partner, humans hide severe punishment, although their observed cooperativeness is decisive. *Proceedings of the National Academy of Science, 108,* 18307–18312.

Sattler, D. N., & Kerr, N. L. (1991). Might versus morality explored: Motivational and cognitive bases for social motives. *Journal of Personality and Social Psychology, 60,* 756–765.

Singer, T., Seymour, B., O'Doherty, J. P., Stephan, K. E., Dolan, R. J., & Frith, C. D. (2006). Empathic neural responses are modulated by the perceived fairness of others. *Nature, 439,* 466–469.

Van Lange, P. A. M., Joireman, J., Parks, C. D., & Van Dijk, E. (2013). The psychology of social dilemmas: A review. *Organizational Behavior and Human Decision Processes, 120,* 125–141.

Van Lange, P. A. M., Ouwerkerk, J. W., & Tazelaar, M. J. A. (2002). How to overcome the detrimental effects of noise in social interaction: The benefits of generosity. *Journal of Personality and Social Psychology, 82,* 768–780.

Yamagishi, T. (1986a). The provision of a sanctioning system as a public good. *Journal of Personality and Social Psychology, 51,* 110–116.

Yamagishi, T. (1986b). The structural goal/expectation theory of cooperation in social dilemmas. *Advances in Group Processes, 3,* 51–87.

Yamagishi, T. (1988a). Seriousness of social dilemmas and the provision of a sanctioning system. *Social Psychology Quarterly, 51,* 32–42.

Yamagishi, T. (1988b). The provision of a sanctioning system in the United States and Japan. *Social Psychology Quarterly, 51,* 265–271.

PART ONE
The Workings of Reward and Punishment

2 When Punishment Supports Cooperation: Insights from Voluntary Contribution Experiments*

LOUIS PUTTERMAN

Abstract
Recent years have seen an outpouring of research by economists on the role of punishment in supporting voluntary collective action. This research parallels increased interest within biology and psychology about the role that propensities to engage in punishment may have played in the evolution of cooperative behaviors. Following the initial demonstration that opportunities to punish dramatically altered well-known results in experiments without punishment, research focused on topics including (a) the impact of punishment on efficiency; (b) how punishment's cost affects its efficacy; (c) the extent to which punishment is strategically motivated; (d) what explains "misdirected" punishment; (e) the impact of opportunities to engage in counter-punishment and in other punishment of higher order; and (f) the circumstances under which subjects opt to allow punishment to be given. In this chapter, I discuss all of these issues, but focus more on (d)—(f) in which many of the investigations are more recent.

A theme of my discussion will be how certain factors appear to promote successful cooperation by facilitating coordination of the actors with respect both to base level cooperation decisions (contributions) and punishment decisions. Major candidates for the coordinating role are social norms which might be brought into the laboratory by subjects in some but not other societies, opportunities to engage in communication, and richer information settings, including ones permitting multiple orders of punishment on the basis of relatively full information about both contribution and punishment decisions. While I will mainly be dealing with laboratory experiments, I will discuss correspondence or lack of correspondence to real world environments, both contemporary and in our evolutionary past, so that the applicability of this body of research to relevant social issues remains within the frame of my discussion.

BEGINNINGS

Although the recent economics literature on cooperation and punishment has a variety of antecedents, its immediate starting point was the appearance in 1999 of a soon-to-be-published working paper by Ernst Fehr and Simon Gächter,

---

*Draft of chapter for Van Lange, Rockenbach and Yamagishi, eds., *Social Dilemmas: New Perspectives on Reward and Punishment*.

"Cooperation and Punishment in Public Goods Experiments." Among the most closely related antecedents were Yamagishi (1986) and Ostrom, Walker and Gardner (1992), but these seemed to have limited impact in economics. Yamagishi's experiment differed from Fehr and Gächter's in that it involved asymmetric marginal payoffs, it predetermined that punishment would go to a group's lowest contributor, and in it the amount of punishment was determined jointly, rather than individually, by another set of voluntary contributions. The latter features resemble those of formal sanction schemes, which are discussed later. Ostrom et al. studied a common pool resource problem which, while sharing many of the social dilemma features of the voluntary contribution mechanism, has tended to be addressed in a separate stream of literature. Also, Fehr and Gächter argued that the willingness to pay for punishment in the Ostrom et al. study was less striking theoretically because subjects interacted without a pre-announced last period, so predictions based on backward unraveling did not technically apply.

Leaving aside these more direct antecedents, interest in motivations for punishment had been stimulated among economists by the large body of ultimatum game results showing willingness to incur a cost to punish apparently unfair offers. Beginning with Güth, Schmittberger and Schwarze (1982), the game invites a proposer to split an endowment with a responder, who can veto the proposal, causing both to receive nothing. Dozens of replications had found most proposers to offer substantially more than the smallest available amount, which in theory should give the responder sufficient incentive not to veto. More pertinently, most responders offered less than 30% of the pie rejected their offers, although this meant leaving with less money and no potential long-term material benefit. These responders were evidently willing to incur a cost for the satisfaction of imposing a larger cost on their counterparts, pointing to a possibly more general willingness to engage in costly punishment of unfair or norm-violating behaviors. In one test of this conjecture, Fehr, Gächter and Kirchsteiger (see also Fehr & Gächter, 1998) introduced punishment opportunities into the gift exchange game studied earlier by Fehr, Kirchsteiger and Riedl (1993). They demonstrated that subjects anticipated the possibility of being punished, that such costly punishment did occur, and that the presence of the punishment option raised the rate of norm adherence (reciprocating a higher wage with higher effort).

The public goods experiment into which Fehr and Gächter (2000a) next introduced punishment opportunities had been extensively studied under the name voluntary contribution mechanism. Many of the prior experiments are summarized in the survey by Ledyard (1995). A group of subjects is formed by the experimenter and each is asked to simultaneously and independently allocate an endowment of points or experimental currency between a private account and a group or public account. Each member receives the same return from allocations to the group account, a return less than that for allocating to her private account but high enough so that each is better off in a full- than in a zero-contributions equilibrium.[1] Standard findings had been that (a) subjects' average contributions

---

1. I will focus on versions of the experiment in which the returns from allocations to the group account are constant and where the endowments and returns are equal for all group members. These symmetric, linear VCMs account for most but not all of the literature.

were typically about half of their endowments, with considerable individual variation in one-time play and in the first period of repeated play, (b) when the game was played a finite number of times, with pre-announced last period, contributions tended to display a declining trend, reaching a low although often still positive average level in the final period, (c) contributions tended to be somewhat higher when group composition was fixed than when it was changing each period, (d) contributions tended to be higher the greater is the private return from contributing to the group account, and (e) contributions rose if play was restarted without prior announcement, even if group composition remained unchanged. Findings (a) and (b) together were sometimes interpreted as indicating that the complete free riding prediction of standard economic theory failed in the short run but was gradually approximated as subjects acquired a better understanding of their situation. However, the other findings suggested that explanations involving preferences not standard in received economic theory, including willingness to cooperate conditional on others doing so or a partially offsetting psychic return from cooperation, held promise.[2]

Fehr and Gächter suggested that the decline in contributions over time could be viewed as resulting from an interaction of fair or cooperatively minded individuals with selfish or opportunistic ones. Without any mechanism to prod the latter into cooperating, the former tended to withdraw their contributions when confronted with evidence that too many members of their group are opportunists, since the propensity to cooperate does not include a desire to be taken advantage of. Adding a punishment stage to the game, they conjectured, would alter the outcome because cooperators could now signal their wish to cooperate without passively enduring others' free-riding. Selfish group members could be induced to contribute if they expected sufficient punishment so that allocating to their private accounts ceased to be profitable.

It is important to focus on the motivation of the pro-social or cooperation-encouraging punisher. The version of standard economic theory in which individuals are not only uniformly rational and self-interested but also have common knowledge of sharing this description predicts no effect of adding opportunities to punish. Although there can be a selfish motive for punishing if it is expected to induce enough additional contributions by other group members, that condition cannot hold in a finitely repeated interaction, according to the standard model. This is because a selfish individual will never punish in the last period, so punishing in the next-to-last period cannot be a credible threat, which makes next-to-last period punishing itself never profitable, and so on. Dropping the common

---

2. Finding (c) suggests subjects inclined to invest in reputations for conditional cooperativeness, which at a minimum violates the strong assumption that all know one another to be perfectly rational and self-interested (money-maximizing) and to have common knowledge of this. Finding (d) violates the standard theory prediction that a subject should contribute nothing so long as the return from contributing is less than that from allocation to her private account, but is consistent with subjects having varying private psychic returns from contributing or displaying cooperativeness. The restart effect suggests that willingness to cooperate is vying with desire to avoid being "suckered" and that many subjects took advantage of an opportunity to "let bygones be bygones."

knowledge assumption and letting individuals harbor doubts that fellow players are perfectly rational and selfish suffices to make punishing by selfish agents rational during repeated play under some circumstances, but punishing in one-shot play or in the known last period of finitely repeated play remains inexplicable without either irrationality or motivations that deviate from strict maximization of own money payoff.

One motivation for punishing in the voluntary contribution game was suggested by Fehr and Schmidt (1999). In their model of biased inequity aversion, many individuals are willing to incur a cost to reduce the income gap between themselves and a higher-earning individual, and some individuals are also willing to incur a cost to reduce the income gap between themselves and a lower-earning individual. The second type of preference can account for contributing to the public good if it is assumed that there is something to get contributing started by at least some group members, since those who contribute the most will earn the least (in the absence of punishment), so an agent with strong enough dislike of inequality in which he is advantaged may raise his own contribution so as to reduce this selfishly advantageous inequality. The first type of preference can account for punishing a low contributor, provided that the cost of punishing is less than the earnings loss to the person targeted.

Another motivation for punishing was suggested by Fehr and Gächter (2000b). They suggested that many individuals have propensities to reciprocate kind or generous behavior with kindness of their own (positive reciprocity) and to reciprocate unkind or ungenerous behavior with their own unkindness (negative reciprocity). An individual holding a strong impulse of positive reciprocity can be expected to contribute to the public good if others do, since this is a way to reciprocate the kindness they exercise through the spill-over effect of their contributions. An individual holding a strong impulse of negative reciprocity can be expected to incur at least a modest cost to punish group members who take advantage of him by not contributing or by contributing substantially less, since the latter members' actions are unkind insofar as they withhold bestowing benefits that they themselves enjoy.

In Fehr and Gächter (2000a), the expectation that many subjects would incur the cost of punishing low contributors was born out. The design had subjects play a contributions game in groups of four for ten periods without punishment opportunities and for ten periods with punishment opportunities, with different orders in different treatments. Both groups of fixed composition and randomly reshuffled groups were studied, as well as a treatment in which subjects were guaranteed never to interact with the same individual twice (a "perfect stranger" treatment) run for only six periods per phase due to limits on size of subject pool and lab. The goal of the latter was to test behavior in strictly one-shot interactions but with opportunities for learning. In all cases, the fall-off in contributions with repetition that is familiar from experiments without punishment was replicated in the no punishment condition but was not present when punishment was permitted, being replaced by a noticeable upward trend in contributions in the partner treatment.

Punishment and its effects on cooperation was particularly noteworthy because the experimenters went to great lengths to shuffle individuals' identities, so that it was impossible to invest in individual reputations, and because the instructions were quite neutral, with subjects having as much opportunity to punish cooperators as to punish free riders. The term "punishment" was avoided, the instructions indeed referring to "assigning points" to the targeted individuals. Significantly, subjects altered their contribution behavior in their first decisions of the punishment condition, before any punishing had been observed, suggesting qualitatively accurate prior beliefs about how punishment would be used. These findings were potentially revolutionary not only for students of collective action, but for those studying many other kinds of social interaction, since tendencies to punish even in end-game situations render realistic the possibility of many outcomes theoretically ruled out by older rational actor models.

Efficacy and Strategic Motivation, and Efficiency

A number of follow-up studies began to circulate almost immediately after Fehr and Gächter's. Sefton, Shupp and Walker (2007), Bochet, Page and Putterman (2006), Bowles, Carpenter and Gintis (2001), and Masclet, Noussair, Tucker and Villeval (2003),[3] each confirmed the basic qualitative finding for a contributions game with punishment opportunities: contributions higher than in a corresponding condition without such opportunities, either rising or at least failing to fall rapidly with repetition, and substantial amounts of costly punishment mostly aimed at low contributors. Each of these studies also explored other issues, and several are returned to subsequently.[4]

One of the first issues investigated was the impact of punishment's cost on both willingness to pay and on responsiveness of contributions. Fehr and Gächter's design involves punishment points purchased at an increasing marginal cost, with a constant proportionate impact on the earnings of the recipient, who loses 10% of his pre-punishment earnings for the period for each point received. A possibly unintended consequence is that punishment costs the punisher less per money unit lost by the recipient the less the recipient's contribution to the group account (Casari, 2005). Although several subsequent studies use the same "punishment technology," others, including Fehr and Gächter (2002), adopt a simpler and, from the latter standpoint, less biased design, which maintains a fixed and uniform ratio between cost to punisher and cost to recipient. By varying this ratio, Anderson and Putterman (2006), Carpenter (2007) and Nikiforakis and Normann (2008) investigate the demand for punishment and find subjects to purchase more of it at a lower price, as would be expected for an ordinary good. Nikiforakis and Normann's between-subject design also shows that whether and to what degree the opportunity to punish changes the declining contribution feature of the finitely repeated voluntary contributions mechanism (VCM) without punishment to the increasing contribution profile found by Fehr and Gächter (2000a) depends on what they call "punishment effectiveness": the loss to a targeted individual per unit spent by the

---

3. Publication year and first circulation are widely separated, in some cases.
4. To keep the scope of the chapter manageable, I will not discuss the comparison of rewards and punishments introduced by Sefton et al., nor the substitution of moral disapproval for punishment studied by Masclet et al.

punisher. Contributions rise with repetition, in their experiment, when the latter value is 3 or 4, are essentially flat when it is 2, and are falling, although less rapidly than in the no punishment condition, when it is 1.

How contributions respond to punishment is studied at the micro level by Önes and Putterman (2007) and Page, Putterman and Garcia (2013) using multivariate regressions. They model the change in an individual's contribution to the group account from the previous to the current period as a function of the relative rank of her contribution during the previous period and the interaction of that rank with the amount of punishment she received. The results show that groups' lowest contributors tend to increase their contributions by a larger amount the more punishment they are given, while their highest contributors tend to *reduce* their contributions more the more they are punished, justifying description of such punishment as "perverse," as discussed further subsequently.

Two related issues considered by early follow-up studies are the extent to which punishment is explained by inequity aversion, and what role is played by the strategic desire to induce an increase in contribution by the targeted individual. The inequity aversion motive in the Fehr-Schmidt model can explain punishment of low contributors only if punishing costs the punisher less than it costs the recipient. In some conditions studied by Anderson and Putterman (2006), Falk, Fehr and Fischbacher (2005), Carpenter (2007), and Nikiforakis and Normann (2008), punishers must pay as much or more than the punishment recipient, however. Non-trivial amounts of punishment occur at these high costs to punishers, although generally at amounts insufficient to cause contributions to be sustained at high levels. This finding indicates that inequity aversion cannot be the only explanation for punishment and that negative reciprocity or an urge to punish norm violation interpretation has broader explanatory range.

The motive behind punishment can be considered strategic if the punisher will have future interactions with the person targeted and thus opportunities to benefit by inducing higher future contributions. That such motives explain some punishment is suggested by the fact of greater punishment in the partner than in the stranger treatments in Fehr and Gächter (2000a)[5], but the presence of substantial punishment in perfect stranger treatments and in strictly one-shot treatments (see Falk et al., 2005) shows that there is also much non-strategic punishment. Other evidence includes the finding that the amount of punishment given is not significantly less in the last period of play).[6] Finally, when subjects were asked to punish in a randomly determined sequence and were shown the amount of punishment given by those whose turns came earlier, those later in the sequence did not punish less, suggesting that giving punishment, rather than simply seeing to it that the recipient received punishment, was desired as an end in itself (see Casari & Luini, 2009).

---

5. See also Balliet, Mulder and Van Lange (2011).
6. This result is shown in Önes and Putterman (2007) in regressions that control for the targeted individual's contribution deviation from the group average, preventing misinterpretation of the uptick in punishment that often accompanies last period free-riding. The same result was found for the data of Page et al. (2005) and Bochet et al. (2006).

The fact that it increases contributions to the public good does not in itself imply that punishment has a net social benefit. Efficiency is increased only if the increase in overall earnings attributable to the higher contributions is sufficient to offset the reduction of earnings incurred by punishers and those punished by them. In Fehr and Gächter's data, this was not the case overall, but it was true of the last periods of play under the punishment condition, and they suggested that it might therefore hold true in the long run. Gächter, Renner and Sefton (2008) demonstrated the accuracy of that conjecture with a replication of the original Fehr-Gächter experiment, differing only in that each phase lasted forty rather than ten periods. Earnings were higher overall in the punishment condition, with this duration of play.

"Misdirected," Counter-, and Higher-order Punishment

While the substantial majority of punishment in most experiments of this literature has been directed at groups' lower contributors, most of it by higher contributors, a non-negligible share of observed punishment in many experiments has been found to be directed at high contributors, most often by low ones. Cinyabuguma, Page and Putterman (2004) called this punishment "perverse" because it tends to reduce group earnings both through its direct effect and through its negative impact on contributions. They computed hypothetical earnings in experiments conducted by their research team and found that although earnings were not higher in a treatment with punishment opportunities than in an otherwise identical treatment without those opportunities, earnings would have been higher absent the perverse punishment events and their effects on contribution decisions.

Herrmann, Thöni and Gächter (2008) investigated the misdirected punishment phenomenon, focusing on the relationship between the contribution levels of punisher and target rather than the latter's relationship to the average in the group as a whole. Denoting any instance in which the punisher's contribution is less than that of the target as "anti-social" punishment,[7] members of their team had found more of it among Russian than in Western subject pools and had proceeded to conduct parallel experiments with student subjects at sixteen sites in fifteen countries. They found mainly "pro-social" punishment of free riders at sites in Western Europe (Copenhagen, St. Gallen, Zurich, Nottingham and Bonn), the U.S. (Boston), Australia (Melbourne) and Korea (Seoul), but relatively high shares of anti-social punishment at sites in Belarus (Minsk), Ukraine (Dnipropetrovs'k), Russia (Samara), Oman (Muscat), Turkey (Istanbul), Greece (Athens) and Saudi

---

7. Suppose that with endowments of 20, the contributions of four subjects in a certain period are 4, 8, 12 and 16. If the contributor of 4 punishes the contributor of 8, it is anti-social punishment by the definition of Herrmann et al., but not perverse punishment by the definition of Cinyabuguma et al. While I have argued elsewhere that the latter definition may be more appropriate if our focus is on the incentive implications of a punishment pattern in experiments like most discussed thus far, where the recipient has no knowledge of who the punishment is from, the two approaches probably overlap in the large majority of cases.

Arabia (Riyadh). Perhaps not surprisingly, they found that the various populations' contribution levels in the punishment condition were inversely related to the proportion of punishment given anti-socially. They documented that shares of anti-social punishment given correlate with country-level measures of norms of civic cooperation and rule of law. This suggests that subjects use punishment opportunities to encourage cooperation more reliably when they bring favorable norms, already well-established in their society, into the lab with them.

Cinyabuguma et al., Falk et al. and Herrmann et al. find evidence that much if not all punishment of cooperators can be explained as attempts to retaliate for punishment received. In almost all of the experiments discussed thus far, subjects are not told who punished them, and identifying numbers or positions on the screen are randomly changed from one period to the next, making it impossible for the subject to be sure that a high contributor in one period was a high contributor in the previous one. Nevertheless, punished low contributors are often observed to themselves engage in costly punishment of a high contributor in the following period, most likely with intent to retaliate.[8]

Nikiforakis (2008) suggested that experiments of the kind discussed so far may give an overly optimistic sense of people's ability to achieve voluntary cooperation with the aid of sanctions because of protection from retaliation afforded by anonymity. He replicated the partner and stranger grouping conditions of Fehr and Gächter (2000a) with a student subject pool in the U.K., adding a treatment in which each period included not only a stage for punishment following the contribution stage, but also a third stage in which subjects learn which group members punished them by how much and can engage in costly counter-punishment. He found that about a quarter of punishments were counter-punished, punishment of free-riding fell, and contributions to the group accounts failed to rise with repetition, unlike the punishment-only treatment. Although average contributions nonetheless exceeded those in the VCM treatment, earnings were lower thanks to the resources spent on punishment and counter-punishment.

Counter-punishment is potentially part of a larger set of actions that can be called "higher-order punishment," meaning punishing of another agent conditioned on that agent's past punishment decisions. If we call punishment based on contribution decisions 1st-order punishment, then that based on 1st-order punishment decisions can be called 2nd-order punishment, and so forth. Henrich and Boyd (2001) suggest that in human evolutionary history, availability of 2nd-order punishing opportunities actually served to promote pro-social 1st order punishment and therefore base-level cooperative actions, since group members would not feel tempted to shirk their obligations to (1st-order) punish a (base-level) free rider, given the expectation of receiving 2nd-order punishment should they do so. Axelrod (1986) suggested that punishing those who fail to punish free-riding is a "meta-norm" that sustains cooperation. Another cooperation-supporting form of

---

8. Falk et al. find that such "spiteful" punishment of high contributors is largely restricted to cases in which punishment effectiveness is high and punishers can therefore increase the earnings gap between themselves and the recipients.

2nd-order punishment would be punishing any group member who (perversely or anti-socially) punished a cooperator.

To investigate when the presence of these opportunities is harmful and when it is helpful to cooperation and efficiency, Cinyabuguma, Page and Putterman (2006), Denant-Boemont, Masclet, and Noussair (2007), and Kamei and Putterman (2013) study variants of the VCM with punishment opportunities in which higher-order punishing opportunities are not restricted to counter-punishment. While the last two papers replicate the qualitative findings of Nikiforakis (2008) when conducting similar treatments, all find that opportunities for higher-order punishment are not *per se* damaging to cooperation and efficiency.[9] Kamei and Putterman (2013) find that both contributions and earnings are significantly higher in a treatment in which subjects are provided with information about all past bilateral punishments and can take that as well as past contributions into account when punishing, as compared with the typical treatment having one punishment stage per period and subsequent scrambling of identities. They conjecture that higher efficiency emerges because full information about the pattern of punishments encourages both contributing and punishing tendencies to converge towards the majority's orientation, which favors cooperation. Counter-punishing is not rare in their data, but it is more common and stronger on average when the punishing act being counter-punished is itself anti-social or perverse rather than pro-social.

Although Kamei and Putterman's findings offer some reassurance that higher-order punishment opportunities need not discourage cooperation, those findings contrast somewhat with results obtained by Nikiforakis and Engelmann (2011), in which subjects are also offered both higher-order punishment opportunities and fuller information about the punishments within their group, yet fail to improve cooperation relative to a treatment with a single punishment stage. The core difference is that whereas in Kamei and Putterman's design, there are never more than three stages to a period—one for contributing, one each for first- and second-order punishing—Nikiforakis and Engelmann's design allows for as many rounds of punishing as subjects choose to engage in (provided they have the funds to cover the cost), with a fresh contribution stage arriving only when any feuds initiated have been fully played out.[10] Although Kamei and Putterman's treatments with fixed subject identifiers also allow feuding to continue over the course of many periods, feuds appear to be uncommon (and are indeed difficult to detect unambiguously) in their data, given that intervening contribution decisions offer alternative explanations for observed punishments. Both situations in which the base-level problem of cooperation can be suspended indefinitely, as in Nikiforakis and Engelmann, and ones in which preoccupation with punishing is attenuated by an ongoing need to attend to the cooperative task that brought individuals together in the first place, as in Kamei and Putterman, may have their real world

---

9. Cinyabuguma et al.'s design has less immediate relevance because only the character of subjects' 1st-order punishing behaviors, not who specifically punished whom, is made known at the 2nd-order punishment stage.

10. Other experiments on feuding include Bolle, Tan and Zizzo (2012), Nicklisch and Wolff (2011), and Nikiforakis, Noussair and Wilkening (2012).

analogues (for the latter case, think of a cooperative work team or partnership). The relevance of the contrasting conclusions of these papers might therefore be argued to be application-specific.

When Do Subjects Choose to Allow Punishment?

By 2005, at least four independent research teams had designed experiments to study subjects' preferences with regard to operating in a sanction-free versus a sanction-permitting environment.[11] Botelho, Costa Pinto, Harrison and Rutström (2005) had subjects engage in play under both conditions, imposed exogenously, and then vote on which to use in a final, higher stakes period. Gürerk, Irlenbusch and Rockenbach (2006) had subjects playing a repeated VCM choose freely each period whether to do so in a group permitting or in one not permitting sanctions. Ertan, Page and Putterman (2009) let subjects determine by vote whether above-average, below-average, and average contributors in their group could receive costly sanctions, revisiting the decision every few periods after viewing feedback on what other groups were choosing and the associated average contributions and earnings. Sutter, Haigner and Kocher (2010) let inexperienced subjects vote once only between punishment, reward, or sanction-and-reward-free play, varying punishment and reward effectiveness across treatments, and also comparing outcomes to those in treatments in which the schemes were imposed exogenously.

In the text of their paper, Botelho et al. emphasized that subjects in Fehr and Gächter's (2000a) treatments had on average earned less when punishment was permitted than in the condition without punishment. Botelho et al. expressed doubt that individuals would want to be governed by such an institution. Consistent with their expectations, their own subjects tended to earn less in their exogenous punishment condition and accordingly almost all groups voted against having punishment opportunities in the high-stakes period. The corresponding question of whether *inexperienced* individuals would vote to permit punishment seemed to be answered similarly: most groups in Sutter et al.'s experiment voted against punishment of low effectiveness (1:1 ratio of punisher to target loss) and *all* groups offered the corresponding choice voted against punishment of high effectiveness (1:3 ratio).

Subjects in Gürerk et al. (2006) and those in Ertan et al. (2009) also initially showed a dislike of the idea of sanctions, with only 37% of subjects selecting to play in a group permitting sanctions in the initial period, in the former, and majorities in only 43% of subject groups choosing to allow any sanctions on their first vote, in the latter. In these experiments in which choice of institution was permitted to change over time, however, an institution permitting punishment came to be favored by a large majority after some periods of play. A theme of Ertan et al. pertinent to the previous section is that while the majority of groups eventually voted to permit punishment of below-average contributors, no group

---

11. In the paragraph and references, I list published versions with later dates of publication.

voted to permit punishment of above-average contributors, and the data showed considerably higher average contributions and earnings when subjects played in a condition in which only below-average contributors can be punished than in the condition without restriction of punishment that their subjects played in an exogenous phase, or other experiments with similar parameters.

■ WHAT DOES PUNISHMENT REPRESENT? IS IT EVER UNDER GROUP CONTROL?

While the experiments just discussed provide insight into individuals' preferences between environments with punishment opportunities and ones without, do group choices between such schemes have any counterpart in the real world? To answer this, we need to also address the prior question: in what if any form do we observe peer-to-peer punishments or sanctions in real life? In modern societies with elaborated legal systems, it is difficult to find examples of collective action settings in which individuals can impose material or pecuniary costs on one another without violating the law,[12] so social sanctions like verbal criticism, snubbing, and ostracism appear to be the most plausible counterparts of laboratory informal sanctions. Since it is reasonable to suppose that such sanctions carry real social and psychic costs to both givers and receivers, their non-pecuniary nature in real life does not in and of itself rule out external validity for experiments that accord to them a monetary representation.[13] More material or physical forms of punishment might occur in societies with less developed legal systems and in more remote locales, and might also have been more common in earlier human societies.

Insofar as informal sanctions are primarily social ones in modern societies, however, some might argue that both group voting on whether to permit them and individual choice between an environment with and one without such punishment opportunities has no real world analogue. It seems possible, however, that groups do meaningfully regulate the degree to which informal sanctions take place by punishing sanctioning that violates explicit or implicit understandings among their members. If the large majority of a group's members agree that "everyone should pull his or her weight" in a joint endeavor, they may also agree that those who take it upon themselves to discipline free riders are to be praised or supported whereas those who fail to engage in such disciplining or who criticize it are to be criticized and resisted. What's referred to as "peer pressure" may be understood as none other than the concerted application of criticism and of a stance of preparedness to criticize by the large majority of a group's members. Decisions on who should and who should not be punished might emerge over time in the course of

---

12. A possible exception is sabotage that workers in a team or partners in an enterprise might inflict on one another, with potentially asymmetric pecuniary consequences.

13. Economists are quite used to writing down models in which value from money and value from an intangible psychic source are interchangeable. Leisure, throughout the modern history of economics, and social utility from, say, the avoidance of inequality, in more recent years, are examples of psychic goods treated as components of individuals' utility functions.

ongoing interactions. Such understandings are also sometimes reached by discussion and vote (Ostrom, 1990).

Informal versus Formal Sanctions

The kind of punishment discussed up to this point is voluntarily given by one group member to another or, in other words, from peer-to-peer or "horizontally." An alternative type of sanctions are punishments, penalties or fines imposed "vertically" by a government, administration, or group acting in concert. The voluntary individual sanctions discussed thus far have sometimes been termed "informal" to distinguish them from the latter alternative, which are called "formal."[14] Many social norms or requirements in modern societies are enforced by governments with the threat of monetary penalties or imprisonment if the individual fails to comply. In many cases, adoption of formal or vertical sanctions is accompanied by outlawing of informal or horizontal ones, which are referred to by pejorative terms such as "vigilantism." Experimental studies of how fines work, e.g., to induce the payment of taxes, are almost as old as the method of experimental economics. But studies that build on the voluntary contributions framework, explicitly compare formal and informal sanction schemes, study choice between the two kinds of schemes, and consider their possible co-existence, appear to be a new development.

A study by Putterman, Tyran and Kamei (2011) in which subjects must vote on components that together comprise a formal sanction scheme in a VCM, was partly motivated by the observation that in many studies of informal sanctions, a quarter to a third of punishment is "misdirected" at high contributors. Given this lack of unanimity about who should be sanctioned when sanctions are up to the individual, we wondered how easily groups could reach decisions about the targeting and intensity of formal sanctions, and whether subjects displaying different orientations with respect to voluntary cooperation and informal sanctioning would also vote differently on the parameters of a formal sanction scheme. Our subjects voted on whether to penalize allocations to their private accounts or those to their group account, on whether to permit some allocation to the account(s) in question to be exempt from taxation and if so how much, and on the maximum penalty, which together with the exemption level determines the penalty rate per unit allocated. As anticipated, subjects who tended to display less cooperative inclinations also voted for inefficient sanction scheme components. Nevertheless, almost all groups' majorities learned to construct fully efficient schemes after a few votes. The outnumbering of "perverse" voting tendencies by group-level majorities as well as learning to improve institutions with time resemble the results in Ertan et al.'s study in which groups voted on who could be informally sanctioned.

Markussen, Putterman and Tyran (forthcoming) let subjects decide between formal, informal, and sanction-free play of a VCM by majority vote, varying the

---

14. Still another terminology would be to call the former "decentralized" and the latter "centralized" sanctions.

available formal scheme across treatments with respect to fixed cost to subjects (more versus less expensive) and strength of sanctions (monetarily deterrent versus non-deterrent). Kamei, Putterman and Tyran (2012) conducted a similar study, but their subjects first voted for either an informal or a formal sanctions scheme, and if the formal option were chosen, its details (including deterrence level) would then be determined in each period through voting. In both studies, there were fixed costs of adopting a formal sanction scheme, corresponding to the costs of manning and operating a state, but these costs always amounted to less than 40% of the gains of shifting the equilibrium from complete free-riding to full contributions, gains that standard economic theory predicts from adopting a deterrent-level sanction. Both studies found formal sanctions to be relatively popular when deterrent and inexpensive, but some groups preferred informal sanctions even then, and most groups preferred informal sanctions when formal ones were non-deterrent, expensive, or both. Both studies also found evidence that informal sanctions were more effectively used when chosen by vote.

Of course, the concern discussed earlier as to whether real world groups can determine the presence or not of informal sanctions also raises questions about experiments in which subjects choose between formal and informal sanctions. If informal sanctions are aspects of the social interaction between individuals that cannot be suppressed by group decision, then the realistic alternatives may simply be informal sanctions alone or formal sanctions added to informal ones. Kube and Traxler (2011) compared VCM play with informal sanctions alone to that with the combination of informal and formal sanctions and found that higher contributions and earnings were achieved with the combination. They argue that the addition of informal sanctions helps to explain why formal but non-deterrent sanctions are often effective—e.g., people may avoid littering despite small expected fines (given low probability of detection) because of the added cost of incurring reproach from bystanders.

Formal sanctions of non-deterrent strength (again, in view of low probabilities of detection and enforcement) are common, perhaps in part because punishments harsh enough to deter non-cooperation or rule-breaking without normative or other aids are viewed as too draconian, especially given chances of error. In addition to complementary informal sanctions, another force that might help confer effectiveness on informal sanctions is the sense of support or of intention to cooperate conveyed by being chosen democratically. Tyran and Feld (2006) show experimentally that non-deterrent formal sanctions significantly raise cooperation when selected by majority voting but not when imposed exogenously by the experimenters. Markussen et al. (forthcoming) confirm this with an added exogenously imposed non-deterrent sanction treatment.

The Benefits of Coordination

Boyd, Gintis and Bowles (2010) argue that the evolution of a propensity to punish free-riding would have been favored if punishers had been able to credibly signal an intention to punish, but then engage in actual punishment only if they found themselves to be in a group containing enough punishers that incurring this cost would ultimately pay off in the form of higher cooperation in the long run. A somewhat similar and recurrent theme in the research of Elinor Ostrom and collaborators, including Ostrom et al. (1992) and Janssen, Holahan, Lee and Ostrom (2010), is that communication about group strategy is often key to successful cooperation.

Voting may also be viewed as a coordination device, and the higher efficiencies achieved when groups choose their schemes by voting in Ertan et al. (2009), Kamei et al. (2012), and Markussen et al. (forthcoming) echo parallel indications of an impact of voting in Tyran and Feld (2006), Sutter et al. (2010) and Kamei (2011). Verbal or text communication has been found to lead to substantially higher levels of cooperation in social dilemma games including VCM experiments (Sally, 1995; Brosig, Ockenfels & Weimann, 2003; Bochet, Page & Putterman, 2006), but examples in which groups use such communication to improve coordination with respect to informal or formal sanction schemes in a VCM are rare thus far.[15]

CONCLUDING REMARKS

The literature discussed in this chapter, growing so rapidly that only a small fraction of it has been referenced here,[16] suggests that models of collective action which ignore the predisposition to punish unfair or free-riding behaviors in social dilemmas, do a poor job of predicting the range of conditions under which people can successfully cooperate. This is potentially good news, given that some of the most serious problems facing our world, including global warming and protection of natural resources, are social dilemmas.

Why are peer-to-peer sanctions and voluntary cooperation needed if governments can in principle induce full cooperation from rational and self-interested individuals by imposing deterrent sanctions on any who fail to cooperate? A first reason may be that sanctions of sufficient strength to be deterrent despite low probability of the violator being caught and punished, might need to be so high as to violate modern standards of acceptability—for instance, long prison terms for litterers or those who ignore stop signs. A second is that many problems of collective action, such as cooperating in the management of a village woodlot or raising effort in an enterprise in response to a group incentive or profit-sharing scheme, are too small in scale and too costly to monitor to be handled by governments at reasonable cost. The issue of up-front cost mentioned previously may apply as well.

Perhaps the most important point to be made is that we need to be wary of invoking government as a *deus ex machina*. That is, the presence of a democratic

---

15. Bochet et al., 2006, find cooperation so high with face-to-face communication in the absence of sanctioning opportunities that the addition of such opportunities makes little difference. In their treatment with text communication and punishment opportunities, subjects hesitate to discuss making the sanctions into a tool for promoting cooperation, instead suggesting that they should be avoided because they waste money. In Bochet and Putterman, 2009, however, sanctions are successfully used in a treatment in which subjects can send promises to contribute specific amounts to the public good: the use of sanctions to punish false promises leads to greater adherence to and hence credibility of promises, and this, along with sanctioning low contributions in general, supports a higher contribution and earnings outcome.

16. Other summaries can be found in Gächter and Herrmann (2008) and Chaudhuri (2011).

and accountable government responsive to a population's will may best be viewed as evidence that a prior collective action problem—the problem of bending once autocratic state machineries to the people's will—has been solved, and that that solution continues to be policed by voluntary collective actions such as citizen political participation, support for an investigative press, and the bestowing of social rewards on honest officials and whistle-blowers. In other words, accountable states could not exist and would soon cease to be accountable without at least a modicum of voluntary collective action to undergird them. If so, government-mandated collective action is a way of leveraging voluntary collective action, not a substitute for it.

REFERENCES

Anderson, C. M., & Putterman, L. (2006). Do Non-strategic Sanctions Obey the Law of Demand? The Demand for Punishment in the Voluntary Contribution Mechanism. *Games and Economic Behavior, 54*, 1–24.

Axelrod, R. (1986). An Evolutionary Approach to Norms. *American Political Science Review, 80*, 1095–1111.

Balliet, D., Mulder, L., & Van Lange, P. (2011). Reward, Punishment, and Cooperation: A Meta-Analysis. *Psychological Bulletin, 137*, 594–615.

Bochet, O., Page, T., & Putterman, L., (2006). Communication and Punishment in Voluntary Contribution Experiments. *Journal of Economic Behavior and Organization, 60*, 11–26.

Bochet, O., & Putterman, L. (2009). Not Just Babble: A Voluntary Contribution Experiment with Iterative Numerical Messages. *European Economic Review, 53*, 309–326.

Bolle, F., Tan, J., & Zizzo, D. (2010). Vendettas. University of Nottingham CeDEx Discussion Paper 2010-02.

Botelho, A., Harrison, G., Costa Pinto, L., & Rutström, E. (2005). Social Norms and Social Choice. Unpublished paper, Dept. of Economics, University of Central Florida.

Bowles, S., Carpenter, J., & Gintis, H. (2001). Mutual Monitoring in Teams: Theory and Evidence on the Importance of Residual Claimancy and Reciprocity. Mimeo, University of Massachusetts and Middlebury College.

Boyd, R., Gintis, H., & Bowles, S. (2010). Coordinated Punishment of Defectors Sustains Cooperation and Can Proliferate When Rare. *Science, 328*, 617–620.

Brosig, J., Ockenfels, A., & Weimann, J. (2003). The Effect of Communication Media on Cooperation. *German Economic Review, 4*, 217–242.

Carpenter, J. (2007). The Demand for Punishment. *Journal of Economic Behavior and Organization, 62*, 522–542.

Casari, M. (2005). On the Design of Peer Punishment Experiments. *Experimental Economics, 8*, 107–115.

Casari, M., & Luini, L. (2009). Cooperation under Alternative Punishment Institutions: An Experiment. *Journal of Economic Behavior and Organization, 71*, 273–282.

Chaudhuri, A. (2011). Sustaining Cooperation in Laboratory Public Goods Experiments: A Selective Survey of the Literature. *Experimental Economics, 14*, 47–83.

Cinyabuguma, M., Page T., & Putterman, L. (2004). On Perverse and Second-Order Punishment in Public Goods Experiments with Decentralized Sanctions. Working Paper 2004-12, Brown University Department of Economics.

Cinyabuguma, M., Page, T., & Putterman, L. (2006). Can Second-Order Punishment Deter Perverse Punishment? *Experimental Economics, 9*, 265–279.

Denant-Boemont, L., Masclet, D., & Noussair, C. N. (2007). Punishment, Counter-punishment and Sanction Enforcement in a Social Dilemma Experiment. *Economic Theory, 33,* 145–167.

Ertan, A., Page, T., & Putterman, L. (2009). Who to Punish? Individual Decisions and Majority Rule in Mitigating the Free-Rider Problem. *European Economic Review, 53,* 495–511.

Falk, A., Fehr, E., & Fischbacher, U. (2005). Driving Forces Behind Informal Sanctions. *Econometrica, 73,* 2017–2030.

Fehr, E., Kirchsteiger, G., & Riedl, A. (1993). Does Fairness Prevent Market Clearing? An Experimental Investigation. *Quarterly Journal of Economics, 108,* 437–460.

Fehr, E., Gächter, S., & Kirchsteiger, G. (1997). Reciprocity as a Contract Enforcement Device—Experimental Evidence. *Econometrica, 65,* 833–860.

Fehr, E., & Gächter, S. (1998). How Effective are Trust- and Reciprocity-Based Incentives? In A. Ben-Ner & L. Putterman, (Eds.), *Economics, Values, and Organization* (pp. 337–363). New York: Cambridge University Press.

Fehr, E., & Gächter, S. (2000a). Cooperation and Punishment in Public Goods Experiments. *American Economic Review, 90,* 980–994.

Fehr, E., & Gächter, S. (2000b). Fairness and Retaliation: The Economics of Reciprocity. *Journal of Economic Perspectives, 14,* 159–181.

Fehr, E., & Gächter, S. (2002). Altruistic Punishment in Humans. *Nature, 415,* 137–140.

Fehr, E., & Schmidt, K. (1999). A Theory of Fairness, Competition, and Cooperation. *Quarterly Journal of Economics, 104,* 817–868.

Gächter, S., & Herrmann, B. (2008). Reciprocity, Culture and Human Cooperation: Previous Insights and a New Cross-Cultural Experiment. *Philosophical Transactions of the Royal Society B* doi:10.1098/rstb.2008.0275.

Gächter, S., Renner, E., & Sefton, M. (2008). The Long-Run Benefits of Punishment. *Science, 322,* 1510.

Gürerk, Ö., Irlenbusch, B., & Rockenbach, B. (2006). The Competitive Advantage of Sanctioning Institutions. *Science, 312,* 108–110.

Güth, W., Schmittberger, R., & Schwarze, B. (1982). An Experimental Analysis of Ultimatum Bargaining. *Journal of Economic Behavior and Organization, 3,* 367–388.

Henrich, J., Boyd, R. (2001). Why People Punish Defectors: Weak Conformist Transmission can Stabilize Costly Enforcement of Norms in Cooperative Dilemmas. *Journal of Theoretical Biology, 208,* 79–89.

Herrmann, B., Thöni, C., & Gächter, S. (2008). Antisocial Punishment across Societies. *Science, 319,* 1362–1367.

Janssen, M., Holahan, R., Lee, A., & Ostrom, E. (2010). Lab Experiments for the Study of Social-Ecological Systems. *Science, 328,* 613–617.

Kamei, K. (2011). Democracy and Resilient Pro-Social Behavioral Change: An Experimental Study. Unpublished paper, Brown University.

Kamei, K., & Putterman, L. (2013). In Broad Daylight: Fuller Information and Higher-order Punishment Opportunities Can Promote Cooperation. Brown University Department of Economics Working Paper 2012-3, revised.

Kamei, K., Putterman, L., & Tyran, J.-R. (2012). State or Nature: Formal vs. Informal Sanctioning in the Provision of Public Goods. Brown University Department of Economics Working Paper 2011-3, revised.

Kube, S., & Traxler, C. (2011). The Interaction of Legal and Social Norm Enforcement. *Journal of Public Economic Theory, 13,* 639–660.

Ledyard, J. (1995). Public Goods: A Survey of Experimental Research. In J. Kagel & A. Roth (Eds.), *Handbook of Experimental Economics* (pp. 111-194). Princeton: Princeton University Press.

Markussen, T., Putterman, L., & Tyran, J.-R. (forthcoming). Self-organization for Collective Action: An Experimental Study of Voting on Sanction Regimes. *Review of Economic Studies* (in press).

Masclet, D., Noussair, C., Tucker, S., & Villeval, M.-C. (2003). Monetary and Nonmonetary Punishment in the Voluntary Contributions Mechanism. *American Economic Review*, 93, 366-380.

Nicklisch, A., & Wolff, I. (2011). Cooperation Norms in Multiple Stage Punishment. *Journal of Public Economic Theory*, 13, 791-827.

Nikiforakis, N. (2008). Punishment and Counter-punishment in Public Goods Games: Can We Really Govern Ourselves. *Journal of Public Economics*, 92, 91-112.

Nikiforakis, N., & Engelmann, D. (2011). Altruistic Punishment and the Threat of Feuds. *Journal of Economic Behavior and Organization*, 78, 319-32.

Nikiforakis, N., & Normann, H.-T. (2008). A Comparative Statics Analysis of Punishment in Public-Good Experiments. *Experimental Economics*, 11, 358-369.

Nikiforakis, N., Noussair, C., & Wilkening, T. (2012). Normative Conflict and Feuds: The Limits of Self-Enforcement. *Journal of Public Economics*, 96, 797-807.

Önes, U., & Putterman, L. (2007). The Ecology of Collective Action: A Public Goods and Sanctions Experiment with Controlled Group Formation. *Journal of Economic Behavior and Organization*, 62, 495-521.

Ostrom, E. (1990). Governing the Commons: The Evolution of Institutions for Collective Action. Cambridge. U.K.: Cambridge University Press.

Ostrom, E., Walker, J., & Gardner, R. (1992). Covenants With and Without a Sword: Self-Governance is Possible. *American Political Science Review*, 86, 404-417.

Page, T., Putterman, L., & Garcia, B. (2013). Voluntary contributions with redistribution: The effect of costly sanctions when one person's punishment is another's reward. *Journal of Economic Behavior and Organization*, 85, 34-48.

Page, T., Putterman, L., & Unel, B. (2005). Voluntary Association in Public Goods Experiments: Reciprocity, Mimi cry and Efficiency. *Economic Journal*, 115, 1032-1053.

Putterman, L., Tyran, J.-R., & Kamei, K. (2011). Public Goods and Voting on Formal Sanction Schemes: An Experiment. *Journal of Public Economics*, 95, 1213-1222.

Sally, D. (1995). Conversation and Cooperation in Social Dilemmas: A Meta-Analysis of Experiments from 1958 to 1992. *Rationality and Society*, 7, 58-92.

Sefton, M., Shupp, R., & Walker, J. (2007). The Effect of Rewards and Sanctions in Provision of Public Goods. *Economic Inquiry*, 45, 671-690.

Sutter, M., Haigner, S., & Kocher, M. (2010). Choosing the Carrot or the Stick?–Endogenous Institutional Choice in Social Dilemma Situations. *Review of Economic Studies*, 77, 1540-1566.

Tyran, J.-R., & Feld, L. P. (2006). Achieving Compliance when Legal Sanctions are Non-deterrent. *Scandinavian Journal of Economics*, 108, 1-22.

Yamagishi, T. (1986). The Provision of a Sanctioning System as a Public Good. *Journal of Personality and Social Psychology*, 51, 110-116.

3 How (and When) Reward and Punishment Promote Cooperation: An Interdependence Theoretical Perspective

■ DANIEL BALLIET AND
   PAUL A. M. VAN LANGE

Abstract
Prior research finds that both rewards and punishment promote cooperation in social dilemmas. We discuss an interdependence theoretical perspective on understanding the proximate psychological mechanisms that underlie how incentives work to promote cooperation. Specifically, we discuss how understanding the specific incentive structure of interdependent social interactions may lead to greater insight into both (a) the use and (b) the effectiveness of incentives in promoting cooperation. We also discuss important implications from understanding various social motives and the perceived motives of others that affect how incentives influence cooperation. By applying an interdependence perspective, we arrive at several new promising directions for future research on incentives and cooperation.

Individuals in relationships, groups, organizations, and societies often face social dilemmas—situations that involve a motivational conflict between choosing to do what is best for oneself or what is best for the collective. Certainly, relationships and groups can benefit when individuals sacrifice some of their immediate direct self-interest in order to behave in a way that is beneficial for the collective. Yet, people do not always choose to cooperate. The fact that people do even cooperate across a broad range of circumstances is quite puzzling to many biological and social scientists. Rational choice theory predicts that people will not cooperate in social dilemmas, unless their own interests are aligned with others (Hargreaves, Heap, & Varufakis, 2004). Moreover, evolutionary theory suggests that the evolution of cooperation amongst unrelated strangers (at least to the extent that we observe it in humans) is difficult to explain in terms of evolutionary processes, although recent advances implicate that it is plausible (Nowak, 2006).

Much research on human cooperation has centered on asking the basic question: Under what conditions will people be willing to cooperate. Numerous solutions have been identified, including communication, small group size, the monitoring of reputation, and framing, to name a few (for reviews, see Balliet, 2010, Gächter & Herrmann, 2009; Weber, Kopelman, & Messick, 2004; Van Lange, Balliet, Parks, & Van Vugt, 2013). More recently, there has been an onslaught of research on **incentives as a solution to social dilemmas.** This research has largely arrived at the conclusion that incentives (both punishments and rewards) are able to increase cooperation in social dilemmas (Fehr & Gächter, 2000; Mulder, 2008; Ostrom, Walker, & Gardner, 1992; Parks, 2000; Rand, Dreber, Ellingsen, Fudenberg, & Nowak, 2009; Yamagishi, 1986, 1988).

Although philosophers (e.g., Hobbes, 1651) and scientists (e.g., Hardin, 1968) have discussed the implications of incentives for cooperation, it was not until Yamagishi's (1986, 1988) pioneering work and the subsequent work of others (e.g., Fehr & Gächter, 2000, 2002; Ostrom et al., 1992) that at least the value of punishment for increasing cooperation became an empirical fact (for recent meta-analyses, see Balliet, Mulder, & Van Lange, 2011; Balliet & Van Lange, 2013a). Although certain theories and research on incentives and motivation may suggest that incentives can undermine autonomy, the intrinsic motivation to cooperate, or result in reactance to the incentive (e.g., Brehm, 1966; Deci & Ryan, 2000), research has largely replicated the finding that both punishments and rewards tend to increase cooperation in social dilemmas (see Gächter, Renner, & Sefton, 2008; Rand et al., 2009). At this point, research is attempting to understand how incentives work to promote cooperation.

Recent views on this issue have approached the topic from an evolutionary perspective. The idea is that evolution may have selected for a disposition to punish noncooperators, so-called strong reciprocity (e.g., Fehr, Fischbacher, & Gächter, 2002). Evolutionary models support the possibility of this potential design feature in humans (Gintis, 2000) and certainly an abundance of cross-cultural data suggests that humans possess a tendency to punish noncooperators, even at a cost to themselves (Henrich et al., 2006, 2010; Herrmann, Thöni, & Gächter, 2008). Much less research, however, has approached understanding the relation between incentives and cooperation using different theoretical perspectives, especially with a strong focus on the proximal causes of the use and effectiveness of incentives to promote cooperation.

The purpose of this chapter is to discuss the implications of interdependence theory, as developed by Kelley and Thibaut (Kelley et al., 2003; Kelley & Thibaut, 1978), for understanding the relation between incentives and cooperation. It is a theory that places particular emphasis on (a) the nature of self-interested behavior (i.e., that human behavior is partially motivated by enhancing own outcomes; the given matrix thesis), (b) the social preferences one may have (i.e., that human behavior is often also motivated by concern for others' outcomes; the transformation of motivation thesis), and (c) **the perceptions of others' social preferences** (i.e., the perceived transformation thesis). As we will discuss, this perspective may provide insight into several new promising directions for future research for both understanding (a) the use of incentives and (b) the effectiveness of incentives to promote cooperation.

■ INTERDEPENDENCE THEORY, INCENTIVES, AND COOPERATION

Interdependence theory is a theory about the structure of social interaction situations. It advances a taxonomy of interaction situations, and outlines the relevance of dimensions such as degree of dependence, degree of conflicting interests, degree of information availability, and the degree to which interdependence extends over time (see Kelley & Thibaut, 1978; Rusbult & Van Lange, 2003). Moreover, the theory goes beyond formally outlining interdependence structures, in that it addresses how people may respond and adapt to others in various interdependence structures. In the following sections we outline three principles of interdependence theory regarding the psychology of interdependent individuals and discuss the implication each has for understanding the relation between incentives and cooperation.

Given Matrix Thesis. Interdependence theory claims that a natural starting point for individuals in an interdependent situation is to consider their own direct self-interest. Such an assumption shares similarities with other frameworks in the social sciences, such as rational choice theory (Hargreaves, Heap, & Varufakis, 2004). An implication of this perspective is that people should be influenced by direct changes to an incentive structure during interdependent situations, such as a social dilemma.

Olson (1965) claimed that incentives could be used to reduce the discrepancy between self-interest and collective interest. In fact, the addition of punishments for noncooperation and rewards for cooperation do indeed reduce this discrepancy (Kollock, 1998). Research has found that direct manipulations to incentive structures that reduce the discrepancy between self-interest and collective interest results in higher rates of cooperation, since self-interest is now more closely aligned with cooperation (Komorita & Parks, 1995; Komorita, Sweeney, & Kravitz, 1980). Indeed, several experimental studies since then provide strong support for this by demonstrating that both rewards (Parks, 2000; Rand et al., 2009) and punishments (Yamagishi, 1988) tend to promote cooperation.

One implication of this perspective is that equivalent rewards and punishments should result in the same increase in cooperation. A recent meta-analysis has concluded that rewards and punishments do not statistically differ in the magnitude of their effect on behavior (Balliet, Mulder, & Van Lange, 2011), especially when both rewards and punishment were administered over several trials of a social dilemma. However, the sample of studies used in the meta-analysis for both rewards and punishment may not be completely symmetrical in the magnitude of the incentives provided across the experiments. At the study level, researchers are able to more strongly control and compare rewards and punishments (of equivalent magnitudes), and this work has resulted in mixed findings. Some studies report that punishments are more effective (Andreoni et al., 2003; Rapoport & Au, 2001; Stern, 1976), whereas other studies suggest that rewards are more effective than punishment (Komorita & Barth, 1985; McCusker & Carnevale, 1995), and some studies suggest that there is no difference between the two incentives in terms of effectiveness (Rand et al., 2009; Sefton, Shupp, & Walker, 2007). Yet, several methodological differences remain amongst these studies that may underlie the mixed results. As such, there is consensus about two conclusions: First, reward and punishment both are effective at promoting cooperation, and second, more research is needed to examine the specific circumstances under which reward versus punishment might be equally or differentially effective.

It is important to also recognize that although rewards and punishments of equivalent magnitudes may have similar effects on behavior, this does not necessarily mean that the psychological response to punishment and reward is equivalent. Moreover, each may have different indirect effects on subsequent cooperation after the removal (or in the absence) of incentives (also see Shinada & Yamagishi, 2008). For example, Mulder and colleagues (2006) find that the presence of a punishment system can undermine the development of trust. Specifically, people trust others less in a group when at an earlier point in time there was a sanctioning system promoting group cooperation, but the system was later removed, compared to a situation when no sanction ever existed to regulate cooperation. This may be because people perceive that others cooperate out of their own self-interest when a sanctioning system is present, but in the absence of a sanctioning system people are perceived to cooperate out of concern for the group.

Indeed, interdependence theory (e.g., Balliet & Van Lange, 2013b), along with other theories of trust (e.g., Yamagishi, 2011), suggest that trust is only relevant to situations with stronger conflicting interests, because these situations allow people to express their concern for the well-being for the relationship or group. As Yamagishi (2011) notes, the presence of an incentive system for cooperation promotes assurance, not trust. Moreover, Chen, Pillutla, and Yao (2009) have replicated and extended these results to apply to the use of rewards—so both punishments and rewards may similarly undermine the development of trust. Thus, although both rewards and punishments can similarly promote cooperation by reducing the conflict of interests people face in situations, they can also have similar indirect effects on trust. Moreover, there may be additional differential indirect effects, such as punishments (as opposed to rewards) may initiate feuds (e.g., antisocial punishment, Herrmann et al., 2008; Fehr & Rockenbach, 2003), undermine intrinsic motives for fairness or altruism, and/or punishment may result in a stronger reactance to the incentive.

These later points imply that there may be important differences between the direct impact of punishment and reward on promoting cooperation, beyond focusing purely on the implications for an individual's direct self-interest. Several important individual and social processes may alter the impact of both rewards and punishment on cooperation. Importantly, beyond examining the implications of rewards and punishment on the interdependence structure of social interactions, interdependence theory considers how people understand the situation with different motives (beyond self-interest) and the importance of how people perceive others' motives in these social interactions, and as we discuss subsequently, both these issues may have implications for understanding the workings of incentives to promote cooperation.

Transformation of Motivation Thesis. In a proximate sense, people are not always attempting to maximize their own personal well-being, without the consideration of others. According to interdependence theory, although people may have an immediate reaction to the situation to consider their own self-interest, people may also bring to the situation other social motives that may influence the way they perceive a situation and how they eventually behave. Specifically, while the theory suggests that people initially begin to think about an interdependent situation in terms of self-interest, individuals can transform their motivation based on broader considerations, such as taking into account others' outcomes.

Indeed, the past 40 years of research on human cooperation has arrived at a general consensus that people do indeed consider others' outcomes when making interdependent decisions, such as in social dilemmas (see Balliet, Parks, & Joireman, 2009; Fehr & Schmidt, 1999). Research on social values, social motives, and social preferences find that a significant number of people do often prefer to cooperate in one-shot anonymous social dilemmas (e.g., Fischbacher & Gächter, 2010)—an observation that is incongruent with a perspective that people are always just focusing on their own outcomes during social dilemmas. Several social motivations may underlie a tendency to prefer cooperation, specifically a motivation to maximize joint gain and/or maximizing equality in outcomes (inequality aversion) (Van Lange, 1999). Importantly, social motives may affect both the use of incentives *and* how people respond to incentives.

According to interdependence theory, social motives (e.g., maximizing joint gain or equality) become especially important for determining behavior in situations that involve a conflict between self and collective interests (Balliet & Van Lange, 2013b; Kelley et al., 2003). Importantly, supporting or contributing to an incentive system that either punishes defectors and/or rewards cooperators can be costly and pose a second-order social dilemma (Yamagishi, 1988). When incentives are costly, then it is in each individual's self-interest not to provide any incentives, but to benefit on the increased levels of cooperation as a result of others providing incentives. Thus, since the decision to provide costly sanctions is itself a social dilemma, then according to interdependence theory, social motives should predict decisions to engage in the costly punishment of norm violators.

Indeed, people who tend to maximize collective outcomes or equality in outcomes may be more inclined to punish noncooperators (Dawes, Fowler, Johnson, McElreath, & Smirnov, 2007; Fowler, Johnson, & Smirnov, 2005; Johnson et al., 2009). Specifically, Dawes and colleagues (2007) found that people are willing to punish people in a so-called random income game, whereby participants in a group of four are randomly assigned a specific amount of money by a computer. In this experiment, people were willing to pay a cost to either take money away from the high-earners and/or give money away to the low-earners. The authors take this as support for the position that egalitarian motives may underlie the distribution of punishments in prior experimental research. Indeed, Johnson and colleagues (2009) have also found that people who tend to take money away from high-earners in the random income game are more likely to punish noncooperators (and so high-earners) in a public goods experimental design. These findings support the position that a social motive, such as egalitarianism, may direct the use of punishment (and possibly rewards) in social dilemmas. Another motivation that often correlates with an egalitarian motive is the motive to maximize joint gain (Van Lange, 1999), yet research has not addressed how this motive may underlie punishing noncooperators or rewarding cooperators. Perhaps people with this motive are more likely to reward than punish, since this strategy is maximizing joint outcomes—a possibility for future research to explore.

Differences in motives and specific goals that people bring to social dilemmas may also influence who responds to being punished with subsequent cooperation. Punishment may provide important situational feedback that enables people to adjust their behavior to better achieve their goals. This topic has received some attention in prior research. For example, people with a prosocial motive may desire to cooperate, but nonetheless they may not do so because they fear that others will take advantage of their cooperation (Pruitt & Kimmel, 1977). Prosocial (yet fearful) defectors may respond quite differently to punishment compared to individuals who defect to maximize their own outcome. Specifically, among prosocial defectors, punishment may increase expectations that others are willing to cooperate and may even induce guilt, and both expectations and guilt may encourage subsequent cooperation.

Free-riders who defect out of self-interest, however, may be more likely to respond to the magnitude of the punishment. If punishment is too small, it may pay to continue to defect, but if punishment is too large, then it would pay to cooperate. Prior research has found that small penalties may decrease cooperation, compared to larger penalties (Gneezy & Rustichini, 2000; Tenbrunsel, & Messick, 1999), but this effect may be limited to understanding how self-interested free-riders respond to being punished. People with competitive goals, however, may instead be induced to cooperate through observing others maximizing their relative payoffs by being rewarded for cooperating (or potentially reduced relative earnings through punishment). These individuals may be motivated to compete with others for being the most cooperative when the rewards for cooperation are substantial. How social motives (and specific interaction goals) affect responses to rewards and punishment is a promising new direction for future research.

Perceived Transformation of Motivation Thesis. Not only do individual motives matter, but how people perceive the motives of others during interdependent social interactions matters for understanding how people behave during social dilemmas. People understand when others sacrifice their own self-interest and engage in cooperative behaviors that benefit relationships, groups, and organizations. Thus, people may be responsive to the perceived transformation of motives of others that underlies cooperative behavior. For example, when people perceive that their partner sacrificed their self-interest in a specific situation to do what was best for a relationship, then the perceptions of the benevolent motives that underlie their behavior may subsequently increase trust in a partner (e.g., Wieselquist, Rusbult, Agnew, & Foster, 1999). We suspect that the process of the perceived motives of others may have important consequences for understanding the relation between incentives and cooperation.

Much prior research has examined the effect of peer punishment and reward on cooperation. For example, in the well-replicated paradigm developed by Fehr and Gächter (2000; 2002), a group of four individuals plays a public goods dilemma and then learns how much its group members contributed (or not) to the public good. Afterwards, each group member has an opportunity to pay a cost to punish the other group member(s). In this situation, the perceived motives of the punisher may matter for how people respond to being punished. When people perceive that another person is punishing them because they are concerned about the collective outcome, this may have the effect of promoting cooperation. So what helps to communicate that people are punishing or rewarding out of concern for collective outcomes?

In a recent meta-analysis, Balliet, Mulder, and Van Lange (2011) argued that the extent to which incentives are costly to deliver will indicate that people are providing incentives out of concern for the collective. This is because people have to sacrifice their immediate self-interest to pay a cost to punish others for not contributing to the public good. When people pay this cost, others may perceive that they are genuinely concerned about the collective outcome. Yet, when punishment is free or less costly to administer, then this may less clearly communicate that a person is providing an incentive out of concern for collective outcomes. The meta-analysis compared the effect of both rewards and punishments on cooperation in studies that made the incentives either costly or free to administer. The results were that both types of incentives were more effective when they were costly, compared to free, to administer. One interpretation is that people are more likely to perceive costly incentives as caused by a concern for collective outcomes and that this may encourage subsequent cooperation and the emergence of group norms of cooperation. In the absence of communicating that incentives are delivered out of concern for collective outcomes, incentives may be less effective.

When people are able to communicate that their behavior is directed by concern for collective outcomes, this may have a positive impact on both cooperation and the effectiveness of punishments in promoting cooperation. In fact, this may be why communication is generally more effective than incentives for increasing cooperation in experimental social dilemmas (Balliet, 2010) and why allowing communication with the use of incentives is more effective at increasing cooperation compared to a situation that only allows for incentives (Janssen, Holahan, Lee, & Ostrom, 2010; Ostrom et al., 1992). When people are able to communicate why they have delivered punishments for noncooperation and rewards for cooperation, this may communicate that the behaviors were directed by prosocial motives, which may enhance trust in others and facilitate subsequent cooperation.

In fact, research does suggest that people are inclined to perceive costly punishment of others as the result of benevolent motives. For example, Barclay (2006) found that people tend to perceive altruistic punishers as more trustworthy, but that this effect was limited to when punishment was directed toward free-riders. This may be taken as indirect evidence that people perceive that benevolent motives underlie the willingness to engage in the costly punishment of others. Moreover, Nelissen (2008) found that people grant greater reputational benefits to punishers who pay a greater cost to punish others. People who paid a greater cost in punishing noncooperators were preferred as partners in a subsequent trust game. Clearly, these findings reveal that people are responsive to the perceived motives of others who deliver incentives and that the perception of benevolent motives that underlies the delivery of incentives may result in positive reputations and how others continue to interact with the punisher. Although this conclusion is already well-supported by prior research, more research is needed to directly measure the perceived motives of both the delivery of rewards and punishment and how variation in the perceived motives of people who provide incentives relates to how second and third parties subsequently think about and interact with that person.

FEATURES OF INTERDEPENDENCE

A novel feature of interdependence theory, relative to other theories in the social sciences, is that it provides a conceptual framework for understanding the structure of outcomes for interdependent social interactions. By analyzing features of an outcome matrix, and related representations of interdependence, interdependence theory proposes six dimensions that might underlie interaction situations (see Kelley et al., 2003). Specifically, the dimensions that characterize interdependence structures include the level of dependence, asymmetry of dependence, basis of dependence, degree of conflicting interests, temporal structure, and information availability (for an overview see, Van Lange & Balliet, 2013). Next, we will illustrate and suggest various lines of research that are relevant to interdependence theoretical principles—specifically that these dimensions are essential to understand how people might react to norm violations, such as tendencies toward free-riding.

In the following sections we outline some directions for future research on incentives for cooperation across a broader domain of social situations, and illustrate that the mechanics of reward and punishment are strongly shaped by two dimensions of interdependence: (a) the degree to which interests are conflicting (a classic dimension of interdependence theory), and (b) the future (time-extendedness) of the interdependence (a dimension that has been conceptualized more recently by interdependence theory, Kelley et al., 2003).

DEGREE OF CONFLICTING INTERESTS

Social dilemmas, by definition, involve some degree of conflicting outcomes between persons facing the dilemma. However, the degree of conflict varies across social dilemmas, both inside and outside the lab (Balliet & Van Lange, 2013b; Rapoport & Chammah, 1965). How situations vary along this underlying dimension may have important implications for understanding the workings of punishment and reward for promoting cooperation.

As mentioned earlier, one principle of interdependence theory is that people initially interpret social interdependence in terms of self-interest—and one implication of this perspective is that people are responsive to changes in the structure of outcomes during interdependent situations. This implies that people will be more cooperative in situations that involve less conflict between self and collective interests. As noted earlier, a robust finding is that people tend to be more cooperative when they interact in a situation with a low degree of conflict of interests (Komorita & Parks, 1995). People also tend to expect more cooperation from others in situations with low conflict (Krueger, DiDonato, & Freestone, 2012). For example, Balliet, Li, and Joireman (2011) report that 95% (n = 66) of participants playing a maximizing difference game choose to cooperate, a situation when cooperation is in the self-interest of each participant. However, only 49% (n = 95) of participants choose to cooperate in the prisoner's dilemma and a similar percentage of people expected that amount of cooperation from others.

Thus, in situations that involve greater degrees of conflict of interests, there is a less uniformed set of expectations for the behavior of others, which may indicate less strongly shared expectations for behavior (or social norms), relative to when people interact in situations approaching coordination games. When self-interest is nearly or actually aligned with cooperation, then people have strong expectations for behavior, resulting in a strong social norm (i.e., a strong situation, Cooper & Withey, 2009). For example, when the costs for self are exceptionally large, and benefits for the collective small, then people may find a noncooperative choice somewhat understandable. But it is more counter-normative if one does not make a contribution, at a small cost to self, that would yield enormous benefits to the collective (e.g., Joireman et al., 2003).

Much prior research has discussed the role of incentives in promoting norms of cooperation (e.g., Fehr & Fischbacher, 2004). However, no previous research has addressed the consequences of the degree of conflicting interests for the use and effectiveness of incentives to promote cooperation. We argue that specific norms for behavior may be energized when people hold strong expectations for behavior, and believe that most others think the same way too. For example, people are unlikely to reward others for behaving according to expectations in such a situation. However, people will be strongly motivated to punish others who violate this social norm. Comparing the maximizing difference game to the prisoner's dilemma game, Balliet, Li, and Joireman (2011) found that people self-reported a greater desire for revenge towards a noncooperative partner in the maximizing difference game, and that the difference was explained by stronger expectations for cooperation, compared to the prisoner's dilemma. Additionally, at least one study has found that people do indeed punish more when there is less, compared to greater, conflict of interests in a public goods dilemma (Carpenter, 2007). That is, when contributions to the public goods were more valuable (high MPCR), then people were willing to punish noncooperators more than when contributions were less valuable to the public good (low MPCR). These findings support the position that there may be stronger norms that are sustained by the use of punishment in situations with lower degree of conflicting interests.

So what happens to the use of punishment in situations with an increasing degree of conflict of interests and norms become less clear? Relative to situations with less conflict, situations with greater conflict should elicit less desire to punish noncooperators, but potentially a greater willingness to reward cooperators. When people expect others to cooperate, they may still understand that in general people expect others not to cooperate (and choose not to cooperate themselves), and so this situation involves less shared consensus about behavior (i.e., a weak social norm). In this context, people who expect others to cooperate may signal their desire to cooperate by rewarding others who do cooperate. In this context, punishment may not be as effective a tool to promote cooperation, because it may spark negative reactions to punishment, such as retaliation (Denant-Boemont, Masclet,

& Noussair, 2007). Thus, an interesting implication is that the willingness to use punishment to promote cooperation may increase as a function of the increase in correspondence of interests in a social dilemma, but that the use of rewards may increase with a decrease in the correspondence of interests (i.e., in situations with a greater conflict between self-interest and collective interest).

TEMPORAL STRUCTURE

Beyond the degree of conflicting interests, other structural dimensions may hold important implications for understanding how specific features of the person and situation may systematically alter the use and effectiveness of rewards and punishments in promoting cooperation. We would like to note the importance of the temporal structure of the situation. Social interactions can vary in terms of being a one-shot encounter with no future interactions, to being a social interaction embedded in a relationship with a past history and perceived future. Previous scholars have noted that possible future interactions can hold important consequences for understanding cooperation (e.g., Axelrod, 1984). Less work, however, has discussed how this future may (or may not) affect the workings of rewards and punishment in promoting cooperation—although much work across studies has either studied the effect of sanctions in either one-shot interactions or repeated interactions (see Balliet, Mulder, & Van Lange, 2011).

Gächter, Renner, and Sefton (2008) examined how the effect of punishment on cooperation differed depending on the number of iterations of a specific interaction. That study found that punishments were most effective over the long-term and they argued that this provided some evidence for punishments being efficient solutions to cooperation. A recent meta-analysis also finds that both punishments and rewards are more effective when administered over several repeated trials of a dilemma, compared to one-shot dilemmas (Balliet, Mulder, & Van Lange, 2011). Specifically, they found that punishments were least effective in one-shot dilemmas, slightly more effective in repeated interactions with a new partner on each trial, and most effective on repeated interactions between the same partners over time. Thus, there is evidence that the temporal structure may have important consequences for both the efficiency and effectiveness of sanctions for promoting cooperation, but little theoretical attention has been paid to how this structural feature of the situation may exert these effects.

Interdependence theory suggest that features of the person or situation that are relevant to affecting the trade-offs between a smaller immediate gain and a larger delayed reward may affect choice in situations with an extended temporal structure (Kelley et al., 2003). For example, such situations allow for the expression of specific dispositions, such as conscientiousness, self-control, and concern for future consequences (e.g., Joireman et al., 2012). During one-shot interactions these traits may not relate to either cooperation or a willingness to engage in costly punishment, but during repeated interactions it may be that these traits become relevant to predicting cooperation and the use of costly sanctions. Moreover, features of the situation that make people aware of the long-term consequences of their own behavior may encourage both cooperation and the use of costly incentives to promote cooperation (e.g., Balliet & Ferris, 2012). Additionally, Van Lange, Klapwijk, and Van Munster (2011) have demonstrated that people highly concerned with their own outcomes during social interactions are sensitive to the temporal structure of the situation, with these individuals being more cooperative in situations that involve repeated interactions (perhaps because they perceive that it is in their long-term self-interest to cooperate). Future research may test if this is also the case for the willingness to provide sanctions to promote cooperation. One implication would be that people should be willing to pay a higher cost to punish defectors during interactions with a longer extended future. Lastly, punishments may be most effective over time in the context of repeated interactions between the same partners because several psychological processes are affected by this structural feature of the situation, such as an ability to develop reputations and the efficient emergence of social norms. Future research on this issue will benefit by attempting to simultaneously measure and control for each of these possible reasons why an extended future makes sanctions more efficient and effective in promoting cooperation.

■ COMPARISON OF INTERDEPENDENCE THEORY WITH OTHER THEORETICAL FRAMEWORKS

Interdependence theory is similar to various theories of social behavior that assume that self-interest is a strong motivator of human behavior. For example, like many formulations of game theory, rational choice theory, and classic economic theory, interdependence theory assumes that humans approach decisions with an initial response based on self-interest. Interdependence theory also assumes that people can transform their initial self-interested preferences in a situation based on broader, social and temporal considerations, such as concern for others' outcomes, egalitarianism, and future outcomes (Van Lange, 1999). As such, interdependence theory shares notions with extended models of social preferences, as advanced by, for example, Fehr and Schmidt (1999), and more recently, by Fischbacher and Gächter (2010). Thus, these latter perspectives tend to emphasize self-interest *and* social preferences to explain social behavior.

Still there are at least three differences in emphasis. One difference is that interdependence theory assumes that the social preferences take a variety of forms, including cooperation (enhancement of own and others' outcomes), and equality (minimization of absolute differences in outcomes for self and others); and there may also be preferences that are not other-regarding, including competition (or spite, enhancement of relative advantage over others' outcomes). Under some specific circumstances, altruism (enhancement of others' outcomes) and aggression (minimization of others' outcomes) can help explain behavior in interdependence situations (see Van Lange & Balliet, 2013). A second difference is that interdependence theory emphasizes the importance of others' perceived transformation of motivation. People tend to think about how others' behaviors are directed by intentions and pay close attention to how others' behavior deviates from self-interest and how this may reflect social motives underlying behavior. A third difference is that interdependence theory focuses on how the structure of interdependent outcomes are determined and can afford what person and situational factors influence behavior. Indeed, we previously discussed here two such dimensions in greater detail—degree of conflicting interest and temporal structure (while other dimensions have not been discussed, such as degree of dependence or information availability). Interdependence theory may be viewed as an integrative theory that seeks to understand the structure of interdependent situations ("the games"), what they afford in terms of psychological process (e.g., transformations, or social preferences), and how that structure in combination with others' behavior may inform us about others' goals (e.g., perceived transformations, or perceived social preferences).

INTERDEPENDENCE THEORY AS A TOOL TO UNDERSTAND LAB/FIELD DISCREPANCY

Social interactions during lab-based studies differ substantially from interactions in the "wild life." According to interdependence theory (Kelley et al., 2003; Van Lange & Balliet, 2013), any differences in the interdependence structure of these interactions may have profound influences on behavior. Recently, Guala (2012) has reviewed studies on the use of costly punishment in both lab and field studies and concluded that while costly punishment is a robust phenomenon in the lab, costly punishment is rarely documented in anthropological field studies. However, Guala may overlook some important differences between the social interdependence between lab and field studies and this may provide several clues for the observed differences between these contexts.

For example, as illustrated previously, single-trial versus repeated interaction (i.e., *temporal structure*) is one of the key features of interdependence. As a case in point, in small communities, people typically know each other, have a history of social interaction experiences, and may have formed strong attachments to (some) other members of their community. In contrast, in the lab, researchers have almost exclusively relied on strangers, because, as the reasoning holds, strangers allow us to exclude the "noise" that comes from experiences outside of the lab. Moreover, there is almost always an interdependent future ahead for people as members of ongoing groups or communities, but such an interdependent future is severely limited in the lab. A future of interdependence might be abstract, but it brings about feelings of dependence in the future, feelings of uncertainty (continuity and change), but most importantly, a mindset whereby the "shadow of the future" (Axelrod, 1984) exerts influences on the motives and behavior of individuals (for recent evidence, see Balliet & Ferris, 2013; Van Lange et al., 2011).

Another situational feature of interdependence theory is *information availability*, and this dimension is also relevant to lab-based situations (at least, as studied so far) and the situations we encounter outside of the lab in ongoing groups and communities. For example, there is little doubt that the "rules of the game" are clearer in the lab than outside of the lab. Moreover, people often do not exactly know what other people want, or how much they want it, or how costly a particular action is for others (or even for themselves). And also in ongoing groups and communities, there are often asymmetries such that some public goods are much more important to some than to others (e.g., the public good of a library is more important to the educated than the not so educated). This implies that some people might feel a little indifferent (or independent) whereas others feel very strongly about the quality of libraries—in interdependence theoretical terms, people differ in their level of dependence. And among those who do not care about libraries, they may face strongly conflicting interests—others might want a nice, costly library, but for them a library does not provide any substantial benefits. To summarize, even if we take a parsimonious view, social dilemmas in "real life" differ from most lab situations in terms of (a) temporal structure, (b) information availability, and (c) symmetrical dependency, as well as other possible structural interdependence features.

These differences in interdependence features not only directly affect cooperation, but are also relevant to understanding the workings of rewards and punishment, as suggested previously. To further illustrate, information availability may affect punishments of noncooperators. Costly punishment may be less likely to be used if one is not completely confident that another person intentionally acted as a noncooperator. For example, in everyday life, unintended errors, or noise, are quite commonplace, in that external barriers prevented a person from translating his or her cooperative intentions into cooperative action. Indeed, one may accidentally say the wrong thing, push the wrong button—or arrive late because of a traffic jam that was not really foreseeable (e.g., Van Lange, Ouwerkerk, & Tazelaar, 2002). Given that people at some level are likely to realize that particular outcomes (e.g., delayed meeting because of traffic jam) are not intentional, it is likely that people might give each other the benefit of the doubt. And in light of incomplete information, gathering more information about the intentionality of a particular outcome or action (e.g., Why were you late?) seems a more sensible strategy than to punish.

CONCLUDING REMARKS

Prior research on rewards and punishment in promoting cooperation has used a public good paradigm with a well-defined structure of interdependence. However, according to interdependence theory, differences in the interdependence structure underlying public good dilemmas may influence not only (a) cooperation, but also (b) the willingness to use reward and punishment to promote cooperation, and (c) the effectiveness of these incentives.

According to this perspective, one promising direction for future research would be to vary systematically certain structural features of the situation (e.g., the degree of conflicting interest, temporal structure, and information uncertainty) to understand the impact that these structural dimensions may have on determining the use and effectiveness of sanctions in promoting cooperation. As outlined previously, interdependence theory also outlines some psychological processes that may influence both the use and effectiveness of rewards and punishments in promoting cooperation. According to this perspective, self-interest is the point of departure for individual decision making during interdependent decisions and this has the important implication that people are responsive to structural changes to interdependence, especially with regards to any reduction in the degree to which interests are conflicting. People are more likely to cooperate when there is less discrepancy between self-interest and collective interest, and both rewards and punishments may, in part, promote cooperation by reducing this discrepancy in the interdependence structure.

Interdependence theory also suggests that preferences broader than self-interest (social preferences or social motives) are important for how individuals interpret and respond to situations with conflicting interests. For example, people who are attempting to either maximize collective outcomes or maximize equality in outcomes may be more likely to engage in the second-order cooperation of punishing noncooperators and rewarding cooperators. Moreover, social motives may partially determine the standards that influence the way people interpret and respond to the situational feedback of punishment and rewards. We raise the possibility that individuals with prosocial motives may be more likely to respond to being punished by increasing expectations of others' cooperation, by feeling increased guilt for their failure to cooperate, or both.

Besides these psychological processes that might underlie sanctions and cooperation, a major innovation of interdependence theory, beyond existing theories in the social sciences, is that it provides a taxonomic approach of social situations that may guide predictions about behavior across a wide range of social contexts. In this chapter, we discuss how the degree of conflicting interests and the temporal structure may impact the use and effectiveness of incentives, but other structural dimensions may also have important implications.

Interdependence theory may also be useful in understanding why sanctions exert a different affect on behavior in separate situations. We illustrate this point by discussing the differences observed across both lab and field studies on costly punishment and cooperation. This approach may also extend to understanding discrepancies between lab studies that employ different methodologies (e.g., different MPCR in public goods dilemmas). The general point is that theory and research may benefit by moving beyond studying a single (fixed) interdependence structure, such as the prisoner's dilemma or public goods dilemma, but may profit by manipulating certain structural features of these social dilemmas.

Clearly, these paradigms have proven to be exceptionally useful to studying cooperation, but outside the lab and in the "wild," people are exposed to a much broader range of interdependence structures that may have important consequences for sanctions and cooperation. Indeed, if one of the goals of science is to provide a comprehensive understanding of human cooperation, then considering a broader range of social interaction situations will be one important direction for future research.

REFERENCES

Andreoni, J., Harbaugh, W., & Versterlund, L. (2003). The carrot or the stick: Rewards, punishments, and cooperation. *American Economic Review, 93*, 893–902.

Axelrod, R. (1984). *The evolution of cooperation*. New York, NY: Basic Books.

Balliet, D. (2010). Communication and cooperation in social dilemmas: A meta-analytic review. *Journal of Conflict Resolution, 54*, 39–57.

Balliet, D., & Ferris, D. L. (2013). Ostracism and prosocial behavior: A social dilemma analysis. *Organizational Behavior and Human Decision Processes, 120*, 298–308.

Balliet, D., Li, N. P., & Joireman, J. (2011). Relating trait self-control and forgiveness among prosocials and proselfs: A test of compensatory and synergistic models. *Journal of Personality and Social Psychology, 101*, 1090–1109.

Balliet, D., Mulder, L. B., & Van Lange, P. A. M. (2011). Reward, punishment, and cooperation: A meta-analysis. *Psychological Bulletin, 137*, 594–615.

Balliet, D., Parks, C., & Joireman, J. (2009). Social value orientation and cooperation in social dilemmas: A meta-analysis. *Group Processes and Intergroup Relations, 12*, 533–547.

Balliet, D., & Van Lange, P. A. M. (2013a). Trust, punishment and cooperation across 18 societies: A Meta-analysis. *Perspectives on Psychological Science, 8*, 363–379.

Balliet, D., & Van Lange, P. A. M. (2013b). Trust, conflict, and cooperation: A meta-analysis. *Psychological Bulletin, 139*, 1090–1112.

Barclay, P. (2006). Reputational benefits for altruistic punishment. *Evolution and Human Behavior, 27*, 325–344.

Brehm, J. W. (1966). *A Theory of Psychological Reactance*. Oxford, England: Academic Press.

Carpenter, J. P. (2007). Punishing free-riders: How group size affects mutual monitoring and the provision of public goods. *Games and Economic Behavior, 60*, 31–51. doi:10.1016/j.geb.2006.08.011

Chen, X., Pillutla, M. M., & Yao, X. (2009). Unintended consequences of cooperation inducing and maintaining mechanisms in public goods dilemmas: Sanctions and moral appeals. *Group Processes and Intergroup Relations, 12*, 241–255. doi:10.1177/1368430208098783

Cooper, W. H., & Withey, M. J. (2009). The strong situation hypothesis. *Personality and Social Psychology Review, 13*, 62–72.

Dawes, C. T., Fowler, J. H., Johnson, T., McElreath, R., & Smirnov, O. (2007). Egalitarian motives in humans. *Nature, 446*, 794–796.

Deci, E. L., & Ryan, R. M. (2000). The "what" and "why" of goal pursuits: Human needs and the self-determination of behavior. *Psychological Inquiry, 11*, 227–268. doi:10.1207/S15327965PLI1104_01

Denant-Boemont, L., Masclet, D., & Noussair, C. N. (2007). Punishment, counterpunishment, and sanction enforcement in a social dilemma experiment. *Economic Theory, 33*, 145–167. doi:10.1007/s00199-007-0212-0

Fehr, E., & Fischbacher, U. (2004). Social norms and human cooperation. *Trends in Cognitive Science, 8*, 185–190. doi:10.1016/j.tics.2004.02.007

Fehr, E., Fischbacher, U., & Gächter, S. (2002). Strong reciprocity, human cooperation, and the enforcement of social norms. *Human Nature, 13*, 1–25. doi:10.1007/s12110-002-1012-7

Fehr, E., & Gächter, S. (2000). Cooperation and punishment in public goods experiments. *The American Economic Review, 90*, 980–994.

Fehr, E., & Gächter, S. (2002). Altruistic punishment in humans. *Nature, 415*, 137–140. doi:10.1038/415137a

Fehr, E., & Rockenbach, B. (2003). Detrimental effects of sanctions on human altruism. *Nature, 422*, 137–140.

Fehr, E., & Schmidt, K. M. (1999). A theory of fairness, competition, and cooperation. *The Quarterly Journal of Economics, 114*, 817–868. doi:10.1162/003355399556151

Fischbacher, U., & Gächter, S. (2010). Social preferences, beliefs, and the dynamics of free riding in public goods experiments. *American Economic Review, 100*, 541–556.

Fowler, J. H., Johnson, T., & Smirnov, O. (2005). Egalitarian motives and altruistic punishment. *Nature, 433*. doi:10.1038/nature03256

Gächter, S., & Herrmann, B. (2009). Reciprocity, culture and human cooperation: Previous insights and a new cross-cultural experiment. *Philosophical Transactions of the Royal Society Biological Sciences, 364*, 791–806. doi:10.1098/rstb.2008.0275

Gächter, S., Renner, E., & Sefton, M. (2008). The long-run benefits of punishment. *Science, 322*, 1510. doi:10.1126/science.1164744

Gintis, H. (2000). Strong reciprocity and human sociality, *Journal of Theoretical Biology, 206*, 169–179.

Gneezy, U., & Rustichini, A. (2000). A fine is a price. *Journal of Legal Studies, 29*, 1–17.

Guala, F. (2012). Reciprocity: Weak or strong? What punishment experiments do (and do not) demonstrate. *Behavioral and Brain Sciences, 35*, 1–15.

Hardin, G. (1968). The tragedy of the commons. *Science, 162*, 1243–1248.

Hargreaves Heap, S. P., & Varoufakis, Y. (2004). *Game theory: A critical text (2nd Ed.)*. London, UK: Routledge.

Henrich, J. et al. (2006). Costly punishment across human societies. *Science, 312*, 1767–1770.

Henrich, J. et al. (2010). Markets, religion, community size, and the evolution of fairness and punishment. *Science, 327*, 1480–1484.

Herrmann, B., Thöni, C., & Gächter, S. (2008). Antisocial punishment across societies. *Science, 319*, 1362–1367. doi:10.1126/science.1153808

Hobbes, T. (1651). *Leviathan*. Cambridge: Cambridge University Press.

Janssen, M. A., Holahan, R., Lee, A., & Ostrom, E. (2010). Lab experiments for the study of social-ecological systems. *Science, 328*, 613–617.

Johnson, T., Dawes, C. T., Fowler, J. H., McElreath, R., & Smirnov, O. (2009). The role of egalitarian motives in altruistic punishment. *Economics Letters, 102*, 192–194.

Joireman, J. A., Kuhlman, D. M., Van Lange, P. A. M., Doi, T., & Shelley, G. P. (2003). Perceived rationality, morality, and power of social choice as a function of interdependence structure and social value orientation. *European Journal of Social Psychology, 33*, 413–437.

Joireman, J., Shaffer, M., Balliet, D., & Strathman, A. (2012). Promotion orientation leads future oriented people to exercise and eat healthy: Evidence from a two-factor consideration of future consequences-14 scale. *Personality and Social Psychology Bulletin, 38*, 1272–1287.

Kelley, H. H., Holmes, J. G., Kerr, N. L., Reis, H. T., Rusbult, C. E., & Van Lange, P. A. M. (2003). *An atlas of interpersonal situations*. Cambridge, UK: Cambridge University Press.

Kelley, H. H., & Thibaut, J. W. (1978). *Interpersonal relations: A theory of interdependence*. New York, NY: Wiley.

Kollock, P. (1998). Social dilemmas: The anatomy of cooperation. *Annual Review of Sociology, 24*, 183–214.

Komorita, S. S., & Barth, J. M. (1985). Components of reward in social dilemmas. *Journal of Personality and Social Psychology, 48*, 364–373. doi:10.1037/0022-3514.48.2.364

Komorita, S. S., & Parks, C. D. (1995). *Social Dilemmas*. Boulder, CO: Westview Press.

Komorita, S. S., Sweeney, J., & Kravitz, D. A. (1980). Cooperative choice in the n-person prisoner's dilemma situation. *Journal of Personality and Social Psychology, 38*, 504–516. doi:10.1037/0022-3514.38.3.504

Krueger, J. I., DiDonato, T. E., & Freestone, D. (2012). Social projection can solve social dilemmas. *Psychological Inquiry, in press.*

McCusker, C., & Carnevale, P. J. (1995). Framing in resource dilemmas: Loss aversion and the moderating effects of sanctions. Organizational. *Behavior and Human Decision Processes, 61,* 190–201. doi:10.1006/obhd.1995.1015

Mulder, L. B. (2008). The difference between punishments and rewards in fostering moral concerns in social decision making. *Journal of Experimental Social Psychology, 44,* 1436–1443. doi:10.1016/j.jesp.2008.06.004

Mulder, L. B., van Dijk, E., De Cremer, D., & Wilke, H. A. M. (2006). Undermining trust and cooperation: The paradox of sanctioning systems in social dilemmas. *Journal of Experimental Social Psychology, 42,* 147–162. doi:10.1016/j.jesp.2005.03.002

Nelissen, R. M. A. (2008). The price you pay: cost-dependent reputation effects of altruistic punishment. *Evolution and Human Behavior, 29,* 242–248.

Nowak, M. (2006). Five rules for the evolution of cooperation. *Science, 314,* 1560.

Olson, M. (1965). *The logic of collective action: Public goods and the theory of groups.* Cambridge: Harvard University Press.

Ostrom, E., Walker, J., & Gardner, R. (1992). Covenants with and without the sword: Self-governance is possible. *American Political Science Review, 86,* 404–417.

Parks, C. D. (2000). Testing various types of cooperation rewards in social dilemma. *Group Processes and Intergroup Relations, 3,* 339–350. doi:10.1177/1368430200003004001

Pruitt, D. G., & Kimmel, M. J. (1977). Twenty years of experimental gaming: Critique, synthesis, and suggestions for the future. *Annual Review of Psychology, 28,* 363–392. doi:10.1146/annurev.ps.28.020177.002051

Rand, D. G., Dreber, A., Ellingsen, T., Fudenberg, D., & Nowak, M. A. (2009). Positive interactions promote public cooperation. *Science, 325,* 1272–1275. doi:10.1126/science.1177418

Rapoport, A., & Au, W. T. (2001). Bonus and penalty in common pool resource dilemmas under uncertainty. *Organizational Behavior and Human Decision Processes, 85,* 135–165. doi:10.1006/obhd.2000.2935

Rapoport, A., & Chammah, A. M. (1965). *Prisoner's dilemma: A study in conflict and cooperation.* Ann Arbor, MI: University of Michigan Press.

Rusbult, C. E., & Van Lange, P. A. M. (2003). Interdependence, interaction, and relationships. *Annual Review of Psychology, 54,* 351–375. doi:10.1146/annurev.psych.54.101601.145059

Sefton, M., Shupp, R., & Walker, J. M. (2007). The effect of rewards and sanctions in provision of public goods. *Economic Inquiry, 45,* 671–690. doi:10.1111/j.1465-7295.2007.00051.x

Shinada, M., & Yamagishi, T. (2008). Bringing back the leviathan into social dilemmas. In A. Biel, D. Eek, T. Garling, & M. Gukstafsson (Eds.), *New Issues and Paradigms in Research on Social Dilemmas* (pp. 93–123). New York, NY: Springer.

Stern, P. C. (1976). Effect of incentives and education on resource conservation decisions in a simulated common dilemma. *Journal of Personality and Social Psychology, 34,* 1285–1292. doi:10.1037/0022-3514.34.6.1285

Tenbrunsel, A. E., & Messick, D. M. (1999). Sanctioning systems, decision frames, and cooperation. *Administrative Science Quarterly, 44,* 684–707.

Van Lange, P. A. M. (1999). The pursuit of joint outcomes and equality in outcomes: An integrative model of social value orientation. *Journal of Personality and Social Psychology, 77,* 337–349. doi:10.1037/0022-3514.77.2.337

Van Lange, P. A. M., & Balliet, D. (2013). Interdependence Theory. In J. A. Simpson & J. F. Dovidio (Eds.), *Handbook of Personality and Social Psychology* (Vol. 2). Washington: APA.

Van Lange, P. A. M., Balliet, D., Parks, C., & Van Vugt, M. (2013). *Social Dilemmas: Understanding the Psychology of Human Cooperation*. New York: Oxford University Press.

Van Lange, P. A. M., Klapwijk, A., & Van Munster, L. M. (2011). How the shadow of the future might promote cooperation. *Group Processes and Intergroup Relations*. Advance online publication. doi:10.1177/1368430211402102

Van Lange, P. A. M., Ouwerkerk, J. W., & Tazelaar, M. J. A. (2002). How to overcome the detrimental effects of noise in social interaction: The benefits of generosity. *Journal of Personality and Social Psychology, 82*, 768–780. doi:10.1037//0022-3514.82.5.768

Weber, M., Kopelman, S., & Messick, D. M. (2004). A conceptual review of decision-making in social dilemmas: Applying a logic of appropriateness. *Personality and Social Psychology Review, 8*, 281–307. doi:10.1207/s15327957pspr0803_4

Wieselquist, A., Rusbult, C. E., Foster, C. A., & Agnew, C. R. (1999). Commitment, pro-relationship behavior, and trust in close relationships. *Journal of Personality and Social Psychology, 77*, 942–966. doi:10.1037/0022-3514.77.5.942

Yamagishi, T. (1986). The provisioning of a sanctioning system as a public good. *Journal of Personality and Social Psychology, 51*, 110–116. doi:10.1037/0022-3514.51.1.110

Yamagishi, T. (1988). Seriousness of social dilemmas and the provision of a sanctioning system. *Social Psychology Quarterly, 51*, 32–42.

Yamagishi, T. (2011). *Trust: The evolutionary game of mind and society*. New York, NY: Springer.

4 Regulating the Regulation: Norms about Punishment

■ PONTUS STRIMLING AND
KIMMO ERIKSSON

Abstract

Rules about punishment dictate how one must behave to ensure that one's punishment behavior is not met with social disapproval. These rules can be both prescriptive, telling us when we have to punish and how much we must punish at a minimum, and restrictive, telling us when we cannot punish or what the maximum punishment can be. In this chapter we investigate the general features of these rules, focusing on punishment of norm violations in social dilemmas.

Researchers have often viewed the provision of punishment as a costly public good that must itself be enforced, creating a second order social dilemma that requires prescriptive norms for people to "cooperate", i.e., to punish. We argue that this is a misunderstanding of the nature of punishment and go through theoretical reasons for why prescriptive rules about punishment might not be important. Instead, we discuss the reasons that *restrictive* norms could benefit the group and review experiments where this is shown to be the case.

Finally we report the results of four surveys that use real world situations to assess people's views about punishment in several countries. We find that punishment behavior is regulated by generally agreed upon views (i.e., norms), which are largely restrictive rather than prescriptive. Results show a strong consistency across scenarios and countries, indicating that these norms follow general principles.

■ **INTRODUCTION**

Rules that govern behavior are ubiquitous within every human society and include both formal rules written down in law books and *norms*[1]. Transgressions against these rules can be punished to ensure that the transgressor goes back to acting according to the rules. These punishments are in and of themselves behaviors that are governed by rules of their own and the structure of these punishment-related rules is the topic of this chapter.

There are two important questions about norms surrounding punishment: First, if it is costly for the individual to punish, how do groups make sure that punishment is carried out? Second, if punishment is costly for the group, then how do groups limit that cost? These two questions lead us to investigate two different types of rules: prescriptive rules, which will tell people what they should do, and restrictive rules, that tell people what they are not allowed to do.

---

1. We define norm as an established standard of behavior shared by members of a social group to which each member is expected to conform.

A special set of situations where punishment is believed to be important are *social dilemmas*. These are situations where individual interests are in conflict with the interest of the group. These situations are important and provide the context for the vast majority of research on sanctions, both punishment and rewards. Although the main focus of this chapter is on social dilemmas, it should be noted that behavioral rules cover a host of different strategic situations and that we see no reason to believe that the structure of rules surrounding punishment would differ depending on the underlying situation. For example, traffic violations are punished whether they are social dilemmas (for instance, speeding) or coordination games (which side of the road to drive on).

While there are studies of what formal punishments people believe are fair when it comes to people breaking the laws of a society (Hamilton & Rytina, 1980; Warr et al., 1983), we have found no prior work on norms about informal punishments. This is surprising, not least because there is much research on how norms govern behavior in many situations, including social dilemmas (e.g., by Robert Cialdini and his colleagues), and there is some research on the use of informal sanctions (e.g., by Markus Brauer and his colleagues). The aim of this chapter is to present our initial explorations of what norms about informal sanctions look like. Our focus is on the extent to which rules about punishment in social dilemmas are prescriptive or restrictive. Before we present the empirical findings we will review the theoretical arguments for and against prescriptive and restrictive rules.

■ REASONS FOR AND AGAINST PRESCRIPTIVE RULES

In the case of social dilemmas there is a well-known theoretical argument that makes a prediction about what norms will surround punishment. Punishment is assumed to be costly to the punisher, at the very least in terms of the opportunity cost of not spending the time and energy on something else. Because of this cost, individually rational agents will not punish voluntarily. Assuming punishment to be directed against agents who do not behave in the interest of the group, punishment will deter selfish behavior and thereby lead to an increase of the group's welfare in the long run. Thus, the provision of punishment is a public good, but because it is costly, it will not be provided by agents unless there is a second level of norms regulating that you must punish (or you will be punished yourself). This is known as the second order problem (e.g., Elster, 1989; Yamagishi, 1986). This argument leads to the prediction that, in the context of social dilemmas, the general character of norms about punishment will be prescriptive, making it obligatory to punish those who do not act in the interest of the group.

There are several reasons to be doubtful about the assumptions behind this prediction. Consider the assumption that punishment will not be provided unless somehow enforced. This assumption has been shown to be invalid in a large number of experiments in which participants in social dilemmas have been given the option to contribute to the punishment of others at a cost to themselves; a robust finding is that a substantial proportion of participants voluntarily do so (e.g., Fehr

& Gächter, 2002; Ostrom, Walker, & Gardner 1992; Yamagishi, 1986). Thus, it seems that no enforcement is needed for a substantial proportion of people to be willing to engage in punishment of others.

Now consider the assumption that the provision of punishment is a public good. Data relevant to this issue exist from many laboratory studies of punishment in the public goods game (PGG). Participants in this game receive an endowment in each round. This endowment can be kept as private property or invested in a common good that is equally beneficial to all group members, regardless of their contribution. After each round, participants can choose to spend some of their resources on punishing others. The general finding is that contributions go up when punishment is introduced. However, because of the costs of punishment, this increase in contributions does not automatically translate to increased group payoff. An extensive meta-analysis of these studies only finds tentative evidence for an increase in group payoff and only several rounds after punishment was introduced (Balliet et al., 2011). Furthermore, since the choice of targets of punishment is left up to the individual, there is no guarantee that it will be directed against those who contributed least to the common good. Experiments in some countries find that punishment is often used against those who contribute much to the common good, which tends to result in contributions no higher than in a no-punishment treatment and a negative effect of punishment on group payoff (Herrmann, Thöni, & Gächter, 2008). Finally, even when there is an advantage of having punishment in the first place, this can be eradicated if the punished party has the possibility of taking revenge for being punished (Nikiforakis, 2008). To summarize these findings in laboratory experiments, the provision of punishment on a voluntary basis often has bad consequences for the group payoff and there is no general evidence that punishment is a public good in these settings.

Interestingly, the theoretical view of the goodness of voluntary punishers in public goods games is typically not shared by the actual participants of experiments. When people only play one round of PGG they rate punishers negatively on a range of personality features including trustworthiness and likability (Kiyonari & Barclay, 2008). However, when the subjects play several rounds of PGGs they start to evaluate the punishers as more trustworthy but not as nicer (Barclay, 2006). When there was an opportunity to directly reward or punish the players who punished in previous rounds, they were actually given *less rewards* and *more punishment* than the people who did not punish; these results were not always significant but they were consistent across three experiments (Kiyonari & Barclay, 2008). In an experiment by Cinyabuguma et al. (2006) where each round of PGG was followed by two rounds of punishment, first stage punishers attracted more, not less, second stage punishment. (It should be noted that some of the second stage punishment in this latter study could be due to revenge; however, revenge is not a possible explanation for the results of Kiyonari and Barclay.)

Even if punishers are not directly rewarded it is possible that they could receive indirect rewards by being a preferred partner in other games from which they might benefit. Testing this idea, Horita (2010) had subjects read about a PGG in which there was one punisher and one non-punisher and decide which of these individuals they would rather be partnered with in a series of games. Preferences were found to differ between two classes of games. In games where *the partner would be in a position to provide resources to the participant* (e.g., if the partner was to be the dictator in a dictator game with the participant as the recipient[2]), the punisher tended to be the preferred partner. In contrast, in games where *the participant would be in a position to provide resources to the partner* (e.g., if the partner was to be the recipient in a dictator game with the participant as the dictator), the non-punisher tended to be the preferred partner. Thus, it seems that punishers are not preferred partners in those games where they could be rewarded.

While all of the abovementioned studies centered on punishment in a public goods game, Rob Nelissen (2007) looked at how people viewed third party punishers in a dictator game[3]. He found that people saw these punishers as more fair, friendly, and generous and that they were entrusted with more money in a trust game. Thus, it would seem that the view of third-party punishers is more positive than the view of peer punishers in PGG.

In conclusion, studies of how punishers are viewed indicate that they are generally not well liked and are not rewarded for being punishers. A notable exception is the study of third-party punishers. Our interpretation of this discrepancy is that third-party punishers have been given a special role whose task it is to mete out punishment, whereas in PGG all participants are peers. We shall return to this very important distinction presently.

■ REASONS FOR AND AGAINST RESTRICTIVE RULES

If the decision to break the rules is determined by a calculation of the risk of getting caught times the cost of being punished, one might expect that more severe punishment would make people cheat less. However, there are good reasons not to believe in such a simple relationship. One obvious reason is that people often do not behave as rational agents—but even under the assumption of rational agents, the total strategic structure may be such that the degree of punishment does not affect equilibrium levels of cheating (Eriksson & Strimling, 2012; Weissing & Ostrom, 1991). Further, even if there was a monotone relationship between punishment degree and the amount of rule breaking, it might still be that higher punishment is undesirable. One reason is that it is typically desirable that the punished party becomes a productive member of the group, which could be impeded by too severe punishment. Another reason is that the punished party will sometimes be wrongfully accused, in which case all of the cost to the punished is a waste. People may have good reason to doubt that those who voluntarily punish others have made an impartial and knowledgeable assessment of the long-term benefits for the group. After all, people may well make the alternative

---

2. In a dictator game, one player (the dictator) is endowed with tokens while the second player (the recipient) is not. The dictator can then choose how he wants to distribute those tokens between himself and the recipient.

3. Third party punishment means that a third player can punish the dictator by removing some of his tokens after the distribution decision has been made.

interpretation that voluntary punishers are angry and act on a personal desire to punish. Such an interpretation would be consistent with psychological research on anger and punishment. For instance, people tend to act on anger whether it is rational or not to do so (Lerner & Tiedens, 2006). Brain imaging studies show that people may derive personal satisfaction from punishing others (de Quervain et al., 2003; Singer et al., 2006). We shall return to how people view punishers in one of the studies we report later in this chapter.

One way of restricting punishment rights is to centralize them to a single agent, regardless of who is to be punished. Laboratory experiments have shown that restriction of punishment rights increases the efficiency of use of punishment, both when rights are centralized to one punishing agent (Baldassarri & Grossman, 2011; O'Gorman, Henrich, & Van Vugt, 2009) and when rights are decentralized so that every agent punishes one other agent (Eriksson, Strimling, & Ehn, 2013). These findings support the notion that low levels of punishment are optimal for the group, and that norms that restrict punishment could serve a general purpose of lowering levels of punishment to less destructive levels.

CONCLUSION

There seems to be no evidence that rules prescriptive of punishment are necessary in order to get some people to punish. Nor is there any evidence that people who choose not to punish are seen as rule-breakers. In contrast, restrictions on punishment can increase group benefit. However, the empirical literature is focused on situations in which everyone is allowed to punish. It is possible that if punishment rights are indeed restricted to specific positions, the need for prescriptive rules about punishment increases to make sure that everyone who has the punishment position actually punishes. To investigate this, we look both at situations where there are specific punishment positions and situations where there are none.

Research from Markus Brauer's group indicates that positions must be taken into consideration in theorizing about punishment: Both potential punishers and potential punishees perceive differences in roles as extremely important in regards to who can legitimately sanction deviant behavior (Chaurand & Brauer, 2008; Nugier et al., 2007). Perceived legitimacy, in particular a shared sense of legitimacy, creates voluntary compliance with norms (Tyler, 1997; Zelditch & Walker, 1984).

As we mentioned previously, there are signs that people's view of punishers change over the course of several rounds of games played in laboratory experiments. One interpretation of this finding is that people are used to one set of norms and the more time they spend in the laboratory the more time they have to develop new norms. To ensure that we are studying real-world norms our surveys present situations that are common in the real world rather than abstract games.

EMPIRICAL STUDIES OF NORMS ABOUT USE OF INFORMAL SANCTIONS

As mentioned, we have found no research focused on norms that regulate the use of informal sanctions in social dilemmas (or in any other situation in which there are norms about behavior). Here we report our own initial explorations in the form of four survey studies. They deal with the following four questions:

1. Is every group member allowed to voluntarily punish a selfish individual or is the right to punish restricted to group members in certain roles?
2. Given that group members in certain roles have the right to voluntarily punish a selfish individual, are they also allowed to choose any level of punishment that they want or are there restrictions on the severity of punishments?
3. When no group member has a special role, how are voluntary punishers regarded compared to those who do not voluntarily punish a selfish individual?
4. When no group member has a special role, does legitimacy of punishment of a selfish individual depend on it being collectively managed rather than individually volunteered?

The studies used scenarios chosen to represent three basic types of social dilemmas: depletion of a common resource, free-riding on a joint effort, and pollution of a common environment. Similarly, studies used punishments taken from the realm of punishments available outside the laboratory. To demonstrate that these scenarios tap into the same psychological mechanisms that laboratory experiments do, the third study also included an abstract social dilemma of the kind used in laboratories, where both payoffs and punishments are given in terms of money.

Surveys were administered online to participants recruited through the Amazon Mechanical Turk (https://www.mturk.com).[4] Users of the Mechanical Turk can come from any country in the world, allowing us to examine norms in more than one culture. Data came primarily from the United States and India, as the vast majority of Turk users are located in these countries. For Study 1 we managed to recruit respondents from many countries across all continents. For Study 4, a Swedish sample of university students complemented the American and Indian Turk users.

■ STUDY 1: ARE PUNISHMENT RIGHTS RESTRICTED TO CERTAIN INDIVIDUALS?

The first study is taken from Eriksson, Strimling, and Ehn (2013); for details, we refer to the original paper. The survey was completed by 528 participants (63% male; mean age 30 years) of mixed educational backgrounds. Based on country of residence, they were divided into six subsamples of unequal size: Asia (N = 213), Europe (N = 170), North America (N = 67), Latin America (N = 27), Africa (N = 26), Australia and New Zealand (N = 25).

The questionnaire presented three scenarios (see Appendix). The first scenario described two families dining together and discovering that one of the children

---

4. Online surveys using the Mturk have been found to be a source of reliable data (Buhrmester, Kwang, & Gosling, 2011).

has already eaten the sweets meant for dessert (*depletion of a common resource*); the child could potentially be sanctioned, punished or rewarded, by the child's siblings, by the child's parents, or by the other parents. The second scenario described a hospital ward where one nurse has come in to work very late which forces the other nurses to work extra hard (*free-riding on a joint effort*); the late-coming nurse could potentially be sanctioned by the head nurse or by another nurse with a degree from a prestigious school. The third scenario described a student apartment where one of several roommates has made a mess in a common area (*pollution of a common environment*); the messy roommate could potentially be sanctioned by another roommate or by a visitor.

Respondents were asked for each scenario whether "situations more or less like this scenario (where your answer would be the same) are common," using a five-point response scale from -2 = *very uncommon* to 2 = *very common*.

For each specified party, respondents judged the appropriateness of that party punishing/reprimanding the selfish behavior, compared to not reacting at all, on a five-point scale between -2 = *highly inappropriate* and 2 = *highly appropriate*. The alternative response of praising/rewarding unselfish behavior was judged on the same scale.

Results of Study 1

For each of the three scenarios, around two thirds of all respondents thought that situations similar to those in the scenarios were quite common or very common (the two highest points on the five-point response scale). There were no significant differences between geographical subsamples. In other words, these everyday social dilemmas were recognized across many cultures.

Use of rewards was typically judged as inappropriate for *all* involved parties in all scenarios, with the exception of the head nurse for whom it was weakly appropriate to use rewards. Use of punishment was also judged as inappropriate except for certain preferred parties: the roommate in the making-a-mess scenario, the head nurse in the coming-late scenario, and the child's parent in the eating-the-sweets scenario (in which the child's sibling was judged somewhere between appropriate and inappropriate as a punisher). To quantify this pattern, three domain indices were computed for each participant: *reward by any party* (average judgment of 7 items; α = 0.64; $M = -0.27$, $SD = 0.93$); *punishment by a non-preferred party* (average judgment of 3 items; α = 0.57; $M = -0.68$, $SD = 0.91$); *punishment by a preferred party* (average judgment of 3 items; α = 0.81; $M = 1.18$, $SD = 0.81$). The item "punishment by the child's sibling" was excluded. As illustrated in Figure 4.1, every geographical subsample judged punishments by non-preferred parties as inappropriate.

■ STUDY 2: IS THE SEVERITY OF PUNISHMENT RESTRICTED?

The second survey was completed by 100 participants (56% male; mean age 30 years) of mixed educational backgrounds, from United States (N = 50)

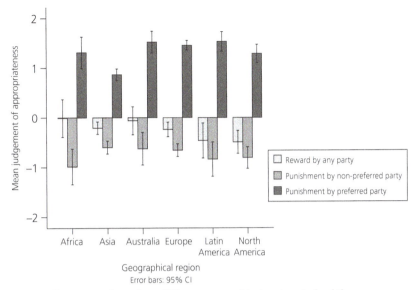

Figure 4.1 How respondents from different geographical regions judged the appropriateness of sanctions in Study 1. Bars show average judgments, across all three scenarios, of rewards by any party, punishments by a non-preferred party, and punishments by a preferred party.

and India (N = 50). Respondents were presented with the same three scenarios as in Study 1: making-a-mess, coming-late, and eating-the-sweets (see Appendix). They were told to imagine that the roommate in the making-a-mess scenario, the head nurse in the coming-late scenario, and the child's parent in the eating-the-sweets scenario (i.e., the roles that were identified as preferred punishers in Study 1) reacted to the selfish individual ("S") in either of five different ways:

1. not reacting at all;
2. explaining to S that what S did was wrong;
3. same as (2) but also yelling at S;
4. same as (3) but also slapping S;
5. same as (4) but also beating S with a stick.

For each reaction, respondents were asked how this would affect their view of the punisher: *negative* (coded -1), *neutral* (coded 0), or *positive* (coded +1).

Results of Study 2

Results were similar for all three scenarios. The only reaction that tended to affect people's view of the punisher positively was to just explain that the selfish behavior was wrong. Yelling tended to be neutral in its effect on people's view of the punisher. People's view of the punisher tended to be negatively affected if the punisher did not react at all, and the tendency was even more negative

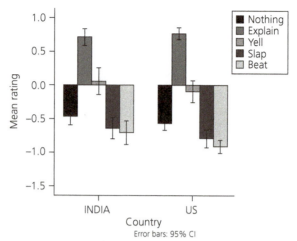

Figure 4.2 How respondents in Study 2 judged voluntary punishers depending on the severity of the punishment.

if the punisher used the more severe punishments of slapping or beating. The response pattern is illustrated in Figure 4.2, showing the mean ratings for each reaction across the three scenarios. Note how responses were very similar between Indian and American participants.

■ STUDY 3: HOW ARE VOLUNTARY PUNISHERS REGARDED COMPARED TO NON-PUNISHERS?

The third survey was completed by 200 participants (54% male; mean age 31 years) of mixed educational backgrounds, from United States (N = 100) and India (N = 100). It focused on situations where group members are not distinguished by any differences in roles, which is the typical setup in laboratory experiments.

The three scenarios from the previous studies were adapted so that there were no cues to distinguish between group members (see Appendix). For every scenario, we then described one group member who decided to let the selfish behavior go (i.e., a non-punisher), and another group member who decided to yell about the selfish behavior (i.e., a voluntary punisher). The decision to use yelling as punishment in these scenarios was based on the finding in Study 2 that yelling tended to be neutrally viewed when done by a preferred punisher.

A fourth scenario, in which a typical abstract social dilemma was described, mimicked laboratory experiments (see Appendix). Each of three participants could give away money that would then be doubled and split between the other two participants, after which decisions they could punish each other by paying an amount to deduct three times the same amount from the punishee of their choice. As in the previous scenarios, the scenario described one selfish person, one non-punisher and one punisher.

The order of scenarios was counterbalanced, so that the experiment scenario was presented either first or last with 100 participants in each condition. For each scenario, respondents compared the punisher against the non-punisher on seven traits, on a five-point scale coded from -2 = *definitely [the non-punisher]* to 2 = *definitely [the punisher]*. The seven items were:

1. you would prefer to spend time with;
2. most likely to punish people unfairly;
3. most likely to adhere to standard norms of behavior;
4. most likely to be an angry person;
5. most likely to take others' interests into account;
6. most likely to create bad morale in the group;
7. most trustworthy.

Results of Study 3

There were no order effects, so we present the results for the pooled data. Results were similar for all four scenarios and both countries, as illustrated in Figure 4.3. Respondents tended to prefer to spend time with non-punishers; they also tended to find non-punishers most likely to adhere to standard norms of behavior, to take others' interests into account, and to be trustworthy. Punishers, on the other hand, tended to be viewed as most likely to punish other people unfairly, to be angry people, and to create bad morale in the group.

STUDY 4: COLLECTIVELY MANAGED VS. INDIVIDUALLY VOLUNTEERED PUNISHMENT

The fourth survey was completed on paper by 18 Swedish students of computer science and online by 100 participants (54% male; mean age 31 years) of mixed educational backgrounds from United States (N = 50) and India (N = 50). The aim of this study was to investigate the legitimacy of individual voluntary punishment compared to collectively managed punishment.

The survey presented four variations of a scenario where a group has a joint task that requires multiple meetings. One group member tends to come late to these meetings and, in the end, this group member has to buy coffee for everyone in the group. This involves three steps: *decision on the norm* (that it is unacceptable to come late), *decision on the punishment* (that latecomers must buy coffee for everyone in the group), and *execution of the punishment* (ensuring that the latecomer buys coffee for everyone). One variation of the scenario had all these steps managed collectively by the group; the other three variations had a single individual, Eric, voluntarily stepping in instead of the collective, either in the last step or earlier in the first or second steps (see Appendix). The order of scenario variations was counterbalanced.

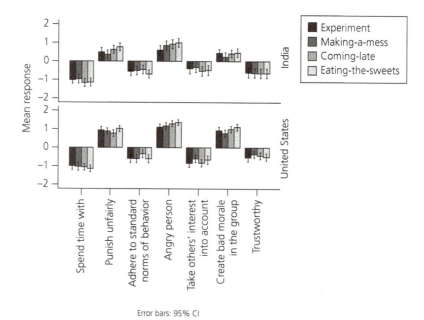

Figure 4.3 How respondents in Study 3 judged voluntary punishers compared to non-punishers on four positive and three negative items. The figure show the results for all four scenarios.

Respondents were asked, for each scenario variation, whether they found Eric's behavior to be OK. A response scale from -3 = *definitely not OK* to 3 = *definitely OK* was used. The same question was then asked about the group's behavior.

Results of Study 4

Eight respondents were excluded because they gave the exact same response to all questions, indicating that they had not paid attention. All three countries showed the same pattern: When the individual, Eric, manages every step involved in punishment, his behavior tended to be viewed as not OK (i.e., below the midpoint of zero). Eric's behavior tended to be viewed as more OK when more steps were managed collectively rather than by Eric, see Figure 4.4. The group's behavior was also viewed as more OK the more steps were managed collectively.

■ DISCUSSION

Across scenarios and cultures, we found remarkable consistency of norms regarding informal punishment. In the two studies with distinguishable roles we found evidence both for prescriptive norms (i.e., views that a certain party ought to punish) and restrictive norms (i.e., views that a certain party ought

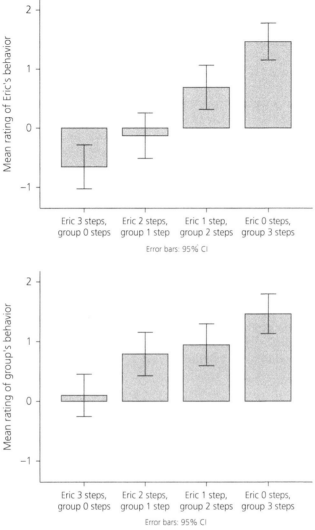

Figure 4.4 How respondents in Study 4 judged an individual punisher's (Eric) behavior and the group's behavior, depending on how many punishment decisions were made by the group (instead of Eric alone).

not to punish) present, whereas in the situations without distinguishable norms we found only restrictive norms.

Norms in Social Dilemmas with Distinguishable Roles

Studies 1 and 2 investigated social dilemmas in which involved parties had different roles with respect to the person who behaved selfishly. To have the right to punish in these situations, it was not sufficient to be part of the group that suffered from the selfish behavior. Involved parties tended to be normatively constrained from punishing unless they had a special role. In this special role, people would tend to view you negatively if you do not punish at all, but even more so if you use a punishment that is too severe. Therefore, there are both prescriptive and restrictive norms occurring. The socially acceptable behavior is to punish only if you are in the punishing role and for that punishment to be deemed by the group as an appropriate amount, not too little nor too much.

While humans seem to have a knack for picking up norms, there is reason to believe that it is still difficult to learn whether or not you have the right position to punish, or what the right amount of punishment is. We expect norms to be inferred from experience to no little extent. Direct experience can be relied on when you infer a norm about a common behavior. However, norm-breaking is typically rare (or else we would not call it a norm), so punishment for norm violation will be rare. In addition, the behavior expected of you is dependent on your position within the situation, so you can only rely on the punishment behavior you have observed for that specific position. Thus, for any given situation in which you could potentially punish someone, people will typically suffer a lack of previous experience on how to behave in that particular situation. They can therefore be expected to draw on their experiences from other punishment situations and assume that analogous norms hold also in the present situation. In other words, in order for there to be unspoken norms about punishment, these norms need to be easily generalizable or people will simply not know them. This could explain why there is so little difference in attitude towards punishment between our different scenarios.

Laws About Punishment

A special case in which there are distinguishable roles is formal law. There are prescriptive and restrictive principles in criminal laws both now and historically. The idea that every criminal act has both a minimum and maximum punishment is found in all law books, even those of the very first laws in which every law is a description of a specific infringement and the exact punishments it merits (Jarrick & Bondesson, 2011).

The law often restricts people from using certain behaviors (e.g., violence) to punish each other. This principle is explicit already in the Tang Code (624 a.d.), in which it is stated that a person who acts outside of the law to revenge the death of his parents should be punished by lifetime banishment (Johnsson, 1997). Conversely, failing to fulfill the punishment duty of one's position carries penalties in most societies that employ an institutionalized justice system.

Norms in Social Dilemmas with No Distinguishable Roles

Studies 3 and 4 investigated social dilemmas in homogeneous groups. These surveys showed that individual members who voluntarily punish others are viewed negatively in various ways. Study 4 showed that the preferred alternative is for the group to manage punishment as a collective. This is consistent with anthropological studies of real world punishment in small-scale societies (Guala, 2012).

While collectively managed punishment may have advantages over individually managed punishment in terms of optimizing the level of punishment, it is clear from Study 3 that efficiency is not the only concern people have about voluntary punishers. Individual punishers tended to be regarded as angry persons who were not acting in the interests of others and likely to use punishment unfairly and create bad morale in the group. Voluntary punishers were not even regarded as trustworthy in this survey. This is consistent with previous findings of punishers being judged as trustworthy only if participants had played the public goods game several times (Barclay, 2006).

The results of our surveys were remarkably constant not just across scenarios but also across cultures. This stands in stark contrast with other norms, such as norms regarding punctuality, where there are often substantial differences between countries (Levine et al., 1980). Of course, it is possible that this universality across cultures holds only for the particular scenarios we happened to use. Even so, the indication that there might be human universals in norms regulating punishment is enough to warrant future studies.

CONCLUDING REMARKS

In this chapter we have investigated what norms surround punishment. In survey-based research we found, throughout the world, the existence of norms that heavily restrict punishment. To a lesser extent we found norms that make punishment obligatory. Situations were viewed differently depending on whether everyone involved were in the same position (colleagues, siblings or friends) or whether someone had an elevated position (a teacher, a parent, or a boss). Norms that restrict punishment were found in both cases, but norms that make punishment obligatory were found only in situations where someone had a special position (and then only that person was obligated to punish). The finding of no obligations to punish in the case where there are no positions might to some extent depend on the limited number of scenarios we used. Perhaps there exist other scenarios without special positions where some punishment is seen as obligatory. However, even if this is the case, those norms would have to be different from the norms about situations where people with special positions are expected to hand out punishment.

This leaves would-be punishers in a precarious position. They must be sensitive to norms that tell them not to punish too much as well as to norms that tell them not to punish too little, and sensitive to how this depends on their position in the group. The opportunity to see and learn norms surrounding punishment only arises when someone has broken a norm for how to behave in the first place. This gives anyone who is learning punishment norms fewer occasions to learn what the acceptable behavior is compared to other norms. Nonetheless, we found remarkable agreement on the norms, not just within countries but also across countries. We suggested that the solution to this paradox might be that punishment norms become generalizable between situations, as people have no choice but to generalize.

The findings in this chapter stand in stark contrast to the notion that punishment, in itself, is seen as a public good. The most positive interpretation of how people view punishment is as a double-edge sword that may benefit the community by ensuring that people adhere to norms, but harmful when overused or used by the wrong person. The surveys conducted here do not address whether or not punishers are altruistic or even see themselves as altruistic. Instead, they join an increasing number of studies that find that others often view punishers in a negative light. However, in a new experiment we have found that the individuals who punish behavior that is harmful to the group are, to a large extent, the same individuals who punish behavior that benefits the group (details available from the authors). This suggests a general lack of altruistic motivations among punishers that would help explain *why* people tend to view them so negatively.

REFERENCES

Baldassarri, D., & Grossman, G. (2011). Centralized sanctioning and legitimate authority promote cooperation in humans. *Proceedings of the National Academy of Sciences, 108*, 11023–11027.

Balliet, D., Mulder, L. B., & Van Lange, P. A. M. (2011). Reward, punishment, and cooperation: A meta-analysis. *Psychological Bulletin, 137*, 4.

Barclay, P. (2006). Reputational benefits for altruistic punishment. *Evolution and Human Behavior, 27*, 5, 325–344.

Buhrmester, M. D., Kwang, T., & Gosling, S. D. (2011). Amazon's Mechanical Turk: A new source of inexpensive, yet high-quality, data? *Perspectives on Psychological Science, 6*, 3–5.

Chaurand, N., & Brauer, M. (2008). What determines social control? People's reactions to counternormative behaviors in urban environments. *Journal of Applied Social Psychology, 38*, 1689–1715.

Cinyabuguma, M., Page, T., & Putterman L. (2006). Can second-order punishment deter perverse punishment? *Experimental Economics, 9*, 265–279.

de Quervain, D. J.-F., Fischbacher, U., Trever, V., Schellhammer, M., Buck, A., & Fehr, E. (2004). The neural basis of altruistic punishment. *Science, 305*, 1254–1258.

Elster, J. (1989). *The cement of society: A study of social order.* Cambridge: Cambridge University Press.

Eriksson, K., & Strimling, P. (2012). The hard problem of cooperation. Plos ONE, 7 (7):e40325. doi:10.1371/journal.pone.0040325.

Eriksson, K., Strimling, P., & Ehn, M. (2013). Ubiquity and efficiency of restrictions on informal punishment rights. *Journal of Evolutionary Psychology, 11*(1), 17–34.

Fehr, E., & Gächter, S. (2002). Altruistic punishment in humans. *Nature, 415*, 137–140.

Guala, F. (2012). Reciprocity: weak or strong? What punishment experiments do (and do not) demonstrate. *Behavioral and brain sciences, 35*, 1–59.

Hamilton. V. L., & Rytina, S. (1980). Social Consensus on Norms of Justice: Should the Punishment Fit the Crime? *American Journal of Sociology, 85*, 5, 1117–1144.

Herrmann, B., Thöni, C., & Gächter, S. (2008). Antisocial punishment across societies. *Science, 319*, 1362–1367.

Horita, Y. (2010). Punishers May Be Chosen as Providers But Not as Recipients. *Letters on Evolutionary Behavioral Science, 1*, 6-9.

Jarrick, A., & Wallenberg-Bondesson, M. (2011). Flexible Comparativeness: Towards Better Methods for the Cultural Historical Study of Laws—And Other Aspects of Human Culture. In A. M. Forssberg, M. Hallenberg, O. Husz & J. Nordin (Eds.), *Organizing History. Studies in Honour of Jan Glete*. Lund: Nordic Academic Press.

Johnson, W. (1997). *The T´ang Code, Volume II: Specific Articles*. Princeton University Press.

Kiyonari, T., & Barclay, P. (2008). Cooperation in social dilemmas: Free riding may be thwarted by second-order reward rather than by punishment. *Journal of personality and social psychology, 95*, 4.

Lerner, J. S., & Tiedens, L. Z. (2006). Portrait of the angry decision maker: how appraisal tendencies shape anger's influence on cognition. *Journal of Behavioral Decision Making, 19*, 115-137.

Levine, R. V., West, L. J., & Reis, H. T. (1980). Perceptions of time and punctuality in the United States and Brazil. *Journal of Personality and Social Psychology, 38*, 4.

Nelissen, R. (2008). The price you pay: cost-dependent reputation effects of altruistic punishment. *Evolution and Human Behavior, 29*, 242-248.

Nikiforakis, N. (2008). Punishment and counter-punishment in public good games: can we really govern ourselves? *Journal of Public Economics, 92*, 91-112.

Nugier, A., Niedenthal, P. M., Brauer, M., & Chekroun, P. (2007). Moral and angry emotions provoked by informal social control. *Cognition and Emotion, 21*, 1699-1720.

O'Gorman, R., Henrich, J., & Van Vugt, M. (2009). Constraining free riding in public goods games: designated solitary punishers can sustain human cooperation. *Proceedings of the Royal Society B, 276*, 323-329.

Ostrom, E., Walker, J., & Gardner, R. (1992). Covenants with and without a sword: Self-governance is possible. *American Political Science Review, 86*, 404-417.

Singer, T., Seymour, B., O'Doherty, J. P., Stephan, K. E., Dolan, R. J., & Frith, C. D. (2006). Empathic neural responses are modulated by the perceived fairness of others. *Nature, 439*, 466-469.

Tyler, T. R. (1997). The psychology of legitimacy. *Personality and Social Psychology Review, 1*, 323-344.

Warr, M., Meier, R., & Erickson, M. (1983). Norms, Theories of Punishment, and Publicly Preferred Penalties for Crimes. *Sociological Quarterly, 24*, 75-91.

Weissing, F., & Ostrom, E. (1991). Irrigation institutions and the games irrigators play: Rule enforcement without guards. In *Game Equilibrium Models II: Methods, Morals, and Markets.* (pp. 188-262). Springer Berlin Heidelberg.

Yamagishi, T. (1986). The provision of a sanctioning system as a public good. *Journal of Personality and Social Psychology, 51*, 110-116.

Zelditch, M., Jr., & Walker, H. A. (1984). Legitimacy and the stability of authority. *Advances in Group Processes, 1*, 1-25.

APPENDIX

SCENARIOS USED IN STUDIES 1 AND 2

Eating-the-sweets: At a gathering of two families, one of the children (Kevin) has eaten up the sweets that everyone in the two families was supposed to share after dinner. Both families are around when this is discovered.

Coming-late: At the hospital, one nurse (Rachel) did not show up until very late one day; in the meantime, the others had to work extra hard. Other nurses, of varying educational background, as well as the head nurse (Rachel's supervisor) are around when this is discovered.

Making-a-mess: In a student apartment, one of the students who lives there (Cath) has created a mess. Both Cath's roommate and a visitor of the roommate are around when this is discovered.

SCENARIOS USED IN STUDY 3

Eating-the-sweets: At a gathering of a few classmates after lectures, one of them (Kevin) has eaten the sweets that everyone was supposed to share. Upon noticing this, the other classmates have different reactions: Paul decides to let it go, whereas Ron decides to yell at Kevin.

Coming-late: At the hospital, one nurse (Rachel) did not show up until very late one day; in the meantime, the other nurses in her team had to work extra hard. When Rachel eventually arrived, the other nurses had different reactions: Sarah decides to let it go, whereas Maria decides to yell at Rachel.

Making-a-mess: In a student apartment, one of the students who lives there (Cath) has created a mess. Her two roommates have different reactions: Jennie decides to let it go, whereas Frances decides to yell at Cath.

Experiment: An economics experiment involves three participants. Everyone is given 10 dollars that they can choose to keep or voluntarily give away to the others. Every dollar they give away is matched by the experimenter. This means that if a participant gives away a certain amount, both the others receive that amount in full. After these decisions have been made, they can sacrifice some money to deduct from someone else's earnings: For every dollar they sacrifice, three dollars are deducted from the participant of their choice. In the experiment, Carl and Peter both gave away some money, Mark did not give away anything. Carl decides to let it go, whereas Peter decides to sacrifice 2 dollars in order to deduct 6 dollars from Mark.

SCENARIOS USED IN STUDY 4

Individual decides norm and punishment and executes punishment: At the first meeting, the group member Eric thinks about the importance of arriving on time and decides for himself that coming late is unacceptable. Eric then finds John and tells him that he has come up with a suitable punishment: Each time

John comes late in the future he must buy coffee for the entire group. As it happens, John comes late to a couple of the following meetings, and each time Eric makes sure John buys coffee for the entire group.

Group decides norm, individual decides punishment and executes punishment: At the first meeting, the entire group discusses the importance of arriving on time and jointly decides that coming late is unacceptable. One group member, Eric, then finds John and tells him that he has come up with a suitable punishment: Each time John comes late in the future he must buy coffee for the entire group. As it happens, John comes late to a couple of the following meetings, and each time Eric makes sure John buys coffee for the entire group.

Group decides norm and punishment, individual executes punishment: At the first meeting, the entire group discusses the importance of arriving on time and jointly decides that coming late is unacceptable. The group jointly decides on a suitable punishment for latecomers: Each time John comes late in the future he must buy coffee for the entire group. As it happens, John comes late to a couple of the following meetings, and each time one of the other group members (called Eric) makes sure John buys coffee for the entire group.

Group decides norm and punishment and executes punishment: At the first meeting, the entire group discusses the importance of arriving on time and jointly decides that coming late is unacceptable. The group jointly decides on a suitable punishment for latecomers: Each time John comes late in the future he must buy coffee for the entire group. As it happens, John comes late to a couple of the following meetings, and each time the other group members (one of whom is called Eric) together make sure John buys coffee for the entire group.

5 For the Common Good? The Use of Sanctions in Social Dilemmas

■ ERIC VAN DIJK, LAETITIA B. MULDER, AND ERIK W. DE KWAADSTENIET

Abstract

Sanctions (i.e., rewards and punishments) are often proposed as straightforward solutions to promote cooperation and prevent noncooperation. The effects of sanctions are, however, complex. Whereas sanctions may often work, the literature on sanctioning behavior also shows that sanctions may backfire. In this chapter, we present our research program to reveal the psychological processes that underlie these negative effects. In doing so, we also discuss the conditions that should be met for sanctions to work. In addition, we discuss the psychological processes that determine whether or not people want to use sanctions as a means to increase cooperation.

The term "social dilemma" refers to the conflict people may experience between choosing for their own interest, or for the collective interest (Dawes, 1980). Social dilemmas would not have received such great attention, if people would always cooperate and go for the collective interest. Real life examples like overfishing, and excessive energy consumption not only show that people are often inclined to put their own interest first. They also show the negative consequences of doing so. How can we promote cooperation? One possible solution that almost immediately comes to mind is to use sanctions, either negative (punishments, fines for those who do not cooperate) or positive (rewards, bonuses for those who do cooperate). Such sanctions basically aim to change the payoff structure of the dilemma people face to increase the relative attractiveness of cooperation over noncooperation.

Numerous studies have shown that rewards and punishments can indeed be effectively used to increase levels of cooperation (Balliet, Mulder, & Van Lange, 2011; Eek, Loukopoulos, Fujii, & Gärling, 2002; Fehr & Gächter, 2002; McCusker & Carnevale, 1995; Wit & Wilke, 1990; Yamagishi, 1986, 1992). This is not to say that sanctions are always successful. Sometimes sanctions are ineffective because the sanctions are too small to motivate cooperation; and sometimes people feel that the chances of detection (due to imperfect monitoring) are simply too low. Sanctions even run the risk of being counter-effective in the sense that they may lower cooperation rather than increase cooperation (e.g., Fehr & Rockenbach, 2003; Gneezy & Rustichini, 2000; Mulder, Van Dijk, De Cremer, & Wilke, 2006a; Tenbrunsel & Messick, 1999).

In this chapter we will briefly review this research and its mixed findings on the (in)effectiveness of sanctions. In doing so, we will not only discuss the potential consequences of sanctions (positive or negative), but also raise the question to what extent people take these consequences into account when considering to install sanctions. As such, we address the underlying motivations of sanctioning behavior, and provide a social-psychological perspective on the use of sanctions.

THE CONSEQUENCES OF SANCTIONS

As noted previously, various experimental studies have shown that sanctioning systems can successfully increase cooperation in social dilemmas. These insights are generally obtained by comparing the willingness to cooperate in settings with versus without sanctioning systems. In the early psychological studies on sanctions, the main focus was on the effects of sanctions that are administered by a central authority, also referred to as centralized sanctions (e.g., Balliet et al., 2011). In such studies, sanctions were, for example, imposed by a leader. In more recent years, these studies have been supplemented with research on settings where individual group members can punish each other (e.g., Fehr & Gächter, 2000), also referred to as decentralized sanctions (Balliet et al., 2011).

The recent meta-analysis of Balliet et al. (2011) indicated that both types of sanctions can—and often do—promote cooperation. It should be noted, however, that sanctions also have their drawbacks and, as such, may sometimes be counterproductive. Two important drawbacks that have been documented are that sanctions may undermine the willingness to cooperate by (a) inducing a business frame and (b) reducing interpersonal trust.

Eliciting a Business Frame

That sanctions may induce people to evaluate and define their decisions in business terms rather than ethical terms was demonstrated in a study by Tenbrunsel and Messick (1999). In a simulated setting, participants were put in the role of manager of a factory and were asked to what extent they would set their chimney scrubbers into action, and thereby reduce toxic emissions (i.e., the cooperative, environmentally friendly behavior). In the absence of sanctions, people viewed this decision as a basically ethical or environmental decision in which running the scrubbers would be the "right" thing to do. When a financial sanction was installed for not running the scrubbers, however, things changed. Then, people started thinking of the decision as a business decision rather than an ethical or environmental decision. When the financial sanction was small, this even decreased the extent to which people chose to run the scrubbers because even with the small sanction they could obtain higher outcomes by not running the scrubbers.

Another illustration of this framing effect of sanctions comes from a field study by Gneezy and Rustichini (2000). In their study, parents were fined if they picked up their children late from the day care center. Interestingly, this fine actually increased rather than decreased the number of parents picking up their children late. The explanation for this effect was that the fine altered the parents' perception of the situation. As Gneezy and Rustichini (p. 14) put it, the perception was changed to "The teacher is taking care of the child in much the same way as she did earlier in the day. In fact, this activity has a price (which is called a 'fine'). Therefore, I can buy this service as much as needed." Instead of seeing it as a sign of moral disapproval, the parents thus regarded the fine as a reasonable price to pay in exchange for the teacher looking after their children after closing time. These studies suggest that a financial punishment may remove the moral aspects of a decision, and thereby crowd out the intrinsic motivation to cooperate (see also Deci, Koestner, & Ryan, 1999).

In our own research program we provided further insight in this phenomenon by studying the effect that sanctions may have on people's moral emotions. Moral emotions such as guilt and shame are potential motivators of moral behavior, and are thereby linked to the well-being of others (Haidt, 2003; see for an overview on moral emotions e.g., Tangney, Stuwig, & Mashek, 2007). In the context of social dilemmas, these insights suggest a link between moral emotions and the importance people attach to the collective interest. In Mulder and Van Dijk (2012) we recently used this assumed link to explain and demonstrate the undermining effect of sanctions. In particular, we wondered whether sanctions could reduce the moral emotions people experience. For this purpose, we presented participants with a setting in which they had to indicate how they would feel after being noncooperative or cooperative. Corroborating the assumed link between the importance of the collective interest and moral emotions, the results showed that people reported feeling more guilty and ashamed after noncooperation than after cooperation. Whereas these findings might not come as a surprise, the more interesting finding was that this effect was reduced when there had been a fine on noncooperation. Put differently, one could argue that the installment of a sanction had reduced the experience of moral emotions after noncooperation. All this suggests that sanctions can undermine the moral underpinning of behavior. In the case of social dilemmas, it may undermine the feeling that it is wrong to put one's own interests first.

Reducing Interpersonal Trust

We discussed how sanctions may undermine the motivation of the decision-maker. In addition to this direct effect on the individual decision-maker, the detrimental effects of sanctions may also operate in a more indirect way, via our perceptions of other people. Sanctions may undermine the trust we have in others. In Mulder et al. (2006a) we showed this negative effect on interpersonal trust in a two-trial public good experiment. In the first trial of the public good dilemma, half of the participants learned that there was a punishment on noncooperation, whereas the other half were told that there was no punishment on noncooperation. In the second round, all participants faced a setting without a sanctioning system. This meant that for those who had not experienced a sanctioning system on trial 1, the situation remained the same. For those who had experienced a sanctioning system, however, things did change: They now found themselves in a situation where they and their fellow group members could no longer be punished for their decisions.

The results showed that especially those who faced the situation where a once-installed sanctioning system (trial 1) was lifted (on trial 2) no longer trusted their fellow group members. That is, compared to the participants who had never experienced a sanctioning system, they expected lower levels of cooperation from their fellow group members. Apparently, the mere existence of a sanctioning system may communicate that the group needs such extrinsic measures to ensure cooperation (see also Mulder, Van Dijk, Wilke, & De Cremer, 2005). The mere presence of a sanctioning system may communicate to people that the sanctions are there for a reason; it may thus communicate "Careful, without sanctions people do not cooperate."

Note that in this way, the installment of sanctioning systems may not only decrease people's trust in other group members' intrinsic motivation to cooperate (Chen, Pillutla, & Yao, 2009; Mulder et al., 2006a). By implication, it means that sanctioning systems may create their own need. By inducing distrust, sanctioning systems may lead people to conclude that they need the system *because* others cannot be trusted. Once installed, one may even need to maintain the sanction because lifting the sanction may create its own self-fulfilling prophecy: Cooperation will go down as a result of mutual distrust. A recent study showed that this is no different for rewards (Irwin, Mulder, & Simpson, 2012): Rewards as well as punishments are regarded as extrinsic motivators for cooperation, and thus undermine trust in other people's (intrinsic) motivation to cooperate.

So What?

Readers may argue that the drawbacks we described may not be a problem as long as the sanction is large enough, is not removed, and behavior is fully monitored. Under such circumstances, it may not matter so much whether or not a sanction undermines either the moral frame or trust in cooperative motives: After all, people may then cooperate for mere instrumental reasons. However, the drawbacks of sanctions may come forward in unexpected ways. For one thing, it may induce people to evade the sanction by turning to alternative ways of defection. Take for example the social dilemma of garbage reduction in which people face the decision to reduce their garbage or not. A sanction may be installed that entails charging a fine for every kilogram of garbage that people produce above a certain threshold. At first glance, such a simple system may seem perfect in the sense that garbage of all citizens is weighed and people automatically will be charged accordingly. However, this system may not only stimulate citizens to reduce their garbage, it may also trigger them to think about ways to work around the fine without having to reduce their garbage. For example, they may throw their garbage into the bushes or at illegal dump sites (Miranda & Aldy, 1998; see also Kim, Chang, & Kelleher, 2008).

In Mulder, Van Dijk, de Cremer, and Wilke (2006b) we revealed this evasion of sanctions in an experimental paradigm in which we compared a traditional public good setting in which people only had two options with a setting in which people had three options. In the traditional public good setting, participants could allocate endowments to their own account (and further their own interest), or to a collective account (and further the collective interest). In the three-option setting, we added a third option, which for the current purposes can be labeled as the evasion option (we did not use this label in the study itself). This evasion option was in fact worse for the collective than the other two options, comparable to the situation of illegal dumping: it directly reduced the collective outcomes.

The results of this study showed that the negative sanction on self-interested behavior was highly effective in the 2-option case; there, it reduced allocations to the own account and increased contributions to the collective account. In the 3-options case, the same sanction did again reduce the direct allocations people made to their own account. However, it did not increase allocations to the collective account. Instead, it increased allocations to the evasion account, and in the end the sanction thus only harmed the collective. With this setup we were able to demonstrate that sanctions may backfire in subtle ways. Sanctions that seem successful because they reduce the behavior they target, may at the same time promote evasive behavior that in the end may even be worse for the collective.

The story so far suggests that it is too simplistic to see sanctions as an easy solution to promote cooperation. One could even say that our research program primarily paints a pessimistic picture about the effects of sanctions. This, however, is not the picture we wish to present. Sanctioning noncooperative behavior also has positive consequences. After all, sanctions communicate moral norms. In law, regulations and sanctions have the expressive function of showing what is morally right or wrong (McAdams, 2000) and, as such, express disapproval of noncooperation by others (Cooter, 1998; Williams & Hawkins, 1986). Hence, sanctions may have the power to increase people's awareness that cooperation is the "morally right" thing to do (Mulder, 2009).

So, a sanction is more like a double-edged sword. On the one hand, it communicates disapproval of noncooperative behavior, thereby strengthening the social norm of cooperation. On the other hand, it can have the adverse effects we described previously. It is therefore important to identify the conditions that determine whether sanctions have adverse effects or whether they are successful in increasing pro-social behaviors. In our research program, we identified and addressed two such moderators: (a) the size of the sanction, and (b) trust in the sanctioning authority.

Sanction Size

One straightforward way to overcome the potential drawbacks of sanctions is to make the sanction so high that it counteracts any possible drawbacks. Indeed, the fact that sanctions may evoke a business frame may not be problematic at all, if the sanction makes cooperation more attractive to the individual than noncooperation. In other words, one could make the sanction so high that even a self-interested businessman would conclude that it is better to cooperate. In fact, this is what Tenbrunsel and Messick (1999) showed in the chimney scrubbers study discussed previously.

Here, we would like to stress that the size of a sanction can do much more than just change the relative attractiveness of noncooperation vs. cooperation. People may use the size as a cue to determine the immorality of noncooperation. To see how, you only need to think back to your teenage years. A message that you were grounded probably more strongly communicated to you that your parents disapproved of your behavior than a message that you had to go to bed early. In a similar vein, large sanctions on noncooperation may provide a stronger signal that it is immoral not to cooperate than small sanctions. Mulder, Verboon and De Cremer (2009) studied the influence of sanction size on people's perceptions of noncooperation in a setting where participants could further the outcomes of others (by allocating lottery tickets). Their findings resembled the teenage years example: Large sanctions on noncooperation (i.e., not allocating lottery tickets to others) enhanced people's perception that noncooperation was considered morally wrong by the sanctioning authority. Moreover, large sanctions enhanced the participants' own perceptions of noncooperation as being morally wrong.

Trust in Authorities

Considering that sanctions may communicate disapproval of noncooperation, it is important that such a message is accepted and adopted by responders. Centralized sanctions are often installed by an authority such as the government, a teacher, or a manager, etcetera. Trust in such authorities has been shown to affect the influence of the imposed sanction. In research by Mulder, Van Dijk and De Cremer (2009), we used the 3-option setting that we had introduced in Mulder et al. (2006b); i.e., the setting in which we previously were able to show that with an option to evade, sanctions may be counter-effective and hurt rather than promote the collective interest. This time, however, we varied the information participants had about the authority. The participants either learned that the sanction was installed by an authority who had the collective interest in mind (a trustworthy, pro-social leader), or that it was installed by an authority who had his/her own interests in mind (an untrustworthy, self-interested leader). Despite the presence of an alternative option to dodge the sanction, people generally cooperated when the sanction was installed by a trustworthy, pro-social leader. In contrast, when the sanction was installed by an untrustworthy, self-interested leader, people tended to choose the alternative noncooperative option and dodged the sanction, especially when their general trust in authorities was also low. Apparently, trust in the authority may be seen as a pointer in the right (collective) direction, and may help to foster a moral norm of cooperation (see also Muehlbacher, Kirchler, & Schwarzenberger, 2011; Wahl, Kastlunger, & Kirchler, 2010).

■ THE (UN)WILLINGNESS TO SANCTION

The findings we reviewed so far suggest that sanctions may work by increasing the relative attractiveness of cooperation, but at the same time may undermine cooperation by evoking a business frame and undermining interpersonal trust.

To counteract such concerns, sanctions need to be: (a) installed by authorities that are perceived as pro-social and trustworthy, and (b) large enough to express moral disapproval. These preconditions may make sanctions a successful means to increase cooperation.

Note, however, that up till now we mainly focused on the effects that sanctions may or may not have once they are installed. To instigate these effects, however, sanctions must first be installed and administered. A critical question therefore remains: Are people actually willing to sanction others? Addressing this question is important, if only for the obvious reason that sanctions can only show their effects if someone has decided to install them. Governments need to decide whether or not to impose sanctions on their citizens; managers in organizations need to decide on whether or not to give their employees bonuses, etcetera.

So when and how do people decide to sanction? It is surprising to see that the question of the willingness to sanction, the prerequisite for any effect of sanctions, has long remained unaddressed. A notable exception was Yamagishi (e.g., 1986, 1988), who studied the willingness to install sanctioning systems as a function of people's expectations and, for example, found that people are more willing to contribute to sanctioning systems if they fear or expect that others would not cooperate. These findings suggest that people see sanctions as an instrumental means to increase cooperation.

This does not, however, necessarily imply that people will always be willing to administer sanctions. By imposing punishments on others, one directly harms their outcomes. In general, people are reluctant to harm others (see e.g., the "do-no-harm principle" Baron, 1995) so one should have good reasons for doing so. Occasional defection may sometimes be tolerated (Stouten, De Cremer & Van Dijk, 2009; see also Chen & Bachrach, 2003). But when fellow group members repeatedly jeopardize the collective interest, and repeatedly free-ride on others' cooperativeness, the willingness to sanction increases.

An important aim of sanctioning noncooperation is to promote cooperation. Indeed, research on altruistic punishment (e.g., Fehr & Gächter, 2000, 2002; Gürerk, Irlenbusch, & Rockenbach, 2006) identified the willingness to punish noncooperators as a prerequisite for the evolution of cooperation (Fowler, 2005). In this research, participants often encounter a large number of trials, which allows for cooperation to develop. In general, such studies reveal that people are willing to altruistically give up resources to punish others who do not contribute to the collective interest, and that this mechanism of altruistic punishment is indeed effective in increasing cooperation. Fehr and Gächter (2000) assigned participants to ten rounds with and ten rounds without a sanctioning system. During the rounds with the sanctioning system, participants could reduce the outcomes of those who did not contribute. This reduction was not only costly to the punished person, but also to the punisher. The results, first of all, showed that the sanctioning systems successfully induced people to further the collective interest. More importantly, however, these results showed that people were willing to give up their own resources to punish low contributors (i.e., participants engaged in costly punishment; see also Ostrom, Walker & Gardner, 1992).

In a study by Gürerk et al. (2006) participants anonymously interacted in a 30-trial public good dilemma. On each trial, participants first chose whether they wanted to play the dilemma with a sanctioning institution or without a sanctioning institution. Subsequently, participants played the dilemma. If they had opted for the sanctioning institution, they could then subsequently punish others for their noncooperation or reward them for cooperation. Initially, only about one-third of the participants preferred to enter the sanctioning institution. Over time (i.e., over trials), however, this proportion increased, and more and more people entered the sanctioning situation, leading to an increase in cooperation and collective outcomes.

People thus seem aware of the potential instrumental benefits of punishing defection, and seem—to some extent—willing to sanction consistent defection. Interestingly, research also shows that people do not indiscriminately punish all defectors. For instance, Shinada, Yamagishi and Ohmura (2004) observed that participants were more likely to punish noncooperative in-group members than noncooperative out-group members; a finding they explained by suggesting that punishment is primarily used to maintain cooperation within one's own system of social exchange. Put differently, people may sanction to the extent that it is instrumental to increase the outcomes of their own group.

Note, however, that instrumentality is a tricky concept. Evolutionary explanations—which lie at the basis of many of the economic studies on the development of sanctioning systems—do not necessarily imply that decisions are *motivated* by considerations of instrumentality and concerns for the collective. Just as the ant may not evaluate its contribution to the ant pile in terms of instrumentality, people may not always have the collective interest in mind when sanctioning others. Other motives than instrumentality may play an important role as well. For instance, research on retribution has suggested that people may punish norm violators in order to give them their just deserts (e.g., Carlsmith, 2006; Carlsmith, Darley, & Robinson, 2002). This interpretation implies that people are not always concerned about the future consequences of punishment, and whether or not it will increase cooperation. Rather, the decision to punish may "simply" be driven by a motive to restore justice. This drive may be instrumental in the sense that it may result in a higher level of cooperation, but it does not imply that the decision to sanction was made with such instrumentality in mind. In our own line of research we draw special attention to the importance of emotions as drivers of sanctions.

The Emotional Basis of Sanctions

Norm transgressions, like violations of the equity norm, are often met with anger and punishment. Even more so, the anger we feel is often the fuel for the punishment. As such, anger after a norm violation has also been described as the proximate mechanism underlying punishment (Fehr & Gächter, 2002). The anger that we experience when confronted with noncooperative behavior is, however, not only a direct consequence of the violation itself. Our reactions are also influenced by who we are. Eisenberger, Lynch, Aselage, and Rohdieck (2004) showed that people differ in their endorsement of the negative reciprocity norm (i.e., the belief prescribing that negative behavior should be reciprocated with retribution), and that the anger people feel after norm violations is positively related to their endorsement of this negative reciprocity norm.

The link between anger and the endorsement of the negative reciprocity norm suggests that sanctions may often take the form of revenge and retribution. Justice restoration and retribution as motives for sanctioning imply a more affective than rational basis for the willingness to sanction. Indeed, it has been suggested that people sometimes derive pleasure from punishing defectors. In support of this idea, De Quervain et al. (2004) showed that the punishment of defectors activates the anterior dorsal striatum, i.e., a brain region that was implicated in other fMRI research in making decisions that are motivated by anticipated rewards (e.g., O'Doherty, Dayan, Schultz, Deichmann, Friston, & Dolan, 2004).

In our own research program (Stouten, De Cremer, & Van Dijk, 2005) we were able to demonstrate that negative emotional reactions towards non-cooperators are influenced by people's social value orientations. Social value orientations are individual differences in the relative importance assigned to outcomes for the self versus outcomes for others in interdependent situations (Kuhlman & Marshello, 1975; Messick & McClintock, 1968). People who have a preference for furthering their self-interest are generally referred to as proselfs, and people who have a preference for furthering the interests of the collective are generally referred to as prosocials (for an overview on social values see e.g., Van Lange, De Cremer, Van Dijk, & Van Vugt, 2007). Both proselfs and prosocials may react with anger to norm violations, but as Stouten et al. demonstrated, the basis of this anger may differ. In a public good setting, they showed that proselfs were primarily angry at non-cooperators if this noncooperation had had a negative impact on their own outcomes. In contrast, prosocials responded in anger to noncooperative others even if the noncooperation had not affected their own outcomes. Apparently, emotional responses to noncooperation can have their basis in moral concerns (for prosocials) or more egoistic concerns (for proselfs).

Emotional reactions may also change and develop with age. In Van den Bos, Van Dijk, and Crone (2012) we investigated the responses of participants from different age groups, ranging from late childhood to early adulthood, to violations of trust in a repeated trust game. The results indicated that with increasing age, both the anger towards and the punishment of noncooperative players decreased. This pattern fits with the notion that, with age, the ability to regulate negative affect increases, implying that the decision to punish becomes less emotion-driven over time.

So what about the positive? Since most sanctioning studies exclusively focused on punishments, much less is known about the emotions that underlie people's decisions to reward (i.e., positive sanctions). Are decisions to reward cooperation also emotion-driven? This is one of the questions we intend to answer in a new line of research. In De Kwaadsteniet, Rijkhoff, and Van Dijk (2013), we reported a first study on the emotional underpinnings of rewards. In this experimental study, participants (as third-parties) observed the outcomes of a social dilemma in which members differed in terms of cooperation. In contrast to the bulk of sanctioning studies where people can punish those who do not cooperate, here participants could reward the cooperative members. The results indicated that participants were willing to reward cooperation, with higher rewards being assigned to the more cooperative members. Moreover, the results showed that the rewards were driven by positive emotions, such as pride, elation and satisfaction. While these findings suggest a similar (emotion-based) process for rewards as for punishments, more research is needed. For instance, since (emotional) reactions to negative events are generally stronger than reactions to positive events (see e.g., Baumeister, Bratslavsky, Finkenauer, & Vohs, 2001; Wason, 1959), one may wonder whether responses to noncooperation are stronger than responses to cooperation, and if so, if punishments are more emotion-driven than rewards. We are currently setting up studies to investigate these questions.

In this research, we also want to address another issue. Previous research (including our own) on the willingness to sanction was mainly focused at increasing the understanding of decisions to sanction. Note, however, that it is equally interesting and relevant to understand why people would decide *not* to sanction. This is not a trivial issue, as the questions we pose ourselves strongly determine the answers we obtain. To illustrate, if we restrict ourselves to asking why people would punish others for their noncooperation, it should not come as a surprise that the answers only address the basis for punishment. We punish because we want to increase cooperation, or because we are angry. Does this mean that if we decide not to punish that apparently we do not care about increasing cooperation, or that we are not angry when we are confronted with noncooperation? Maybe. But then again, maybe not. Research has shown that people are not very supportive of those who punish others (e.g., Kiyonari & Barclay, 2008; Horita, 2010). Anticipation of these effects may induce people to refrain from punishing others (even if they are angry at those who do not cooperate). In addition, research has shown that people often adhere to the "do-no-harm principle" (Baron, 1995; Van Beest, Van Dijk, De Dreu, & Wilke, 2005), meaning that they are reluctant to lower the outcomes of others. Based on this principle, one may wonder whether a decision not to punish non-cooperators may reflect an aversion to harm others. In other words, the fear or aversion to hurt someone may play a role in the decision *not* to punish. The reluctance to punish incidental noncooperation, that we discussed previously, would fit with such an account.

More generally, this reasoning implies that people may be reluctant to use sanctions to the extent that they feel these sanctions are unjustified. Here too, one may wonder whether this will have a similar effect on punishment decisions as on reward decisions. As our discussion so far illustrates, prior research on sanctions in social dilemmas mostly presented participants with situations in which they had complete information about others' cooperative behavior. Thus, participants knew for certain whether another person had cooperated or not. In real-life, however, certainty is more likely to be the exception than the rule (for an overview on uncertainty effects in social dilemmas, see Van Dijk, Wit, Wilke, & Budescu, 2004). Uncertainty can take many forms. Here, we consider "noise," which refers to uncertainty about whether others actually cooperated or not (e.g., Tazelaar, Van Lange, & Ouwerkerk, 2004; Van Lange, Ouwerkerk, & Tazelaar, 2002).

We propose that decision-makers require more certainty to punish others than to reward others. More specifically, we suggest that especially under situations of noise people will show a relative preference for rewards over punishments. Our reasoning is again based on the "do-no-harm-principle" (Baron, 1995; Van Beest et al., 2005) which shows that—in the absence of additional reasons that might justify such behavior—people are more reluctant to lower others' outcomes than they are willing to increase others' outcomes. In a similar vein, we suggest that people may be more reluctant to "unjustly" punish someone for alleged noncooperation than to "unjustly" reward someone for alleged cooperation. The reluctance to punish in noisy settings is then the direct result of the fact that noise increases the chance of unjustly rewarding or punishing others (i.e., a violation of the just desert motive; Carlsmith, 2006; Carlsmith et al., 2002). Consider, for example, a noisy situation with a 20% chance that a person who presumably cooperated in fact did not cooperate, and a similar chance that a person who presumably did not cooperate in fact did cooperate. In such situations, one runs a 20% chance to unjustly punish or reward someone. Under such conditions, we suggest that the relative preference may tilt more towards rewarding, because the negative consequences of unjust punishments appear higher than the negative consequences of unjust rewards. Put differently, this also means that people require more certainty for installing punishments than for rewards. In a recent set of studies we provided first support for this reasoning, and indeed found that participants required a higher level of certainty for punishments than for rewards. Moreover, participants indicated anticipated guilt over unjust sanctioning as more important for punishments than for rewards (Van Dijk, De Kwaadsteniet, & Mulder, 2009). Apart from showing the importance of anticipated guilt as a motive, these findings show that it is fruitful to not only consider people's motives to sanction, but also their motives *not* to sanction.

■ CONCLUDING REMARKS

Sanctions are generally seen as rather simple and straightforward solutions to address the problem of noncooperation. If the problem is that people prefer noncooperation over cooperation, it is almost a no-brainer to suggest that sanctions might help. Lowering the attractiveness of the noncooperation (by punishing) and increasing the attractiveness of cooperation (by rewarding) should improve things for the better.

In a way, the initial studies on sanctioning systems reflected the simplistic view that sanctions mainly worked by affecting the relative attractiveness of the two options (cooperate vs. not cooperate). More and more, however, research has come to reveal the complexity of sanctions. This complexity can be seen as a manifestation of the psychology of sanctions.

When it comes to the effects of sanctions, a complicating factor is that sanctions may not only change the relative attractiveness of the two options, but also the *weights* we assign to both components. While in objective terms, sanctions may make cooperation more attractive, sanctions may undermine the importance people assign to furthering the collective interest. By undermining people's internal motivation to cooperate (i.e., by reducing the weight they put on the collective interest), sanctions may sometimes change things for the worse. In addition, sanctions may affect the motivation we attribute to others. By reducing the weights we assume others put on the collective interest, sanctions may lower interpersonal trust. As a result, sanctions may sometimes backfire, and hurt rather than promote the collective interest.

Large sanctions and trustworthy authorities may help, but their crucial importance for making sanctions work—although demonstrated in research—is not yet common knowledge. When sanctions backfire, this often comes as a surprise to those who install the sanctions (see e.g., Gneezy and Rustichini's [2000] day care example). To anticipate such effects, one needs to understand the psychology of sanctions.

The same goes for the use of sanctions. To understand why and when people use sanctions (be it positive or negative), it is not sufficient to point to the instrumentality of sanctions. The conclusion that people punish to increase cooperation (or decrease noncooperation) is appealing in its simplicity, but does not capture all of the psychology of sanctioning behavior. For example, to understand whether or not people sanction, we also need to understand the emotions they feel when being confronted with noncooperation or cooperation. By also wondering why people might refrain from imposing sanctions, we may increase our understanding of sanctioning behavior even further.

Of course, we realize that the complexity that psychology brings to the sanctioning literature also comes at a cost. Here we can only agree with Thaler's (1992, p. 198) remark when he discussed the benefits of bringing psychology into economics: "Rational models tend to be simple and elegant with precise predictions, while behavioral models tend to be complicated, and messy, with much vaguer predictions. But, look at it this way. Would you rather be elegant and precisely wrong, or messy, and vaguely right?" As this quote illustrates, we should embrace the complexity that the current insights offer. When it comes to considering the use of sanctions to solve real-life social dilemmas we need to further explore the conditions under which sanctions may or may not work. Eventually, these insights will evolve in a more accurate account of behavior, and thereby offer a better prospect to solve social dilemmas.

REFERENCES

Balliet, D., Mulder, L. B., & Van Lange, P. A. M. (2011). Reward, punishment, and cooperation: A meta-analysis. *Psychological Bulletin, 137*, 594–615.

Baron, J. (1995). Blind justice: Fairness to groups and the do-no-harm principle. *Journal of Behavioral Decision Making, 8*, 71–83.

Baumeister, R., Bratslavsky, E., Finkenauer, C., & Vohs, K. D. (2001). Bad is stronger than good. *Review of General Psychology, 5*, 323–370.

Carlsmith, K. M. (2006). The roles of retribution and utility in determining punishment. *Journal of Experimental Social Psychology, 42*, 437–451.

Carlsmith, K. M., Darley, J. M., & Robinson, P. H. (2002). Why do we punish?: Deterrence and just deserts as motives for punishment. *Journal of Personality and Social Psychology, 83*, 284–299.

Chen, X. P., & Bachrach, D. (2003). Tolerance of free riding: The effects of defection size, defection pattern and social orientation. *Organizational Behavior and Human Decision Processes, 90,* 139–147.

Chen, X. P., Pillutla, M. M., & Yao, X. (2009). Unintended consequences of cooperation inducing and maintaining mechanisms in public goods dilemmas: Sanctions and moral appeals. *Group Processes & Intergroup Relations, 12,* 241–255.

Cooter, R. D. (1998). Expressive law and economics. *Journal of Legal Studies, 27,* 585–608.

Dawes, R. M. (1980). Social dilemmas. *Annual Review of Psychology, 31,* 169–193.

Deci, E. L., Koestner R. M., & Ryan R. A. (1999). Meta-analytic review of experiments examining the effect of extrinsic rewards on intrinsic motivation. *Psychological Bulletin, 125,* 627–668.

De Kwaadsteniet, E. W., Rijkhoff, S. A. M., & Van Dijk, E. (2013). Adherence to equality as a benchmark for punishment and reward: The moderating role of uncertainty in social dilemmas. *Organizational Behavior and Human Decision Processes, 120,* 251–259.

De Quervain, D. J.-F., Fischbacher, U., Treyer, V., Schellhammer, M., Schnyder, U., Buick, A., & Fehr, E. (2004). The neural basis of altruistic punishment. *Science, 305,* 1254–1258.

Eek, D., Loukopoulos, P., Fujii, S., & Gärling, T. (2002). Spill-over effects of intermittent costs for defection in social dilemmas. *European Journal of Social Psychology, 32,* 801–813.

Eisenberger, R., Lynch, P., Aselage, P., & Rohdieck, S. (2004). Who takes the most revenge? Individual differences in negative reciprocity norm endorsement. *Personality and Social Psychology Bulletin, 30,* 787–799.

Fehr, E., & Gächter, S. (2000). Cooperation and punishment in public goods experiments. *American Economic Review, 90,* 980–994.

Fehr, E., & Gächter, S. (2002). Altruistic punishment in humans. *Nature, 415,* 137–140.

Fehr, E., & Rockenbach, B. (2003). Detrimental effects of sanctions on human altruism. *Nature, 422,* 137–140.

Fowler, J. H. (2005). Altruistic punishment and the origin of cooperation. *Proceedings of the National Academy of Sciences, 102,* 7047–7049

Gneezy, U., & Rustichini, A. (2000). A fine is a price. *Journal of Legal Studies, 29,* 1–17.

Gürerk, Ö., Irlenbusch, B., & Rockenbach, B. (2006). The competitive advantage of sanctioning institutions. *Science, 312,* 108–111.

Haidt, J. (2003). Elevation and the positive psychology of morality. In C. L. Keyes & J. Haidt (Eds.), *Flourishing: Positive psychology and the life well-lived* (pp. 275–289). Washington, DC: American Psychological Association.

Horita, Y. (2010). Punishers may be chosen as providers but not as recipients. *Letters on Evolutionary Behavioral Science, 1,* 6–9.

Irwin, K., Mulder, L. B., & Simpson, B. (2012). *The detrimental effects of sanctions on intra-group trust: A comparison between punishments and rewards.* Manuscript submitted for publication.

Kim, G. S., Chang, Y. J., & Kelleher, D. (2008). Unit pricing of municipal solid waste and illegal dumping: An empirical analysis of Korean experience. *Environmental Economics and Policy Studies, 9,* 167–176.

Kiyonari, T., & Barclay, P. (2008). Cooperation in social dilemmas: Free riding may be thwarted by second-order reward rather than by punishment. *Journal of Personality and Social Psychology, 95,* 826–842.

Kuhlman, D. M., & Marschello, A. (1975). Individual differences in game motivation as moderators of preprogrammed strategic effects in prisoner's dilemma. *Journal of Personality and Social Psychology, 32,* 922–931.

McAdams, R. H. (2000). An attitudinal theory of expressive law. *Oregon Law Review, 79*, 339–390.

McCusker, C., & Carnevale, P. J. (1995). Framing in resource dilemmas: Loss aversion and the moderating effects of sanctions. *Organizational Behavior and Human Decision Processes, 61*, 190–201.

Messick, D. M., & McClintock, C. G. (1968). Motivational basis of choice in experimental games. *Journal of Experimental Social Psychology, 4*, 1–25.

Miranda, M. L., & Aldy, J. E. (1998). Unit pricing of residential municipal solid waste: Lessons from nine case study communities. *Journal of Environmental Management, 52*, 79–93.

Muehlbacher, S., Kirchler, E., & Schwarzenberger, H. (2011). Voluntary versus enforced tax compliance: Empirical evidence for the "slippery slope" framework. *European Journal of Law and Economics, 32*, 89–97.

Mulder, L. B. (2009). The two-fold influence of sanctions on moral norms. In D. De Cremer (Ed.), *Psychological perspectives on ethical behavior and decision making* (pp. 169–180). Charlotte, NC: Information Age Publishing.

Mulder, L. B., & Van Dijk, E. (2012). *When sanctions undermine our moral emotions*. Unpublished manuscript.

Mulder, L. B., Van Dijk, E., & De Cremer, D. (2009). When sanctions that can be evaded still work: The role of trust in leaders. *Social Influence, 4*, 122–137.

Mulder, L. B., Van Dijk, E., De Cremer, D., & Wilke, H. A. M. (2006a). Undermining trust and cooperation: The paradox of sanctioning systems in social dilemmas. *Journal of Experimental Social Psychology, 42*, 147–162.

Mulder, L. B., Van Dijk, E., De Cremer, D., & Wilke, H. A. M. (2006b). When sanctions fail to increase cooperation in social dilemmas: Considering the presence of an alternative option to defect. *Personality and Social Psychology Bulletin, 32*, 1312–1324.

Mulder, L. B., Van Dijk, E., Wilke, H. A. M., & De Cremer, D. (2005). The effect of feedback on support for a sanctioning system in a social dilemma: The difference between installing and maintaining the sanction. *Journal of Economic Psychology, 26*, 443–458.

Mulder, L. B., Verboon, P., & De Cremer, D. (2009). Sanctions and moral judgments: The moderating effect of sanction severity and trust in authorities. *European Journal of Social Psychology, 39*, 255–269.

O'Doherty, J., Dayan, P., Schultz, J., Deichmann, R., Friston, K., & Dolan, R. J. (2004). Dissociable roles of ventral and dorsal striatum in instrumental conditioning. *Science, 304*, 452–454.

Ostrom, E., Walker, J., & Gardner, R. (1992). Covenants with and without a sword; Self-governance if possible. *American Political Science Review, 86*, 404–417.

Shinada, M., Yamagishi, T., & Ohmura, Y. (2004). False friends are worse than bitter enemies: "Altruistic" punishment of in-group members. *Evolution and Human Behavior, 25*, 379–393.

Stouten, J., De Cremer, D., & Van Dijk, E. (2005). All is well that ends well, at least for proselfs: Emotional reactions to equality violation as a function of social value orientation. *European Journal and Social Psychology, 35*, 767–783.

Stouten, J., De Cremer, D., & Van Dijk, E. (2009). Behavioral (in)tolerance of equality violation in social dilemmas: When trust affects contribution decisions after violations of equality. *Group Processes and Intergroup Relations, 12*, 517–531.

Tangney, J. P., Stuewig, J., & Mashek, D. J. (2007). Moral emotions and moral behavior. *Annual Review of Psychology, 58*, 345–372.

Tazelaar, M. J. A., Van Lange, P. A. M., & Ouwerkerk, J. W. (2004). How to cope with "noise" social dilemmas: The benefits of communication. *Journal of Personality and Social Psychology, 87,* 845–859.

Tenbrunsel, A. E., & Messick, D. M. (1999). Sanctioning systems, decision frames, and cooperation. *Administrative Science Quarterly, 44,* 684–707.

Thaler, R. H. (1992). *The winner's curse; Paradoxes and anomalies of economic life.* Princeton: Princeton University Press.

Van Beest, I., Van Dijk, E., De Dreu, C. K. W., & Wilke, H. A. M. (2005). Do-no-harm in coalition formation: Why losses inhibit exclusion and promote fairness cognitions. *Journal of Experimental Social Psychology, 41,* 609–617.

Van den Bos, W., Van Dijk, E., & Crone, E. A. (2012). Learning whom to trust in repeated social interactions: A developmental perspective. *Group Processes and Intergroup Relations, 15,* 243–256.

Van Dijk, E., De Kwaadsteniet, E. W., & Mulder, L. B. (2009). How certain do we need to be to punish and reward in social dilemmas? Presentation at the 13th international Conference on Social Dilemmas, August 20–24. Kyoto, Japan.

Van Dijk, E., Wit, A., Wilke, H., & Budescu, D. V. (2004). What we know (and do not know) about the effects of uncertainty on behavior in social dilemmas. In R. Suleiman, D. V. Budescu, I. Fischer, & D. M. Messick (Eds.), *Contemporary psychological research on social dilemmas* (pp. 315–331). Cambridge University Press.

Van Lange, P. A. M., De Cremer, D., Van Dijk, E., & Van Vugt, M. (2007). Self-interest and beyond: Basic principles of social interaction. In A. W. Kruglanski & E. T. Higgins (Eds.), *Social psychology: Handbook of basic principles* (2nd ed, pp. 540–561). New York: Guilford.

Van Lange, P. A. M., Ouwerkerk, J., & Tazelaar, M. (2002). How to overcome the detrimental effects of noise in social interaction: The benefits of generosity. *Journal of Personality and Social Psychology, 82,* 768–780.

Wahl, I., Kastlunger, B., & Kirchler, E. (2010). Trust in authorities and power to enforce tax compliance: An empirical analysis of the "slippery slope framework". *Law & Policy, 32,* 383–406.

Wason, P. C. (1959). The processing of positive and negative information, *The Quarterly Journal of Experimental Psychology, 11,* 92–107

Williams, K. R., & Hawkins, R. (1986). Perceptual research on general deterrence: A critical review. *Law and Society Review, 20,* 545–572.

Wit, A., & Wilke, H. (1990). The presentation of rewards and punishments in a simulated social dilemma. *Social Behaviour, 5,* 231–245.

Yamagishi, T. (1986). The provision of a sanctioning system as a public good. *Journal of Personality and Social Psychology, 51,* 110–116.

Yamagishi, T. (1988). The provision of a sanctioning system in the United States and Japan. *Social Psychology Quarterly, 51,* 265–271.

Yamagishi, T. (1992). Group size and the provision of a sanctioning system in a social dilemma. In W. B. G. Liebrand, D. M., Messick, & H. A. M. Wilke (Eds.), *Social dilemmas: Theoretical issues and research findings* (pp. 267–287). Oxford, England: Pergamon Press.

PART TWO

The Organization of Reward and Punishment

6 Promoting Cooperation: The Distribution of Reward and Punishment Power

■ DANIELE NOSENZO AND MARTIN R. SEFTON

Abstract
Recent work in experimental economics on the effectiveness of rewards and punishments for promoting cooperation mainly examines decentralized incentive systems where all group members can reward and/or punish one another. Many self-organizing groups and societies, however, concentrate the power to reward or punish in the hands of a subset of group members ('central monitors'). We review the literature on the relative merits of punishment and rewards when the distribution of incentive power is diffused across group members, as in most of the extant literature, and compare this with more recent work and new evidence showing how concentrating reward/punishment power in one group member affects cooperation.

■ INTRODUCTION

Social dilemmas stem from the misalignment of individual and group incentives. The optimal decision of a self-interested individual is in conflict with what is best from a societal view. A classic example, and one that we focus on here, is the situation where individuals can voluntarily contribute to public good provision. While all members of a group benefit when an individual contributes to the public good, each individual in the group has a private incentive to free-ride. Standard economic theory, based on the assumption that individuals maximize their own payoff, predicts under-provision relative to the social optimum. There is a long tradition in economics of studying mechanisms that may improve matters, for example by introducing externally-imposed incentives to encourage contributions and discourage free-riding, such as subsidies to contributors or taxes on free-riders. Chen (2008) describes many of these mechanisms and reviews related experimental research.

An important alternative approach relies on self-governance (Ostrom, 1990). Here, rather than relying on externally-imposed incentives, groups may design institutional arrangements that let individual group members set and enforce their own norms of cooperation, by voluntarily rewarding fellow group members who contribute and/or by punishing those who free-ride. Most of the literature in economics has focused on arrangements that involve decentralized incentive systems, whereby all group members can monitor and reward/punish each other. However, in many settings the power to reward or punish is not distributed equally across all group members, and is often concentrated in the hands of a central monitor. This raises a natural question of how the distribution of reward and punishment power affects their success in promoting cooperation.

The focus of this article is to address this question. To do this, in Section 2 we survey the existing experimental economics literature on decentralized and centralized incentive systems. We focus on discretionary incentives, where group members can voluntarily reward or punish others as opposed to externally-imposed incentives, where group members react to institutionalized rewards and/or punishments.[1] In Section 3, we report a new experiment that examines the relative success of decentralized and centralized rewards and punishments in sustaining cooperation. Section 4 offers some concluding comments on the broader implications of these findings.

THE USE OF INCENTIVES TO PROMOTE COOPERATION IN PUBLIC GOODS GAMES

One of the most extensively used frameworks for the study of cooperation in groups is the 'public goods game' (PGG, henceforth). There are n players, each endowed with E tokens. Each player chooses how many tokens to place in a 'private account' and how many to place in a 'group account'. A player receives a monetary payoff of α from each token placed in her private account. Each token a player contributes to the group account generates a return $n\beta$, which is equally shared among all n members of the group. Thus, from each token she contributes to the group account, a player receives a monetary payoff of β. The game is parameterized such that players have a private incentive to allocate all tokens to private accounts ($\beta < \alpha$), whereas the group as a whole would maximize monetary payoffs if all players fully contributed to the group account ($n\beta > \alpha$). Thus, tokens placed in the group account are akin to contributions to a public good, and this game captures the tension between private and collective interests, which lies at the heart of social dilemmas.[2]

A large number of economic experiments have studied behavior in the PGG (see Chaudhuri, 2011; Ledyard, 1995 for reviews of the literature). A stylized finding is that, although individuals do make positive contributions to the public good, contribution levels typically fall substantially short of the socially efficient level. Moreover, contributions tend to decline with repetition, and full free-riding often prevails towards the end of an experiment. Thus, incentives to free-ride undermine cooperation in PGGs, and the design of institutional arrangements that induce individuals to eschew narrow self-interest and promote cooperation is thus an important issue, which has attracted ubiquitous interest among behavioral scientists.

---

1. Examples of institutionalized incentives are studied in Andreoni and Gee (2012); Croson et al. (2007); Dickinson and Isaac (1998); Dickinson (2001); Falkinger et al. (2000); Fatás et al. (2010). Also related is Yamagishi (1986), where players can contribute to a centralized 'sanctioning fund,' which is then used to mete out sanctions on low contributors (see also Sigmund et al., 2010).

2. This framework in which tokens are allocated between private and group accounts was introduced by Marwell and Ames (1979); Isaac et al. (1984) modified their design to introduce the version described here.

In this section we review two such arrangements: the use of *sanctions* against free-riders vis-à-vis the use of *rewards* for cooperators. In particular, we will review evidence from economic experiments on the effectiveness of punishment and reward incentives when these are administered through a decentralized system, whereby each group member monitors and sanctions/rewards other group members, or through a centralized system, whereby the power to administer the incentives is concentrated in the hands of a restricted number of group members.

Standard theory predicts that the opportunity to punish or reward other group members will have no effect on cooperation: costly punishment/reward reduces earnings and so should not be used by a self-interested individual. Knowing this, individuals should not be deterred from pursuing their selfish interests by the threat of punishment, or the promise of rewards. Nevertheless, as we discuss in the next sub-section, the availability of punishments and/or rewards can promote cooperation and increase public good provision relative to settings where discretionary incentives are unavailable.

Decentralized (Peer-to-Peer) Punishments and Rewards

Most of the economics literature has focused on *decentralized (peer-to-peer) incentives*, which can be used by all group members to reward or punish each other. The vast majority of studies have focused on punishment incentives (e.g., Fehr & Gächter, 2000; Fehr & Gächter, 2002).[3] Fehr and Gächter (2000), for example, use a two-stage PGG. In the first stage, players choose a contribution level, as in the standard game described earlier. In the second stage, players learn the contributions of the other members of their group and then simultaneously decide whether to assign 'punishment tokens' to each group member. Each assigned token is costly to both the punishing and the punished player. The availability of peer-to-peer punishment is found to significantly increase contributions relative to the standard PGG: averaging across all periods and treatments reported in Fehr and Gächter (2000), players contribute about 25% of their endowment in the game without punishment, and 67% in the game with punishment.[4] Moreover, the availability of punishment incentives stabilizes cooperation: in the games with punishment, contributions do not decrease as in the standard game without punishment, and can increase over time to converge to nearly full cooperation. These findings have been widely replicated in the literature (for recent surveys see, e.g., Chaudhuri, 2011; Gächter & Herrmann, 2009; Shinada & Yamagishi, 2008), and suggest that decentralized punishment systems can provide powerful incentives to cooperate in social dilemmas.

---

3. There are parallel literatures focusing on punishment incentives in other related social dilemmas, such as common pool resource dilemmas (Ostrom et al., 1992) or prisoner's dilemmas (Caldwell, 1976).

4. Punishment opportunities increase contributions both in a "partner" treatment, where players are matched with the same other group members repeatedly, and a "stranger" treatment, where players are re-matched into new groups after each period, though contributions are lower in the latter treatment.

The effectiveness of punishment incentives has also been shown to vary with the punishment technology. In particular, the use of a punishment token imposes costs on both punisher and punishee, and cooperation rates are generally higher and more stable with higher impact-to-cost ratios (e.g., Egas & Riedl, 2008; Nikiforakis & Normann, 2008). 'Low-power' punishments with a 1:1 impact-to-cost ratio are not always successful in encouraging cooperation in PGGs. For example, while Masclet and Villeval (2008) and Sutter et al. (2010) find that 1:1 punishments significantly increase contributions relative to a standard PGG with no punishment, Egas and Riedl (2008), Nikiforakis and Normann (2008) and Sefton et al. (2007) find that 1:1 punishments are ineffective.

In contrast to the abundant evidence on the effectiveness of punishments, the use of rewards to promote cooperation has received less attention in the experimental literature. Sefton et al. (2007) studied a two-stage PGG where, in the first stage, players choose a contribution to the public good and, in the second stage, after having observed others' contributions, players can assign 'reward tokens' to each other. Each token assigned is costly to the rewarding player (her earnings decrease by $0.10), and increases the earnings of the rewarded player (also by $0.10). Sefton et al. (2007) find that the availability of rewards increases contributions relative to a standard PGG with no rewards or punishments, although the effect is small (subjects contribute 43% of their endowment in the standard PGG and 59% in the game with rewards) and is statistically significant only at the 10% level. Moreover, rewards do not stabilize cooperation: in the last period of the game with rewards, contributions are actually lower (albeit not significantly so) than in the standard game with no punishment/reward incentives.

Other studies have confirmed that when rewards are pure monetary transfers between players, as in Sefton et al., they have only a weak (and mostly statistically insignificant) impact on cooperation rates in PGG experiments (Drouvelis & Jamison, 2012; Sutter et al., 2010; Walker & Halloran, 2004). However, if the impact of the reward on the rewarded player's payoff exceeds the cost of using the instrument, rewards have been found to be effective in encouraging cooperation (Rand et al., 2009 and Sutter et al., 2010, both using 'high-power' rewards with a 3:1 impact-to-cost ratio). Moreover, high-power rewards are as effective as high-power punishments (Drouvelis, 2010; Rand et al., 2009; Sutter et al., 2010).[5]

These findings point to a potential limitation on the use of rewards to encourage cooperation in social dilemmas: rewards can be expected to be effective only when the cost of assigning the reward is outweighed by the benefits that accrue to the recipient of the reward. While there may be situations where recipient's valuation of the reward exceeds the cost of delivering it (e.g., the awards and perks used in employee recognition programs usually impose modest costs on the firm but may have special value to employees), in many settings rewards that generate direct net benefits may be unavailable.

---

5. For a review of the relative effectiveness of peer rewards and peer punishment see Milinski and Rockenbach (2012). See Balliet et al. (2011) for further discussion and for a meta-analysis of the effectiveness of discretionary and non-discretionary incentives.

In summary, the findings in the literature suggest that both peer-to-peer punishments and rewards can effectively promote cooperation in social dilemmas.[6] Crucial to the effectiveness of either instrument is the ratio of the benefit/cost of receiving the reward/punishment to the cost of delivering it. High-power rewards and punishments are both beneficial for cooperation. For a given effect on cooperation, rewards have an efficiency-advantage over the punishment instrument, since the mere use of high-power rewards raises joint payoffs (e.g., Rand et al., 2009; Sutter et al., 2010). In contrast, punishment can enhance efficiency only if the efficiency gains from higher contributions exceed the social loss associated with the use of the instrument (see, e.g., Ambrus & Greiner, 2012; Gächter et al., 2008; Herrmann et al., 2008). Thus, while the instruments may be similarly effective in raising contribution levels, (high-power) rewards may be preferred to sanctions on efficiency grounds. On the other hand, there is mixed evidence that low-power punishments are effective in raising contributions in PGG experiments, and low-power rewards have largely been found to be ineffective.

Centralized Punishments and Rewards

While the literature reviewed previously suggests that peer-to-peer incentives can successfully promote cooperation, there are also settings where they fail to do so. One problematic aspect of the use of peer-to-peer rewards and punishments is that some players may misuse incentives and actually use them to undermine cooperation. For instance, several experiments with peer-to-peer punishment have documented the existence of 'antisocial' or 'perverse' punishment, whereby sanctions are used against contributors rather than free-riders with detrimental effects on cooperation (see, for example, Herrmann et al., 2008; Gächter & Herrmann, 2009; or Gächter & Herrmann, 2011).[7] A second issue concerns the potential inefficiencies that may arise if individuals fail to coordinate their punishment or rewarding activities such that too much (or too little) punishment and/or rewarding are meted out. This may be particularly problematic in the case of an excessive use of punishment, due to its associated social inefficiencies. The coordination problems

---

6. Some studies have examined whether the joint availability of punishments and rewards can further increase cooperation. Results are mixed. Sefton et al. (2007) find that contributions are highest when group members can use both instruments. Rand et al. (2009) find that combining punishments and rewards does not lead to higher contributions than when only punishment or only rewards can be used. Finally, in Drouvelisand Jamison (2012), contributions are higher when both instruments are available than when only rewards are available, but the joint availability of punishments and rewards does not increase contributions relative to a treatment where only punishment is available. (However, note that in their experiment the punishment instrument displays a 3:1 impact-to-cost ratio, while the reward instrument has a 1:1 ratio.)

7. Several studies have examined whether further punishment stages, in which players can punish punishing behaviors, may be a way to discipline perverse or anti-social punishment. Cinyabuguma et al. (2006) find that allowing such "second-order punishment" has little effect in deterring perverse punishment, and in fact they observe another form of perverse second-order punishment where the punishers of free-riders are punished. Moreover, Denant-Boemont et al. (2007) and Nikiforakis (2008) find that allowing second-order punishment can even have a negative effect on cooperation.

may be further aggravated by the existence of a (second-order) free-rider problem in the use of incentives: since punishing and/or rewarding others is costly, each individual would prefer that someone else bears the burden of enforcing the norm of cooperation (Elster, 1989; Fehr & Gächter, 2002).

Perhaps as a consequence of these difficulties, some groups and societies have developed *centralized systems* to administer incentives. In such systems, the role of disciplining group members is delegated to one or more authority figures ('monitors') that have exclusive use of the punishment and/or reward instruments. Ostrom (1990), for example, discusses the case of the Hirano, Nagaike and Yamanoka villages in Japan, where the monitoring and sanctioning functions were delegated to 'detectives' who patrolled the communally owned lands and collected fines from villagers caught using the lands without authorization. In some villages, the role of 'detective' was taken up by all eligible male villagers on a rotating basis.[8] Pirate societies are another example of self-organizing groups facing social dilemmas (e.g., in the provision of effort during a plunder) who delegated the administration of discipline to a central authority. The power *"to allocate provisions, select and distribute loot (...) and adjudicate crew member conflicts/administer discipline"* was transferred from pirate crews into the hands of elected quartermasters, who, together with ship captains, acted as 'social leaders' in pirate societies (Leeson, 2007, p. 1065; see also Leeson, 2009). A further, more contemporary example of centralized incentive systems can be found in the arrangement of team incentives in organizations, where the role of administering reward and punishment incentives to team members is concentrated in the hands of a team leader or supervisor.

Delegation of the disciplining power to a central monitor can successfully solve some of the issues of peer-to-peer incentives outlined previously. For example, centralizing the use of incentives may eliminate or reduce the inefficiencies arising from the miscoordination of punishing/rewarding activities. The second-order free-riding problem may also be mitigated in the sense that, although the use of incentives is still costly, monitors know that they cannot free-ride on others' monitoring efforts. Moreover, the effectiveness of the punishment and reward instruments may increase when the use of the instruments is centralized. For instance, a monitor who can make a coordinated use of the group resources that are earmarked for the disciplining activity may be able to inflict a harsher punishment upon a free-rider than if the sanctioning resources are diffused across group members. Similarly, the disciplining effect of rewards may increase if these are concentrated in the hands of a monitor who has discretion to allocate or withhold the funds from group members.

On the other hand, there are also potential disadvantages associated with centralized incentive systems. Installing a central monitor to administer the group punishing/rewarding resources does not solve the issue of whether the incentives will be used in the best interest of the group. In fact, monitors may face stronger incentives than group members to abuse their power. For example, monitors may be tempted to underuse the resources earmarked for the monitoring and

---

8. Similar positions of 'guards' have been created by self-organizing groups for the management of irrigation and forestal systems (see Ostrom, 1990; Ostrom, 1999).

disciplining activities if they are residual claimants of such resources. Analogously, monitors may be tempted to overuse the resources at their disposal, e.g., if they can keep a share of the fines collected from the sanctioned individuals. This discussion highlights the importance of keeping monitors accountable to the group for their activities (Ostrom, 1990). A further issue, discussed in Balliet et al. (2011), regards the relation between monitors and group members. If monitors are perceived as 'out-groups', who are extraneous to the group, this may undermine group cohesion with negative effects on cooperation.

Overall, the previous discussion raises interesting questions about the relative effectiveness of centralized incentive systems vis-à-vis decentralized systems in social dilemma settings. Surprisingly, very few experimental studies in economics have focused on centralized punishment and reward systems.[9] One such study is van der Heijden et al. (2009), who examine a team production setting where team members automatically receive an equal share of the team output irrespective of their contribution to team production. This setting is analogous to the public goods setting, and complete free-riding is the unique equilibrium. Van der Heijden et al. (2009) compare this setting to one where the distribution of team output is not automatic, but instead is administered by a 'team leader'. The team leader can monitor other team members' contributions and decide how to allocate team output amongst team members. In this setting, team leaders face the temptation to keep the whole team output for themselves, and thus it is unclear whether they can successfully promote cooperation. In fact, van der Heijden et al. (2009) find that the introduction of a team leader significantly increases average team contributions by 73%, and team earnings by 37%. However, not all teams perform well under a team leader: cooperation breaks down when team leaders abuse their power and distribute output unfairly among team members.

Another study focusing on centralized incentives is Gürerk et al. (2009). They study a team production game where, after all team members have made a contribution to team production and received an equal share of team output, one team member (the team leader) receives a monetary budget that she can use to discipline team members. Team leaders can choose the type of incentives that they will have available in the game: they can choose to discipline team members using either punishments or rewards. Gürerk et al. (2009) find that team leaders are initially reluctant to choose the punishment instrument, and almost all team leaders commit to using the reward instrument instead. However, rewards are less effective than punishments in encouraging team members to contribute: contributions decline over time when rewards are used, whereas there is an increasing trend in contributions under punishment incentives. As a consequence, leaders' preference for rewards tends to diminish over time.[10]

---

9. Eckel et al. (2010) study a "star-network" setting where one player occupies a central position, but that player can be punished as well as punish. Thus, although punishment power is asymmetrically distributed across group members, it is not centralized in the hands of one player. Similarly, Leibbrandt et al. (2012) and Nikiforakis et al. (2010) study punishment mechanisms with asymmetric (but not centralized) distributions of the power to punish.

10. A similar finding is reported in Gürerk et al. (2006) for decentralized incentive systems.

These two studies suggest that centralized incentive systems can successfully promote cooperation in social dilemmas. Nevertheless, some of the empirical findings (e.g., the heterogeneity in team success under leaders in van der Heijden et al., 2009) highlight the concerns discussed previously about the potential pitfalls of centralized systems. Moreover, since neither study includes treatments where subjects can mutually monitor and punish/reward each other, it is difficult to draw conclusions about the relative success of centralized systems vis-à-vis decentralized systems.

Two recent studies which do include a comparison between centralized and decentralized incentive systems are O'Gorman et al. (2009) and Carpenter et al. (2012). Both studies focus on punishment incentives. O'Gorman et al. (2009) study a PGG with two types of sanctioning systems: one treatment uses the standard mutual monitoring system (peer-to-peer punishment), whereas the other treatment uses a centralized monitoring system whereby only one group member (randomly selected each period) can punish group members. O'Gorman et al. (2009) find that in a treatment without punishment, contributions display the usual decreasing trend over time, and average contributions are significantly lower than in either punishment treatment. Contributions do not differ significantly between the centralized and peer-to-peer punishment treatments, but average earnings are significantly higher with centralized punishment than with peer-to-peer punishment, suggesting that a more coordinated use of punishment power can reduce efficiency losses.

Carpenter et al. (2012) also study a PGG and compare a treatment with peer-to-peer punishment and a treatment where the monitoring and punishment power is concentrated in the hands of one group member. In contrast to O'Gorman et al. (2009), Carpenter et al. (2012) report higher contributions under peer-to-peer punishment (where subjects on average contribute 56% of their endowment) than in the treatment with centralized punishment (where average contributions are 33% of the endowment). Average earnings are also higher under peer-to-peer than centralized punishment. There are several differences in the experimental designs of the O'Gorman et al. (2009) and Carpenter et al. (2012) studies, but perhaps a potential explanation for the different findings reported in the two studies is that in O'Gorman et al. (2009), the role of central monitor was randomly assigned to a new subject in each new round of play, whereas in Carpenter et al. (2012), roles remained constant throughout the experiment. Assigning the role of central monitor on a rotating basis, as in O'Gorman et al. (2009), may attenuate the negative impact that the appointment of a 'bad monitor' (e.g., a monitor who never sanctions free-riding) may have on contribution dynamics, and may thus explain the different success of the centralized system across the two studies.[11]

---

11. Baldassarri and Grossman (2011) study a rather different sort of centralized punishment institution where a third-party (i.e., a player external to the group who neither contributes nor benefits from contributions) is responsible for punishment. They find that centralized punishment is most effective where the third-party is elected rather than randomly appointed. Relatedly, Grechenig et al. (2012) study a centralized punishment institution where a player external to the group controls the allocation of group members' punishment resources. Their focus, however, is on group members' choices between this centralized-punishment institution and standard decentralized and no-punishment institutions. In the setting most similar to those studied in O'Gorman et al. (2009) and Carpenter et al. (2012), they find that subjects prefer decentralized punishment to centralized and no-punishment institutions.

While the studies reviewed previously shed some light on the effectiveness of centralized incentives systems in sustaining cooperation in social dilemmas, several important questions remain unanswered. First, while the studies by O'Gorman et al. (2009) and Carpenter et al. (2012) allow a comparison between centralized and decentralized punishment systems, we are not aware of any study comparing centralized and decentralized reward systems. Second, with the exception of van der Heijden et al. (2009), all other studies have examined 'high-power' incentives (with either a 3:1 or 2:1 impact-to-cost ratio). As discussed in the previous sub-section, 'high-power' peer-to-peer punishments and rewards are usually very successful in encouraging cooperation in social dilemmas, and so it seems that there may be little scope for centralized systems to improve over this. An interesting question is whether concentrating punishment/reward power can improve the success of incentives in environments where peer-to-peer incentives have been less successful in encouraging cooperation. In this sense, the result reported in van der Heijden et al. (2009) that concentrating rewards in the hands of a leader is beneficial for cooperation is interesting because most of the literature on 1:1 peer-to-peer rewards find them to be ineffective, and so this suggests that concentrating reward power may increase the effectiveness of the instrument. In the next section we report a new experiment to shed light on some of these questions.

THE EFFECTIVENESS OF CENTRALIZED VERSUS DECENTRALIZED INCENTIVES: NEW EVIDENCE

Design and Procedures

The new experiment used 150 volunteer participants, randomly matched into three-person groups.[12] All groups played a two-stage PGG, repeated over ten periods in fixed groups. In stage one, each player received an endowment of 20 tokens and had to choose how many to allocate to a public account and how many to keep in a private account. A player earned 3 points for each token she kept in her private account, and 2 points from each token allocated to the public account (regardless of which group member had contributed it). At the end of the stage, players were informed of the decisions and earnings of each group member. In stage two, 24 additional tokens were given to each group and these could be used to either increase own-earnings, or reward or punish other group members, depending on treatment. At the end of stage two, players were informed of the stage two decisions and earnings of each group member. Players were then informed of their total earnings for the period, these being the sum of their earnings from the two stages.

Altogether we had five treatments, with ten groups in each treatment. In our *Baseline* treatment, 8 stage-two tokens were placed in each player's private account,

---

12. The experiment was conducted in multiple sessions in the CeDEx computerized laboratory at the University of Nottingham in Spring 2012. Subjects were recruited using ORSEE (Greiner, 2004) and the software was written in z-Tree (Fischbacher, 2007). A copy of experimental materials is available in the Appendix.

yielding 3 points per token. In our mutual monitoring treatments, each player was given 8 stage-two tokens that could be kept in a private account, yielding 3 points per token, or assigned to other group members. In our *Mutual-Punish* treatment, a token assigned to a group member reduced her earnings by 3 points, while in our *Mutual-Reward* treatment, each stage two token assigned to a group member *increased* her earnings by three points. Based on the previous research discussed earlier, we expected that the effect of allowing 1:1 rewards or punishment would be quite weak, allowing for the possibility that concentrating reward/punishment power would increase the effectiveness of rewards or punishment.

In our central monitoring treatments, all punishment/reward power was concentrated in the hands of one randomly-assigned group member (this was the same group member in all ten periods). This group member (the 'central monitor') was given 24 tokens in stage two, and these could be placed in her private account, yielding 3 points per token, or assigned to other group members. Assigning a token reduced the assignee's earnings by three points in the *Central-Punish* treatment, and increased her earnings by three points in the *Central-Reward* treatment.[13]

Our parameters were chosen to satisfy two criteria that we considered may be important for the successful administration of incentives. First, we chose parameters to give central monitors the *ability to discipline*. A group member can increase her stage one earnings by 20 points by keeping all her tokens rather than contributing them. We wanted to give the central monitor sufficiently many stage two tokens so that she could reduce a free-rider's stage two earnings by at least 20 points by withholding rewards in the *Central-Reward* treatment. With 24 stage two tokens, a monitor could employ a strategy of rewarding full contributors with 8 tokens and withholding rewards from free-riders. Against this strategy, a defector gains 20 points in stage one and loses 24 points in stage two, and so this strategy effectively disciplines free-riders. Second, we wanted to give central monitors an *incentive to discipline*. Since the central monitor could free-ride in stage one and keep all her stage two tokens, giving a payoff of at least $(20 \times 3) + (24 \times 3) = 132$ points, we wanted the payoff from full contribution and an equal allocation of reward tokens to be higher than this. With our parameters, the central monitor receives $(60 \times 2) + (8 \times 3) = 144$ points when the group contributes fully and she rewards equally.

Results

As seen in Figure 6.1, our *Baseline* treatment exhibits the standard pattern observed in previous public goods experiments. Average contributions start out around 60% of endowments and steadily decline with repetition to 20% of endowments in period ten. Across all rounds participants contribute, on

---

13. In addition to earnings from each period we gave each participant an initial point balance of 320 points (which covered any potential losses in the treatments allowing punishment). At the end of a session the initial balance plus accumulated point earnings from all periods was converted into cash at a rate of £0.75 per point. Participants earned, on average, £11.10 for a session lasting between 30 and 60 minutes.

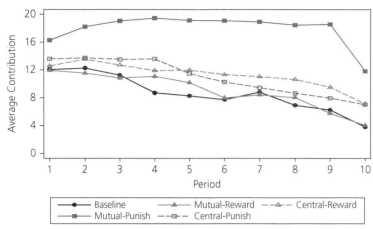

Figure 6.1 Average contributions to public good across periods.

average, 43% of their endowments. Relative to this, we find that peer punishment is highly effective. Averaging across all periods, participants contribute 89% of their endowments in the *Mutual-Punish* treatment. This difference in average contributions is highly significant (p = 0.001).[14] In contrast, peer rewards are ineffective: average contributions in the *Mutual-Reward* treatment are 45% of endowments, not significantly different from *Baseline* (p = 0.821). These findings are qualitatively consistent with the findings from exogenous 1:1 treatments reported in Sutter et al. (2010). However, punishment is much more effective in our study, perhaps reflecting the stronger punishment technology.[15]

Turning to our *Central-Punish* treatment, we find that concentrating punishment power reduces the effectiveness of punishment. Contributions are 55% of endowments in *Central-Punish*, significantly lower than in *Mutual-Punish* (p = 0.038). In fact, when punishment is left to a central monitor, average contributions are not significantly different from *Baseline* (p = 0.571). Concentrating reward power, on the other hand, results in a small, but insignificant, increase in contributions. Average contributions in *Central-Reward* are 56% of endowments, not significantly different from *Mutual-Reward* (p = 0.406) or *Baseline* (p = 0.406).

Differences between the *Mutual-Punish* treatment and the other treatments are also evident in Figure 6.2, which shows the distribution of contributions, pooling over all periods. While in the *Mutual-Punish* treatment only 5% of decisions were to contribute zero, in all other treatments around 30% of contribution decisions result in extreme free-riding. At the other extreme, in the *Mutual-Punish* treatment players contribute 20 tokens 78% of the time, twice as often as in any other treatment. In turn, full contributions are twice as frequent in the centralized

---

14. All p-values are based on two-sided Wilcoxon rank-sum tests, treating each group as a unit of observation.

15. In their study, the gain to a player from free-riding completely rather than contributing fully was 8 experimental currency units, whereas the most punishment that a player could receive was 3 experimental currency units.

98 ■ Reward and Punishment in Social Dilemmas

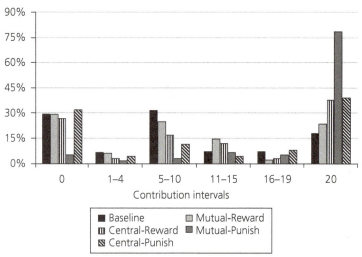

Figure 6.2 Distribution of individual contributions to public good.

monitoring treatments as in *Baseline* (39% in *Central-Punish*, 38% in *Central-Reward*, and 18% in *Baseline*).

Differences between treatments seem most strong for the case of maximal contributions. While the proportion of maximal contributions is significantly higher in *Mutual-Punish* than *Baseline* (p = 0.001), the differences between proportions in the centralized monitoring treatments and *Baseline* are not significant (*Central-Reward* versus *Baseline*, p = 0.255; *Central-Punish* versus *Baseline*, p = 0.128). The reason for this is not so much the size of the effect (though, as Figure 6.2 shows, there is a considerable difference in this respect), but rather the reliability of the effect. In nine of ten *Mutual-Punish* groups, maximal contributions are observed as often as not, while the same can be said of only one *Baseline* group. In the centralized monitoring treatments there is more heterogeneity. In each treatment there are four groups that look like *Mutual-Punish* groups in terms of their propensity to contribute fully, and six groups that look like *Baseline* groups.

This heterogeneity across groups in contribution behavior translates into heterogeneity in earnings. In principle, a group could earn as much as 144 points per group member per period, and in fact two groups in *Mutual-Punish* achieved this, but there was considerable variability in actual earnings among the other groups. Figure 6.3 presents box-and-whiskers diagrams for the distribution of group earnings, where the box shows the lower quartile, median, and upper quartile of attained group earnings.[16]

Relative to *Baseline*, earnings are higher and less variable in the *Mutual-Punish* treatment. It is worth noting that even in the short horizon of the experiment, earnings are significantly higher in *Mutual-Punish* than *Baseline* (p = 0.008). The

---

16. The whiskers represent the lowest (highest) observation still within 1.5 times the inter-quartile range of the lower (upper) quartile. One outlier is indicated in the Punish treatment.

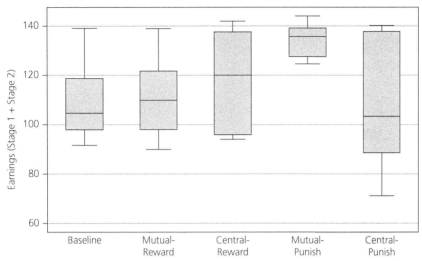

Figure 6.3 Box plots of group performance. Group performance is measured by earnings per group member per period.

diagrams also show that centralized monitoring leads to more variable group performances than the other treatments. Apparently, when placed in the role of central monitor, some players used the strategy of contributing fully and disciplining free-riders, and successfully managed a cooperative group. At the same time, other central monitors failed either because they used punishments or rewards ineffectively, or because they did not try to use them at all. This result underlines the importance of differences in leadership qualities across individuals. This was previously noted by van der Heijden et al. (2009), who also observed a mixture of 'good' and 'bad' leaders. Overall leadership seemed much more effective in their study, although the power technology of the leaders is very different across studies. An interesting avenue for further research could be to identify the psychological mechanisms underlying differences in leadership quality.

Next, we examine how rewards and punishments were directed. Figure 6.4 shows that the number of reward/punishment tokens a subject receives is sensitive to how her contribution relates to the average contribution of the rest of her group.

The patterns in the mutual monitoring treatments are similar to previous experiments. Group members are punished more heavily the lower is their contribution relative to the average contributed by the rest of their group, and rewards are mainly targeted at those who contribute at or above the average contributed by the rest. However, large deviations below the average of others' contributions are punished more heavily than cooperators are rewarded. On average, if a player free-rides rather than contributes fully in a group where the others contribute fully, she receives more than 20 points of punishment in *Mutual-Punish*, but forgoes far less than 20 points of rewards in *Mutual-Reward*. There is a noticeable difference in the way incentives are used in the *Central-Punish* treatment, where punishments are more frequently meted out against group members who contribute above the

100 ■ Reward and Punishment in Social Dilemmas

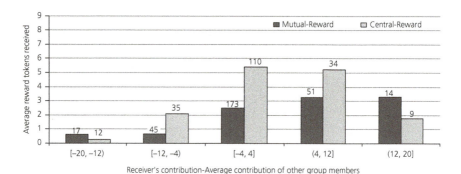

Figure 6.4 Reward/punishment tokens received. Numbers above bars indicate the number of cases in each interval.

group average. Such anti-social punishment has been shown to be detrimental to cooperation in mutual monitoring environments (see section 2).[17]

The effectiveness of punishment and rewards depends crucially on how players respond to the use of these incentives. Figure 6.5 shows how individuals change their contributions in response to punishment/reward received in the previous period. We distinguish between those subjects who give less than, the same as, and more than, the group average. In the punishment treatments, those who contribute less than the group average tend to increase their contribution in response to being punished. In *Mutual-Punish*, there is very little punishment of those who contribute at or above the average of the rest of their group, but in *Central-Punish*

---

17. Although some potential explanations for anti-social punishment cannot operate in a centralized monitoring environment (e.g., revenge for being punished in previous periods, or pre-emptive retaliation by free-riders who expect to get punished), some others can (e.g., a dislike of non-conformism). It is difficult to explain why anti-social punishment is more prevalent with centralized as opposed to mutual monitoring. One possibility is that players can discipline anti-social punishers in the mutual monitoring environment by punishing them in subsequent periods, while the central monitor does not have to fear punishment. If so, then this suggests that the possibility to discipline central monitors (for example by voting them out of office) might reduce anti-social punishment by central monitors. We chose to appoint central monitors randomly for purposes of experimental control, but future research could examine how the effectiveness of central monitors depends on the way they are appointed.

The Distribution of Reward and Punishment Power ■ 101

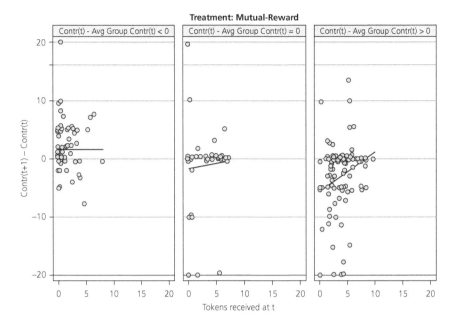

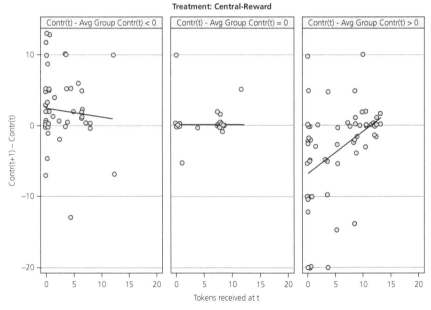

Figure 6.5 Response to reward/punishment tokens received. For each treatment we show three separate OLS regression lines, one based on data from players who contributed less than the average of the other members of their group (leftmost panel), one for players who contributed the same as the average of the other group members (middle panel), and one for players who contributed more than the average of the other group members (rightmost panel).

102 ■ Reward and Punishment in Social Dilemmas

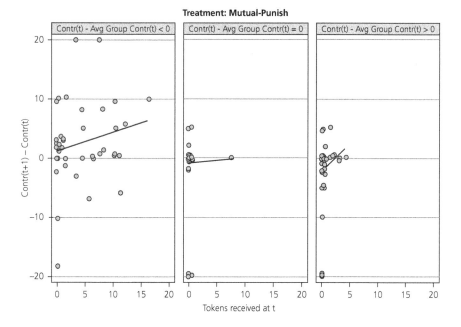

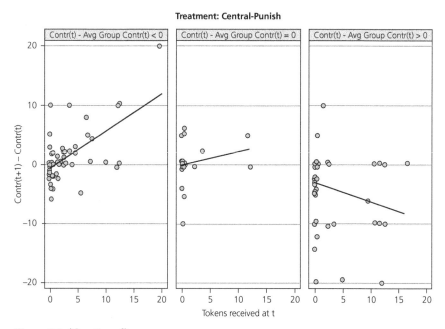

Figure 6.5 (Continued)

these players are sometimes punished and they tend to respond by decreasing their contribution. In the reward treatments, those that contribute less than the average of the rest of their group do not change their contribution much, while those who contribute at or above the average of the rest of the group tend to decrease their contribution if they don't get rewarded. This asymmetry in the response to rewards may explain why they have little impact in sustaining cooperation.

In summary, our new experiment finds that peer-to-peer punishment is an effective mechanism for promoting cooperation, whereas peer-to-peer rewards are much less effective. Our treatments with concentrated reward/punishment power were designed so that central monitors had both an incentive to induce cooperation, and sufficient resources to be able to incentivize cooperation, by other group members. Nevertheless, cooperation in these treatments is not significantly higher than in our Baseline.

CONCLUSIONS

We reviewed evidence on the effectiveness of discretionary incentives to promote cooperation. A large literature in economics shows that decentralized (peer-to-peer) punishments can be effective in raising contributions and earnings. Previous studies have emphasized the importance of high-power incentives and/or long time horizons for the success of punishment institutions. Our new experiment shows that punishments can be effective even within a context of a 'low power' incentive system (with a 1:1 impact-to-cost ratio) and short horizon (10 periods). Indeed, somewhat surprisingly, peer-to-peer punishment elicited (and maintained) high levels of cooperation from very early in the game, indicating that the threat of punishment seems almost instantly recognized by our subjects. Peer-to-peer rewards, on the other hand, have not been studied as extensively. While high-power rewards are as effective as high-power punishments, most studies find that low-power rewards are ineffective. Our new experiment with low-power rewards confirms this.

Our primary focus, however, is to compare these decentralized incentive systems with centralized systems. Centralized systems have natural manifestations in the organization of teams and small groups and societies, where the administration of incentive power is delegated to subsets of group members (which we refer to as 'central monitors'). Perhaps surprisingly, centralized systems have been relatively overlooked in the literature. Existing evidence suggests that concentrating incentive power may enhance efficiency. However, some of the findings caution that conferring all reward or punishment power on one individual is risky: some individuals are found to abuse (or, at least, fail to use effectively) their incentive power, with detrimental consequences for cooperation. Our new experiment finds that concentrating punishment power clearly reduces its effectiveness, while concentrating reward power slightly raises its effectiveness, albeit not significantly.

The poor performance of centralized institutions in our setting may partly reflect the specific details of the decision environment studied in our experiment. For example, for centralized institutions to be successful, central monitors must have a sufficient incentive to use rather than keep for themselves the group resources earmarked for the disciplining activity. This "incentive to discipline" is sensitive to the parameters of the decision environment. For example, in our setting the incentive to discipline increases with the size of the group, *ceteris paribus*. Thus, centralized institutions may be found to be more effective in settings where central monitors control larger groups. Another condition for centralized institutions to be successful is that central monitors have sufficient disciplining power to induce a player who only cares about her own material payoff to contribute. This "ability to discipline" is also sensitive to the parameters of the decision setting. For example, in our experiment the ability to discipline increases in the amount of resources earmarked for the disciplining activity. Thus, central monitors may be more successful in settings where they control a larger amount of resources.

Our new experiment also finds considerable heterogeneity in group performance when power is centralized: while some groups perform well under a central monitor, in other groups central monitors simply keep to themselves resources that can be used to discipline others. To the extent that central monitors advance their own material payoff by keeping these resources and not using them to incentivize cooperation through the disciplining of free-riders, this can be viewed as an abuse of their power. This highlights the importance of designing appropriate constraints to the ability of monitors to abuse their power. Centralized systems should not be transformed into autocratic systems where monitors cannot be held accountable for their use of group resources. On the contrary, centralized systems should have built-in mechanisms to allow group members to oversee the conduct of those who are empowered with disciplining authority.

Another source of failure in our central monitoring treatments comes from monitors who use the resources erratically and thus fail to establish a clear norm of cooperation. This creates uncertainty about whether actions will be punished and/or rewarded, and this may undermine the usefulness of incentives. Such uncertainty could be reduced if monitors could use other devices (such as communication) to induce norms of cooperation and explain the likely consequences of adhering or deviating from these norms. Nevertheless, we suspect that some monitors would still fail even with unlimited opportunities to communicate their intentions.

This points to the importance of selecting the right individuals for the role of monitor. Thus, how monitors are appointed is an important feature of centralized systems. For example, systems where the monitoring role is assigned to group members on a rotating basis may limit the negative impact of 'bad monitors,' and thus have an advantage over systems with consolidated power positions. The appointment of central monitors through democratic elections (as it happened for captains and quartermasters in pirate societies) may be another mechanism that allows group members to screen out candidate monitors who are likely to abuse their power.

JEL Classification Numbers: C72; H41.

ACKNOWLEDGEMENTS

We thank Paul van Lange, Michalis Drouvelis, Jan Potters, Abhijit Ramalingam and seminar participants at the University of East Anglia for useful comments.

We acknowledge the support of the Leverhulme Trust (ECF/2010/0636) and the Network for Integrated Behavioural Science (ES/K002201/1).

REFERENCES

Ambrus, A., & Greiner, B. (2012). Imperfect Public Monitoring with Costly Punishment— An Experimental Study. *American Economic Review, 102*(7), 3317–3332.

Andreoni, J., & Gee, L. K. (2012). Gun for hire: Delegated enforcement and peer punishment in public goods provision. *Journal of Public Economics, 96*(11–12), 1036–1046.

Baldassarri, D., & Grossman, G. (2011). Centralized sanctioning and legitimate authority promote cooperation in humans. *Proceedings of the National Academy of Sciences, 108*(27), 11023–11027.

Balliet, D., Mulder, L. B., & Van Lange, P. A. M. (2011). Reward, punishment, and cooperation: A meta-analysis. *Psychological Bulletin, 137*(4), 594–615.

Caldwell, M. D. (1976). Communication and sex effects in a five-person Prisoner's Dilemma Game. *Journal of Personality and Social Psychology, 33*(3), 273–280.

Carpenter, J., Kariv, S., & Schotter, A. (2012). Network architecture, cooperation and punishment in public good experiments. *Review of Economic Design, 16*(2–3), 93–118.

Chaudhuri, A. (2011). Sustaining cooperation in laboratory public goods experiments: a selective survey of the literature. *Experimental Economics, 14*(1), 47–83.

Chen, Y. (2008). Incentive-compatible Mechanisms for Pure Public Goods: A Survey of Experimental Research. In C. R. Plott & V. L. Smith (Eds.), *Handbook of Experimental Economics Results*, (Vol. 1, pp. 625–643). Amsterdam: North-Holland.

Cinyabuguma, M., Page, T., & Putterman, L. (2006). Can second-order punishment deter perverse punishment? *Experimental Economics, 9*(3), 265–279.

Croson, R., Fatás, E., & Neugebauer, T. (2007). Excludability and contribution: a laboratory study in team production. CBEES Working paper 07–09, University of Texas, Dallas.

Denant-Boemont, L., Masclet, D., & Noussair, C. N. (2007). Punishment, counterpunishment and sanction enforcement in a social dilemma experiment. *Economic Theory, 33*(1), 145–167.

Dickinson, D. L. (2001). The carrot vs. the stick in work team motivation. *Experimental Economics, 4*(1), 107–124.

Dickinson, D. L., & Isaac, R. M. (1998). Absolute and relative rewards for individuals in team production. *Managerial and Decision Economics, 19*(4–5), 299–310.

Drouvelis, M. (2010). The Behavioural Consequences of Unfair Punishment. University of Birmingham Department of Economics Discussion Paper 10-34.

Drouvelis, M., & Jamison, J. (2012). Selecting Public Goods Institutions: Who Likes to Punish and Reward? Federal Reserve Bank of Boston, WP No. 12-5.

Eckel, C. C., Fatás, E., & Wilson, R. (2010). Cooperation and Status in Organizations. *Journal of Public Economic Theory, 12*(4), 737–762.

Egas, M., & Riedl, A. (2008). The economics of altruistic punishment and the maintenance of cooperation. *Proceedings of the Royal Society B—Biological Sciences, 275*, 871–878.

Elster, J. (1989). *The cement of society. A study of social order.* Cambridge: Cambridge University Press.

Falkinger, J., Fehr, E., Gächter, S., & Winter-Ebmer, R. (2000). A simple mechanism for the efficient provision of public goods: Experimental evidence. *American Economic Review, 90*(1), 247–264.

Fatás, E., Morales, A. J., & Ubeda, P. (2010). Blind justice: An experimental analysis of random punishment in team production. *Journal of Economic Psychology, 31*(3), 358-373.

Fehr, E., & Gächter, S. (2000). Cooperation and punishment in public goods experiments. *American Economic Review, 90*(4), 980-994.

Fehr, E., & Gächter, S. (2002). Altruistic punishment in humans. *Nature, 415*(6868), 137-140.

Fischbacher, U. (2007). z-Tree: Zurich toolbox for ready-made economic experiments. *Experimental Economics, 10*(2), 171-178.

Gächter, S., & Herrmann, B. (2009). Reciprocity, culture, and human cooperation: Previous insights and a new cross-cultural experiment. *Philosophical Transactions of the Royal Society B—Biological Sciences, 364*(1518), 791-806.

Gächter, S., & Herrmann, B. (2011). The limits of self-governance when cooperators get punished: Experimental evidence from urban and rural Russia. *European Economic Review, 55*(2), 193-210.

Gächter, S., Renner, E., & Sefton, M. (2008). The long-run benefits of punishment. *Science, 322*, 1510.

Grechenig, K., Nicklisch, A., & Thöni, C. (2012). Information-sensitive Leviathans: The Emergence of Centralized Punishment. Mimeo, University of Lausanne.

Greiner, B. (2004). An Online Recruitment System for Economic Experiments. In *Forschung und wissenschaftliches Rechnen. GWDG Bericht 63*, ed. K. Kremer and V. Macho, 79-93. Göttingen: Ges. für Wiss. Datenverarbeitung.

Gürerk, Ö., Irlenbusch, B., & Rockenbach, B. (2006). The competitive advantage of sanctioning institutions. *Science, 312*(108), 108-111.

Gürerk, Ö., Irlenbusch, B., & Rockenbach, B. (2009). Motivating teammates: The leader's choice between positive and negative incentives. *Journal of Economic Psychology, 30*(4), 591-607.

Heijden, E. van der, Potters, J., & Sefton, M. (2009). Hierarchy and opportunism in teams. *Journal of Economic Behavior & Organization, 69*(1), 39-50.

Herrmann, B., Thöni C., & Gächter, S. (2008). Antisocial punishment across societies. *Science, 319*, 1362-1367.

Isaac, R. M., Walker, J. M., & Thomas, S. H. (1984). Divergent Evidence on Free Riding—an Experimental Examination of Possible Explanations. *Public Choice, 43*(2), 113-149.

Ledyard, J. O. (1995). Public goods: A survey of experimental research. In A. E. Roth & J. H. Kagel (Eds.), *The Handbook of Experimental Economics* (pp. 111-181). Princeton: Princeton University Press.

Leeson, P. T. (2007). An-arrgh-chy: The Law and Economics of Pirate Organization. *Journal of Political Economy, 115*(6), 1049-1094.

Leeson, P. T. (2009). The calculus of piratical consent: the myth of the myth of social contract. *Public Choice, 139*(3), 443-459.

Leibbrandt, A., Ramalingam, A., Sääksvuori, L., & Walker, J. M. (2012). Broken Punishment Networks in Public Goods Games: Experimental Evidence. Jena Economic Research Paper 2012-004.

Marwell, G., & Ames, R. (1979). Experiments on the provision of public goods I: Resources, interest, group size, and the free-rider problem. *American Journal of Sociology, 84*(6), 1335-1360.

Masclet, D., & Villeval, M. C. (2008). Punishment, inequality, and welfare: a public good experiment. *Social Choice and Welfare, 31*(3), 475-502.

Milinski, M., & Rockenbach, B. (2012). On the interaction of the stick and the carrot in social dilemmas. *Journal of Theoretical Biology, 299*, 139–143.

Nikiforakis, N. (2008). Punishment and counter-punishment in public good games: Can we really govern ourselves? *Journal of Public Economics, 92*(1–2), 91–112.

Nikiforakis, N., & Normann, H. (2008). A comparative statics analysis of punishment in public goods experiments. *Experimental Economics, 11*(4), 358–369.

Nikiforakis, N., Normann, H.-T., & Wallace, B. (2010). Asymmetric Enforcement of Cooperation in a Social Dilemma. *Southern Economic Journal, 76*(3), 638–659.

O'Gorman, R., Henrich, J., & van Vugt, M. (2009). Constraining free riding in public goods games: designated solitary punishers can sustain human cooperation. *Proceedings of the Royal Society B-Biological Sciences, 276*(1655), 323–329.

Ostrom, E. (1990). *Governing the commons: The evolution of institutions for collective action, the political economy of institutions and decisions.* Cambridge: Cambridge University Press.

Ostrom, E. (1999). Coping with Tragedies of the Commons. *Annual Review of Political Science, 2*(1), 493–535.

Ostrom, E., Walker, J. M., & Gardner, R. (1992). Covenants with and without a sword—Self-governance is possible. *American Political Science Review, 86*(2), 404–417.

Rand, D. G., Dreber, A., Ellingsen, T., Fudenberg, D., & Nowak, M. A. (2009). Positive Interactions Promote Public Cooperation. *Science, 325*(5945), 1272–1275.

Sefton, M., Shupp, R., & Walker, J. M. (2007). The effect of rewards and sanctions in provision of public goods. *Economic Inquiry, 45*(4), 671–690.

Shinada, M., & Yamagishi, T. (2008). Bringing Back Leviathan into Social Dilemmas. In A. Biel, D. Eek, T. Gärling, & M. Gustafsson (Eds.), *New Issues and Paradigms in Research on Social Dilemmas* (pp. 93–123). New York: Springer.

Sigmund, K., Silva, H. D., Traulsen, A., & Hauert, C. (2010). Social learning promotes institutions for governing the commons. *Nature, 466*(7308), 861–863.

Sutter, M., Haigner, S., & Kocher, M. G. (2010). Choosing the Carrot or the Stick? Endogenous Institutional Choice in Social Dilemma Situations. *Review of Economic Studies, 77*(4), 1540–1566.

Walker, J. M., & Halloran, M. A. (2004). Rewards and sanctions and the provision of public goods in one-shot settings. *Experimental Economics, 7*(3), 235–247.

Yamagishi, T. (1986). The provision of a sanctioning system as a public good. *Journal of Personality and Social Psychology, 51*(1), 110–116.

APPENDIX—EXPERIMENTAL INSTRUCTIONS [ALL TREATMENTS]

INSTRUCTIONS

Welcome!

You are about to participate in a decision-making experiment. Please do not talk to any of the other participants until the experiment is over. If you have a question at any time please raise your hand and an experimenter will come to your desk to answer it.

At the beginning of the experiment you will be matched with two other people, randomly selected from the participants in this room, to form a group of three. **The composition of your group will stay the same throughout the experiment**, i.e., you will form a group with the same two other participants during the whole experiment. Each person in the group will be randomly assigned a role, either 'group member A,' 'group member B,' or 'group member C.' **Your role will stay the same throughout the experiment**. Your earnings will depend on the decisions made within your group, as described in the following paragraphs. Your earnings will not be affected by decisions made in other groups. All decisions are made anonymously and you will not learn the identity of the other participants in your group. You will be identified simply as 'group member A,' 'group member B,' and 'group member C.'

At the beginning of the experiment, you will be informed of your role and given an initial balance of 320 points. The **experiment will then consist of 10 periods**, and in each period you can earn additional points. At the end of the experiment, each participant's initial balance plus accumulated point earnings from all periods will be converted into cash at the exchange rate of 0.75 pence per point. Each participant will be paid in cash and in private.

DESCRIPTION OF A PERIOD

Every period has the same structure and has two stages.

Stage One

In Stage One of each period you will be endowed with 20 tokens.

You must choose how many of these tokens to allocate to a group account and how many to keep in your private account.

Similarly, the other two members of your group will be endowed with 20 tokens each and must choose how many tokens to allocate to the group account and how many to keep in their private accounts.

You will make your decision by entering the number of tokens you allocate to the group account. Any tokens you do not allocate to the group account will automatically be kept in your private account. You enter your decisions on a screen like the one shown in the following photo/illustration.

STAGE ONE

You have to decide how many tokens to allocate to the group account
Any tokens you do not allocate to the group account are automatically kept in your private account

Your endowment   20
How many tokens do you want to allocate to the group account? ____

SUBMIT

Appendix Figure 6.1 Stage One Screenshot (all treatments).

Earnings from Stage One will be determined as follows:
For each token you keep in your private account you will earn 3 points.
For each token you allocate to the group account, you and the other two members of your group will earn 2 points each.
Similarly, for each token another group member keeps in his or her private account this group member will earn 3 points, and for each token he or she allocates to the group account all three group members will earn 2 points each.
Your point earnings from Stage One will be the sum of your earnings from your private account and the group account.
Thus:

Your point earnings from Stage One = 3 x (number of tokens kept in your private account) + 2 x (total number of tokens allocated to the group account by yourself and the other two members of your group).

Before we describe Stage Two we want to check that each participant understands how earnings from Stage One will be calculated. To do this we ask you to answer the questions in the following section. In a couple of minutes the experimenter will check your answers. When each participant has answered all questions correctly, we will continue with the instructions.

■ STAGE ONE QUESTIONS

1. How many periods will there be in the experiment? ____
2. How many people are in your group (including yourself)? ____
3. Will you be matched with the same or different people in every period? (circle one)
   SAME DIFFERENT
4. Suppose in Stage One of a period each group member allocates 0 tokens to the group account.
   How many tokens does A keep in his or her private account? ____
   What will be A's earnings from his or her private account? ____
   What is the total number of tokens allocated to the group account? ____

What will be A's earnings from the group account? _____
What will be A's earnings from Stage One? _____

5. Suppose in Stage One of a period each group member allocates 20 tokens to the group account.
   How many tokens does A keep in his or her private account? _____
   What will be A's earnings from his or her private account? _____
   What is the total number of tokens allocated to the group account? _____
   What will be A's earnings from the group account? _____
   What will be A's earnings from Stage One? _____

6. Suppose A allocates 16 tokens to the group account, B allocates 10 tokens to the group account, and C allocates 4 tokens to the group account.
   How many tokens does A keep in his or her private account? _____
   What will be A's earnings from his or her private account? _____
   What is the total number of tokens allocated to the group account? _____
   What will be A's earnings from the group account? _____
   What will be A's earnings from Stage One? _____

■ [BASELINE]

Stage Two

At the beginning of Stage Two you will be informed of the decisions made by each group member and their earnings from Stage One in a screen like the one in the following photo/illustration.

In Stage Two of each period you will be endowed with 8 additional tokens. These will automatically be placed in your private account from which you earn 3 points per token. Thus you will earn an additional 24 points in Stage Two.

Similarly, the other group members will be endowed with 8 additional tokens each, which will be automatically placed in their private accounts from which they earn 3 points per token. Thus the other group members will earn an additional 24 points each in Stage Two.

Neither you nor the other group members make any decisions in Stage Two.

Appendix Figure 6.2 Stage Two Screenshot (Baseline treatment).

Ending the Period

At the end of Stage Two the computer will inform you of your total earnings for the period. Your period earnings will be the sum of your earnings from Stage One and Stage Two.

At the end of period 10 your accumulated point earnings from all periods will be added to your initial balance of 320 points to give your total point earnings for the experiment. These will be converted into cash at the exchange rate of 0.75 pence per point. Each participant will be paid in cash and in private.

[MUTUAL-PUNISH/MUTUAL-REWARD]

Stage Two

At the beginning of Stage Two you will be informed of the decisions made by each group member and their earnings from Stage One.

In Stage Two of each period you will be endowed with 8 additional tokens. You must choose how many of these to use to [punish] [reward] group members and how many to keep in your private account.

Similarly, the other group members will be endowed with 8 additional tokens each and must choose how many of these to use to [punish] [reward] group members and how many to keep in their private accounts.

You make your decision by completing a screen like the one in the following photo/illustration. You choose how many tokens to assign to each group member. You can assign tokens to yourself if you want. Any of the 8 additional tokens not assigned will automatically be kept in your private account. You cannot assign more than 8 tokens in total.

STAGE TWO

The Table below shows the number of tokens allocated by each group member to the group account in Stage ONE.
The Table also shows the earnings of each group member from Stage ONE.

In Stage TWO you are endowed with 8 additional tokens.
You can use these tokens to punish group members. Any tokens you do not assign will be placed in your private account.
Enter a number from 0 to 8 inclusive in each field. You cannot assign more than 8 tokens in total.

	Tokens allocated to group account in Stage ONE	Earnings from Stage ONE	Tokens you assign to this group member
YOU	xxx	xxx	
group member ix	xxx	xxx	
group member jx	xxx	xxx	

Appendix Figure 6.3 Stage Two Screenshot (Mutual treatments).

Earnings from Stage Two will be determined as follows:

For each additional token you keep in your private account you will earn 3 points.

For each token you assign to a group member that group member's earnings will be [reduced] [increased] by 3 points.

Similarly, for each additional token another group member keeps in his or her private account this group member will earn 3 points, and for each token he or she assigns to a group member that group member's earnings will be [decreased] [increased] by 3 points.

Thus:

Your point earnings from Stage Two = 3 x (number of additional tokens kept in your private account) [-] [+] 3 x (total number of tokens assigned to you by all group members in Stage Two).

We want to check that each participant understands how their earnings from Stage Two will be calculated. To do this we ask you to answer the questions in the following paragraph. In a couple of minutes the experimenter will check your answers. When each participant has answered all questions correctly we will continue with the instructions.

Stage Two Questions

Suppose in Stage Two of a period A assigns 2 tokens to B and 2 tokens to C. B assigns 2 tokens to B and 6 tokens to C. C assigns 8 tokens to B.

1. How many tokens does A keep in his or her private account? _____
2. What is the total number of tokens assigned to A? _____
3. What will be group member A's earnings from Stage Two? _____
4. How many tokens does B keep in his or her private account? _____
5. What is the total number of tokens assigned to B? _____
6. What will be group member B's earnings from Stage Two? _____
7. How many tokens does C keep in his or her private account? _____
8. What is the total number of tokens assigned to C? _____
9. What will be group member C's earnings from Stage Two? _____

Ending the Period

At the end of Stage Two the computer will inform you of all decisions made in Stage Two and the earnings of each member of your group for Stage Two. The computer will then inform you of your total earnings for the period. Your period earnings will be the sum of your earnings from Stage One and Stage Two.

At the end of period 10 your accumulated point earnings from all periods will be added to your initial balance of 320 points to give your total point earnings for the experiment. These will be converted into cash at the exchange rate of

0.75 pence per point. [Although your earnings in some periods may be negative, your initial balance ensures that your final earnings for the experiment cannot be negative.] Each participant will be paid in cash and in private.

■ **[CENTRAL-PUNISH/CENTRAL-REWARD]**

Stage Two

At the beginning of Stage Two you will be informed of the decisions made by each group member and their earnings from Stage One.

In Stage Two of each period group member A will be endowed with 24 additional tokens. Group member A must choose how many of these to use to [punish] [reward] group members and how many to keep in his or her private account. Group members B and C do not make any decisions in Stage Two.

If you are group member A, you make your decision by completing a screen like the one in the following photo/illustration. You choose how many tokens to assign to each group member. You can assign tokens to yourself if you want. Any of the 24 additional tokens not assigned will automatically be kept in your private account. You cannot assign more than 24 tokens in total.

Earnings from Stage Two will be determined as follows:

For each additional token A keeps in his or her private account he or she will earn 3 points.

For each token A assigns to a group member that group member's earnings will be [decreased] [increased] by 3 points.

Thus:

A's point earnings from Stage Two = 3 x (number of additional tokens kept in A's private account) [–] [+] 3 x (number of additional tokens A assigns to himself or herself)

Appendix Figure 6.4 Stage Two Screenshot (Central treatments).

B's point earnings from Stage Two = [–] [+] 3 x (number of additional tokens assigned to B by group member A).

C's point earnings from Stage Two = [–] [+] 3 x (number of additional tokens assigned to C by group member A).

We want to check that each participant understands how their earnings from Stage Two will be calculated. To do this we ask you to answer the questions in the following section. In a couple of minutes the experimenter will check your answers. When each participant has answered all questions correctly we will continue with the instructions.

Stage Two Questions

Suppose in Stage Two of a period A assigns 12 tokens to B and 8 tokens to C.

1. How many tokens does A keep in his or her private account? _____
2. What is the total number of tokens assigned to A? _____
3. What will be group member A's earnings from Stage Two? _____
4. What is the total number of tokens assigned to B? _____
5. What will be group member B's earnings from Stage Two? _____
6. What is the total number of tokens assigned to C? _____
7. What will be group member C's earnings from Stage Two? _____

Ending the Period

At the end of Stage Two the computer will inform you of all decisions made in Stage Two and the earnings of each member of your group for Stage Two. The computer will then inform you of your total earnings for the period. Your period earnings will be the sum of your earnings from Stage One and Stage Two.

At the end of period 10 your accumulated point earnings from all periods will be added to your initial balance of 320 points to give your total point earnings for the experiment. These will be converted into cash at the exchange rate of 0.75 pence per point. [Although your earnings in some periods may be negative, your initial balance ensures that your final earnings for the experiment cannot be negative.] Each participant will be paid in cash and in private.

■ **[ALL TREATMENTS]**

Beginning the Experiment

If you have any questions please raise your hand and an experimenter will come to your desk to answer it.

We are now ready to begin the decision-making part of the experiment. Please look at your computer screen and begin making your decisions.

7 Broadening the Motivation to Cooperate: Revisiting the Role of Sanctions in Social Dilemmas

XIAO-PING CHEN, CAROLYN T. DANG, AND FONG KENG-HIGHBERGER

Abstract
Previous research examining the effects of sanctioning in social dilemmas have found that while they are effective in inducing individual cooperation in the short term, their long-term effects could be detrimental (e.g., Chen, Pillutla, & Yao, 2009). While researchers have identified both structural and motivational reasons for this, the structural and motivational approaches have been examined in isolation from one another. In addition, most sanctioning research has focused on monetary, short-term, and individual-based ways to induce cooperation. In this chapter, we integrate the structural and motivational approaches to examine how sanctions may better induce cooperation. In so doing, we propose the further exploration of long-term cooperation through the usage of sanctions that are: non-monetary, group-based, decentralized, and not focused on immediate reinforcement strategies.

INTRODUCTION

Social dilemmas are situations in which people face a conflict between maximizing individual interest and maximizing collective interest. Social dilemmas are ubiquitous in all aspects of life. They range from large global issues like air pollution, forest depletion, overpopulation, and the shortage of water, to more geographically contained problems such as military arms races between countries or price wars between companies, to more localized issues such as failed group or community projects. While the scale of the dilemma, the magnitude of the damage, or the seriousness of the consequences might be different in each of these dilemmas, there is at least one commonality they all share: the decision maker (whether it be an individual, organization, or country) needs to decide whether or not, or how much money, time, and effort to contribute, to preserve the common resource, to establish or maintain peace or profit, or to make the group and community project successful.

It is also evident that the actions of one single decision maker cannot accomplish the goals individually, for the collective actions of all involved determine whether the goals are achieved. For instance, when one contributes everything but no one else is doing so, this individual's contribution is likely to be wasted.

On the other hand, when one does not contribute anything but everyone else (or the majority of others) is contributing a great deal, the goals will be achieved, and the person who does not contribute will still receive the maximum benefit. Therefore, there seem to be two main conflicting rationalities involved in a social dilemma: an individual rationality that one should not contribute anything to protect self-interest, and a collective rationality that all should contribute to have the common good available for everyone's benefit.

Since preserving common resources, maintaining world peace, having a healthy profit, and completing group/community projects are so important for the betterment of human life and the sustainability of human survival, identifying ways to induce cooperation (or contribution) are imperative for social scientists. Scholars have identified structural and motivational means to increase cooperation in social dilemmas (Yamagishi, 1984). Structural approaches focus on changing the contextual factors or key objective parameters of the dilemma to provide more incentives for cooperation. Such approaches include changing the payoff matrix for cooperative and defective choices, changing the payoff allocation rules, or introducing sanction systems. On the other hand, the motivational approaches focus on changing the psychological states of the people in the dilemma so that they are more willing to cooperate. Such approaches include raising the trust level among members, increasing identity level with the collective, or making people believe that their contribution is vital to the success of the collective.

In our chapter, we focus on integrating the structural and motivational approaches in order to advance the social dilemma literature. Currently, scholars have tended to view the structural and motivational approaches to be somewhat interdependent in that structural changes often induce motivational/psychological changes, and for the effects of structural changes to sustain, motivational changes must happen. Though this comprehensive view is clearly supported by the research findings on the effects of sanctions on cooperation induction in social dilemmas (Chen, Pillutla, & Yao, 2009; Mulder, van Dijk, De Cremer, & Wilke, 2006), we explore ways in which the structural and motivation perspectives can be integrated.

First, we review the literature's traditional focus on the effects of monetary sanctions on short-term cooperation. Then, we offer three alternative perspectives to broaden the scope of sanctioning and cooperation to include non-monetary incentives, namely justice-related and ethical viewpoints, to induce long-term cooperation. Finally, we propose four non-traditional ways of implementing sanctions to potentially optimize long-term cooperation, specifically: 1) decentralized sanctions, 2) non-monetary sanctions, 3) collective performance-based sanctions, and 4) long-term oriented sanctions. In conclusion, we are hopeful that further exploration of these non-traditional sanctioning systems may broaden the potential for finding effective, efficient, and long-term solutions to social dilemmas.

■ SANCTIONS AND COOPERATION

In examining factors that would increase cooperation and deter defection, researchers have paid attention to the role of sanctions. Generally speaking, sanctions refer to rewards or punishments that are imposed on individuals who commit certain actions or behaviors. Within the context of social dilemmas, sanctions can be *penalty* or *reward* oriented (Messick & Brewer, 1983). In penalty sanctions, individuals are punished if they defect (e.g., forced to pay a fine). In reward sanctions, individuals are rewarded if they cooperate (e.g., receive a monetary payment). The rationale behind the cooperation-inducing effects of sanctions is that they change the pay-off structure of the social dilemma. Specifically, the incentive of defecting is decreased due to the potential punishment or reward, thereby making cooperation the relatively more attractive option between the two.

Empirical studies on the utility of sanctions have shown them to be a powerful means to increase cooperation (see Balliet, Mulder, & Van Lange, 2011, for a meta-analysis). In a classic study by Yamagishi (1986), it was demonstrated that sanctioning systems not only exerted a positive and direct effect on cooperation, but also had an indirect and positive effect on cooperation. In terms of the direct effect, Yamagishi showed that high sanctioning caused individuals to cooperate because of the anticipated higher cost for the individual for not cooperating, which was what was intended by the structural changes. The indirect effect, however, occurred through participants' expectations that other members' would also cooperate due to the sanctioning system in place. In other words, the presence of the sanctioning system induced changes in the psychological state of the participants and assured them that others would also be incentivized to cooperate, which in turn increased participants' own levels of cooperation.

In further validating the effectiveness of sanctions for cooperation induction, Eek et al. (2002) examined the role of intermittent monetary costs in defecting. They found that participants were more likely to defect when there was no monetary cost for doing so, but were less likely to defect when they themselves or others involved in the social dilemma were charged a high monetary cost. In fact, experiments 1 and 2 showed that 90% and 60%, respectively, of participants defected when there was no cost imposed on defecting. However, if they themselves or others were charged a high cost, then defection rates decreased. In explicating the theoretical rationale for the findings, Eek et al. (2002) conjectured that a spillover effect occurred, which is when an individual who sees another person being fined for defection assumes that this other person will cooperate more, which in turn increases the individual's own level of cooperation. According to the authors, this fits with Pruitt and Kimmel's (1977) goal expectation theory.

The notion that monetary sanctions induce cooperation received support in another study by McCusker and Carnevale (1995). In two experiments, they demonstrated that in the commons dilemmas, the use of large monetary penalties (e.g., total amount of sanctioning system subtracted from participants' personal fund) and reward sanctions (e.g., total amount of sanctioning system added to participants' personal fund) increased cooperative behaviors. The theoretical rationale for this was that monetary rewards and punishment made individuals more cognitively risk averse. This risk aversion then made individuals more inclined to cooperate.

The studies discussed previously thus seem to suggest that sanctions exert a positive effect on cooperation partly because they alter, to some extent, people's motivation for cooperation. However, in examining closely the types of sanctions that have been used in these studies, a common theme emerges: that the sanctions are all *centralized* (provided by external forces), *monetary based*, targeted towards *individuals*, and designed to provide *immediate reinforcement*. For example, in Eek et al.'s (2002) study, the sanctions for defecting were set up by the experimenter, monetarily based, and targeted towards the individual participant. In McCusker and Carnevale's (1995) study, the sanctions occurred immediately after defection (i.e., participants were punished immediately after defecting), and were also set up by the experimenters, and monetarily and individually focused. To what extent do these types of sanctions ensure cooperation over a longer period of time?

In addressing this question, researchers have studied how sanctions affect cooperation in multi-stage social dilemmas and found that while sanctions may be effective in inducing individual cooperation in the short-run, the benefits are limited to the immediate future. Indeed, researchers have conjectured that sanctions that are centralized, monetary based, individual-targeted, and immediately implemented could have detrimental effects over time because the psychological changes induced by such sanctions are often in the opposite direction for long-term effectiveness (e.g., Chen et al., 2009; Mulder et al., 2006). One explanation for this is that such sanctions are likely to lead people to make external attributions for their behavior (Kelley, 1967). In the social dilemma situation, it is likely that people would say "I cooperate because my boss required me to do so," or "I cooperate because I wanted to get a reward," or "I cooperate because I wanted to avoid punishment." It is evident that the more external forces are available to explain one's behavior, the more likely people will use these sources. The unintended consequences of such sanctions are likely heightened extrinsic but reduced intrinsic motivation for cooperation (Deci, Koestner, & Ryan, 1999). As a result, once the sanctions are removed, the extrinsic motivation no long exists, and people stop being cooperative.

Another explanation for the long-term detrimental effects of such sanctions is that they cause individuals to cognitively re-frame the situation in economic rather than social terms, which then decreases cooperation. For example, a study by Pillutla and Chen (1999) demonstrated that framing a situation in an economic context, rather than a noneconomic context, decreased cooperation. In their study, they presented participants with a scenario in which they were either an investment manager making an investment decision (economic context), or a representative of a factory making a decision about a social event (noneconomic context). They found that participants behaved more competitively in the economic context compared to the noneconomic context. The findings thus suggest that monetary incentives may induce an economic frame of mind, which over time may decrease cooperation.

In building upon the work by Pillutla and Chen (1999), other researchers have found support for the effects of sanctions on individuals' frame of reference and their subsequent cooperation behaviors. For example, Tenbrunsel and Messick (1999) showed in two studies that the economic frame of mind associated with monetary sanctioning systems caused individuals to focus on the fines (costs) associated with defecting, rather than the ethical or moral reasons for cooperation. Mulder et al. (2006) further demonstrated that the economic frame of mind associated with sanctions caused individuals to lose trust in other individuals. Specifically, in a series of three experiments, they showed that when there was a sanction on defection, an individual's trust that others are internally motivated to cooperate was undermined. This occurred even when initial trust in others was high. This study thus showed that sanctions caused people to believe that others around them were less internally and inherently motivated to cooperate.

Beyond the effects of sanctions on individuals' cognitive frames, other researchers have shown that sanctions could cause individuals to focus too much on their immediate selfhood and neglect both the welfare of social others and the larger social community. In an experiment conducted by Fehr and Rockenbach (2003), the authors demonstrated that sanctions could destroy altruistic cooperation almost completely by making individuals more self-interested. In another experiment by Bell, Petersen, and Hautaluoma (1989), the authors showed through a laboratory simulation of the commons dilemma that punishment of one type of behavior could actually increase the occurrence of a selfish alternative. In the simulation, three-person groups harvested points from a slowly regenerating central pool. Points were placed in each person's personal pool, which other participants could steal from. They found in their experiment involving 270 students that punishing overconsumption in the commons dilemma caused individuals to focus more on their own welfare and self-interest. The result of this was an increase in the theft of other participants' personal point pool. The findings thus showed that though the sanctions decreased the amount of overconsumption, participants began to steal from other participants in order to maintain their own self-interests.

OTHER MOTIVATIONS UNDERLYING SANCTIONS

The research findings reviewed previously suggest that sanctions may have both positive and/or negative consequences for cooperation. What accounts for this duality? As we have suggested in the previous discussion, the benefits of sanctions may be limited to the short term. Thus, if the goal of the sanction is to instill cooperation immediately, then the use of sanctions (particularly monetary and individually focused sanctions) may be particularly effective. However, social dilemmas are complicated situations that require more long term-oriented thinking. Indeed, in looking at current social dilemmas facing society today (e.g., climate change, public resources, etc.), it appears as though cooperation needs to be instilled over a longer period of time. Sanctions should thus be oriented in a way to ensure maximum cooperation not just in the short term, but in the long term as well.

In considering how to better structure sanctions for cooperation, we suggest that one way to make sanctions more effective is to broaden their scope. In particular, we suggest that research on sanctions move away from monetary, individual, and short-term incentives, which have been the core features upon which researchers have examined sanctions and how sanctions have been implemented.

As an alternative perspective, we review different theoretical perspectives that show how sanctions could be broadened to include other motivating forces. By considering these forces, we argue that sanctions could be better structured and implemented to motivate long-term cooperation, while at the same time minimizing costs and negative side-effects.

The Just Desserts Perspective. The decision to punish a defector (or reward a cooperator) need not be motivated only by monetary and individual incentives. Indeed, different theoretical perspectives suggest that more other-oriented and long-term forces may motivate the use of sanctions. One perspective that points to a more other-oriented motivation behind sanctions is the *just desserts* perspective. The just desserts perspective argues that individuals are motivated to punish noncooperators (e.g., free riders and defectors) out of the need to maintain justice, or to right a wrong that has been committed (Carlsmith, Darley, & Robinson, 2002). The central tenet of the theory is that the punishment imposed on a non-cooperator should depend on the three distinct yet interrelated facets.

First is the *magnitude* of the harm inflicted on other individuals or entities. The argument here is that to the extent that the harm inflicted is large (e.g., stealing large amounts of money), then the punishment or sanction should also be large. The second facet focuses on the *intent* behind the violator's actions. The rationale is that individuals whose intentions were malevolent should be punished to a greater extent. Indeed, there exist instances when harm is accidentally inflicted onto another individual. This rationale thus suggests that punishments should be meted out based on the violator's intentions. The third facet concerns the *circumstances* in which the violation took place. For example, a person who steals money to live a lavish lifestyle should be punished more harshly than a person who steals money to help his or her impoverished family. In the latter case, there is an extenuating circumstance in that the person is trying to aid his or her family. In the former case, there is no extenuating circumstance justifying the stealing.

These three facets suggest that sanctions are motivated by considerations that may be motivated by other-regarding orientations and justice. When deciding how to punish a non-cooperator, for instance, individuals may be attuned to the magnitude of the non-cooperator's actions on the welfare of other individuals. In addition, individuals may also be attuned to how other individuals may benefit from the non-cooperator's actions (e.g., the case of the person stealing to provide for his/her family). Regardless of the facets that one focuses on, the three elements of the just desserts perspective suggest that individuals are attuned to both the welfare of other individuals, as well as the larger social justice cause, when deciding how to punish offenders.

Numerous studies have found support for this theoretical perspective (e.g., Carlsmith, 2006; Darley, Sanderson, & LaMantia, 1996; LeBoeuf, Carlsmith, & Darley, 2001), suggesting that sanctions could be motivated by individuals' larger focus on social justice. For example, in a series of three experiments, Carlsmith et al. (2002) found that when deciding what the punishment should be for prototypical wrongdoings, participants were highly sensitive to factors uniquely associated with the just desserts perspective (e.g., seriousness of the offense, moral trespass). Indeed, even when participants were told to focus on deterrence factors when making their punishment decisions (e.g., frequency of offense), participants' sentencing decisions were still driven by just desserts concerns.

The Altruistic Punishment Perspective. The *altruistic punishment* perspective further suggests that sanctions may be motivated by a more other-oriented and long-term focus. Altruistic punishment refers to instances when individuals choose to punish noncooperators even if the punishment yields no immediate benefit for the punisher themselves (Fehr & Gächter, 2002). In an anthropological study involving 15 populations from five continents, researchers showed that all 15 populations engaged in altruistic punishment, though to varying degrees (i.e., some populations engaged in more altruistic punishment than others) (Henrich, McElreath, Barr, et al., 2006).

In empirical studies, researchers have found further support for the use of altruistic punishment. For example, in a study involving third-party punishment, where the third-party participants are "unaffected" by the behaviors of those involved in the interactions, Fehr and Fischbacher (2004) found that nearly two-thirds of third-party participants who observed the dictator game decided to punish dictators who transferred less than half their endowments. Thus, individuals engaged in altruistic punishment even despite the fact that they were not directly harmed by the noncooperators' behaviors (Fehr & Fischbacher, 2004). According to researchers, the motivation for engaging in altruistic punishment may be to benefit future interaction partners of the punishee. In other words, individuals will punish the offender so that the offender will not defect in future interactions with other individuals (e.g., Fehr & Gächter, 2002).

Other researchers have suggested that altruistic punishment may be driven by individuals' emotional reactions to injustice. Seip, van Dijk, and Rotteveel (2009), for example, contend that the experience of anger associated with witnessing non-cooperative behaviors (e.g., witnessing dictators in the dictator game transferring less than half their endowment) provided the "'extra fuel' necessary for people to punish free riders even if it is costly and does not yield any material benefits" for the individual (p. 191). Thus, even though individuals may be completely detached from the social dilemma situation, the anger associated with witnessing non-cooperation can motivate the use of sanctions.

Indeed, from the neuroscience perspective, it is perhaps unsurprising that individuals feel anger when witnessing injustice inflicted on others. Research on the neuroscience of empathy, for example, has shown that sharing the emotions of others (e.g., feeling angry when witnessing a dictator keep more than half of his/her endowment) is associated with the activation of neural structures that are also active during the individual's own first-hand emotional experience (Singer & Lamm, 2009). In other words, feeling empathic towards others seems to be an almost automatic and natural reaction (e.g., Singer et al., 2004). The just desserts and altruistic punishment perspectives therefore both demonstrate that sanctions need not be motivated by individual, short-term, and monetary benefits. Rather, decisions to inflict sanctions may be motivated by individuals' commitments to more other-oriented and long-term outcomes (e.g., commitment to justice and ensuring that future interaction partners are benefitted).

The Moral Emotion Perspective. Research on *moral emotions* further suggests that more other-oriented and long-term forces can motivate sanctions. Moral emotions are defined as emotions related to the interest and welfare of other individuals (e.g., anger, shame, guilt, disgust) (Haidt, 2003). As discussed in the previous section, researchers have already demonstrated the role that anger plays in individuals' decisions to punish defectors (e.g., Pillutla & Murnighan, 1996; Sanfey, Rilling, Aronson, Nystrom, & Cohen, 2003). Aside from anger, researchers have begun to explore the role of guilt in punishment decisions. According to Baumeister, Stillwell, and Heatherton (1994), guilt arises from interpersonal transactions including interpersonal transgressions and positive inequities. It is an unpleasant emotional experience, and can be detrimental to the individuals' overall well-being.

From an evolutionary standpoint, guilt serves various relationship-enhancing functions, such as: motivating individuals to treat interpersonal others well, motivating individuals to avoid transgressions against social others, and minimizing inequities. In the context of social dilemmas, researchers have shown that feelings of guilt may be elicited when individuals perceive themselves to be responsible for meting out punishment (e.g., the moderator for an argument involving two individuals). In such situations, people may decide to punish the offender in order to ensure that they themselves do not feel guilty for the inequities inflicted on social others. In other words, punishing the offender ensures that the individual is *not* committing a transgression towards those who were harmed by the offender's actions. In this case, guilt-induced sanctions restore a sense of justice among group members in general and the victim in particular. In empirically validating the role that both guilt and anger play in sanctions, Nelissen and Zeelenberg (2009) found in two experiments that third-party punishments are indeed independently motivated by both anger and guilt. In particular, the researchers found that experiences of anger and guilt mediated individuals' decisions to inflict punishment on defectors, such that when guilt and anger were inhibited experimentally, this reduced punishment.

The previous discussion thus suggests that the motivations behind sanctions extend beyond individual and monetary forces. Indeed, the theoretical perspectives presented previously show that individuals are attuned to larger social issues, the welfare of others, and moral and ethical factors when deciding how to mete out punishments and rewards. Given this, we thus argue that sanctions should be broadened to include motivation forces beyond individual and monetary incentives. If individuals in general are attuned to and motivated by the welfare of not just themselves, but of the larger group and social issues, then sanctions could be structured in such a way as to tap into these alternative motivational forces.

■ SANCTIONS PROMOTING SUSTAINABLE COOPERATION

We therefore propose that cooperation could be induced by focusing on both structural and motivational elements that tap at more other-oriented, prosocial, and long-term orientations. In particular, we propose four types of new sanctioning systems, (a) decentralized (as opposed to centralized) rewards or punishments, (b) non-monetary rewards or punishments, (c) group-based rewards or punishments, and (d) long-term rewards or punishments.

Sanctions with decentralized rewards or punishments. Decentralized sanctions refer to rewards or punishments provided by individuals who participate in the dilemma themselves and have equal roles (Balliet et al., 2011). In other words, instead of having sanctions imposed by external forces, people involved in the social dilemma voluntarily form self-governing systems to protect the long-term collective interest; it is "mutual coercion mutually agreed-upon" in Hardin's (1968) terms. In this sense, the peer-to-peer sanctions in Fehr and his colleagues' study (1992) are examples of decentralized sanctions. Even though setting up such systems constitutes a second-order dilemma for all (Yamagishi, 1986), such decentralized sanction systems have demonstrated efficiency and effectiveness (Ostrom, 1990).

Based on the extensive field research by Ostrom and colleagues (1990), several principles need to be followed when designing effective decentralized sanction systems. There should be (1) clearly defined boundaries regarding who has the rights to withdraw resources from common public resources; (2) congruence between appropriation and provision rules restricting time, place, technology, quantity of resource units and requiring labor, material, and/or money and the local condition; (3) collective-choice arrangements so that most individuals can participate in modifying the operational rules; (4) monitoring the common public resource conditions and appropriate behaviors; and (5) graduated sanctions such that the appropriators who violate operational rules will be sanctioned on the basis of the seriousness and context of the offense. It is evident that these principles ensure that people involved in social dilemmas are intrinsically motivated to protect their long-term collective interest, that they take responsibility in setting and modifying the operating rules, and that they are willing to input time, effort and/or money to monitor individual behavior so that appropriate sanctions will be applied to those who deserve them. It seems that there are two major psychological mechanisms underlying the effectiveness of the decentralized sanctioning systems: one is that such systems induce intrinsic motivation and the other is that such systems are in complete alignment with the just desserts perspective.

A recent meta-analysis study (Balliet et al., 2011) provided further quantified evidence to support the decentralized sanction systems. After meta-analyzing studies involving 187 effect sizes, the authors found that the punishment-cooperation association was significantly stronger in a decentralized system compared to a centralized system, even though the difference was not significant for the rewards-cooperation effect size.

Sanctions with non-monetary rewards or punishments. As discussed earlier, the sanctions used in previous studies are all related to monetary payment, which sensitizes individual value of money rather than the value of intangible rewards such as recognition or reputation. We propose that if non-monetary rewards or punishments are introduced into the sanctioning system, they will be more effective in sustaining cooperation for primarily two reasons. First, they are more likely to induce intrinsic motivation for cooperation; and second, they are more likely to induce moral emotions towards non-cooperation.

The Goal/Expectation Theory of cooperation in social dilemmas (Pruitt & Kimmel, 1977; Chen et al., 2009) states that an individual's contribution towards the provision of a public good is a function of their expectations about how much others in the group will contribute. When individuals expect others to contribute more (less) towards the provision of a public good, they will subsequently contribute more (less), and these expectations are likely to be influenced by the attributions individuals make regarding others' contributing behavior.

Non-monetary rewards (such as public recognition) or punishments (such as bad reputation) are likely to guide people's attention to intrinsic reasons for cooperation; they are also likely to induce moral emotions toward non-cooperative behaviors. Even though public recognition or reputation is not inherently intrinsic, it is different from monetary reward in two important ways. First is its tangibility, and second is its subjectivity. While the monetary reward or punishment is tangible and objectively present, a public recognition or disapproval is not. Therefore, when a person attributes his/her own cooperation to reasons for getting public recognition or approval, it is likely because the person would like to believe that he/she is a cooperative person and cooperation is good for the society. That is, a non-monetary sanction system is more likely to make people attribute their own and others' cooperative behavior as caused by intrinsic rather than extrinsic factors. As a result, they feel good about themselves and tend to trust others more in future dilemma situations.

Empirical evidence that supports our reasoning can be found in several studies (e.g., Masclet, Noussair, Tucker, & Villeval, 2003). For example, in the second experiment conducted by Masclet et al. (2003), they introduced "non-monetary" punishment in which the suggested punishment points did not reduce the payoff of any agent, but were used to register disapproval of others' contribution levels. They found that the existence of the possibility of "non-monetary" punishment alone increased the average level of contributions and earnings, though by less than the monetary punishment. The authors conclude that the increase in cooperation by monetary punishment may be partly due to the opportunity for others to express their disapproval of free riding behavior.

A field study regarding conservation of water in a community revealed similar findings. In this study, the researchers used local newspapers to publish the names of who consumed the most and least amount of water, and they found that the consumption rate decreased dramatically (Maki, Hoffman, & Berk, 1978). In this case, it is the reputation at stake for these residents, and it proved effective in promoting conservation behaviors. Another classic study (Freedman & Fraser, 1966) on compliance behavior of citizens of a community also demonstrated that the internal identity of being a good citizen served as a driving force for people to engage in citizen-like behaviors such as cooperating with the researcher to put signs in their front yard to promote safe driving behavior. An even more interesting finding from Chen et al. (2009) was that a moral appeal from a group leader not only induced, but also sustained, a high level of cooperation in a group that faced a social dilemma, because the moral appeal increased the trust level among group members.

Sanctions targeted toward the collective. While research on individualized sanctions has made substantial progress, the research on collective sanctions, systems where rewards or punishments are based on group performance (Heckathorn, 1990), has been quite limited. Collective sanctions have primarily been studied in sociology (e.g., Heckathorn, 1988, 1990, 1996) and law (e.g., Levinson, 2003), but minimally in organizational behavior in the context of network governance (e.g., Jones, Hesterly, & Borgatti, 1997). In spite of Kollock's mentioning collective sanctions as "an area ripe for research" (p. 206) in his widely cited review of social dilemmas (1998), it has received little attention in social psychology, especially in the context of public goods dilemma. We propose that sanctions toward the collective may be a more effective type of motivation that could sustain cooperative behaviors in that such sanctions are likely to be perceived as guided by cooperative motives (e.g., Kelley et al., 2003; Mulder & Nelissen, 2010; Van Lange & Rusbult, 2011). Moreover, while collective sanctions are extrinsic on the surface (e.g., monetary rewards and punishments), they may also create simultaneous forms of intrinsic motivation through group identification and intergroup competition.

Sanctions targeted toward the collective rather than an individual are likely to focus people's attention on the group interest rather than on their self-interest, which is likely to create a feeling of "common fate." Numerous studies on group communications have shown that when members of a group have a chance to discuss the nature of the dilemma faced by the group as a whole, they are likely to develop identification toward the group, feel as part of the group, and regard group interest as more important than self-interest (Brewer & Kramer, 1986; Chen & Yao, 2004; Dawes, van de Kragt, & Orbell, 1988). Moreover, the effects of group identity on cooperation induction are well documented by many researchers (Chen, 1996; Dawes et al., 1988; Kerr & Kaufman-Gilliland, 1994). Finally, Harrison & Price, Gavin, and Florey's (2002) study on team diversity and group functioning demonstrates how stronger reward contingencies, defined as the degree to which outcomes for individual members depend on outcomes for their team, stimulate collaboration.

The second mechanism through which the collective sanction may induce a long-term cooperation is shifting members' perspective from the individual level goal/expectation, where individuals expect other group members to contribute more (less) towards the provision of the public good, to a group level goal/ expectation. That is, group members will pay more attention to how other groups will be able to establish or maintain their public goods. In other words, sanctions towards the collective shift the public goods dynamic from an interpersonal competition dynamic to an intergroup competition dynamic.

In a study conducted by Bornstein & Ben-Yossef (1994), the authors found that subjects were almost twice as likely to cooperate in the Intergroup Prisoner's Dilemma (IPD) team game than to a structurally identical (single-group) Prisoner's Dilemma (PD) game, in spite of the following facts: (a) the cost of cooperation for the individual group member was identical in both games, (b) the external benefit to the individual's group resulting from a cooperative choice was also identical, and (c) cooperation in the intergroup dilemma was collectively deficient whereas in the single-group dilemma it was collectively optimal. This study seems to indirectly, though arguably strongly, support the benefits of collective sanctions over individualized sanctions, since collective sanctions make the group's perspective salient, while individualized sanctions make the individual's perspective salient. Furthermore, the collective sanctions should remain effective even after being removed, since this removal will not remove the intrinsic motivating factors to contribute, only the extrinsically motivating ones.

On the other hand, we recognize that there might be a dark side associated with the collective sanction method. One such dark side is the close monitoring of each other's actions within the group, when extending to multiple aspects of a member's life, could suffocate group members' freedom of choice beyond cooperation in social dilemmas.

Sanctions toward long-term outcomes. As indicated earlier, the sanctioning system is often designed to provide immediate reinforcement rather than future outcome in previous studies. We propose that if an element of long-term outcome is introduced, the sanctioning system will be more effective in sustaining individual cooperation because it highlights the prospects of the future and the just desserts perspective in people's minds.

One type of long-term sanctions can be in the form of a decreasing amount of monetary payoff for defection, or of an increasing amount of monetary payoff for cooperation, specified as a function of the number of trials involved in the dilemma game. Another type of long-term sanctioning system can be in the form of rewarding cooperation or punishing defection in future rounds of games, rather than in the current round or the next immediate round. Of course, one condition for the long-term sanctioning system to work is the premise that all involved in the social dilemma are staying in the dilemma situation to the end, and there is no escape for anyone to get out of the situation.

Both types of sanctioning systems are likely to extend people's focus on a longer-term horizon. The classic finding from studies examining the effects of short-term versus long-term horizon is the "shadow of the future" phenomenon (Axelrod, 1984). When a one-shot game is played, the majority chooses to defect, but when multi-trial games are played or when the end round of a game is unknown to the players, people's cooperation rate is much higher (Bó, 2005).

We explicate several reasons for why a shadow of the future or a long-term oriented sanctioning system is important to induce and sustain cooperation. One reason is related to the opportunity for reciprocity. Reciprocity is one of the most pervasive universal principles for human interaction (Gouldner, 1960) and has been demonstrated to be most effective in inducing cooperation in a 2-person prisoner's dilemma (Axelrod, 1984). When people are locked in a situation for long-term interaction, they will expect their deeds to be reciprocated by others: when they do good to others, others will return the favor; whereas if they do bad to others, others can retaliate. There is therefore little reason to defect in the first place.

Another related reason is the reputation effect, that is, a bad reputation as a non-cooperator will follow the non-cooperator and evoke negative moral emotions from others, who would likely exercise altruistic punishment (Fehr & Gächter, 2002). Research on indirect reciprocity (Wedekind & Milinski, 2000) has assumed that people may gain a positive reputation if they cooperate and a negative reputation if they do not, and has shown that people are more likely to cooperate with others who made donations to charities (Milinski, Semmann, & Krambeck, 2002). The interesting finding on the effects of presenting subtle cues of being watched—by means of an image of a pair of eyes on people's donation behavior (Bateson, Nettle, & Roberts, 2006)—further suggests the ubiquitous effects of reputational mechanisms.

A third reason for the positive effectiveness of a long-term sanctioning system to sustain cooperation may be related to the just deserts perspective. A strong signal from such a system is that justice will be served in the long run. Specifically, those who cooperate or sacrifice self-interest in the short term will be rewarded in the long run; and no matter how much one benefits from making a defective choice in the short-term, everyone (including the short-term beneficiary) will suffer the disastrous outcomes in the end. Simply put, no one can escape from the negative consequences resulting from non-cooperative behaviors. With the long-term perspective ever present, people are likely to behave according to long-term rather than short-term rationality.

DISCUSSION AND PROPOSITION

In this chapter, we reviewed the literature on the effects of sanctions (rewards and punishments) in the social dilemma, discussed the common theme embedded in the majority of these studies, introduced new theoretical perspectives on punishment, and proposed four new sanctioning systems that may be able to induce short-term cooperation, but also to sustain its effects for long-term collective interests. In this section, we summarize our main points and highlight the major theoretical and practical contributions we intend to make.

Previous research examining the effects of sanctioning in social dilemmas has found that sanctioning systems are effective in inducing individual cooperation in the short term (Balliet et al., 2011); however, its long-term effects could be detrimental (Chen et al., 2009; Mulder et al., 2006). We conjecture that a comprehensive view regarding the unintended consequences of a centralized, monetary-based, individual-targeted, or immediately provided sanction system is related to the *interdependent* nature of the structural and motivational changes. Simply put, any changes made to the structure of a social dilemma would induce psychological changes in the individuals who are in the dilemma, and it is these psychological changes that directly influence how people react/behave in the face of the structural changes.

Based on this comprehensive view, it is conceivable that one of the explanations for the short-term effective but long-term defective sanction system is related to the heightened external attribution people make in the presence of sanctions (Kelley, 1967); as a result, people reduce trust in others because there are additional external reasons for cooperation (Chen et al., 2009). Second, monetary-based sanctions sensitize individual value of money rather than the value of intangible rewards such as recognition, social approval, or reputation. Third, the individual targeted sanctions highlight the importance of self-interest rather than the importance of the collective interest or the interdependence between the self and collective interest. Finally, the sanctioning system that is often designed to provide immediate reinforcement makes salient the urgency of getting rewards or avoiding punishments, shifts people's focus to short-term outcomes, and leaves the future outcome out of the picture.

These analyses lead to our propositions of four sanctioning systems that will be more effective in sustaining cooperation in social dilemmas:

> *Proposition 1:* Compared to a centralized sanctioning system, a decentralized system is more effective in sustaining cooperation, because it is more likely to induce intrinsic motivation for cooperation and is more aligned with the just desserts perspective.
>
> *Proposition 2:* Compared to a monetary sanctioning system, a non-monetary system is more effective in sustaining cooperation, because it is more likely to induce intrinsic motivation for cooperation and trust in others.
>
> *Proposition 3:* Compared to an individual performance-based sanctioning system, a collective performance-based system is more effective in sustaining cooperation, because it is more likely to induce the "common fate" feeling or group identity in the individuals, and it is more likely to heighten the "intergroup competition" mindset in group members.
>
> *Proposition 4:* Compared to an immediate reinforcement sanctioning system, a long term-oriented system is more effective in sustaining cooperation, because it shifts people's focus to long-term outcomes, and it provides opportunities for people to reciprocate and to build their reputations.

Our propositions make several important contributions to advance the theory in the sanction-cooperation literature. First, we bridge the gap between the structural approach, often advocated by economists and sociologists, and the motivational approach, often advocated by social psychologists, to propose a comprehensive view to solve social dilemmas using sanctions. This view requires researchers to pay attention to both tangible and intangible reasons for cooperation, and suggests that it is often the intangible reasons that will stand the test of time in promoting cooperation.

Second, we identify the psychological mechanisms underlying the sanction effects on cooperation: intrinsic motivation, trust, just desserts, group identity, opportunity for reciprocity and reputation building, etc. Doing so allows us to provide reasonable explanations not only for why sanctions are effective in inducing cooperation in the short term, but also for why they are ineffective in sustaining cooperation in the long term. More importantly, based on these analyses, we are able to create new effective solutions for sustaining cooperation in social dilemmas in which a long-term collective outcome is at least as, if not more, important than the short-term individual benefit.

Third, we integrate the theoretical perspectives on why people punish noncooperators into the development of our propositions. The just desserts perspective, the altruistic punishment perspective, and the moral emotional perspective provide foundations to explain the deep and complex motives of human behavior. While self-interest is often the focal basis for human behavior, people are also social beings who care about others and the public. This tension manifests most strongly and explicitly in a social dilemma when noncooperators receive extra benefits at the expense of cooperators' contribution. Our propositions suggest that sanctioning systems that bring out the prosocial motives in human beings will go a long way to sustain cooperation.

Finally, the practical implications of our propositions are evident, since each of them can be easily applied to any situation that involves the conflict between maximizing individual and maximizing the collective interest. Moreover, the new sanctioning systems we propose can also be used in combination to further enhance their effectiveness. For example, a sanction system can be both non-monetary and collective performance-based, or even contain all four elements: decentralized, non-monetary, collective performance-based, and long term-oriented. We believe that such sanction systems will truly achieve what we have been intending to achieve: long lasting cooperation that will prevent disastrous outcomes from happening. In this sense, we are hopeful that large-scale issues like air pollution, more geographically contained problems such as price wars between companies, and more localized issues such as failed group or community projects can be better addressed.

REFERENCES

Axelrod, R. (1984). *The Evolution of Cooperation*. New York: Basic.

Balliet, D., Mulder, L. B., & Van Lange, P. A. M. (2011). Reward, punishment, and cooperation: A meta-analysis. *Psychological Bulletin*, *137*(4), 594–615. doi: 10.1037/a0023489

Bateson, M., Nettle, D., & Roberts, G. (2006). Cues of being watched enhance cooperation in a real-world setting. *Biology Letters*, *2*(3), 412–414. doi: 10.1098/rsbl.2006.0509

Baumeister, R. F., Stillwell, A. M., & Heatherton, T. F. (1994). Guilt: An interpersonal approach. *Psychological Bulletin*, *115*(2), 243–267. doi: 10.1037/0033-2909.115.2.243

Bell, P. A., Petersen, T. R., & Hautaluoma, J. E. (1989). The Effect of Punishment Probability on Overconsumption and Stealing in a Simulated Commons1. *Journal of Applied Social Psychology*, *19*(17), 1483–1495. doi: 10.1111/j.1559-1816.1989.tb01460.x

Bó, P. D. (2005). Cooperation under the shadow of the future: experimental evidence from infinitely repeated games. *The American Economic Review*, *95*(5), 1591–1604.

Bornstein, G., & Ben-Yossef, M. (1994). Cooperation in Intergroup and Single-Group Social Dilemmas. *Journal of Experimental Social Psychology*, *30*(1), 52–67. doi: 10.1006/jesp.1994.1003

Brewer, M. B., & Kramer, R. M. (1986). Choice behavior in social dilemmas: Effects of social identity, group size, and decision framing. *Journal of Personality and Social Psychology*, *50*(3), 543–549. doi: 10.1037/0022-3514.50.3.543

Carlsmith, K. M. (2006). The roles of retribution and utility in determining punishment. *Journal of Experimental Social Psychology*, *42*(4), 437–451. doi: 10.1016/j.jesp.2005.06.007

Carlsmith, K. M., Darley, J. M., & Robinson, P. H. (2002). Why do we punish?: Deterrence and just deserts as motives for punishment. *Journal of Personality and Social Psychology*, *83*(2), 284–299. doi: 10.1037/0022-3514.83.2.284

Chen, X.-P. (1996). The Group-Based Binding Pledge as a Solution to Public Goods Problems. *Organizational Behavior And Human Decision Processes*, *66*(2), 192–202. doi: 10.1006/obhd.1996.0048

Chen, X. P. (1999). Work team cooperation: The effects of structural and motivational changes. In M. Foddy, M. Smithson, M. Hogg., & S. Schneider (Eds.), *Resolving Social Dilemmas: Dynamic, Structural, and Intergroup Aspects* (pp. 181–192). Philadelphia, PA: Psychology Press.

Chen, X.-P., Pillutla, M. M., & Yao, X. (2009). Unintended Consequences of Cooperation Inducing and Maintaining Mechanisms in Public Goods Dilemmas: Sanctions and Moral Appeals. *Group Processes & Intergroup Relations*, *12*(2), 241–255. doi: 10.1177/1368430208098783

Chen, X. P., & Yao, X. (2004). Re-examine the communication effects in social dilemmas: Sustainability and explanations. Presented at the annual conference of Academy of Management, New Orleans.

Darley, J. M., Sanderson, C. A., & LaMantia, P. S. (1996). Community Standards for Defining Attempt. *American Behavioral Scientist*, *39*(4), 405–420. doi: 10.1177/0002764296039004005

Dawes, R. M. (1980). Social dilemmas. *Annual Review of Psychology*, *31*, 169–193.

Dawes, R. M., van de Kragt, A. J., & Orbell, J. M. (1988). Not me or thee but we: The importance of group identity in eliciting cooperation in dilemma situations: Experimental manipulations. *Acta Psychologica*, *68*, 83–97.

Deci, E. L., Koestner, R., & Ryan, R. M. (1999). A meta-analytic review of experiments examining the effects of extrinsic rewards on intrinsic motivation. *Psychological Bulletin*, *125*(6), 627–668. doi: 10.1037/0033-2909.125.6.627

Eek, D., Loukopoulos, P., Fujii, S., & Gärling, T. (2002). Spill-over effects of intermittent costs for defection in social dilemmas. *European Journal of Social Psychology*, *32*(6), 801–13. doi: 10.1002/ejsp.122

Fehr, E., & Fischbacher, U. (2004). Third-party punishment and social norms. *Evolution and Human Behavior*, *25*(2), 63–87. doi: 10.1016/s1090-5138(04)00005-4

Fehr, E., & Gachter, S. (2002). Altruistic punishment in humans. [10.1038/415137a]. *Nature*, *415*(6868), 137–140.

Fehr, E., & Rockenbach, B. (2003). Detrimental effects of sanctions on human altruism. [10.1038/nature01474]. *Nature*, *422*(6928), 137–140.

Freedman, J. L., & Fraser, S. C. (1966). Compliance without pressure: The foot-in-the-door technique. *Journal of Personality and Social Psychology*, *4*(2), 195–202. doi: 10.1037/h0023552

Gouldner, A. W. (1960). The Norm of Reciprocity: A Preliminary Statement. *American Sociological Review*, *25*(2), 161–178.

Haidt, J. (2003). The Moral Emotions. In R. J. Davidson, K. R. Scherer, K. R., & H. H. Goldsmith, (Eds.), *Handbook of affective sciences*, (pp. 852–870). Oxford: Oxford University Press.

Hardin, G. (1968). The tragedy of the commons. *Science*, *162*, 1243–1248.

Harrison, D. A., Price, K. H., Gavin, J. H., & Florey, A. T. (2002). Time, Teams, and Task Performance: Changing Effects of Surface- and Deep-Level Diversity on Group Functioning. *The Academy of Management Journal*, *45*(5), 1029–1045.

Heckathorn, D. D. (1988). Collective Sanctions and the Creation of Prisoner's Dilemma Norms. *American Journal of Sociology*, *94*(3), 535–562.

Heckathorn, D. D. (1990). Collective Sanctions and Compliance Norms: A Formal Theory of Group-Mediated Social Control. *American Sociological Review*, *55*(3), 366–384.

Heckathorn, D. D. (1996). The Dynamics and Dilemmas of Collective Action. *American Sociological Review*, 61(2), 250–277.

Henrich, J., McElreath, R., Barr, A., Ensminger, J., Barrett, C., Bolyanatz, A., ...Ziker, J. (2006). Costly Punishment across Human Societies. *Science*, 312(5781), 1767–1770.

Jones, C., Hesterly, W. S., & Borgatti, S. P. (1997). A General Theory of Network Governance: Exchange Conditions and Social Mechanisms. *The Academy of Management Review*, 22(4), 911–945.

Kelley, H. H. (1967). Attribution Theory in Social Psychology. *Nebraska Symposium on Motivation*, 15, 192–238.

Kelley, H. H., Holmes, J. G., Kerr, N. L., Reis, H. T., Rusbult, C. E., & Van Lange, P. A. M. (2003). *An atlas of interpersonal situations*. Cambridge, England: Cambridge University Press.

Kerr, N. L., & Kaufman-Gilliland, C. M. (1994). Communication, commitment, and cooperation in social dilemma. *Journal of Personality and Social Psychology*, 66(3), 513–529. doi: 10.1037/0022-3514.66.3.513

Kollock, P. (1998). Social Dilemmas: The Anatomy of Cooperation. *Annual Review of Sociology*, 24(1), 183–214. doi: doi:10.1146/annurev.soc.24.1.183

LeBoeuf, R. A., Carlsmith, K. M., & Darley, J. M. (2001). Emerging from the doghouse: Multiple mechanisms through which apologies repair relationships. Paper presented at the Society for Personality and Social Psychology, San Antonio, TX. Poster retrieved from

Levinson, D. J. (2003). Collective Sanctions. *Stanford Law Review*, 56(2), 345–428.

Maki, J. E., Hoffman, D. M., & Berk, R. A. (1978). A time series analysis of the impact of a water conservation campaign. *Evaluation Quarterly*, 2, 107–118.

Masclet, D., Noussair, C., Tucker, S., & Villeval, M.-C. (2003). Monetary and Nonmonetary Punishment in the Voluntary Contributions Mechanism. *The American Economic Review*, 93(1), 366–380.

McCusker, C., & Carnevale, P. J. (1995). Framing in Resource Dilemmas: Loss Aversion and the Moderating Effects of Sanctions. *Organizational Behavior And Human Decision Processes*, 61(2), 190–201. doi: 10.1006/obhd.1995.1015

Messick, D. M., & Brewer, M. B. (1983). Solving Social Dilemmas: A Review. In L. Wheeler & P. Shaver (Eds.), *Annual Review of Personality and Social Psychology* (pp. 11–44). Beverly Hills, CA: Sage.

Milinski, M., Semmann, D., & Krambeck, H.-J. (2002). Reputation helps solve the /`tragedy of the commons/'. [10.1038/415424a]. *Nature*, 415(6870), 424–426.

Mulder, L., & Nelissen, R. (2010). When Rules Really Make a Difference: The Effect of Cooperation Rules and Self-Sacrificing Leadership on Moral Norms in Social Dilemmas. *Journal of Business Ethics*, 95(0), 57–72. doi: 10.1007/s10551-011-0795-z

Mulder, L. B., van Dijk, E., De Cremer, D., & Wilke, H. A. M. (2006). Undermining trust and cooperation: The paradox of sanctioning systems in social dilemmas. *Journal of Experimental Social Psychology*, 42, 147–162.

Nelissen, R. M. A., & Zeelenberg, M. (2009). When guilt evokes self-punishment: Evidence for the existence of a Dobby Effect. *Emotion*, 9(1), 118–122. doi: 10.1037/a0014540

Ostrom, E. (1990). *Governing the Commons: The Evolution of Institutions for Collective Action*. New York: Cambridge University Press.

Pillutla, M. M., & Chen, X.-P. (1999). Social Norms and Cooperation in Social Dilemmas: The Effects of Context and Feedback. *Organizational Behavior And Human Decision Processes*, 78(2), 81–103. doi: 10.1006/obhd.1999.2825

Pillutla, M. M., & Murnighan, J. K. (1996). Unfairness, Anger, and Spite: Emotional Rejections of Ultimatum Offers. *Organizational Behavior And Human Decision Processes*, *68*(3), 208–224. doi: 10.1006/obhd.1996.0100

Pruitt, D. G., & Kimmel, M. J. (1977). Twenty Years of Experimental Gaming: Critique, Synthesis, and Suggestions for the Future. *Annual Review of Psychology*, *28*(1), 363–392. doi: 10.1146/annurev.ps.28.020177.002051

Sanfey, A. G., Rilling, J. K., Aronson, J. A., Nystrom, L. E., & Cohen, J. D. (2003). The Neural Basis of Economic Decision-Making in the Ultimatum Game. *Science*, *300*(5626), 1755–1758.

Seip, E. C., van Dijk, W. W., & Rotteveel, M. (2009). On Hotheads and Dirty Harries. *Annals of the New York Academy of Sciences*, *1167*(1), 190–196. doi: 10.1111/j.1749-6632.2009.04503.x

Singer, T., & Lamm, C. (2009). The Social Neuroscience of Empathy. *The Year in Cognitive Neuroscience*, *1156*(81), 81–96.

Singer, T., Seymour, B., O'Doherty, J., et al. (2004). Empathy for pain involves the affective but not the sensory components of pain. *Science*, *303*, 1157–1161.

Tenbrunsel, A. E., & Messick, D. M. (1999). Sanctioning Systems, Decision Frames, and Cooperation. *Administrative Science Quarterly*, *44*(4), 684–707.

Van Lange, P. A. M., Joireman, J., Parks, C. D., & van Dijk, E. (in press). The Psychology of Social Dilemmas: A Review. *Organizational Behavior and Human Decision Processes*.

Van Lange, P. A. M., & Rusbult, C. E. (2011). Interdependence theory. In P. A. M. Van Lange, A. W. Kruglanski & E. T. Higgins (Eds.), *Handbook of Theories of Social Psychology* (Vol. 2, pp. 251–272). Thousand Oaks, CA: Sage.

Wedekind, C., & Milinski, M. (2000). Cooperation through Image Scoring in Humans. *Science*, *288*(5467), 850–852.

Yamagishi, T. (1984). Development of distribution rules in small groups. *Journal of Personality and Social Psychology*, *46*(5), 9.

Yamagishi, T. (1986). The provision of a sanctioning system as a public good. *Journal of Personality and Social Psychology*, *51*(1), 110–116. doi: 10.1037/0022-3514.51.1.110

Yamagishi, T., & Sato, K. (1986). Motivational bases of the public goods problem. *Journal of Personality and Social Psychology*, *50*, 67–73.

8 Leadership, Reward and Punishment in Sequential Public Goods Experiments

■ MATTHIAS SUTTER[1] AND
M. FERNANDA RIVAS[2]

Abstract
We study the effects of reward and punishment as instruments for leadership in sequential public goods games. In particular, we embed reward and punishment into a broad research project that investigates the effects of leadership in the provision of public goods by examining (i) the relative importance of reward and punishment as leadership devices, (ii) whether endogenous leadership is more efficient than exogenously enforced leadership, and (iii) whether leaders contributing last, instead of first, also increase contributions. The experimental results are: (i) Reward options yield lower contributions than punishment through exclusion. (ii) Endogenous leadership is much more efficient than exogenously imposed leadership. (iii) Having sequential contributions of group members is not beneficial in itself for contributions since groups where the leader contributes as the last member do not contribute more than groups without a leader. As such, these results illuminate the relative benefits of reward and punishment as instruments for leaders. Yet, while these instruments seem to increase the hierarchical power of the leader, volunteering to be the leader of the group—thereby sacrificing own payoffs to achieve a common goal—seems to increase his persuasive power to convince the followers to contribute to the public good. This happens due to a selection bias—more cooperative members volunteer to be leaders—and due to a stronger response of followers to a voluntary leader than to an externally imposed leader. This has immediate implications for organizations.

JEL classification: C72, C92, H41

■ **INTRODUCTION**

Leadership is a key concept in the management of companies and work teams. Typically, leadership implies that one person in a company or a team takes over responsibility and takes the lead by taking action in a given situation. In recent years, the economics literature, in particular the experimental part of it, has carefully and extensively studied how and why leadership can work, most prominently in situations that resemble social dilemmas and where free-riding

---

1. European University Institute Florence and University of Cologne. Corresponding address: European University Institute, Department of Economics, Via della Piazzuola 43, I-50133 Firenze. e-mail: matthias.sutter@eui.eu.
2. Middle East Technical University—Northern Cyprus Campus. email: rivas@metu.edu.tr.

is a tempting alternative to cooperation. In this chapter, we present a series of experimental studies designed to examine under which conditions, and with which prerequisites, leadership can help resolve social dilemmas.

In the economics literature, leadership is typically studied in the context of sequential public goods experiments. Broadly speaking, the literature suggests that leadership by setting a good example (of being cooperative) has a positive influence on the behavior of others (who follow the leader) even when contractual relationships or hierarchical authority are absent (see Villeval, 2012, for a recent survey). It has been found that sequential contributions in public goods experiments can increase the overall level of contributions, in particular if leaders provide a good example by contributing high amounts. In asymmetric information settings—where leaders have private information about the marginal returns from contributing or where endowments are asymmetric—leadership has been identified to have a positive effect on the overall level of contributions because it serves as a signaling device for information transmission (Potters et al., 2007) or endowment levels (Levati et al., 2007). In symmetric information settings—where all group members know the marginal value of the public good—conditional cooperation (Fischbacher et al., 2001) or positive reciprocity (Fehr & Gächter, 2000) have been invoked as driving factors which can explain the very high positive correlations between leaders' and followers' contributions. Since such high correlations can be considered a very robust phenomenon (see, e.g., Moxnes & van der Heijden, 2003; Gächter & Renner, 2004; Potters et al., 2005; Güth et al., 2007; Gächter et al., 2012; Haigner & Wakolbinger, 2010; Kumru & Vesterlund, 2010), it follows that high contributions of leaders (i.e., those who contribute first) trigger, on average, high contributions of followers (those who contribute after the leader). This pattern establishes a positive role of leadership in voluntary contribution games that share the characteristics of a social dilemma.

So far, the papers dealing with the consequences of sequential contributions of leaders and followers have concentrated on (i) whether sequential contributions through leadership have a positive effect on overall contributions in comparison to simultaneous contributions (answer: "Yes," almost always significantly; see Moxnes & van der Heijden, 2003; Gächter & Renner, 2004; Potters et al., 2005; Duffy et al., 2007; Güth et al., 2007; Pogrebna et al., 2011), (ii) whether followers condition their contributions on leaders' decisions ("Yes," but they contribute systematically less than leaders; see Güth et al., 2007; Gächter et al., 2012), (iii) whether followers infer information from leaders' contributions if the latter are better informed ("Yes"; see Potters et al., 2007), (iv) whether leaders with a sanctioning device (of excluding followers from the group) trigger higher contributions from followers than leaders without formal power ("Yes"; see Güth et al., 2007). In this chapter, we are presenting a series of experiments that provides a framework to examine the effects of leadership more broadly than has been achieved in single papers listed so far. We aim to answer the following questions with our series of experiments.

Question (A): Are leaders with an option to reward other group members as effective as leaders with a sanctioning device?

Question (B): Does it make a difference whether leaders volunteer to be leaders or whether they are forced exogenously to contribute before others?

Question (C): What are the consequences if leaders contribute *after* the followers instead of before them?

Question (A) addresses whether the carrot (i.e., reward) or the stick (i.e., punishment) at a leader's disposal yield different levels of cooperation in groups. Of course, several papers have studied the consequences of reward or punishment in public goods games, however only in a setting where all group members can reward or punish each other and where there is not a single leader who can decide whether or not to reward or punish other group members. In the context without a leader, a reward mechanism has been found to increase the level of cooperation in comparison to a situation without reward, but punishment seems to be a more efficient—and more stable—mechanism to induce cooperation (Andreoni et al., 2003; Gürerk et al., 2006; Sefton et al., 2007; Sutter et al., 2010; Balliet et al., 2011). So far, however, there is no paper that combines the issue of leadership in sequential public goods games with an option for the leader to reward other group members, even though it seems obvious that leaders in a group may resort to rewards (e.g., public recognition) to motivate other group members. We find that punishment works better than reward, but that leadership with reward is still clearly preferable to having no leader at all.

Question (B) examines the importance of providing a good example voluntarily, instead of being forced exogenously. As such, this question addresses whether endogenously chosen leadership has a positive effect on the level of cooperation in a group. Arbak and Villeval (2013) have addressed the issue of endogenous leadership for the first time. They have set up groups of three subjects. Each of them can volunteer as leader in a two-stage public goods game. The leader's contribution in the first stage is announced to the other group members who can then decide on their contribution in the second stage. If two or three group members volunteer as leader, then only one is picked randomly. Arbak and Villeval (2013) find in their experiment with random rematching that about one quarter of subjects is willing to serve as leader (which is typically costly since followers contribute on average less than leaders). Hence, about 56% of groups have a leader across the 30 rounds of the experiment. While the main focus of the paper by Arbak and Villeval (2013) is on examining the reasons why subjects volunteer as leaders, they also try to assess the effects of endogenous leadership by comparing their benchmark treatment to a treatment with imposed leadership, finding that endogenous leadership yields higher contributions on average. However, the comparison is partly confounded by the fact that in the treatment with exogenously imposed leadership there is a leader in 100% of cases, which means that the differences between the endogenous and exogenous leadership treatment may be caused by the voluntary leadership of leaders in the endogenous treatment or the differences between both treatments in having a leader at all in a group. We try to account for this confound in the following way.[3] We will consider one treatment where one group member may opt to serve as leader of the group by contributing to the public good before other group members do. We then compare this treatment with a control treatment where the leader is determined exogenously in exactly the same order as in the endogenous treatment. This means that when there is no leader in a given period and group in the endogenous treatment, we will also have no leader in this period in a matched group with exogenously imposed leadership. We find that voluntary leadership increases contributions significantly, while leadership itself (i.e., the sequential contribution to the public good) need not have a positive effect (compared to a standard public goods game without leadership).

Question (C) investigates the effects of letting one group member contribute *after* the other group members instead of before the others. This question addresses the issue whether sequentiality itself (in whichever order) has a positive effect on contributions in a public goods experiment. It seems reasonable that group leaders may not always go ahead by providing an example—hoping that other group members follow it—but they sometimes wait for other group members to decide and react to their behavior instead. We are not aware of any study on leadership with a reverse structure where the leader contributes as the last group member. We compare a treatment with the leader contributing as the last one with a control treatment without a leader, finding that contributing last does not increase the level of cooperation in comparison to the control condition without leadership. Hence, reverse leadership by being the last one to contribute is no means for establishing cooperation. Rather, our experiments show that leaders should go first, do that voluntarily, and be equipped with reward and/or punishment devices. We call these findings the dos and don'ts of leadership.

The rest of the paper is organized as follows: In the following section we introduce the public goods game. Section 3 presents the experimental design. Results are reported in section 4. A conclusion is offered in section 5.

■ THE BASIC PUBLIC GOODS GAME

The basic game is a standard voluntary contribution mechanism (VCM, hereafter). We set up groups of 4 members who interact for T periods. In every period each member is endowed with an initial endowment e, that he can keep for himself or contribute to the public good, where member i's contribution in period t has to satisfy $0 \leq c_{it} \leq e$. The sum of individual contributions in period t is denoted by $C_t = \sum_{i=1}^{4} c_{it}$. Payoffs in period t are given by:

$$u_{it}(c_{it}, C_t) = e - c_{it} + \beta C_t$$

where $0 < \beta < 1 < 4\beta$. The latter implies that the dominant strategy for a payoff-maximizing subject is to contribute zero to the public good and keep e for himself, while the social optimum is to contribute everything to the public good, because this yields earnings of $4\beta e > e$ per member.

---

3. We draw on previously published material in Rivas and Sutter (2011) for answering question (B).

THE EXPERIMENT

Treatments

In order to address our research questions (A) to (C) we have designed the following six experimental treatments[4]:

1. *CONTROL.* This is the standard VCM introduced previously. In this treatment all four group members contribute simultaneously to the public good. Hence, there is no leader present in the group.
2. *REWARD.* In this treatment, one group member is randomly determined at the beginning of the experiment to be the leader for the whole experiment. In each period the leader has to make his contribution first, which is then communicated (in anonymous form) to the other group members. Only then the other members decide simultaneously on their contribution. After all group members have made their contributions, the leader gets informed about all contributions and may reward one of the other members with 10 ECU (experimental currency units). The reward is costly for the leader and for the non-rewarded members, as each of them has to pay costs of 2 ECU.
3. *EXCLUSION.* Like in treatment *REWARD*, there is a fixed leader who contributes before the other group members. After observing the other members' contributions, the leader may (but need not) exclude one of them from the group for the next period. In case of an exclusion, the group consists of only three members in the next period. The exclusion is costly for the excluded member—because he cannot benefit from the public good in the next period—and for the non-excluded members, including the leader, as the exclusion reduces the number of potential contributors to the public good.
4. *ENDOGENOUS.* In this variation of the VCM, any group member can choose in each single period to become the leader by being the first one to contribute to the public good. Once one member makes a contribution, it is communicated to the other group members who then have to contribute simultaneously. In case no group member volunteers to be the leader and contribute first within the first 15 seconds of a period, then there is no leader and all members have to contribute simultaneously (i.e., independently of each other and without knowing what any other member has done in the respective period). Note that in the latter case, the conditions in treatment *ENDOGENOUS* are identical to those in treatment *CONTROL*.
5. *EXOGENOUS.* This treatment is a replication of treatment *ENDOGENOUS*, subject to the following modification. The role of leader in each period is determined exogenously by using the endogenously evolved patterns of leadership in treatment *ENDOGENOUS*. To be precise, the four members of a group k in treatment *ENDOGENOUS* were labeled as members 1 to 4. For each

---

4. Treatments CONTROL and EXCLUSION are identical to treatments introduced in Güth et al. (2007). For the data analysis of these treatments, we report the data already presented in Güth et al. (2007). Treatment CONTROL here is denoted as treatment C, and EXCLUSION is denoted as SLf in Güth et al. (2007). Treatments ENDOGENOUS and EXOGENOUS are taken from our earlier work in Rivas and Sutter (2011).

period we recorded which member—if any—volunteered to be the leader. This endogenously evolved sequence of leaders in a group k was then implemented exogenously in one group in treatment *EXOGENOUS*. By doing so, we can control the sequence in which single group members are leaders in a group, and we can check whether an identical sequence of group members being leaders has different effects, contingent on leadership having emerged endogenously (in *ENDOGENOUS*) or having been enforced exogenously (in *EXOGENOUS*).

6. *LAST*. Like in *REWARD* and *EXCLUSION*, one group member is randomly determined as a leader. However, the leader does not contribute before the other group members, but *after* them. This means that the three "normal" group members contribute simultaneously, and that the leader gets informed about their contributions before deciding on his own. Contrary to *REWARD* and *EXCLUSION* the leader has no incentive devices available in *LAST*.

Note that for answering our research question (A) on the comparative effects of rewards and sanctions we will compare contribution levels in treatments *CONTROL*, *REWARD* and *EXCLUSION*. Question (B) on the effects of voluntariness can be resolved by checking the differences between treatments *CONTROL*, *ENDOGENOUS* and *EXOGENOUS*. Question (C) on the influence of a reverse sequential order of contributions will be addressed by comparing treatments *CONTROL* and *LAST*.

One should also bear in mind that if subjects are rational and profit-maximizing, then their dominant strategy is to contribute zero in the public goods game, irrespective of the treatment. Rewards do not change this standard prediction because reward is costly. By applying backward induction, it can then be shown that leaders have no incentive to reward other group members, which in turn implies that group members have no incentive to contribute positive amounts. In *EXCLUSION* the leader is indifferent between excluding or not a follower, since he expects the follower to contribute zero anyway.

Procedures

Each treatment consists of $T = 24$ periods throughout which group composition never changes (partner design). We use $e = 25$ and $\beta = 0.4$. In treatments *REWARD*, *EXCLUSION*, *ENDOGENOUS*, and *LAST* there are two parts. Until period 16 the design is as explained in the previous subsection. Before periods 17 and 21, however, subjects can vote whether they want to have (or allow the existence of) a leader or not in periods 17 to 20, and 21 to 24, respectively. The group has a leader—or the possibility of having a leader in *ENDOGENOUS*—only if all four group members vote for leadership, otherwise the members have to contribute simultaneously to the public good in the respective four-period phase.[5]

---

5. Note that in treatments *REWARD* and *EXCLUSION* group members vote on whether the fixed leader continues to be leader. In treatment *ENDOGENOUS*, voting for leadership means that in periods 17-20 or 21-24 it shall also be possible that one group member volunteers to contribute first. In treatment *EXOGENOUS* there is no need for a ballot.

The experiment was computerized (using z-Tree, Fischbacher, 2007) and all sessions were conducted at the Max Planck Institute of Economics in Jena (Germany). Table 1 shows the number of groups (of four subjects each) in the different treatments.

A total of 384 students with different majors participated in the experiment. To ensure full understanding, all subjects had to answer control questions before the experiment started. At the end of each period, subjects were informed about the contributions of every group member (identified by the member number) as well as their own profits. After the voting stage before periods 17 and 21, subjects were informed whether or not leadership had received unanimous support.

For the final payment we randomly chose one period from each block of four periods (i.e., periods 1-4, 5-8, 9-12, 13-16, 17-20, and 21-24). The exchange rate was 1 ECU (experimental currency unit) = 0.06 euro, yielding average earnings of 14 euro (including a 2.50 euro show-up fee) per subject.

RESULTS

Question (A): The Effects of Leadership, Reward and Exclusion

Contributions

Table 8.1 presents the average contributions and standard deviations in all six treatments. In this subsection we consider the data from treatments *CONTROL, REWARD* and *EXCLUSION*, and only the first 16 periods (since we will analyze the voting phase in subsection 4.1.4). The average contributions in *CONTROL* are around 40% of a subject's endowment. They are considerably higher both in *REWARD* (around 55%) and *EXCLUSION* (around 80%). Figure 8.1 shows the time trend of contributions. In *CONTROL* and *REWARD* we see a typical downward trend of contributions. In *EXCLUSION*, however, contributions are stable at a very high level. Table 8.2 shows how frequently leaders reward or punish followers. The difference is remarkable as the average relative frequency of reward is 0.41, but only 0.12 for punishment through exclusion.

Table 8.3 shows the results of a random effects Tobit estimation where the dependent variable is the contribution to the public good. The independent variables are the period, dummies for *REWARD* and *EXCLUSION*, a dummy for being the leader in the group, and several interaction variables. Groups with leaders that have a reward option have significantly higher contributions than we observe in the *CONTROL*-treatment without a leader. Exclusion power, however, yields the highest contributions, and the contributions in *EXCLUSION* are significantly higher than in *REWARD*. Together with the evidence presented in Table 8.2, we can conclude that the effect of exclusion does not rely on a high frequency of exclusions. Instead, the mere existence of the possibility of being excluded is a strong motivation for contributing high amounts. Judging from the evidence

TABLE 8.1 *Number of groups, average contributions and earnings in ECU, and frequency of approving leadership*

	# of groups	Period 1-16 Avg. contribution	(Std.dev.)	Period 17-24 Avg. contribution	(Std.dev.)	Freq. approving leadership Period 17	Period 21	Average earnings Period 1-16
CONTROL	14	10.04	(8.91)	4.96	(7.56)	—	—	31.02
REWARD	19	14.16	(9.76)	8.70	(9.60)	26.3%	47.4%	33.91
EXCLUSION	14	20.78	(7.16)	16.70	(9.90)	57.1%	64.3%	36.68
ENDOGENOUS	17	15.70	(8.97)	10.95	(9.81)	41.2%	58.8%	34.42
EXOGENOUS	14	8.74	(8.50)	4.12	(5.84)	—	—	30.24
LAST	18	10.88	(8.43)	7.86	(8.20)	11.1%	16.7%	31.53

in Figure 8.1 and Table 8.2, though, it seems as if the average contributions in the *REWARD*-treatment are strongly correlated with the relative frequency with which the leader rewards a group member (correlation coefficient = 0.43, $p < 0.05$). Contrary to punishment then, the reward option has to be used in order to stimulate higher contributions.

Our estimates show that across periods there is a significant decline in contributions in *CONTROL* and *REWARD*, but not in *EXCLUSION*. Hence, only the exclusion option yields stable contributions over time. Leaders do not contribute significantly more than the other group members. However, the average contribution of leaders in *REWARD* (*EXCLUSION*) is 16.16 ECU (21.82 ECU), while followers contribute only 13.50 ECU (20.65 ECU). The correlation between leaders'

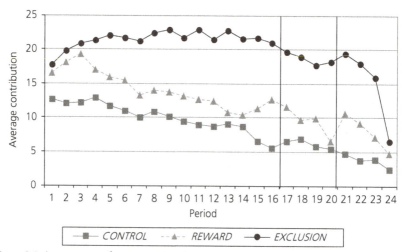

Figure 8.1 Average contributions in *CONTROL, REWARD* and *EXCLUSION*.

TABLE 8.2 *Frequency leaders decide to reward/exclude a follower*

Period	Frequency leader decided to reward a follower	Frequency leader decided to exclude a follower
1	0.63	0.14
2	0.63	0.07
3	0.53	0.14
4	0.26	0.07
5	0.58	0.14
6	0.37	0.07
7	0.37	0.07
8	0.26	0.29
9	0.37	0.21
10	0.42	0.14
11	0.37	0.14
12	0.32	0.21
13	0.42	0.14
14	0.26	0.00
15	0.42	0.07
16	0.32	0.00
Average	0.41	0.12

TABLE 8.3 *Estimation of the contribution in CONTROL, REWARD and EXCLUSION*

Random effect Tobit Regression		
Dependent variable: contribution	Coefficient	Std.Err
REWARD	6.99***	2.50
EXCLUSION	10.69***	2.78
Subject is leader	1.49	4.04
Subject is leader*REWARD	2.27	5.23
Period	−0.64***	0.07
Period*REWARD	−0.19*	0.10
Period*EXCLUSION	1.39***	0.13
Constant	15.07***	1.78
Number of observations	2981	
Number of groups	188	

***signif. at 1% level *signif. at 10% level

and followers' contributions is positive and highly significant in both treatments.[6] We summarize this subsection as follows:

> *Result 1: Having a leader with reward possibilities or a leader with exclusion power yields higher contributions, compared with a control treatment without leader. However, exclusion as a sanctioning device is more effective than a reward option.*

6. The Pearson correlation coefficient between the leader's and the followers' contributions is 0.681 in REWARD and 0.831 in EXCLUSION (p-values = 0.00).

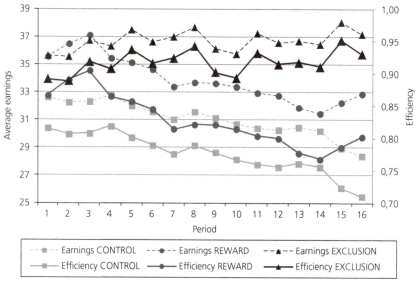

Figure 8.2 Average earnings and efficiency in CONTROL, REWARD and EXCLUSION.

Efficiency

Measuring efficiency as the actually obtained earnings as a percentage of the maximum possible earnings, we find that average efficiency is highest in EXCLUSION (92%), intermediate in REWARD (83%), and lowest in CONTROL (78%). Maximum earnings in EXCLUSION and CONTROL are 40 ECU per group member and period if every subject contributes the full endowment and nobody is excluded. In REWARD the maximum earnings are achieved when every subject contributes the full endowment and one subject is rewarded with 10 ECU—which costs 6 ECU to the group—yielding 41 ECU per group member and period. Figure 8.2 shows the average earnings (with dotted lines) and efficiency (with solid lines) by period.

Result 2: EXCLUSION yields the highest efficiency, while REWARD and CONTROL do not differ significantly with respect to efficiency.

Causes and Consequences of Being Rewarded or Excluded

In the following, we examine which group members are rewarded, respectively excluded, and how these members react to reward or exclusion. Figure 8.3 shows how the relative frequency of reward or exclusion depends on the rewarded or excluded member's contribution in relation to the other group members' contributions. The pattern is straightforward. The less a group member contributes in relation to the other group members, the more (less) likely this

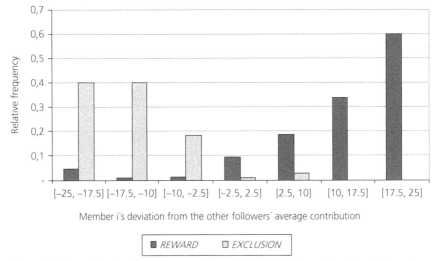

Figure 8.3 Reward and exclusion depending on the deviation from the other followers' contributions.

member is excluded (rewarded). Hence, leaders condition reward or exclusion on relative contributions.[7]

Table 8.4 confirms the basic insights from Figure 8.3 by reporting the results from a panel Probit estimation of the probability of being rewarded, respectively excluded. The independent variables are the positive and negative deviation from the other followers' and the leader's contribution, and the period.

The Probit estimation on the left-hand side of Table 8.4 shows that the probability of being rewarded increases with the positive deviation from the other followers' contribution, and decreases across periods. The higher the negative deviation from the leader's contribution, the higher the probability of being excluded, as can be seen on the right-hand side of Table 8.4. The deviation from the leader's contribution (other followers' contribution) is not significant for *REWARD* (*EXCLUSION*). Figure 8.2 suggests that both probabilities are influenced by the deviation from other followers' contributions. One explanation for not finding that both deviations influence both probabilities lies in the high correlation between the deviation from the other followers' and the leader's contributions, both of which are considered in the estimation. Across periods, the likelihood of rewarding is significantly decreasing, whereas the likelihood to punish via exclusion is basically constant.

---

7. Like Fehr and Gächter (2000), we also observe a positive, but relatively small number of low contributors who punish high contributors. Herrmann et al. (2008) use the term antisocial punishment for such cases, and they demonstrate that antisocial punishment is widespread around the world. Nikiforakis (2008) shows that the positive effects of a punishment device on contributions in a group may be contained if counter-punishment is possible.

TABLE 8.4 *Estimations of the probability of being rewarded/excluded*

	Random Effect Probit Regressions			
Dependent variable	Subject rewarded		Subject excluded	
	Marginal effect	Std.Err.	Marginal effect	Std.Err.
Positive deviation from other followers	0.01***	0.02	−0.02	0.06
Negative deviation from other followers	−0.04	0.03	−0.01	0.06
Positive deviation from leader	0.02	0.02	0.05	0.09
Negative deviation from leader	−0.02	0.02	0.13**	0.06
Period	−0.03**	0.01	−0.03	0.03
Number of observations	912		645	
Number of groups	57		42	

***signif. at 1% level **signif. at 5% level

Table 8.5 shows the effects of being rewarded or excluded on a member's contribution in the next period. We show random effects Tobit regressions where the dependent variable is the contribution to the public good. The independent variables in *REWARD* are a dummy variable that indicates if the subject was rewarded in the previous period, a dummy variable that takes value 1 if another group member was rewarded in the previous period, the contribution of the group lagged by one period, a dummy variable that indicates if the subject is a leader, and the period. In *EXCLUSION* we use a dummy if the subject was excluded the previous period, and a dummy indicating if another group member was excluded the previous period, keeping the other variables identical to the regression for *REWARD*.

TABLE 8.5 *Estimations of the effect of being rewarded/excluded*

	Random effect Tobit Regression				
Dependent variable: contribution	Treatment: REWARD		Dependent variable: contribution	Treatment: EXCLUSION	
	Coefficient	Std.Err.		Coefficient	Std.Err.
Subject was rewarded pervious period	4.00***	1.57	Subject was rewarded pervious period	5.17***	1.87
Other subject was rewarded pervious period	2.44**	1.11	Other subject was rewarded pervious period	1.43	1.33
Group contribution previous period	0.15***	0.02	Group contribution previous period	0.27***	0.02
Subject is leader	3.97	3.00	Subject is leader	1.29	2.61
Period	−0.61***	0.10	Period	0.21***	0.08
Constant	11.21***	2.37	Constant	5.23**	2.45
Number of observations	1140		Number of observations	813	
Number of groups	76		Number of groups	56	

***signif. at 1% level **signif. at 5% level   ***signif. at 1% level **signif. at 5% level

Both reward and exclusion yield higher contributions of the affected group member in the next period. If a subject was rewarded with 10 ECU, contributions increase by an estimated 4.00 ECU, while if a subject was excluded, the increase is estimated at 5.17 ECU. Relatively higher contributions within a group in the previous period also have a significantly positive effect on one's own contributions, which is clear evidence of conditional cooperation (Keser & van Winden, 2000; Brandts & Schram, 2001; Fischbacher et al., 2001; Levati & Neugebauer, 2004; Kocher et al., 2008; Fischbacher & Gächter, 2010). The dummy for the leader is not significant, confirming our findings in Table 8.3. We summarize this subsection as follows:

Result 3: The higher the positive (negative) deviation from the leader's or other group members' contributions, the higher the probability of being rewarded (excluded). Group members who are rewarded or excluded for one period react by choosing significantly higher contributions in the next period.

Periods 17-24

In this subsection we take a brief look at the data of periods 17 to 24. As indicated in Table 8.1, the overall order of contributions across treatments is perfectly preserved in periods 17-24, compared to periods 1-16. Considering periods 17-24 allows for an insightful relation of the contributions within a group in periods 1-16 and the likelihood of voting for leadership in periods 17-20 and 21-24. Figures 8.4 and 8.5 plot the average contributions in periods 1-24 for those groups that accepted leadership twice or once in periods 17-24 and those groups that failed twice to accept leadership. It is obvious from Figure 8.4 that successful groups in periods 1-16 of the *REWARD*-treatment are those that succeed to keep a leader in periods 17-24, which suggests that success breeds success, since leadership leads to higher contributions, and higher contributions make leadership more likely. Those groups that did not accept any leader in periods 17-24 are those that had the lowest contributions in periods 1-16. As shown in Figure 8.5, the relationship between contributions in periods 1-16 and the frequency of choosing a leader is less separating for *EXCLUSION*, but it keeps the same general pattern. Those groups that veto a leader permanently in periods 17-24 are those that have the lowest contributions in periods 1-16. This indicates that bad experiences with leaders in periods 1-16 backfire when leadership can be chosen endogenously.

Table 8.6 reports a random effects Probit regression of the likelihood of voting for a leader in period 17 and period 21. The independent variables are being a leader in periods 1-16, one's own contributions, the other group members' contributions, and the standard deviation of contributions within a group in periods 1-16. The latter variable is intended to capture whether strong heterogeneity of group members with respect to contributions has an impact on the likelihood to vote for a leader, controlling for the average level of contributions. However, this variable is not significant. It turns out that the likelihood to vote for a leader is significantly increasing with the other group members' contributions and that it is higher in period 21

146 ■ Reward and Punishment in Social Dilemmas

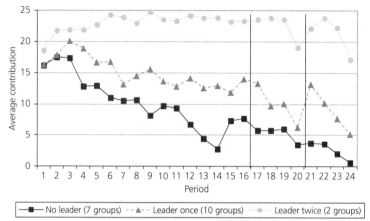

Figure 8.4 Average contribution in *REWARD* by type of group.

than in period 17. The latter might be due to the bad experiences with no leader in periods 17-20. The former result shows that more cooperative groups are more likely to have a leader. We summarize this subsection as follows:

> *Result 4*: Voting behavior in periods 17 and 21 depends strongly on behavior in periods 1 to 16. More cooperative groups are more likely to vote for leadership. Failing to accept a leader has high efficiency costs.

Question (B): The Effects of Voluntary Leadership

In this subsection we analyze whether voluntary leadership—in the absence of reward or punishment opportunities—may have different effects from enforcing leadership exogenously. For this purpose, we compare treatments

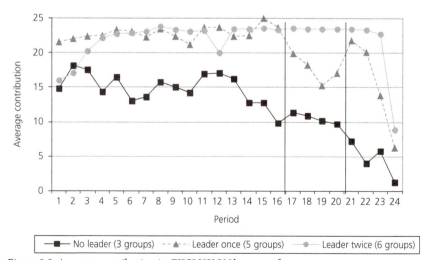

Figure 8.5 Average contribution in *EXCLUSION* by type of group.

TABLE 8.6 *Estimation of the probability of voting for a leader*

Random Effects Probit Regressions	Periods 17 and 21	
Dependent variable	Vote for leader	
	Marginal effect	Std.Err.
Subject was leader periods 1-16	−0.36	0.29
Avg own contribution periods 1-16	0.03	0.03
Avg others' contribution periods 1-16	0.07**	0.03
Std.dev. of group contrib periods 1-16	−0.01	0.06
EXCLUSION	−0.09	0.31
Periods 21	0.59***	0.22
Number of observations		254
Number of groups		132

***signif. at 1% level **signif. at 5% level

ENDOGENOUS and *EXOGENOUS*, and each of them with *CONTROL*. Table 8.1 shows that the average contributions in *ENDOGENOUS* are about 50 percent higher than in *CONTROL* and almost 80 percent higher than in *EXOGENOUS*. The frequency of the number of times a subject is the leader of her group has an average of 3.88 and a maximum of 11 times. No group failed to have a leader in more than 3 periods out of 16 periods.

Figure 8.6 displays the intertemporal development of contributions, indicating that average contributions are in each single period clearly highest if leadership is taken over voluntarily in *ENDOGENOUS*.

Table 8.7 reports a random effects Tobit regression, showing a statistically significant positive treatment effect of voluntary leadership in *ENDOGENOUS*. There is also a significant difference between *EXOGENOUS* and *CONTROL*, but in the opposite direction. Recall that the sequence of group members acting as leaders in *EXOGENOUS* is determined by a matched group in *ENDOGENOUS*. Hence, groups in *EXOGENOUS* also have leaders, but this forced leadership does not raise contributions above the level prevailing in *CONTROL*; on the contrary, it decreases contributions.

Table 8.7 also indicates that leaders contribute significantly more than followers and that the difference in contributions of leaders and followers is smaller in *ENDOGENOUS*. Contrary to Arbak and Villeval (2013), we find that voluntary leadership not only shifts the level of contributions upwards, but also it decreases the difference between leaders' and followers' contributions. In *EXOGENOUS*, the followers' average contributions (7.79 ECU) are equivalent to 67% of the leaders' contributions (11.58 ECU), while in *ENDOGENOUS* the followers' contributions (15.34 ECU) correspond to 85% of the leaders' contributions (17.96 ECU).

One explanation for the difference in the contributions of leaders between the two treatments is that in *ENDOGENOUS* the most generous subjects are likely to volunteer as leaders while in *EXOGENOUS* selfish subjects could be randomly chosen to be the leader.[8] Another explanation is that leaders anticipate that followers

---

8. Gächter et al. (2012) find that since many followers are conditionally cooperative, groups perform best when the leader is a high contributor (in the role of follower).

148 ■ Reward and Punishment in Social Dilemmas

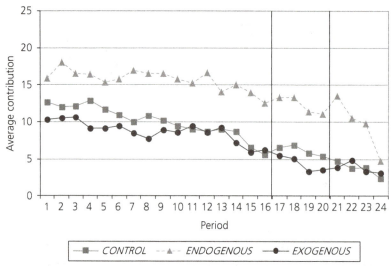

Figure 8.6 Average contributions in CONTROL, ENDOGENOUS and EXOGENOUS.

will **reciprocate the leader's contribution more when leaders volunteer** to be leaders than in the case when they are exogenously chosen to be leaders, and therefore leaders set more cooperative examples in ENDOGENOUS than in EXOGENOUS.

Figure 8.7 shows the average earnings and efficiency of the three treatments. Both variables attain their maximum in ENDOGENOUS, followed by EXOGENOUS and CONTROL, which are very similar.

Figure 8.8 separates the groups in ENDOGENOUS by the number of periods in which a group had a leader in periods 1-16. Note that no group ever had a leader in less than in 13 out of 16 periods, and that most groups had a leader in 15 or 16 periods.

TABLE 8.7 *Estimation of the contribution in CONTROL, ENDOGENOUS, and EXOGENOUS*

Random effect Tobit Regression		
Dependent variable: contribution	Coefficient	Std.Err.
ENDOGENOUS	5.95***	2.25
EXOGENOUS	−6.59***	2.33
Subject is leader	6.83***	0.79
Subject is leader	−2.62**	1.10
Period	−0.62***	0.07
Period	0.30***	0.09
Period	0.27***	0.10
Constant	14.92***	1.64
Number of observations	2880	
Number of groups	180	

***signif. at 1% level **signif. at 5% level

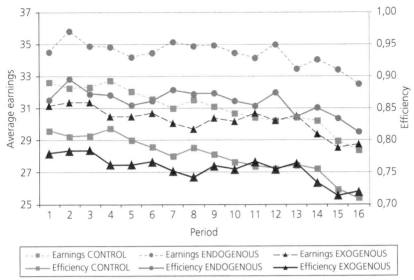

Figure 8.7 Average earnings and efficiency in *CONTROL*, *ENDOGENOUS* and *EXOGENOUS*.

Despite these seemingly small differences in the frequency of voluntary leadership, Figure 8.8 has a clear message. Those groups with voluntary leadership in each single period have clearly the highest contributions. The group with the most frequent failure of voluntary leadership performs worst with respect to contributions. The failure to have a voluntary leader in each single period of periods 1-16 continues to have detrimental effects on contributions also in periods 17-24, as Figure 8.8 indicates.

We summarize this subsection as follows:

> *Result 5: Voluntary leadership increases contributions significantly. Groups in which members volunteer in each single period for leadership have the highest contributions. Exogenously forced leadership decreases contributions below the level prevalent without leadership.*

Question (C): The Effects of Leaders Contributing After the Other Group Members

In this subsection we study whether allowing the leader to observe the contributions of the other group members before taking his decision in *LAST* increases the average contribution of the group. Thus, we address the issue whether sequentiality itself (in whichever order) has a positive effect on contributions in a public goods experiment.

Looking at Figure 8.9 and checking the average contributions reported in Table 8.1 shows that there is no difference in contributions between the *CONTROL*-treatment without leadership and treatment *LAST*. Hence, the sequential contribution procedure in *LAST* does not increase contributions, nor does it decrease them. This is confirmed in the regression results shown in Table 8.8,

150 ■ Reward and Punishment in Social Dilemmas

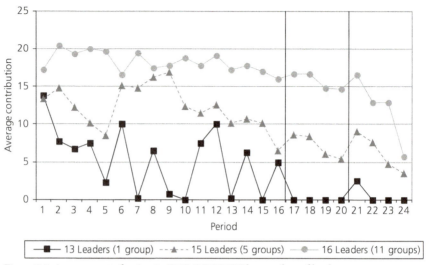

Figure 8.8 Average contribution in *ENDOGENOUS* by number of leaders.

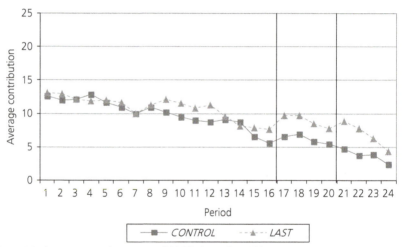

Figure 8.9 Average contributions in *CONTROL* and *LAST*.

where the dummy for *LAST* is not significant.[9] We summarize the findings in this subsection as follows:

> *Result 6:* Sequentiality itself does not raise contributions, because if leaders contribute after the other group members then contributions are not higher than in the benchmark case of no leader in CONTROL.

---

9. Regressions not reported here show that the contributions in *LAST* are significantly smaller than in *REWARD, EXCLUSION* and *ENDOGENOUS*, but not different from those in *EXOGENOUS*. This means that the reverse leadership in *LAST* yields lower contributions than whenever leadership is taken over voluntarily or when a leader has a reward or sanctioning device at his disposal.

TABLE 8.8 *Estimation of the contribution in CONTROL and LAST*

Random effect Tobit Regression		
Dependent variable: contribution	Coefficient	Std.Err.
LAST	1.80	2.00
Subject is leader	−2.19	2.85
Period	−0.53***	0.04
Constant	14.23	0.43
Number of observations	2048	
Number of groups	128	

***signif. at 1% level

DISCUSSION

Social dilemmas are situations characterized by a tension between self-interest and collective welfare. Subjects are tempted to free ride on others contributing as little as possible to a joint project while benefiting from the contributions of the others. In this chapter, we have studied the importance of leadership as a means to deter free-riding and encourage cooperation in social dilemmas. Leadership has been implemented in a very simple form by allowing for sequential contributions to a public good, where the leader either contributes before or after all other group members. We have examined various aspects of leadership that have not been addressed so far in the still growing literature on leadership effects in public goods experiments. In the introduction we have formulated three main research questions. Given our experimental results, we are able to answer these questions now.

Answer (A): Leaders with an option to reward followers are less effective than leaders with a sanctioning device through exclusion. However, leadership with a reward option is still (much) more efficient than a situation without any leader. The main drawback of reward in comparison to punishment is the observation that reward needs to be applied—and potentially increased—permanently, while the mere threat of punishment upholds high levels of cooperation. From this perspective, punishment is more efficient. Nevertheless, our experiment shows that reward and punishment are both useful instruments for leaders to increase contribution levels, and our work contributes to the literature on leadership by being the first one to consider leadership with a reward option for leaders.

Answer (B): Voluntary leadership—even without any reward or sanctioning device—yields clearly higher contributions than the benchmark case without any leader. However, sequential contributions with first contributions by a leader do not raise contributions per se. If leadership is exogenously enforced, contributions are not higher than in the control treatment. Hence, the beneficial effects of leadership depend on leadership being taken over voluntarily. This may be driven by the signal value of voluntary leadership, meaning that leaders who take over responsibility have an option of signaling a strong concern for the well-being of the group (which coincides with efficiency concerns in this case). The positive effects of endogenous (i.e., voluntary) leadership are reminiscent of the positive effects of endogenous institutional choice in public goods experiments documented in Gürerk et al. (2006) and Sutter et al. (2010). Whenever subjects can influence the way the interaction in a social-dilemma situation is structured, this seems to affect their level of cooperation positively, because it seems that endogenous institutions imply stronger commitment and motivation. It seems particularly noteworthy from our findings that endogenous leadership yields even higher contributions than if exogenously determined leaders have a reward device at their disposal. Hence, for the organization of groups it seems important to leave room for leadership to emerge endogenously within groups.

Answer (C): Sequentiality itself does not raise contributions. Hence, introducing a sequence of moves in the private provision of public goods is no universal means of inducing more cooperation. If leaders contribute *after* the other group members then contributions are not higher than in the benchmark case of having no leader at all. It seems reasonable to assume that if leaders contribute last then the other group members may perceive that as a means of control rather than as a leader setting a good example.[10]

Integrating the answers to our three research questions, it seems justified to conclude that the dos of leadership include voluntary leadership and equipping leaders with reward (e.g., public recognition) or sanctioning mechanisms (e.g., fines), whereas the don'ts of leadership are forcing leadership by moving first through an exogenous authority as well as reversing the sequence of leadership by letting the leader contribute after the other group members. These dos and don'ts of leadership have the potential to help companies and groups get out of the trap that is inherent in social dilemmas, i.e., the luring danger that individual self-interest prevails over a group's—or society's—well-being. While leadership has always been acknowledged as an important means to avoid falling into such a trap, our work contributes to a more nuanced understanding of the conditions under which leadership is able to fulfill its promise.

■ CONCLUDING REMARKS

Leadership is a social relation with three main components: the leader, the followers, and the context in which the interaction takes place (Nye, 2010). The leader is the person that helps the group to achieve common goals. He or she can do that using what is sometimes called "soft" and "hard" power (Nye, 2010). Hard power consists of "carrots" and "sticks," while soft power depends on the ability of the leader to convince others to follow him.

We know from previous research that leading by example is a fundamental element of a leader's soft power. Even without communication among the group members, the leader can increase the level of cooperation in a group by setting a

---

10. Previous work by Falk and Kosfeld (2006), for instance, suggests that controlling the actions of others in a principal-agent game may crowd out the intrinsic motivation of agents to behave cooperatively.

good example. In this chapter, we have learned that a group with a leader who has reward opportunities at his disposal can achieve better outcomes in terms of group cooperation than a group without a leader, and that if this leader is provided with a punishment device then the outcome is even better. These findings are relevant for any organization where a leader is exogenously set. Our experiment has shown, however, that rewards (for example through promotion or a bonus payment) need to be applied frequently (or even increased), otherwise they will become ineffective through habit formation. On the contrary, just the mere threat of punishment (for example, firing a worker in a firm) can be enough to influence a group of individuals to achieve a shared goal. This implies that there is an (often overlooked) asymmetry in the effects of punishment and reward. The former does not need to be applied to be potentially effective, while the latter must.

Moreover, we have also learned that if the leader is not externally imposed but he is the member that volunteers to be so, then the group achieves a better outcome. This finding is especially important when we have groups of equals contributing to achieve a common goal. In this case it is recommended that the leader of the group is the member that volunteers to lead or coordinate the group. The reason why such a leader would be a better role model for the other members of the group is potentially twofold. On the one hand, we have a self-selection process where the most altruistic members will volunteer to sacrifice their own payoff in the name of a common goal. On the other hand, most likely the other members of the group will appreciate his efforts and will have a more cooperative behavior than in the case where the leader is exogenously appointed. This suggests that voluntary leadership increases the soft power of the leader, and this is irrespective of hierarchical considerations.

REFERENCES

Andreoni, J., Harbaugh, W., & Vesterlund, L. (2003). The carrot or the stick: Rewards, punishments and cooperation. *American Economic Review, 93*, 893–902.

Arbak, E., Villeval M-C. (2013). Voluntary leadership. Motivation and influence. *Social Choice and Welfare, 40*, 635–662.

Balliet D., Mulder, L. B., & Van Lange, P. A. M. (2011). Reward, punishment, and cooperation: A meta-analysis. *Psychological Bulletin, 137*(4), 594–615.

Brandts, J., Schram, A. (2001). Cooperation and noise in public goods experiments: Applying the contribution function approach. *Journal of Public Economics, 79*, 399–427.

Duffy, J., Ochs, J., & Vesterlund, L. (2007). Giving little by little: Dynamic voluntary contribution games. *Journal of Public Economics, 91*, 1708–1730.

Falk, A., & Kosfeld, M. (2006). The hidden costs of control. *American Economic Review, 96*, 1611–1630.

Fehr, E., & Gächter, S. (2000). Cooperation and punishment in public goods experiments. *American Economic Review, 90*, 980–994.

Fischbacher, U. (2007). Z-tree. Zurich toolbox for readymade economic experiments. *Experimental Economics, 10*, 171–178.

Fischbacher, U., & Gächter, S. (2010). Social preferences, beliefs, and the dynamics of free riding in public goods experiments. *American Economic Review, 100*, 541–556.

Fischbacher, U., Gächter, S., & Fehr, E. (2001). Are people conditionally cooperative? Evidence from a public goods experiment. *Economics Letters, 71*, 397–404.

Gächter, S., Nosenzo, D., Renner, E., & Sefton, M. (2012). Who makes a good leader? Cooperativeness, optimism, and leading-by-example. *Economic Inquiry, 50*, 953–967.

Gächter, S., & Renner, E. (2004). Leading by example in the presence of free rider incentives. Mimeo. University of Nottingham.

Gürerk, Ö., Irlenbusch, B., & Rockenbach, B. (2006). The competitive advantage of sanctioning institutions. *Science, 312* (7 April 2006), 108–111.

Güth, W., Levati, M.-V., Sutter, M., & van der Heijden, E. (2007). Leading by example with and without exclusion power in voluntary contribution experiments. *Journal of Public Economics, 91*, 1023–1042.

Haigner, S., & Wakolbinger, F. (2010). To lead or not to lead. Endogenous sequencing in public goods games. *Economics Letters, 108*, 93–95.

Herrmann, B., Thöni, C., & Gächter, S. (2008). Antisocial punishment across societies. *Science, 319* (7 March 2008), 1362–1366.

Keser, C., & van Winden, F. (2000). Conditional cooperation and voluntary contributions to public goods. *Scandinavian Journal of Economics, 102*, 23–39.

Kocher, M., Cherry, T., Kroll, S., & Netzer, J., Sutter, M. (2008). Conditional cooperation on three continents. *Economics Letters, 101*, 175–178.

Kumru, C. S., & Vesterlund, L. (2010). The effect of status on charitable giving. *Journal of Public Economic Theory, 12*, 709–735.

Levati, M. V., & Neugebauer, T. (2004). An application of the English clock market mechanism to public goods games. *Experimental Economics, 7*, 153–169.

Levati, M. V., Sutter, M., & van der Heijden, E. (2007). Leading by example in public goods experiments with heterogeneity and incomplete information. *Journal of Conflict Resolution, 51*, 793–818.

Moxnes, E., & van der Heijden, E. (2003). The effect of leadership in a public bad experiment. *Journal of Conflict Resolution, 47*, 773–795.

Nikiforakis, N. (2008). Punishment and counter-punishment in public-good games: Can we really govern ourselves? *Journal of Public Economics, 92*, 91–112.

Nye, J. S. Jr. (2010). Power and leadership. In N. Nohria & R. Khurana (Eds.), *Handbook of Leadership. Theory and Practice*. Harvard Business Press.

Pogrebna, G., Krantz, D. H., Schade, & C., Keser, C. (2011). Words versus actions as a means to influence cooperation in social dilemma situations. *Theory and Decision, 71*, 473–502.

Potters, J., Sefton, M., & Vesterlund, L. (2005). After you—Endogenous sequencing in voluntary contribution games. *Journal of Public Economics, 89*, 1399–1419.

Potters, J., Sefton, M., & Vesterlund, L. (2007). Leading-by-example and signaling in voluntary contribution games: An experimental study. *Economic Theory, 33*, 169–182.

Rivas, M. F., & Sutter, M. (2011). The benefits of voluntary leadership in experimental public goods games. *Economics Letters, 112*, 176–178.

Sefton, M., Shupp, R., & Walker, J. M. (2007). The effect of rewards and sanctions in provision of public goods. *Economic Inquiry, 45*, 671–690.

Sutter, M., Haigner, S., & Kocher, M. (2010). Choosing the carrot or the stick?—Endogenous institutional choice in social dilemma situations. *Review of Economic Studies, 177*, 1540–1566.

Villeval, M.-C. (2012). Contributions to public goods and social preferences: Recent insights from behavioral economics. *Revue Economique, 63*, 389–420.

APPENDIX: EXPERIMENTAL INSTRUCTIONS

Appendix contains the instructions (originally in German) we used for the EXCLUSION-treatment. The instructions for the other treatments were adapted appropriately and are available upon request.

Welcome and thanks for participating in this experiment. You receive 2.50 Euro for having shown up on time. If you read these instructions carefully, you can make good decisions and earn more. The 2.50 Euro and all additional amount of money will be paid out to you in cash immediately after the experiment.

During the experiment, amounts will be denoted by ECU (Experimental Currency Unit). ECU are converted to euros at the following exchange rate: 1 ECU = 0.06 Euro.

It is strictly forbidden to communicate with the other participants during the experiment. If you have any questions or concerns, please raise your hand. We will answer your questions individually. It is very important that you follow this rule. Otherwise we must exclude you from the experiment and from all payments.

DETAILED INFORMATION ON THE EXPERIMENT

The experiment consists of 24 separate periods, in which you will interact with three other participants. The four of you form a group that will remain the same in all 24 periods. You will never know which of the other participants are in your group. The group composition is secret for every participant.

WHAT YOU HAVE TO DO

At the beginning of each period, each participant receives an amount of 25 ECU. In the following, we shall refer to this amount as *your endowment*.

Your task (as well as the task of your group members) is to decide **how much of your endowment you want to contribute to a project.** Whatever you do not contribute, you keep for yourself ("ECU you keep").

In every period, your earnings are the sum of the following two parts:

1. the "ECU you keep";
2. the "income from the project."

The "income from the project" is determined by adding up the contributions of the four group members and multiplying the resulting sum by 0.4. That is:

$$\text{Income from the project} = \left[0.4 \times (\text{total group contribution})\right] ECU$$

Each ECU that you contribute to the project raises "income from the project" by 0.4 ECU. Since "income from the project" is the same for all four members of the group (i.e., all receive the same income from the project, as this is determined by the total group contribution), each ECU that you contribute to the project raises your period-earnings as well as the period-earnings of your group members by 0.4 ECU. The same holds for the contributions of your group members: Each ECU that any of them contributes to the project increases "income from the project" (and therefore your earnings) by 0.4 ECU.

The "ECU you keep" is your endowment minus your contribution to the project. Each ECU that you keep for yourself raises "ECU you keep" and your period-earnings by one ECU. Thus, each ECU that you keep yields money for you alone.

■ HOW YOU INTERACT WITH YOUR GROUP MEMBERS IN EACH PERIOD

Within your group, you are identified by a number between 1 and 4. This number will be assigned to you privately at the beginning of the experiment.

Each period consists of the following three stages:

1. One group member first decides about his/her own contribution. In the following, we shall refer to the group member who decides first as the "early contributor."
2. Being informed about the decision of the early contributor, the other three group members decide simultaneously and privately about their own contribution.
3. The early contributor learns about the contribution of the others, and (s)he can decide to exclude at most one of them from the group in the next period.
   - If the early contributor does not exclude anyone, next period's "income from the project" and the earnings you are due in that period are determined as before.
   - If the early contributor excludes someone, in the following period the interacting group members will be three rather than four, and the "income from the project" is determined by adding up only their three contributions. Since the excluded group member stays out of the game, his (her) earnings in the subsequent period are merely equal to his/her endowment (i.e., 25 ECU).

Consider the following example: Member 1 is the early contributor in period 1 and contributes a certain amount. Knowing the contribution of the early contributor, the three other members of the group decide on their contribution, which is then communicated to the early contributor. If the early contributor decides, for instance, to exclude member 2, this means that member 2 is excluded from the group in the next period, i.e., in period 2. Hence, in period 2 only members 1, 3 and 4 interact with each other and their earnings in period 2 are as follows: "*ECU each keeps* + [0.4 × (sum of contributions of members 1, 3, and 4)]." Since member 2 does not participate in the interaction in period 2, (s)he just keeps his/her endowment. Note that member 2 will re-enter the group in period 3.

At the beginning of the experiment, one member of each group is randomly selected to be the "early contributor" for the first 16 periods. The group member who is selected as the early contributor sees this in an "Information Window," which will appear on his/her screen at the beginning of the experiment.

At the end of period 16, there will be two more phases (á four periods). In each of these two phases, group members will have the opportunity to choose themselves whether they want the early contributor to keep on being so or not.

■ HOW YOU CHOOSE WHETHER YOU WANT OR NOT AN EARLY CONTRIBUTOR

In periods 17 and 21, you are requested to indicate whether you want the early contributor to continue being the early contributor or not. If you want him/her to keep on being the early contributor, you must press the "Yes" button on the screen. Otherwise (i.e., if you do not want him/her to be the early contributor), you must press the "No" button.

- If the early contributor receives four "Yeses" (i.e., if (s)he wants as well to be the early contributor), (s)he will be the early contributor in the respective phase, and the sequence of decisions is as described previously.
- Otherwise (i.e., if the early contributor does not receive four "Yeses"), there will no longer be an early contributor, and you as well as your group members must make your contribution decisions simultaneously and privately. This, of course, also means that there will be no opportunity to exclude any group member in this phase.]

■ THE INFORMATION YOU RECEIVE AT THE END OF EACH PERIOD

At the end of each period, you will receive information about the number of ECU contributed by each of your group members as well as about your period-earnings.

■ YOUR FINAL EARNINGS

Your final earnings will be calculated as follows:

1. For each of the six phases of the experiment, one period will be randomly selected.
2. Your earnings in these 6 periods will be added up.
3. The resulting sum will be converted to euros and paid out to you in cash.

Before the experiment starts, we will run a control questionnaire to verify your understanding of the experiment.

Please remain seated quietly until the experiment starts. If you have any questions, please raise your hand now.

i

PART THREE
The Functions of Reward and Punishment In Society

9 Social Decision-making in Childhood and Adolescence

■ EVELINE A. CRONE, GEERT-JAN WILL, SANDY OVERGAAUW, AND BERNA GÜROĞLU

Abstract
This chapter describes several novel lines of research, which have focused on social decision-making and perspective taking across childhood and adolescent development using experimental games. We summarize results from developmental studies using variations of the Dictator Game, the Ultimatum Game, and the Trust Game. A special focus is given to the way cognitive control and perspective taking are implicated in social decision-making, and how these skills develop across adolescence. In addition, we describe insights from cognitive neuroscience studies concentrating on the role of brain regions important for cognitive control and perspective taking, such as the dorsolateral prefrontal cortex (DLPFC) and the temporal parietal junction (TPJ), in social decision-making in children, adolescents and adults. Together, the studies demonstrate a consistent pattern of both increasing strategic motivations and other-oriented concerns in social decision-making across development, which is confirmed by emerging contributions of DLPFC and TPJ. The combination of brain and behavior measures has the advantage of allowing for a deeper understanding of the separable processes involved in the emergence of advanced forms of social decision-making.

■ ADOLESCENCE AS AN IMPORTANT TIME FOR SOCIAL-AFFECTIVE CHANGES

Adolescence is a time of significant social-cognitive and affective changes, and encompasses several social challenges such as developing intimate friendships and gaining peer status (Dahl, 2004; Steinberg et al., 2008). This period is defined as the developmental phase between childhood and adulthood and spans from approximately ages 10 to 20 years. It starts with puberty, during which rising hormone levels trigger a cascade of physical and social-emotional changes, with different time courses for boys and girls (puberty starts approximately 1.5 years earlier for girls than for boys), and with the goal of preparing adolescents for later independence (Shirtcliff, Dahl, & Pollak, 2009). Puberty is followed by mid- to late adolescence, during which adolescents gradually attain mature social goals and eventually reach the legal age for adult responsibilities, such as drinking alcohol, financial independence, voting or getting a driver's license (Steinberg, 2008).

Several studies have reported that during adolescence there is a great improvement in mastery of many cognitive skills, such as the ability to keep multiple pieces of information in working memory (Luna, Padmanabhan, & O'Hearn, 2010), the ability to flexibly switch between multiple tasks (Crone, Bunge, van der Molen, &

Ridderinkhof, 2006) and the ability to inhibit impulsive actions (Durston et al., 2006). These developmental improvements have been captured under the umbrella term 'executive functions', which refers to the ability to keep relevant information online and irrelevant information out of mind in order to achieve long-term goals (Huizinga, Dolan, & van der Molen, 2006).

At the same time, however, it is well documented that during adolescence there is a myriad of changes in decision-making processes which are particularly sensitive to social context, such as increased risk-taking in the presence of friends (Gardner & Steinberg, 2005) and increased sensitivity to social rejection (Cillessen & Rose, 2005; Sebastian, Viding, Williams, & Blakemore, 2010). These developmental sensitivities to affective and social contexts lead to an intriguing paradox in adolescent development. That is to say, under some circumstances, adolescents are compliant, smart, and have the capacity to think about innovative and creative solutions for complex problems, and to think about problems from multiple perspectives. However, under other circumstances, adolescents can react impulsively, without thinking about future consequences of their actions, and show intensified reactions to emotional and social situations. This imbalance is thought to result in several advantages such as explorative learning and adaptive sensation-seeking, but can also lead to serious health problems such as drug abuse, delinquency or social withdrawal (Crone & Dahl, 2012).

Given the strong interplay between cognitive and social-affective development, adolescence is a very important transition period for the development of social values and concern for others. The development of social perspective-taking is one of the core milestones in human development. Perspective-taking is defined here as the ability to understand intentions and goals from a third-person point of view, and the core components mature before the age of 5 years, during which children develop a 'theory of mind' (Wellman, Cross, & Watson, 2001). However, after the age of 5 and particularly during adolescent development, there are continuous changes in how children and adolescents understand and consider intentions of others in social interactions. For example, recent experimental studies have shown that the basic ability to view a situation from the perspective of another person continues to develop in adolescence (Dumontheil, Apperly, & Blakemore, 2010). This is not surprising, given that adolescence is a period with pronounced changes in social orientation and it is likely that many of adults' norms and heuristics in social decision-making are being shaped during adolescence.

The links between cognitive and social development and their specific importance during adolescence have been emphasized already in traditional developmental theories. Selman's (Selman, 1980) work particularly sheds light on the development of perspective-taking and social cognitive abilities during adolescence and focuses particularly on the role of friendships in developing interpersonal understanding. According to his model, friendships are perceived from an egocentric perspective in early childhood; friends are playmates defined by proximity and have no personal thoughts and feelings (Level 0, undifferentiated, ages 3 to 7). The child grows to understand that others have needs and thoughts other than his/her own, but there is no merging and coordination of perspectives (Level 1, unilateral, ages 4 to 9). Due to major cognitive development, the child gains the ability to reflect on his/her behavior as perceived by others and thus recognizes the reciprocity of relationships but cannot yet perceive all perspectives simultaneously from a third-person perspective (Level 2, reciprocal, ages 6 to 12). It is in the next stage that the adolescent can take all perspectives simultaneously and perceive the dyadic relationship between him/her and the interaction partner as an outsider (Level 3, mutual, ages 9 to 15). Finally, the friendship can be recognized as a long-term interdependence and as a dynamic relationship with aspects of dependence and autonomy (Level 4, interdependent, beyond age 12). This framework facilitates the understanding of the development of interpersonal cognition as described by social information processing models (Crick & Dodge, 1994).

This chapter describes several novel lines of research, which have focused on the development of social decision-making and perspective-taking using social dilemma games. These games are particularly informative in studying core components of social decision-making, such as acting upon social norms, fairness considerations, strategic bargaining, trust and reciprocity. We will summarize these recent insights by focusing on variations of the Dictator Game, the Ultimatum Game, and the Trust Game. A special focus is given to the way perspective-taking and cognitive control are needed in social decision-making across adolescence, and how this development takes place.

The current chapter will also describe how social decision-making has been approached from a cognitive neuroscience perspective (Blakemore, 2008). One of the values of a cognitive neuroscience approach is that is allows us to examine how different brain areas contribute to different aspects of decision-making, thereby aiding in the process of dissociation of several subcomponents of decision-making, as well as their developmental trajectory. We will first introduce the current models of social brain development before moving to the development of social decision-making.

MODELS OF SOCIAL BRAIN DEVELOPMENT

Social neuroscience theories have suggested that social decisions made by adults are the result of at least two interacting systems: an emotion-inducing system, which activates primary emotions, and an emotion-regulating system, which is an evolutionarily younger system that distinguishes humans from other animals (Adolphs, 2003; Gallagher & Frith, 2003). The emotion-inducing system, which includes several regions such as the insula, the striatum and the amygdala, is involved in a quick detection of emotional context. The emotion-regulating system allows individuals to control impulses, mentalize about intentions of others and take other people's perspectives, and relies on frontal-cortical areas, including lateral and medial prefrontal cortex (PFC), and on the temporal cortex, including the temporal parietal junction (TPJ) (see Figure 9.1). Prior research has shown a dynamic interplay between these brain regions when making social decisions (Rilling & Sanfey, 2011).

Only recently, researchers have started to examine the development of neural regions involved in social dilemma tasks. The development of social information processing in general has previously been interpreted in the context of the Social

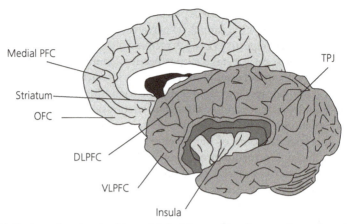

Figure 9.1 Brain regions involved in social decision-making (see text for explanation). PFC = prefrontal cortex. TPJ = temporal parietal junction. OFC = orbitofrontal cortex. DLPFC = dorsolateral prefrontal cortex. VLPFC = ventrolateral prefrontal cortex.

Information Processing Network (SIPN) model (Nelson, Leibenluft, McClure, & Pine, 2005). The SIPN model suggests that social information processing results from three interacting neural 'nodes,' a detection, affective and regulation node. The detection node, which comprises the intraparietal sulcus, superior temporal sulcus (STS), fusiform face area and temporal and occipital regions, detects social properties of a stimulus and is functionally mature before adolescence. The affective node, which includes limbic areas of the brain including the amygdala, ventral striatum, hypothalamus and orbitofrontal cortex, processes the emotional significance of a social stimulus and influences the behavioural and emotional responses to social stimuli. This node is particularly active in early adolescence, possibly under the influence of gonadal hormones. Finally, the cognitive-regulatory node, which consists of the PFC, is important for goal-directed behaviour, impulse control and theory of mind. The latter node is thought to have a gradual and slow developmental trajectory and continues to develop throughout adolescence, and recent studies suggest a similar developmental trajectory for the TPJ (Crone & Dahl, 2012).

These brain regions will be discussed and their developmental patterns will be described in the context of several social dilemma tasks. This integrative approach of combining social experimental, developmental and neuroscience research fields will lead to a new view on the development of social decision-making. In the sections later in this chapter, for each process we will start with a description of behavioral changes in adolescence on specific social dilemma tasks (1) followed by a section on neural regions involved and their developmental patterns (2).

THE DEVELOPMENT OF FAIRNESS CONSIDERATIONS

When making social decisions in which there is a division of goods between two individuals, two motivational aspects are important: interest in your own benefit and concern for others (Van Dijk & Vermunt, 2000). Over the past decades, much research has been conducted to understand the emergence of a sense of fairness across development and in different contexts. Here, we discuss the developmental patterns based on studies employing several experimental investigations of fairness considerations based on the following games, which are described in the order of their complexity: the Dictator Game, the Standard Ultimatum Game, the Mini Ultimatum Game, and the Hidden Ultimatum Game.

The Dictator Game

The Dictator Game (DG) is a simple two-player bargaining game, in which an allocator decides how to split a certain stake (for example, 10 coins). The recipient does not have the possibility to reject the offer made by the allocator, so the proposed division is always divided as suggested by the allocator. It is thought that this game captures an objective indication of the fairness orientation of the allocator (Van Dijk & Vermunt, 2000).

Studies that have compared DG donations in children (as young as 3–6 years), adolescents and adults show that participants of all age groups typically share part of the goods with others (e.g., 20–30%), indicating that they express a concern for the outcomes of others, but they typically do not share half of the goods (50%), indicating that they keep most of the stake for themselves when the recipient has no power (Benenson, Pascoe, & Radmore, 2007; Blake & Rand, 2010; Harbaugh, Krause, & Liday, 2003). The preference for equity (i.e., an equal split of goods), relative to a split which is better for self or a split which is better for the other player, increases between ages 3–8 years (Fehr, Bernhard & Rockenbach, 2008). At the age of approximately 8-9-years children no longer differ from adults in their DG donations to others (Gummerum, Keller, Takezawa, & Mata, 2008; Harbaugh, Krause, & Liday, 2003). Together, these studies suggest that a basic understanding of fairness is already present in early childhood and that fairness concerns develop before early adolescence (ages 8 to 9).

The Standard Ultimatum Game

The Standard Ultimatum Game (UG) is a more complex version of the DG, where the first player (i.e., the proposer) makes an offer to divide a certain stake, for example 10 coins, between the two players. The second player (i.e., the responder) can either accept or reject the proposed division. If the offer is accepted, the coins are divided according to the offer. In case the responder rejects the proposed offer, both players receive nothing (Güth, Schmittberger, & Schwarze, 1982). Thus, this game captures not only fairness, but also strategic motives, because the proposer will make an offer which he believes will be accepted by the responder.

Developmental studies have demonstrated that children between ages 7-10-years make lower offers compared to older adolescents and adults (Harbaugh et al., 2007). Interestingly, children already value equal distributions under the age of six, evidenced by the fact that they do reject unfair offers (Blake & McAuliffe, 2011; Harbaugh et al., 2007; Takagishi, Kameshima, Schug, Koizumi, & Yamagishi, 2010). However, the development of strategic behavior develops quickly between pre-adolescence (7-10-years) and continues to develop during mid- to late adolescence and adulthood, such that adolescents and adults offer strategically more in the UG than in the DG.

That is to say, the DG is often contrasted with the Standard UG in order to have a better understanding of developmental changes in true fairness considerations (DG behavior) and strategic fairness considerations (UG). A recent study that made this comparison showed that children aged 6-13-years did not differ from each other in DG offers. However, in the UG an obvious developmental difference appeared: with age there was an increase in the amount of coins offered by the proposer (Steinbeis, Bernhardt, & Singer, 2012). The increase in UG offers with increasing age is also reported in several other studies that have compared children with adolescents, or children with adults (Güroğlu et al., 2009; Leman, Keller, Takezawa, & Gummerum, 2009; Steinbeis et al., 2012; Harbaugh et al., 2007). These findings have been interpreted as an increase in strategic intentions and perspective-taking during late childhood and adolescence (Crone & Dahl, 2012).

Steinbeis et al. (2012) explained this developmental pattern in terms of an increase in cognitive control. The researchers asked participants to complete the Stop Signal Task in the same experimental setting. This is an inhibitory control task in which participants need to withhold a motoric response when a target changes color. Intriguingly, the individual differences in cognitive control correlated with individual differences in strategic behavior (UG vs. DG). This led to the conclusion that the development of strategic bargaining is possibly associated with a developmental increase in the ability to inhibit selfish impulses.

In summary, even though there is no obvious developmental difference in DG offers in adolescence, strategic fairness considerations as measured in the UG show consistent developmental changes. The largest transition takes place between age 7 and 13 but changes continue to emerge also between childhood and adulthood (Harbaugh et al., 2007; Leman, Keller, Takezawa, & Gummerum, 2008; Steinbeis et al., 2012). Based on these prior studies, we hypothesize that two processes contribute to these developmental changes, an increasing ability to control impulses (Steinbeis et al., 2012) and an increase in perspective-taking. The latter process has been studied in the DG and UG using several manipulations, which are described in more detail later in this chapter.

The Mini UG

The Mini-UG is a simplified version of the UG consisting of four conditions (Falk, Fehr, & Fischbacher, 2003). In each condition the proposer has a set of two fixed distributions to choose from; the responder can again either accept or reject proposed offers. The four conditions each contain the same unfair distribution of the stake (namely the 8/2 distribution with 8 coins for the proposer and 2 for the responder). In each of the four conditions, the alternative division varies: 1) a hyper-fair condition (2/8; 2 coins for the proposer and 8 for the responder), 2) a fair condition (5/5), 3) a hyper-unfair condition (10/0; 10 coins for the proposer and none for the responder), 4) a no-alternative condition (8/2 versus 8/2) (see Figure 9.2A for an example of conditions 1, 2 and 4).

Güroğlu, van den Bos, & Crone (2009) described 3 experiments: proposer mini-DG, proposer mini-UG, and a responder mini-UG, with the aim of providing insight in how fairness considerations, intentionality and strategic thinking develop across adolescent development. The outcomes of the proposer mini-DG once again confirmed the lack of developmental differences between 9-, 12-, 15-, and 18-year olds, consistent with prior studies. The outcomes of the second experiment, proposer mini-UG, showed that, even though strategic behavior was already present at the age of 9, a developmental difference was observed in bargaining behavior in the DG versus the UG. That is to say, in the hyper-fair condition, the 9-, and 12-year-olds made the same offers in both DG as UG, whereas 15-, and 18-year-olds made a clear distinction between the 2 games, which manifested itself in higher offers (more 2/8 offers) in the UG. Finally, results of the responder mini-UG demonstrated that intentions of proposers behind unfair offers were not taken into account in 9-year-olds, whereas from the age of 12 onwards, the rejection rates were influenced by the different options that were available to the proposer. For example, adolescents rejected unfair offers more often when the proposer had a fair distribution as alternative compared to when the proposer had no alternative. Together, these results were taken as **evidence for increased perspective-taking** in adolescence, which resulted in more strategic bargaining.

The Hidden Ultimatum Game

A second useful paradigm to make a distinction between altruistic and strategic considerations is the Hidden Ultimatum Game (Van Dijk, De Cremer, & Handgraaf, 2004). Hidden information means that the **responder is only** informed about a part of the information that is proclaimed to the proposer, whereby the proposer has the ability to use this additional information to his/her own advantage. For example, it can be the case that the proposer has 10 coins to share with the responder, but the responder thinks that there are only 8 coins in the game, and this condition is contrasted with conditions in which there are 10 coins to share with the responder, which is known by both parties (see Figure 9.2B for an example trial).

In case of **complete information conditions** where all information is visible to both parties, offers increased with age (Overgaauw, Güroğlu, & Crone, 2012): an outcome that is consistent to those reported for the standard UG. In contrast, when the proposer makes an offer in the case of hidden information conditions, he/she might be considering the following two options: 1) making an **honest** and thus *truly* **fair offer** based on the total number of coins available (e.g., an offer of 5 coins in this case) or 2) **making a lower offer** based on the number of coins visible to the other player and thus maximizing his/her outcome. This additional information provides the proposer with the opportunity to act with a focus on self-interest maximization where at the same time he/she can make an offer that is *seemingly* fair (e.g., offering 4 coins in this case and keeping the two extra coins for him/herself) (Van Dijk, et al., 2004).

Our findings show that the preference for enlarging one's own outcome by concealing the hidden information is already present in children. Even children from the age of 8 are able to act strategically by using information of hidden coins in their own advantage (Overgaauw, et al., 2012). However, we also found clear differences between children and adults. Children showed only a small decrease in the number of coins offered in the hidden information conditions compared to offers in complete information conditions. Adults, on the contrary, showed a clear distinction between the different conditions by making higher offers in complete information conditions. In other words, in the hidden information condition adults behave in a self-interested, thus strategic, way and make lower offers.

In sum, investigations of several variations of the UG show that there is more self-oriented bargaining behavior before the age of 8 years and increasing understanding of strategic behavior during adolescence. Together, these studies suggest that cognitive control and perspective-taking may be important components of the development of fairness considerations, such that adults inhibit selfish impulses and show more intentionality understanding.

■ NEURAL SUBSTRATES OF FAIRNESS CONSIDERATIONS

Neuroscientific analyses of the standard UG show that an emotion area, the insula, and a regulation area in the PFC, the dorsolateral (DL) PFC, were active when participants experienced unfair decisions by their interaction partners (Sanfey, Rilling, Aronson, Nystrom, & Cohen, 2003). The insula has previously been implicated in primary emotions such as disgust, whereas the DLPFC has been implicated in goal-directed cognitive control (Rilling & Sanfey, 2011). In the study reported by Sanfey et al. (2003), the insula was more active when recipients rejected unfair offers, reflecting the potential emotional basis for rejecting unfairness. In contrast, DLPFC was active when recipients rejected *and* accepted offers, possibly reflecting the cognitive basis of accumulating money. This difference was only observed when participants were playing with another person, and not when they were playing with a computer, emphasizing the social nature of this effect.

The importance of the DLPFC for the cognitive goal of accumulating money was confirmed using transcranial magnetic stimulation (TMS) studies, by showing that temporally altering neuron firing in this region results in an increase in acceptance of unfair offers in humans (Knoch, Pascual-Leone, Meyer, Treyer, & Fehr, 2006). Interestingly, a decision-making game which focused on cooperation rather than rejection (The Prisoners Dilemma Game) demonstrated that the nucleus accumbens, a region in the limbic area which is traditionally associated with reward sensitivity, is more active following mutual cooperation (Rilling, Sanfey, Aronson, Nystrom, & Cohen, 2004). Thus, rejection of unfair proposals and cooperation seem to depend on the same neural mechanisms as those that are sensitive to basic emotional signals of disgust and reward.

A developmental neuroimaging study that compared the UG with the DG, for which the behavioral data were described earlier, showed that children aged 6-13-years activated DLPFC when playing the UG as proposer, but this activation was stronger for the older children (Steinbeis et al., 2012). The extent of this activation correlated with both performance on the Stop Signal Task and strategic behavior (higher offers in UG compared to DG), leading to the conclusion that the development of impulse control is an important component in the development of strategic fairness.

Güroğlu, van den Bos, van Dijk, Rombouts, & Crone (2011) reported partly overlapping findings when they asked children, adolescents and adults to play the mini-UG as responders in the scanner. Consistent with their prior behavioral report (Güroğlu et al., 2009), children rejected unfair offers as often in the condition in which the first player had no alternative as when the first player had a fair alternative, whereas adults rejected unfair offers much less often in the no-alternative condition compared to when there was a fair alternative. In addition, when rejecting unfair offers in the no-alternative condition, adults showed activation in DLPFC and TPJ, regions previously associated with impulse control and perspective-taking, respectively. This activation was less extensive in children and emerged across adolescent development (Güroğlu et al., 2011).

Together, these studies demonstrate that social decision-making is regulated by both emotion-inducing and emotion-regulating brain areas, which make independent contributions to the decision process. These different brain areas have separable developmental time courses, with a relatively slow development of brain areas implicated in impulse control and perspective-taking, such as the DLPFC and the TPJ.

THE DEVELOPMENT OF TRUST AND RECIPROCITY

The different UG versions described previously allow us to study fairness and self-interest in a simple experimental setting. However, in real life, one often needs to make decisions about fairness based on whether one can trust that the other person will reciprocate actions of fairness. These situations put high demands on our ability to think about the other person's intentions (or to take another person's perspective). A task that captures the essentials of trust and reciprocity is the Trust Game (TG) (e.g., Malhotra, 2004; Snijders, 1996; Snijders, & Keren, G., 1999). In this game two players are paired with each other as decision-makers (a trustor and a trustee) over single or numerous trials. The trustor typically makes the first decision, and the trustee observes the trustor's decision before making his/her own decision. More specifically, the trustor can choose between two options: a certain monetary outcome (the "no trust" option), in which both players receive a small reward (e.g., both receive 5 euros), and an uncertain choice (the "trust" option). When the trustor opts for the trust option, the trustee can choose between two options. Either the trustee decides to reciprocate trust, in which case both receive a relatively large reward (e.g., the trustor receives 18 euros and the trustee receives 22 euros) or the trustee decides to defect trust, in which case the trustor receives almost nothing (e.g., 1 euro) and the second player receives a large reward (e.g., 39 euros). The TG is a task that is very suitable to capture the risk to trust on the one hand, and reciprocity or defection on the other hand (see Figure 9.2C for an example).

Developmental studies using the TG showed that trust increases in early adolescence (van den Bos, Westenberg, van Dijk, & Crone, 2010), but most importantly, there is a protracted development of risk-dependent reciprocity. That is to say, when the trustor takes a large risk by trusting the trustee (for example, the trustor may lose a lot when the trustee defects trust), adults typically reciprocate more often than when the trustor does not take a risk (see Figure 9.2C for an example). This pattern suggests that in order to generate positive reciprocal exchanges, or realize "positive reciprocity" (McCabe, Houser, Ryan, Smith, & Trouard, 2001), it is necessary to take a risk or be vulnerable in favor of greater postponed gains from mutual cooperation.

In the study by van den Bos et al. (2010), children aged 9-10-years did not yet demonstrate this risk sensitivity, and across adolescent development (12-22-years) this risk sensitvity slowly emerged (van den Bos et al., 2010). These findings can be interpreted in the context of slowly emerging perspective-taking skills, which increasingly play a role in adolescents' decisions in social interactions. Taken together, the number of studies using the TG to study developmental differences in trust and reciprocity is still relatively small, but studies consistently report a developmental increase in trust and reciprocity in early adolescence, with an increased contribution of perspective-taking in later adolescence and early adulthood.

NEURAL SUBSTRATES OF TRUST DECISIONS

Neuroscientific studies using the TG have demonstrated that in adults, the decision to trust is associated with increased activation in medial PFC when the interaction partner is a human compared to a computer (McCabe, Houser, Ruan, Smith, & Trouard, 2001). Medial PFC is a brain region that is active when individuals think about the mental states of others as well as their own state of mind, or when there is a need to explain and predict behaviors of others by attributing independent mental states, such as thoughts, beliefs and desires (Adolphs, 2003). Several neuroimaging studies have also reported increased activation in medial PFC for social cooperation (Rilling et al., 2002), competition (Gallagher, Jack, Roepstorff, & Frith, 2002), and moral judgement (Greene, Nystrom, Engell, Darley, & Cohen, 2004). Therefore, the medial PFC may have a more general role for predicting future outcomes of interactions.

When adult participants played the TG as trustees, they showed activation in a different set of brain regions, namely in DLPFC and TPJ, regions previously associated with impulse control and perspective-taking (van den Bos, van Dijk, Westenberg, Rombouts, & Crone, 2009). Furthermore, a developmental study demonstrated that the extent of activation in these areas increases across adolescence. Notably, activation in these areas also correlated with individual differences in risk sensitivity, reinforcing the notion that these regions are

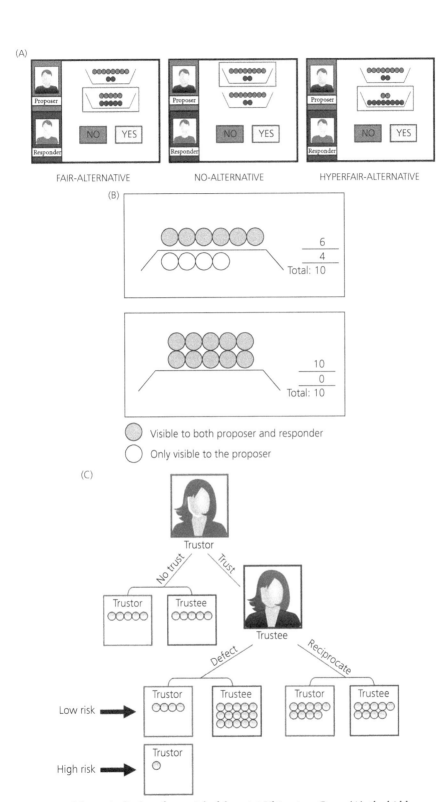

Figure 9.2 Schematic display of one trial of the mini Ultimatum Game (A), the hidden Ultimatum Game (B), and the Trust Game with risk manipulation (C).

important for perspective-taking (van den Bos, van Dijk, Westenberg, Rombouts, & Crone, 2011).

Thus, the neuroscientific studies on the TG provide a highly comparable set of results as what emerged from the UG studies. Receiving unfair offers and receiving trust in one-shot dilemma games results in increased activation in DLPFC and TPJ, which was interpreted in the context that both processes require perspective-taking and cognitive control. Indeed, activation in these regions correlates with behavioral measures of perspective-taking and comes increasingly online during adolescent development (see also Crone & Dahl, 2012).

REPEATED INTERACTIONS

One-shot interactions are crucial for the elicitation of a clean measure of social preferences, i.e., other-regarding motives aimed at increasing or decreasing another individual's welfare (Fehr, 2009). However, social interactions in our daily lives are rarely single encounters. The following section shows that repeated interactions in social dilemma games are a useful method to gain further insights on developmental changes in social learning, e.g., how adolescents learn to deal with negative social experiences, such as ruptured cooperation or social exclusion.

Learning to Bargain

Adult UG bargainers adjust their behavior to their interaction partners' responses and take into account information about what kind of proposals future interaction partners might accept or reject (Duffy & Feltovich, 1999; Fehr & Fischbacher, 2003). Harbaugh et al. (2007) examined the development of these tendencies by investigating how children and adolescents (ages 8–18) learn to bargain in a repeated UG. The experiment consisted of two treatments in which a proposer interacted with five different responders successively in either: 1) a "limited-information" treatment, during which participants could learn about the acceptability of their proposals through direct experience with rejection or acceptance by a responder with whom they would not interact again, or: 2) a "full-information" treatment, during which the participants were additionally informed about what kind of proposals their classmates made and whether these proposals were rejected or not.

The results demonstrated that children and adolescents, like adults, make higher proposals following a rejection and offer less in response to past acceptances. Furthermore, larger proposals made by other proposers led to larger own proposals in the next round, suggesting a role for conformity or social referencing in bargaining behavior in children and adolescents. However, unlike adults (Duffy & Feltovich, 1999), children and adolescents did not use information about whether their peers' proposals were accepted or rejected into their offers. Based on the notion that adult proposers learn from information about which offers from other proposers get rejected, it is likely that this capacity develops during adolescence, but this should be confirmed in future research in which these age groups are directly compared.

Learning to Trust

A related question concerns how adolescents and adults learn to trust when they interact repeatedly with the same interaction partner. Van den Bos, van Dijk and Crone (2011) previously investigated this by giving participants in distinct phases of adolescent development (11-year-old early adolescents, 16-year-old mid-adolescents and 21-year-old late adolescents/young adults) the opportunity to play a repeated TG with three unknown peers who were in fact fictive players with preprogrammed behavior. The participants encountered a trustworthy, neutral and an untrustworthy interaction partner, who reciprocated in 80%, 50% and 20% of the trials, respectively.

Results showed that participants in each age group learned to trust the trustworthy player the most and the untrustworthy player the least. However, the early adolescents showed no change in strategy during the game, whereas the 16-year olds and young adults started to trust the trustworthy player more and the untrustworthy player less. Furthermore, when confronted with betrayal, 11-year-olds mainly kept most of the money to themselves in the following trial instead of sharing again. Older participants, in contrast, more often tried to repair this breach of trust by trusting the player again, despite being defected on the previous trial.

Thus, an increasingly better understanding of the intentions of others and the consequences for others contribute to developmental changes in relation-specific trust.

Punishment and Compensation

What could underlie these developmental increases in the tendency to repair ruptured cooperation? Van den Bos et al. (2011) hypothesized that the development of the ability to control negative emotions associated with betrayal might account for the age-related decline in negative reactions to violated trust. To test this idea, participants were given the opportunity to punish the three different interaction partners in a costly punishment game (Fehr & Gächter, 2002). They could invest some of their earnings from the TG to decrease the outcomes of the other players. For each Euro paid by the participants 3 Euros were subtracted from the other player's profits. The results demonstrated that the participants punished the least trustworthy player the most, and that the 11-year-olds invested more money to punish the untrustworthy player than the mid-adolescents and the adults. Developmental and individual differences in punishment behavior were associated with self-reported levels of anger toward the untrustworthy player. A mediation analysis demonstrated that older participants punished the untrustworthy player less and that this relation was mediated by decreases in anger.

A similar developmental trend in punishing behavior was found in a study investigating the development of sensitivity to social exclusion and punishment of the peers who initiated the exclusion (Gunther Moor et al., 2012). Participants in this study were first included by two peers in a virtual ball-tossing game called Cyberball (Williams, Cheung, & Choi, 2000). In a second game of Cyberball, in which they were coupled with two novel players, they received the ball once at the start of the game, but they were excluded from the ball game in all of the following trials. A myriad of studies has shown that exclusion in Cyberball is as painful as real-life exclusion and leads to the threat of vital needs, such as the need for control and the need to belong as well as lowered mood (Williams, 2007). Following exclusion, people selectively decrease prosocial behavior toward the people who excluded them (Hillebrandt, Sebastian, & Blakemore, 2011).

To investigate developmental differences in the punishment of the peers responsible for exclusion, early adolescents (age 10–12), mid-adolescents (age 14–16) and young adults (18–25) played two games of Cyberball followed by a DG in which they could allocate money to the people who included them (the includers), the people who excluded them (the excluders) and people they had not interacted with before (neutral others). Both adolescents and young adults offered an equal split of the stake to the includers and the neutral others, but selectively punished the excluders by offering them less than half of the stake. Interestingly, young adults behaved slightly more prosocial toward the excluders by more frequent allocations of 40% of the stake instead of allocating 20% like the early- and mid-adolescents (Gunther Moor et al., 2012).

Could this developmental trend be the same in situations in which one is not the victim of a norm violation himself or herself? In a recent study, we investigated this question by giving participants the opportunity to witness an instance of social exclusion as opposed to being excluded themselves (Will, Crone, Van den Bos, & Güroğlu, 2013). In so doing, we were able to investigate developmental differences in both third-party punishment of the excluders and prosocial behavior toward a victim of social exclusion. Participants (age 9 to 22) were first included in a game of Cyberball by two includers and then observed the exclusion of a peer (i.e. the victim) by two excluders. Subsequently, they played two economic games in which they divided money between themselves and the includers, the excluders, and the victim: a standard DG and an Altruistic Punishment/Compensation Game (APCG) (Leliveld, van Dijk, & van Beest, 2012). In the APCG, participants can either do nothing or invest some money, which is then multiplied by 3 and either added to (compensation) or subtracted from (punishment) the other player's total.

The results from the DG showed that there was an age-related increase in money allocated to the victim from age 9 to age 22. Interestingly, instead of a linear decline in punishment behavior with age, we observed a quadratic age-related trend, such that 9-year-olds did not punish the excluders (i.e., they allocated about 40–50% of the stake to both the includers and the victim as well as the excluders). Punishment severity then increased between age 11 and 16 and declined in young adulthood (age 22). Results from the APCG showed the same developmental trajectory, suggesting that the willingness to punish excluders is the same when it is costly to punish. Individual differences in an index of 'state affective perspective-taking' (an estimate of the victim's mood controlled for one's own mood following observed exclusion) predicted both more pronounced compensation of the victims and stronger punishment of the excluders. These results suggest that with increasing age, adolescents are willing to forfeit bigger rewards in order to punish excluders and to compensate victims of social exclusion and that taking the perspective of the victim enhances these decisions.

■ NEURAL CORRELATES OF REPEATED INTERACTIONS

In the prior sections, we summarized studies showing that decisions about trust, reciprocity and fairness can be modulated by prior experiences with people we interact with. When comparing neural activation during repeated interactions, several brain regions respond in a similar way as when playing one-shot games, but there is also additional involvement of regions which are important for learning. For example, Delgado and colleagues (2005) showed in an fMRI study how decisions in a TG and the neural circuitry underlying them can be modulated by the perceived moral character of the trustees. Participants played an iterated TG with three different interaction partners. Each of these players was described to the participants in short biographies that portrayed one player as morally good, one as neutral and one as morally bad. The results showed that despite the fact that each player reciprocated 50% of the time, participants still trusted the morally good partner more often than the other two partners toward the end of the experiment, suggesting that moral information about the people that we interact with can bypass rational taxation of their behavior. Delgado and colleagues (2005) showed that the caudate, a region previously associated with learning, differentiated between positive (being reciprocated) and negative (being defected) feedback during the TG (see also King-Casas et al., 2005). This response was attenuated when the participants interacted with the morally good and bad trustees. This indicates a mechanism for the way moral perceptions might bias our decision-making.

In order to investigate the neural correlates of interactions with personally familiar others, Güroğlu, Klapwijk, & Will (2013) recently conducted a study with young adults (age 20 years) from occupational universities. Sociometric nominations in their classrooms were obtained in order to gain information on the participants' positive (i.e., a friend) and negative (i.e., an antagonist) relationships. After the nominations, participants played multiple rounds of the TG as a trustor with three different interaction partners: two classmates (i.e., the friend and the antagonist) and a confederate who was a third anonymous peer they just met before the scan session. Preliminary findings showed that independent of interaction partner, there was activation in the insula during no-trust choices, and in the medial PFC during trust choices. Interestingly, interactions with the friend involved higher activation of the TPJ and the medial PFC than interactions with the antagonist, suggesting more mentalizing about other during interactions with friends (see also Denny, Kober, Wager, & Ochsner, 2012; Van Overwalle, 2009). Finally, the caudate was also more activated during positive feedback (i.e., reciprocate) following trust choices, as well as during negative feedback (i.e., defect) following no-trust choices, which again signifies the role of the caudate in feedback learning in a social context.

Taken together, the analysis of neural regions involved in repeated interactions again confirms the role of TPJ when there is a need for perspective-taking, such as when thinking about consequences for friends. The repeated interactions illustrate that brain regions, which have previously been associated with non-social learning, such as the caudate, are also involved in social learning. This set of studies illustrates the potential use of real life interactions with known others as a tool for probing the mechanisms of how social interactions with specific interaction partners develop into relationships over time.

IMPLICATIONS AND FUTURE DIRECTIONS

In this chapter, we summarized studies which together show that a basic concern for others is already present from a very young age. That is to say, when administering the DG, even young children already share a proportion of their goods with others, and in this sense they do not differ from adolescents and adults. However, when there is a need for strategic fairness or trust, young children do not yet adapt their social considerations to this changing context as well as adults. This ability emerges slowly during late childhood and continues to refine in adolescence, confirming that this is an important time for the fine-tuning of social considerations in the road to adulthood (Crone & Dahl, 2012).

In addition to the behavioral changes, the investigation of neural patterns revealed a consistent contribution of cortical areas which have previously been associated with cognitive control (DLPFC) and perspective-taking (TPJ) (Rilling & Sanfey, 2011). We showed in this chapter that across paradigms, these regions show a developmental increase in contribution to strategic and other-oriented motives in decision-making. Thus, it is likely that these processes and the underlying neural mechanisms explain a large proportion of variance in the development of fairness and trust considerations.

An interesting new direction in developmental neuroscience studies, which has not yet been well covered in the decision-making studies, is the elevated sensitivity to risks, rewards and losses in adolescence. There are several studies that have demonstrated that in simple reward processing paradigms (such as when winning money in a gambling task) the caudate/striatum is more active in adolescents compared to children and adults. This has been interpreted as an increased sensitivity to affective stimuli, possibly due to the large rise in gonadal hormones associated with puberty (Nelson et al., 2005). Interestingly, these elevated activations in the caudate/striatum are observed to a greater extent under social affective circumstances, for example adolescents take more risks in the presence of peers (Chein, Albert, O'Brien, Uckert, & Steinberg, 2011).

Currently, it is not yet well understood how these variations in affective levels and associated brain activity in the caudate/striatum influence social decision-making behavior and activation in other brain regions such as the DLPFC and TPJ. However, it is likely that these neural responses in affective brain areas influence the way adolescents adapt flexibly to changing social contexts in daily life. One way to investigate this is by studying effects of communicated emotions of others on social decision-making (Lelieveld, Van Dijk, Van Beest, Steinel, & Van Kleef, 2011), by manipulating peer status (Muscatell et al., 2012), or by studying repeated interactions with personally familiar others (Güroğlu & Klapwijk, 2012). The overview of repeated interaction studies revealed that especially the caudate/striatum has an important role in social learning (Delgado et al., 2005), thus, the same region showing elevated responses to rewards in mid-adolescence. This leads to several compelling questions for future research, such as when and how adolescence is a period for developing other-oriented concern and prosocial behavior on the one hand and strategic play on the other hand.

Taken together, it is likely that changes in perspective-taking and cognitive control influence the way social decisions are made during adolescent development. However, at the same time, adolescents navigate this complex phase in life well. For example, new friendships are formed and there is a rapid adaptation to changing social cultures. One underlying mechanism may be this heightened sensitivity to affective cues, which may help them to adapt quickly and flexibly to changing social demands. Future studies should examine how sensitivity to reward and punishment changes during adolescence, and whether there are unique opportunities in adolescent development for attaining status and adaptively exploring their social world. Investigating the role of reward sensitivity in the social decision-making processes in the peer context might be the challenge of studies in the near future.

REFERENCES

Adolphs, R. (2003). Cognitive neuroscience of human social behaviour. *Nature Reviews: Neuroscience, 4*(3), 165–178.
Benenson, J. F., Pascoe, J., & Radmore, N. (2007). Children's altruistic behavior in the dictator game. *Evolution and Human Behavior, 28,* 168–175.
Blake, P. R., & McAuliffe, K. (2011). "I had so much it didn't seem fair": Eight-year-olds reject two forms of inequity. *Cognition, 120*(2), 215–224.
Blake, P. R., & Rand, D. G. (2010). Currency value moderates equity preference among young children. *Evolution and Human Behavior, 31,* 210–218.
Blakemore, S. J. (2008). The social brain in adolescence. *Nature Reviews:Neuroscience, 9*(4), 267–277.
Chein, J., Albert, D., O'Brien, L., Uckert, K., & Steinberg, L. (2011). Peers increase adolescent risk taking by enhancing activity in the brain's reward circuitry. *Dev Sci, 14*(2), F1–F10.
Cillessen, A. H., & Rose, A. J. (2005). Understanding popularity in the peer system. *Current Directions in Psychological Science, 14,* 102–105.
Crick, N. R., & Dodge, K. A. (1994). A review and reformulation of social information-processing mechanisms in children's social adjustment. *Psychological Bulletin, 115,* 74–101.
Crone, E. A., Bunge, S. A., van der Molen, M. W., & Ridderinkhof, K. R. (2006). Switching between tasks and responses: a developmental study. *Dev Sci, 9*(3), 278–287.
Crone, E. A., & Dahl, R. E. (2012). Understanding adolescence as a period of social-affective engagement and goal flexibility. *Nature Reviews: Neuroscience, 13*(9), 636–650.
Dahl, R. E. (2004). Adolescent brain development: A period of vulnerabilities and opportunities. *Annals of the New York Academy of Sciences, 1021,* 1–22.

Delgado, M., Frank, R., & Phelps, E. (2005). Perceptions of moral character modulate the neural systems of reward during the trust game. *Nature Neuroscience, 8*(11), 1611-1618.

Denny, B. T., Kober, H., Wager, T. D., & Ochsner, K. N. (2012). A Meta-analysis of functional neuroimaging studies of self- and other judgments reveals a spatial gradient for mentalizing in medial prefrontal cortex. *Journal of Cognitive Neuroscience, 24*(8), 1742-1752.

Duffy, J., & Feltovich, N. (1999). Does observation of others affect learning in strategic environments? An experimental study. *International Journal of Game Theory, 28*(1), 131-152.

Dumontheil, I., Apperly, I. A., & Blakemore, S. J. (2010). Online usage of theory of mind continues to develop in late adolescence. *Developmental Science, 13*(2), 331-338.

Durston, S., Davidson, M. C., Tottenham, N., Galvan, A., Spicer, J., Fossella, J. A., & Casey, B. J. (2006). A shift from diffuse to focal cortical activity with development. *Dev Sci, 9*(1), 1-8.

Falk, A., Fehr, E., & Fischbacher, U. (2003). On the nature of fair behavior. *Economic Inquiry, 41*, 20-26.

Fehr, E. (2009). Social preferences and the brain. In P. W. Glimcher, C. F. Camerer, E. Fehr & R. Poldrack (Eds.), *Neuroeconomics: Decision Making and the Brain* (pp. 215-232). New York: Elsevier.

Fehr, E., & Fischbacher, U. (2003). The nature of human altruism. *Nature, 425*(6960), 785-791.

Fehr, E., Bernhard, H., & Rockenbach, B. (2008). Egalitarianism in young children. *Nature, 454*, 1079-1083.

Fehr, E., & Gächter, S. (2002). Altruistic punishment in humans. *Nature, 415*(6868), 137-140.

Gallagher, H. L., & Frith, C. D. (2003). Functional imaging of 'theory of mind'. *Trends Cogn Sci, 7*, 77-83.

Gallagher, H. L., Jack, A. I., Roepstorff, A., & Frith, C. D. (2002). Imaging the intentional stance in a competitive game. *Neuroimage, 16*, 814-821.

Gardner, M., & Steinberg, L. (2005). Peer influence on risk taking, risk preference, and risky decision making in adolescence and adulthood: An experimental study. *Dev Psychol, 41*(4), 625-635.

Greene, J. D., Nystrom, L. E., Engell, A. D., Darley, J. M., & Cohen, J. D. (2004). The neural basis of cognitive conflict and control in moral judgement. *Neuron, 44*, 389-400.

Gummerum, M., Keller, M., Takezawa, M., & Mata, J. (2008). To give or not to give: children's and adolescents' sharing and moral negotiations in economic decision situations. *Child Development, 79*, 562-576.

Gunther Moor, B., Güroğlu, B., Op de Macks, Z. A., Rombouts, S. A. R. B., Van der Molen, M. W., & Crone, E. A. (2012). Social exclusion and punishment of excluders: Neural correlates and developmental trajectories. *Neuroimage, 59*(1), 708-717.

Güroğlu, B., & Klapwijk, E. T. (2012). Neural correlates of social interactions with peers. *Manuscript in preparation.*

Güroğlu, B., Klapwijk, E.T., & Will, G.-J. (2013). Trust all, love a few: Neural correlates of social interactions with peers. *Manuscript in preparation.*

Güroğlu, B., van den Bos, W., & Crone, E. A. (2009). Fairness considerations: increasing understanding of intentionality during adolescence. *Journal of Experimental Child Psychology, 104*, 398-409.

Güroğlu, B., van den Bos, W., van Dijk, E., Rombouts, S. A., & Crone, E. A. (2011). Dissociable brain networks involved in development of fairness considerations: Understanding intentionality behind unfairness. *Neuroimage*, *57*, 634–641.

Güth, W., Schmittberger, R., & Schwarze, B. (1982). An experimental analysis of ultimatum bargaining. *Journal of Economic Behavior & Organization*, *3*, 367.

Harbaugh, W. T., Krause, K., & Liday, S. G. (2003). Bargaining by Children. Working paper.

Harbaugh, W. T., Krause, K., & Vesterlund, L. (2007). Learning to bargain. *Journal of Economic Psychology*, *29*, 127–142.

Hillebrandt, H., Sebastian, C., & Blakemore, S. J. (2011). Experimentally induced social inclusion influences behavior on trust games. *Cognitive Neuroscience*, *2*(1), 27–33.

Huizinga, M., Dolan, C. V., & van der Molen, M. W. (2006). Age-related change in executive function: developmental trends and a latent variable analysis. *Neuropsychologia*, *44*(11), 2017–2036.

King-Casas, B., Tomlin, D., Anen, C., Camerer, C. F., Quartz, S. R., & Montague, P. R. (2005). Getting to know you: Reputation and trust in a two-person economic exchange. *Science*, *308*(5718), 78–83.

Knoch, D., Pascual-Leone, A., Meyer, K., Treyer, V., & Fehr, E. (2006). Diminishing reciprocal fairness by disrupting the right prefrontal cortex. *Science*, *314* (5800), 829–832.

Lelieveld, G. J., Van Dijk, E., Van Beest, I., Steinel, W., & Van Kleef, G. A. (2011). Disappointed in you, angry about your offer: Distinct negative emotions induce concessions via different mechanisms. *Journal of Experimental Social Psychology*, *47*, 635–641.

Leliveld, M. C., van Dijk, E., & van Beest, I. (2012). Punishing and compensating others at your own expense: The role of empathic concern on reactions to distributive injustice. *European Journal of Social Psychology*, *42*(2), 135–140.

Leman, P. J., Keller, M., Takezawa, M., & Gummerum, M. (2008). Children's and adolescents' decisions about sharing money with others. *Social Development*, *18*, 711–727.

Leman, P. J., Keller, M., Takezawa, M., & Gummerum, M. (2009). Children's and Adolescents' Decisions about Sharing Money with Others. *Social Development*, *18*, 711–727.

Luna, B., Padmanabhan, A., & O'Hearn, K. (2010). What has fMRI told us about the development of cognitive control through adolescence? *Brain Cogn*, *72*(1), 101–113.

Malhotra, D. (2004). Trust and reciprocity decisions: The different perspectives of trusters and trusted parties. *Organizational Behavior and Human Decision Processes*, *94*, 61–73.

McCabe, K., Houser, D., Ruan, L., Smith, V., & Trouard, T. (2001). A functional imaging study of cooperation in two-person reciprocal exchange. *Proceedings of the National Academy of Sciences of the United States of America*, *98*, 11832–11835.

McCabe, K., Houser, D., Ryan, L., Smith, V., & Trouard, T. (2001). A functional imaging study of cooperation in two-person reciprocal exchange. *Proc Natl Acad Sci U S A*, *98*(20), 11832–11835.

Muscatell, K. A., Morelli, S. A., Falk, E. B., Way, B. M., Pfeifer, J. H., Galinsky, A. D., & Eisenberger, N. I. (2012). Social status modulates neural activity in the mentalizing network. *Neuroimage*, *60*(3), 1771–1777.

Nelson, E., Leibenluft, E., McClure, E. B., & Pine, D. S. (2005). The social re-orietnation of adolescence: a neuroscience perspective on the process and its relation to psychopathology. *Psychological Medicine*, *35*, 163–174.

Overgaauw, S., Güroğlu, B., & Crone, E. A. (2012). Fairness considerations when I know more than you do: Developmental Comparisons. *Frontiers in Psychology*, *3*, 424

Rilling, J. K., Gutman, D. A., Zeh, T. R., Pagnoni, G., Berns, G. S., & Kilts, C. D. (2002). A neural basis for social cooperation. *Neuron*, *35*, 395–405.

Rilling, J. K., & Sanfey, A. G. (2011). The neuroscience of social decision-making. *Annu Rev Psychol, 62*, 23–48.

Rilling, J. K., Sanfey, A. G., Aronson, J. A., Nystrom, L. E., & Cohen, J. D. (2004). The neural correlates of theory of mind within interpersonal interactions. *Neuroimage, 22*, 1694–1703.

Sanfey, A. G., Rilling, J. K., Aronson, J. A., Nystrom, L. E., & Cohen, J. D. (2003). The neural basis of economic decision-making in the Ultimatum Game. *Science, 300*, 1755–1758.

Sebastian, C., Viding, E., Williams, K. D., & Blakemore, S. J. (2010). Social brain development and the affective consequences of ostracism in adolescence. *Brain and cognition, 72*(1), 134–145.

Selman, R. L. (1980). *The growth of interpersonal understanding.* New York: Academic Press.

Shirtcliff, E. A., Dahl, R. E., & Pollak, S. D. (2009). Pubertal development: Correspondence between hormonal and physical development. *Child Dev, 80*(2), 327–337.

Snijders, C. (1996). *Trust and commitments.* Utrecht University.

Snijders, C., & Keren, G. (1999). Determinants of trust. In D. V. Budescu & I. Erev (Eds.), *Games and Human Behavior: Essays in Honor of Amnon Rapoport* (pp. 355–385). Mahway, NJ: Erlbaum.

Steinbeis, N., Bernhardt, B. C., & Singer, T. (2012). Impulse control and underlying functions of the left DLPFC mediate age-related and age-independent individual differences in strategic social behavior. *Neuron, 73*(5), 1040–1051.

Steinberg, L. (2008). *Adolescence.* New York: McGraw-Hill.

Steinberg, L., Albert, D., Cauffman, E., Banich, M., Graham, S., & Woolard, J. (2008). Age differences in sensation seeking and impulsivity as indexed by behavior and self-report: Evidence for a dual systems model. *Dev Psychol, 44*(6), 1764–1778.

Steinbeis, N., Bernhardt, B. C., & Singer, T. (2012). Impulse control and underlying functions of the left DLPFC mediate age-related and age-independent individual differences in strategic social behavior. *Neuron, 73*, 1040–1051.

Takagishi, H., Kameshima, S., Schug, J., Koizumi, M., & Yamagishi, T. (2010). Theory of mind enhances preference for fairness. *Journal of Experimental Child Psychology, 105*(1–2), 130–137.

van den Bos, W., van Dijk, E., Westenberg, M., Rombouts, S. A., & Crone, E. A. (2009). What motivates repayment? Neural correlates of reciprocity in the Trust Game. *Soc Cogn Affect Neurosci, 4*(3), 294–304.

van den Bos, W., van Dijk, E., Westenberg, M., Rombouts, S. A., & Crone, E. A. (2011). Changing brains, changing perspectives: The neurocognitive development of reciprocity. *Psychol Sci, 22*(1), 60–70.

van den Bos, W., Westenberg, M., van Dijk, E., & Crone, E. A. (2010). Development of trust and reciprocity in adolescence. *Cognitive Development, 25*, 90–102.

van den Bos, W., van Dijk, E., & Crone, E. A. (2011). Learning whom to trust in repeated social interactions: A developmental perspective. *Group Processes & Intergroup Relations, 15*, 243–256.

Van Dijk, E., De Cremer, D., & Handgraaf, M. J. J. (2004). Social value orientations and the strategic use of fairness in ultimatum bargaining. *Journal of Experimental Social Psychology, 40*, 697–707.

Van Dijk, E., & Vermunt, R. (2000). Strategy and fairness in social decision making: Sometimes it pays to be powerless. *Journal of Experimental Social Psychology, 36*, 1–25.

Van Overwalle, F. (2009). Social cognition and the brain: A meta-analysis. *Hum Brain Mapp, 30*(3), 829–858.

Wellman, H. M., Cross, D., & Watson, J. (2001). Meta-analysis of theory-of-mind development: the truth about false belief. *Child Development, 72*, 655–684.

Will G.-J., Crone E. A., Van den Bos, W., Güroğlu, B. (2013). Acting on observed social exclusion: Developmental perspectives on punishment of excluders and compensation of victims. *Developmental Psychology.* [Epub ahead of print]. doi: 10.1037/a0032299.

Williams, K. D. (2007). Ostracism. *Annual Review of Psychology, 58*, 425–452.

Williams, K. D., Cheung, C. K. T., & Choi, W. (2000). Cyberostracism: Effects of being ignored over the Internet. *Journal of Personality and Social Psychology, 79*(5), 748–762.

10 Why Sanction? Functional Causes of Punishment and Reward

■ PAT BARCLAY AND TOKO KIYONARI

Abstract

Many disciplines find it puzzling that costly cooperation exists within groups of non-kin. Cooperation can be sustained when noncooperators are punished or when cooperators are rewarded, but these sanctions are themselves costly to provide. As such, we must ask: what forces maintain the existence of sanctioning? Why do people possess a psychology that includes punitive sentiment and a willingness to reward? Many theoretical models rely on "second-order punishment," which means that people will punish those who do not punish noncooperators. However, our review of the evidence suggests that people do not readily do this, and do not particularly like punishers. This calls into question any theories that rely on this second-order punishment. By contrast, people will readily reward those who reward cooperators, which suggests that rewards may function as part of a system of indirect reciprocity where cooperators (and rewarders) are seen as "good," thus worthy of help. So what does sustain punitive sentiment? Punishment may function to signal qualities of the punisher that are otherwise difficult to observe, such as the punisher's trustworthiness or willingness to retaliate against personal affronts. Alternately, punishment may simply be a "Volunteer's Dilemma" where it becomes rational to "volunteer" to punish noncooperators if no one else in the group will. Finally, we discuss how positive and negative sanctions may function differently to maintain large-scale human cooperation, depending on the proportion of cooperators in a population and the necessity for unanimous cooperation. By understanding the forces that sustain people's punitive sentiment and willingness to reward (i.e., the *function* of punishment and reward), we can then harness these forces to promote large-scale cooperation and the provision of public goods.

■ **INTRODUCTION**

Cooperation is a theoretical puzzle in many disciplines. Why would one organism do things that benefit others if doing so is costly? Much research has focused on the psychological mechanisms underlying such help (e.g., Andreoni, 1990; Batson et al., 1997; Cialdini, Brown, Lewis, Luce, & Neuberg, 1997; Cox, 2004). From a functional perspective, why do such cooperative sentiments persist? Why do humans possess psychological mechanisms which cause them to help others? What selective forces cause these sentiments to evolve and/or be learned? Evolutionary researchers often seek to answer these questions of function. By understanding the function(s) of cooperation, it allows us to create situations that will promote cooperation regardless of what specific sentiments trigger cooperation within each individual (Barclay, in press).

Many explanations about the functions of cooperation rely on people being able to target their cooperation towards specific individuals and away from others. For example, reciprocity involves helping those who have specifically helped you (direct reciprocity: Axelrod, 1984; Trivers, 1971) or who have been helpful in general (indirect reciprocity: Alexander, 1987; Nowak & Sigmund, 2005), and avoiding helping people who do not help. However, what happens when cooperative acts cannot be targeted towards specific individuals?

One case where cooperative acts cannot be preferentially targeted towards cooperators is with the provision of public goods. A public good is something that is costly to provide, but once provided, is available to all people regardless of how much each person contributed towards the provision (e.g., Davis & Holt, 1993; Ledyard, 1995). Because all members have equal access to the public good, those who pay the cost of providing public goods will have a lower payoff than non-contributors who do not pay this cost (a.k.a. "free-riders" or defectors). This incentive structure will often result in the underprovision of public goods, a result which has been found in many experiments (see reviews by Ledyard, 1995). A similar situation occurs with resource management because conservation of resources is a public good that everyone benefits from, and a "tragedy of the commons" can occur as individuals follow their rational incentives to overexploit common resources (Hardin, 1968). It is important to solve these twin problems of public goods provision and tragedies of the commons, especially because overuse of natural resources has been implicated in the collapse of some historical societies like the Mayans and Easter Islanders (Diamond, 2005). We will treat these problems equivalently in this chapter because of the similarity in their incentive structures.

As this collection is about peer-to-peer rewards and punishment, readers will not be surprised that these have both been put forth as forces that maintain contributions to public goods. Contributing to public goods can be worthwhile if one can be rewarded sufficiently for doing so. Similarly, free-riding on others' contributions is not worthwhile if one would face punishment for not contributing oneself. Much research has shown that people are willing to pay to sanction others, either through rewards or through punishment, and the majority of studies show that both rewards and punishment can sustain cooperation under some circumstances (e.g., Fehr & Gächter, 2002; Gächter, Renner, & Sefton, 2008; Masclet, Noussair, Tucker, & Villeval., 2003; McCusker & Carnevale, 1995; Nikiforakis & Normann, 2008; Ostrom, Walker, & Gardner, 1992; Rand, Dreber, Ellingsen, Fudenberg, & Nowak, 2009; Rockenbach & Milinski, 2006; Sefton, Shupp, & Walker, 2007; Vyrastekova & van Soest, 2008; Yamagishi, 1986)[1]. We will let others provide a

---

1. Some authors have debated the frequency or effectiveness of punishment (e.g., Guala, 2012), for example by using experiments with unusual methodological constraints that prevent punishers from cooperating (Dreber, Rand, Fudenberg, & Nowak, 2008; Wu et al., 2009). We leave that debate for elsewhere (e.g., see Rankin, dos Santos, & Wedekind, 2009), and instead follow the majority of studies in suggesting that punishment and reward can have some role in supporting cooperation.

more comprehensive review of the existence and effectiveness of punishment and reward, and will instead focus on why people possess such punitive and rewarding sentiment. We will also focus on sanctions provided by individuals ("peer-to-peer sanction") instead of by institutions, as the two types of sanctions may involve different etiologies.

GOALS OF THIS CHAPTER

In this chapter, we will not discuss which specific psychological mechanisms (e.g., which emotions) cause cooperative actions, nor will we discuss which specific emotions cause punishment and reward. These are excellent topics and have been investigated by others (e.g., de Quervain et al., 2004; Fehr & Gächter, 2002; Hopfensitz & Reuben, 2009; Nelissen & Zeelenberg, 2009) and will likely be covered elsewhere in this volume. Instead, we ask: why does punitive sentiment exist at all? Given that it is costly to punish or reward others, why do people possess a psychology which makes them inclined to reward those who provide public goods and punish those who do not? What forces select for and maintain such sentiments? These questions of function are different from and complementary to questions of proximate psychological causation; they are simply at different "levels of analysis" (Tinbergen, 1968; Holekamp & Sherman, 1989).

Evolutionary researchers identify four complementary "levels of analysis" for any behavior (Tinbergen, 1968; Holekamp & Sherman, 1989). Proximate causes are those that occur within an individual, and include: 1) the specific psychological mechanisms (e.g., emotions) triggered in a situation; and 2) the development of those mechanisms within an individual's lifetime (e.g., learning, gene-environment interactions). Ultimate causes are the reasons that those proximate causes exist at all in any member of the species, and include: 3) the phylogeny or evolutionary history of the psychological mechanisms (e.g., what pre-existing features did the psychological mechanism evolve from); and 4) the evolutionary function (e.g., what selective pressures caused that proximate mechanism to evolve and be maintained despite the costs). These levels are not in competition: to truly understand any phenomenon, we need an answer at all four levels.

These different "levels of analysis" are important to clarify because many of the current debates over cooperation and punishment are due to researchers investigating the same phenomenon at different levels of analysis, and then not realizing that others are simply asking different questions (Barclay, 2012). For example, I may punish Fred because I am angry at his non-cooperation (proximate psychological mechanism), and I may possess this anger because it functions to signal my intolerance of exploitation and thus reduces others' attempts to exploit me (potential ultimate function). These two potential "causes" (anger and signaling) are complementary instead of mutually exclusive, and they could both be right—or both be wrong—because they are answers to questions at two of the four different levels of analysis, namely "what is the specific emotion" and "why does it exist." It is this latter question of ultimate functional cause that we address here. Although we will discuss the costs and benefits of sanctioning, we do not suggest that people are consciously responding to these costs and benefits. Instead, these costs and benefits are what allow the underlying psychological mechanisms (e.g., anger, righteous indignation) to arise. We have clarified this here to avoid further confusion over levels of analysis.

WHAT MAINTAINS PEER-TO-PEER SANCTIONING BEHAVIOR?

Peer-to-peer punishment and rewards can support the provision of public goods, but they themselves are costly to provide. These costs can include time, energy, danger, and especially retaliation (e.g., Janssen & Bushman, 2008; Nikiforakis, 2008). As such, we need to ask why people provide such costly sanctions (Yamagishi, 1986). Sanctions benefit all cooperators in a group, but punishers have a lower payoff than non-punishers in their groups who avoid the cost of punishment. Because of this, non-punishers essentially free-ride on the punishment provided by more punitive group members; this behavior has been called "second-order free-riding" (where "first-order free-riding" is failing to cooperate). Game theoretical models and evolutionary simulations show that these second-order free-riders will outcompete those who pay to sanction, which then undermines cooperation in those groups because there is no one to enforce it (Boyd & Richerson, 1992; Henrich & Boyd, 2001; Oliver, 1980; Ostrom, 1990). A similar argument holds for rewarding: if it is costly to reward cooperators, then rewarders will be outcompeted by non-rewarders, unless some other factor counteracts this disadvantage. Thus, to the extent that punishment and reward maintain cooperation, we need to explain what maintains punitive sentiment and the desire to reward.

Second-Order Sanctions

Second-Order Punishment

Some theorists have suggested that punitive sentiment is supported by "second-order punishment" or "meta-norms," which means punishment directed preferentially at "second-order free-riders" (i.e., those who do not punish: Axelrod, 1986; Boyd & Richerson, 1992; Henrich, 2004; Henrich & Boyd, 2001). In these models, "second-order punishment" maintains the "first-order punishment" (i.e., punishment of noncooperators), which is needed to maintain cooperation. Although this argument appears vulnerable to infinite regress (e.g., "third-order punishment" to maintain second-order punishment, and so on), several models rely on the existence of "second-order" punishment of non-punishers (e.g., Axelrod, 1986; Boyd & Richerson, 1992; Brandt, Hauert, & Sigmund, 2006; Fowler, 2005; Henrich, 2004; Henrich & Boyd, 2001; Sober & Wilson, 1999; de Weerd & Verbrugge, 2011). As such, we need to ask: do people tend to punish non-punishers, as predicted by these models?

The evidence to date suggests that people do *not* perform second-order punishment, i.e., they do not particularly punish non-punishers. In the first analysis we know of, Barclay (2006) examined instances of punishment in a standard public goods experiment and found no unambiguous instances of people punishing a group member for failing to punish in a previous round. Nikiforakis (2008) and

Cinyabuguma, Page, & Putterman (2006)[2] both gave experimental participants the opportunity to "counterpunish," i.e., respond to punishment in a second sanctioning opportunity immediately following everyone's first sanctioning decision. They both found that the more a person punishes at the first stage, the more he or she gets punished at the second stage. These two studies suggest that people sanction punishers more than they sanction non-punishers, which is the opposite of what the previous models predict. In contrast to those two studies, Denant-Boemont, Masclet, & Noussair (2007) also allowed participants to counterpunish, but they claimed to find evidence for both retaliation and metanorms, even in the very first round of the experiment. In a type of multiple regression, they found that people who punished more than average at the first stage tended to receive more punishment at the second stage (retaliation), and people who punished less than average at the first stage also received more punishment at the second stage (metanorms). Thus, so far one regression analysis claims to find punishment of non-punishers whereas two do not.

In the most direct test to date, Kiyonari and Barclay (2008) had Canadian students play a public goods game, receive an opportunity to sanction cooperators or noncooperators, and then receive an additional opportunity to sanction partners based on how partners sanctioned. Participants played the game with a free-rider, a cooperator who punished the free-rider, and a cooperator who did not punish. In this direct comparison, non-punishers received no more sanctions than did punishers, and in fact the latter were rated significantly less favorably. This pattern was present in three variations of the experiment, including when the non-punisher was clearly unwilling to use sanctions to support cooperation. Furthermore, these results match similar results in Japan and Belgium (Kiyonari et al., 2004, 2008). These results strongly suggest that people do not preferentially punish non-punishers. As such, these results call into question any model that relies on the existence of second-order punishment to maintain cooperation.

Although there is currently no strong evidence for second-order punishment, at least not in these experimental games, this does not mean it will never be found. There are examples of punishment of non-enforcers in political domains, such as US Senator Joseph McCarthy's accusations of Communism against those who failed to denounce suspected Communists, or the Cuban Liberty and Democratic Solidarity Act of 1996 (a.k.a. the "Helms-Burton Act") which imposes embargoes against companies who fail to embargo Cuba (US Department of State). Both of these examples involve coalitions, which may be relevant, and there are also interesting differences. In the McCarthy example, a failure to sanction was taken as a cue

---

2. Although Cinyabuguma and colleagues (2006) use the phrase "second-order punishment" in their title, they use it very differently than we use it here. They simply mean a second stage of punishing where people can condition their second-stage punishment on others' first-stage punishment of *anyone*. By contrast, we follow evolutionary researchers in specifically referring to the punishment of those who do not punish free-riders. In their results, Cinyabuguma et al. show that people who punish at the first stage tend to receive more punishment at the second stage, not less, so their results are evidence against—not for—the existence of "second-order punishment" in the sense we use the term here.

of one's political sympathies; one can similarly imagine "second-order condemnation" of someone who failed to condemn child molestation. Thus, second-order punishment may only arise when these is a clear need to signal one's dislike of another's actions. Alternately, perhaps second-order punishment only arises when an act of non-cooperation is clearly harmful. In the example of the "Helms-Burton Act," one country's failure to sanction undermines the effectiveness of others' sanctions. Future studies can investigate whether second-order punishment will arise when a failure to punish is a potential cue of coalitional membership or future behavior, and especially when it undermines others' attempts at coercion.

Second-Order Rewards

Second-order sanctions need not be negative. The rewarding of cooperators could be sustained by "second-order rewards," which means rewards preferentially directed at those who reward cooperators. This would naturally occur if rewarding is seen as a good act within a system of indirect reciprocity or generalized exchange, where people gain a good reputation for helping others and are thus more likely to receive help (see Nowak & Sigmund, 2005 for a review). Panchanathan and Boyd (2004) showed that when the provision of public goods is linked to a system of indirect reciprocity, those who provide public goods become more likely to receive help, and those who refuse to help the public providers will lose their reputation and receive less help themselves. There is no problem of infinite regress because systems of indirect reciprocity can be stable unto themselves (Nowak & Sigmund, 2005). Milinski and colleagues have shown that opportunities for indirect reciprocity can support the provision of public goods (Milinski, Semmann, & Krambeck, 2002), including the fight against climate change (Milinski, Semmann, Krambeck, & Marotzke, 2006), as long as people can track reputations about who has contributed and who has not (Semmann, Krambeck, & Milinski, 2004).

Second-order rewards are more likely to support sanctions than is second-order punishment, for several reasons (Kiyonari & Barclay, 2008): (a) rewarders will fare better than punishers because the former receive positive reciprocation whereas the latter experience retaliation (e.g., Cinyabuguma et al., 2006); (b) punishment requires justification to seem appropriate; (c) the same proximate psychological mechanisms are easily co-opted from contributing to rewarding and to second-order rewarding (e.g., liking or empathy towards those who help) whereas this is more difficult with punishment; (d) people will prefer rewarders as partners instead of punishers because the latter can benefit them; and (e) rewards and second-order rewards may even constitute a form of competitive altruism (Barclay, 2011a; Barclay & Willer, 2007). In support of this, Kiyonari and Barclay (2008) show that **people will readily reward rewarders more than non-rewarders, but do not readily punish non-punishers (or reward punishers).**

For rewards to sustain the provision of public goods, provision must be linked to a system of indirect reciprocity (Panchanathan & Boyd, 2004). This means that contributing towards public goods must be seen as good and necessary just as any other act of helping, so people will help public good providers when they are in need. This may require that people recognize that the public good benefits all group members and that failure to contribute harms others (Barclay, 2011b). Once this is common knowledge, good people will be more likely to contribute and no good person will knowingly fail to contribute; this in turn makes reputation systems more effective because rewards and punishment are more likely to go to the appropriate targets. Educating people about such benefits and harms has been successful in the past at promoting reputation systems (see review in Barclay, 2012), and experimental evidence shows that such education enhances the effectiveness of indirect reciprocity at promoting public good provision (Milinski et al., 2006).

Unlike punishment, rewards may involve a time lag: it is easy to cheaply inflict immediate high costs on someone for failing to cooperate, but it may be difficult to cheaply reward them with high benefits immediately (b>c) because they may not immediately need help. Humans likely use placeholders such as verbal rewards and nonverbal displays of gratitude to acknowledge help received, point out indebtedness, and to indicate that the helper is now more likely to receive tangible help in the future. Verbal rewards can thus substitute as proxy rewards until a cooperator later needs help, and should be effective for those who are able to delay gratification. A similar argument would hold for punishment: verbal and nonverbal signs of disapproval may function as proxies for more tangible punishments.

Alternative Explanations for Punishment

Punishment as a Costly Signal

Punishment may function to signal some characteristic about the punisher (Barclay, 2010). For example, some individuals can punish more cheaply or with lower risk of retaliation, e.g., those with high physical ability or social status can punish more easily (Clutton-Brock & Parker, 1995). Consequently, punishing free-riders could be a socially acceptable way of signaling that one has the power to impose costs on others. Audiences would then defer to a punisher out of self-interest, and this would benefit the punisher. Similarly, punishment could signal one's unwillingness to tolerate exploitation: would-be defectors would benefit from cooperating with anyone known to punish defection. In support of this, game theoretical models show that punishment can evolve when people are less likely to defect on individuals who punish defectors (Brandt, Hauert, & Sigmund, 2003; dos Santos, Rankin, & Wedekind, 2011; Hauert, Haiden, & Sigmund, 2004; Sigmund, Hauert, & Nowak, 2001), and experimental work shows that people steal less money from participants who have punished free-riders (Barclay, submitted). This requires no conscious awareness from either punishers or audiences about punishment's signaling properties: as long as there are reputational benefits, then punitive sentiment will arise and persist.

In addition to being triggered by emotions like anger, punishment of free-riders could also be triggered out of concerns for fairness or righteous indignation (Barclay, 2006). In such cases, anyone who punishes free-riders is demonstrating that he or she possesses a sense of justice and dislikes unfairness. If so, then one could trust a punisher more than someone who does not condemn unfairness. Experiments show that people entrust more money to those who have punished free-riders than to those who have not punished (Barclay, 2006; Nelissen, 2008), though this may require exposure to free-riders so that people understand the justification for punishment. Interestingly, there is currently no evidence that people "like" punishers or will reward them (Barclay, 2006; Horita, 2010; Kiyonari & Barclay, 2008); it seems that people trust punishers (which is in their self-interest) but do not pay to reward them (which is not in their self-interest). This may explain another curious difference in the literature: people pay more to punish others when their decisions are observed than when anonymous (Kurzban, DeScioli, & O'Brien, 2007; Piazza & Bering, 2008), but will hide information about their most severe punishments from an observer who could choose them for future interactions (Rockenbach & Milinski, 2011). Of course, if punishment signals toughness, there is no reason to like punishers or choose them, only to defer to them. More research is needed to determine whether punishment is indeed a signal of some traits, and if so, which ones.

Punishment as a Volunteer's Dilemma

Researchers often overestimate the costs of punishment because they compare punishers with non-punishers *in the same group*. This overlooks the fact that punishers personally benefit from the cooperation levels they enforce (West, Griffin, Gardner, 2007). As such, punishers can have higher payoffs than non-punishers *in other groups* (i.e., groups without any punishers). Punishment will arise as long as some competition exists against those outside of one's local group, which is to say that competition is not entirely local (see "scale of competition," West et al., 2006).

It is well-established that punishment is a public good (e.g., Yamagishi, 1986). However, not all public goods have the same incentive structure. Most researchers use social dilemmas where non-cooperation is the dominant response (as in a Prisoner's Dilemma), but there are other types of social dilemmas with slightly different incentive structures[3]. Some public goods are a "Volunteer's Dilemma" (Diekmann, 1985; Murnighan, Kim, & Metzger, 1993), also known as a Snowdrift game, Producer-Scrounger game, Hero game, Brave Leader game, and Dragon-Slayer game (reviewed by Barclay & Van Vugt, in press). In these situations, each person prefers that someone else provide the public good, but would be willing to provide it if no one else will. For example, the two-person Snowdrift Game models a situation where two people are stuck in cars behind a snowdrift: each person would prefer to stay in his car while the other person shovels the snow, but if the other person refuses to shovel, it is better to shovel alone than to stay stranded behind the snowdrift (Doebeli & Hauert, 2005). This is different from the classic Prisoner's Dilemma because non-cooperation is no longer always the best strategy: it pays to "volunteer" to cooperate if no one else will. Research shows that people are more cooperative in social dilemmas that resemble a Snowdrift Game (2 person) or Volunteer's Dilemma (≥2 person) than in classic Prisoner's Dilemmas (Kümmerli et al., 2007).

Punishment may have an incentive structure that is more like a Volunteer's Dilemma than a Prisoner's Dilemma. Punishment is costly, but all cooperators benefit in the long run if free-riders are punished, and this benefit can outweigh the cost of punishing. As such, each person may prefer that *someone else* be the one to pay to punish a free-rider, but each person might be eventually willing to punish if no one else will (Raihani & Bshary, 2011). Thus, punishment is not

---

3. In fact, an N-Person Prisoner's Dilemma is simply a special case of a more general spectrum of social dilemmas, the rest of which all have a mixed equilibrium that includes cooperators and noncooperators (Archetti & Scheuring, 2011).

always as "altruistic" as is sometimes claimed (e.g., Fehr & Gächter, 2002), but can be self-serving (Bshary & Bshary, 2010; Raihani, Grutter, & Bshary, 2010). Punishment functions as a Volunteer's Dilemma: punishers benefit from their actions, but because they also pay a cost, their net benefit is lower than other group members' (Raihani & Bshary, 2011). Thus, we might expect people to refrain from punishment if it looks like someone else will provide the necessary (and costly) punishment (but see Casari & Luini, 2009).

One way to solve the Volunteer's Dilemma with punishment would be to assign the responsibility for sanctioning to a single individual or specialized role (Baldassari & Grossman, 2011; O'Gorman, Henrich, & Van Vugt, 2009; Ostrom, 1990). By putting the onus on that person(s), it reduces the uncertainty about who would volunteer to sanction, and could even increase the likelihood of sanctions occurring. Alternately, when punishment requires coordination by multiple group members, this can reduce the uncertainty over who will punish and can reduce the costs for everyone (Boyd, Gintis, & Bowles, 2010), as well reduce the frequency with which high contributors get punished (Casari & Luini, 2009).

THE CARROT OR THE STICK?

Both punishment and rewards are effective at sustaining cooperation (Fehr & Gächter, 2002; McCusker & Carnevale, 1995; Milinski et al., 2002; Rand et al., 2009; Rockenbach & Milinski, 2006; Sefton et al., 2007; Vyrastekova & van Soest, 2008). When both options are available, people seem to perform both equally at first (Kiyonari & Barclay, 2008), and then use punishment less as cooperation becomes more common and punishment becomes less necessary (Rand et al., 2009; Rockenbach & Milinski, 2006). The psychological literature on learning and operant conditioning suggests that reinforcement-based learning (i.e., reward) is more effective at changing behavior and is more desirable than punishment-based learning (e.g., Skinner, 1971), but research in cooperative games suggests that punishment and reward are equally effective at maintaining cooperation in social dilemmas (meta-analysis: Balliet, Mulder, & Van Lange, 2011).

There is debate over whether punishment provides any collective benefit if rewards are also available. Rand and colleagues (2009) gave participants opportunities to pay to reward and/or punish others after each round of a public goods game, and they found that (in comparison with rewards alone) adding punishment had no additional effect on cooperation and in fact reduced collective welfare. However, this lack of difference could be a ceiling effect, as contributions to the public good approached 90% when either rewards or punishment were present. Conversely, Rockenbach and Milinski (2006) paired public goods games with punishment and/or opportunities for indirect reciprocity, and they found that punishment did increase contributions and collective welfare above and beyond the benefits of rewards alone. In fact, they found that participants came to prefer groups with opportunities for costly punishment and indirect reciprocity over groups without punishment (see also Gürerk, Irlenbusch, & Rockenbach, 2006).

It is possible that punishment and reward may be useful for different things. Punishment is cheaper to use when cooperation is common because fewer people need to be sanctioned, whereas rewards are cheaper when cooperation is rare for the same reason (Oliver, 1980). Similarly, punishment can enforce unanimous cooperation by targeting the few rare defectors (Mulder, 2008), whereas reward may be more effective at initiating cooperation from zero by inspiring the few rare cooperators (Forsyth & Hauert, 2011; Hilbe & Sigmund, 2010). If only a few cooperators are required and additional cooperators would be superfluous (e.g., Volunteer's Dilemmas or other situations with a "provision point"), it would be more efficient to use rewards to stimulate a few cooperators rather than punish all defectors into cooperating unnecessarily. Thus, punishment may be better when cooperation is common and needs to be unanimous, whereas reward may be better when cooperation is less common or does not need to be (e.g., a low "provision point"). These may all be the reasons why institutions such as governments generally focus on punishment for rare crimes of violence or non-cooperation (e.g., tax evasion, pollution, and overharvesting). Similarly, governments focus on incentives (e.g., tax write-offs) to promote charitable donations and other rarer positive acts rather than criminalize a failure to donate.

CONCLUDING REMARKS

To promote cooperation and the provision of public goods, we need to understand what forces select for and maintain cooperative sentiment. This question of *function* is separate from, and complementary to, the question of what the specific cooperative sentiments (and underlying neurological mechanisms) are that trigger cooperation within individuals. It is arguably more effective to alter situations to harness these forces than to focus on directly manipulating proximate psychological mechanisms (Barclay, in press). Because punishment and reward are important in sustaining large-scale cooperation, it is important to understand what forces support the existence of punitive sentiment and a willingness to reward. If our social situations are not conducive to moralistic punishment and rewards via indirect reciprocity, then punishment and reward will likely decrease in frequency and cooperation will subsequently collapse.

Several theoretical models about cooperation rely on non-punishers receiving punishment themselves (e.g., Axelrod, 1986; Boyd & Richerson, 1992; Brandt et al., 2006; Fowler, 2005; Henrich, 2004; Henrich & Boyd, 2001; Sober & Wilson, 1999; de Weerd & Verbrugge, 2011). However, because people do not seem to readily punish non-punishers (Barclay, 2006; Cinyabuguma et al., 2006; Kiyonari & Barclay, 2008; Nikiforakis, 2008; but see Denant-Boemont et al., 2007) we must be hesitant about such models until it is conclusively demonstrated that this "second-order punishment" exists. If it were to be conclusively demonstrated that people do punish those who fail to punish noncooperators, then we should happily reconsider those models. However, until such evidence is found, it would be unwise to rely on any model which depends on this highly equivocal phenomenon. The best places to investigate this may be in coalitions where a single non-punisher undermines the effectiveness of collective punishment (e.g., coalitions), or wherever one's failing to punish an act is taken as a cue of one's tacit approval. Theoreticians and empiricists may instead wish to investigate other factors that are hypothesized to support the existence of punishment, such as a reputation for punishing (Barclay, 2006; Nelissen, 2008) and especially whether punishment is a Volunteer's Dilemma that exists simply because it pays to punish if no one else is willing to (Raihani & Bshary, 2011). If punishment is a Volunteer's Dilemma, then it should be affected by the same factors that affect cooperation in other Volunteer's Dilemmas, such as the group size or individual differences in the cost or benefits of punishing.

From a practical perspective, researchers and policy-makers may want to focus on supporting cooperation via means other than just punishment. Rewards and positive reputation have shown to support cooperation in theoretical work (e.g., Barclay, 2011a; Hilbe & Sigmund, 2010; Panchanathan & Boyd, 2004), laboratory work (e.g., Barclay, 2004; Milinski et al., 2002; Rand et al., 2009), and field research (Bateson, Nettle, & Roberts, 2006; Ernest-Jones, Nettle, & Bateson, 2011; Gerber, Green, & Larimer, 2008). Much research is needed on how to effectively set up systems to allow for positive reputation and to change norms so that people naturally reward those who provide public goods. The benefits for doing so are enormous, though, as public goods may be provided more effectively if we can design social systems that let people gain positive reputations for doing so.

REFERENCES

Alexander, R. D. (1987). *The Biology of Moral Systems*. New York: Aldine de Gruyter.

Andreoni, J. (1990). Impure altruism and donations to public goods: a theory of warm-glow giving. *The Economic Journal, 100*, 464–477.

Archetti, M., & Scheuring, I. (2011). Coexistence of cooperation and defection in public goods games. *Evolution, 65*, 1140–1148.

Axelrod, R. (1984). *The Evolution of Cooperation*. New York, NY: Basic Books.

Axelrod, R. (1986). An evolutionary approach to norms. *American Political Science Review, 80*, 1095–1111.

Baldassari, D., & Grossman, G. (2011). Centralized sanctioning and legitimate authority promote cooperation in humans. *Proceedings of the National Academy of Science of the USA, 108*(27), 11023–11027.

Balliet, D., Mulder, L. B., & Van Lange, P. A. M. (2011). Reward, punishment, and cooperation: a meta-analysis. *Psychological Bulletin, 137*, 594–615.

Barclay, P. (2004). Trustworthiness and Competitive Altruism Can Also Solve the "Tragedy of the Commons." *Evolution & Human Behavior, 25*(4), 209–220.

Barclay, P. (2006). Reputational benefits for altruistic punishment. *Evolution & Human Behaviour, 27*, 344–360.

Barclay, P. (2010). *Reputation and the Evolution of Generous Behavior*. Nova Science Publishers, Hauppauge, NY.

Barclay, P. (2011a). Competitive helping increases with the size of biological markets and invades defection. *Journal of Theoretical Biology, 281*, 47–55.

Barclay, P. (2011b). The evolution of charitable behaviour and the power of reputation. In C. Roberts (Ed.) *Applied Evolutionary Psychology*, (pp. 149–172). Oxford, UK: Oxford University Press.

Barclay, P. (2012). Proximate and ultimate causes of Strong Reciprocity and punishment. *Behavioral and Brain Sciences, 35*(1), 16–17.

Barclay, P. (2012). Harnessing the power of reputation: strengths and limits for promoting cooperative behaviours. *Evolutionary Psychology, 10*(5), 868–883.

Barclay, P. (submitted). "Don't mess with the enforcer": Deterrence as an individual-level benefit for punishing free-riders. Manuscript under review.

Barclay, P., & Van Vugt, M. (in press). The evolutionary psychology of human prosociality: adaptations, mistakes, and byproducts. To appear in D. Schroeder & W. Graziaono (Eds.) *Oxford Handbook of Prosocial Behavior*. Oxford, UK: Oxford University Press.

Barclay, P., & Willer, R. (2007). Partner choice creates competitive altruism in humans. *Proceedings of the Royal Society of London Series B, 274*, 749–753.

Bateson, M., Nettle, D., & Roberts, G. (2006). Cues of being watched enhance cooperation in a real-world setting. *Biology Letters, 2*, 412–414.

Batson, C. D., Sager, K., Garst, E., Kang, M., Rubchinsky, K., & Dawson, K. (1997). Is empathy-induced helping due to self-other merging? *Journal of Personality and Social Psychology, 73*, 495–509.

Boyd, R., Gintis, H., & Bowles, S. (2010). Coordinated punishment of defectors sustains cooperation and can proliferate when rare. *Science, 328*, 617–620.

Boyd, R., & Richerson, P. (1992). Punishment allows the evolution of cooperation (or anything else) in sizable groups. *Ethology and Sociobiology, 13*, 171–195.

Brandt, H., Hauert, C., & Sigmund, K. (2003). Punishment and reputation in spatial public goods games. *Proceedings of the Royal Society of London Series B, 270*, 1099–1104.

Brandt, H., Hauert, C., & Sigmund, K. (2006). Punishing and abstaining for public goods. *Proceedings of the National Academy of Science of the USA, 103*, 495–497.

Bshary, A., & Bshary, R. (2010). Self-serving punishment of a common enemy creates a public good in reef fishes. *Current Biology, 20*, 2032–2035.

Casari, M., & Luini, L. (2009). Cooperation under alternative punishment institutions: an experiment. *Journal of Economic Behavior and Organizations, 71*, 273–282.

Cialdini, R. B., Brown, S. L., Lewis, B. P., Luce, C., & Neuburg, S. L. (1997). Reinterpreting the empathy-altruism relationship: when one into one equals oneness. *Journal of Personality and Social Psychology, 73*, 481–494.

Cinyabuguma, M., Page, T., & Putterman, L. (2006). Can second-order punishment deter perverse punishment? *Experimental Economics, 9*, 265–279.

Clutton-Brock, T. H., & Parker, G. A. (1995). Punishment in animal societies. *Nature, 373*, 209–216.

Cox, J. C. (2004). How to identify trust and reciprocity. *Games and Economic Behavior, 46*, 260–281.

Davis, D. D., & Holt, C. A. (1993). *Experimental Economics*. Princeton, NJ: Princeton University Press.

Denant-Boemont, L., Masclet, D., & Noussair, C. N. (2007). Punishment, counterpunishment and sanction enforcement in a social dilemma experiment. *Economic Theory, 33*, 145–167.

de Quervain, D. J. F., Fischbacher, U., Treyer, V., Schellhammer, M., Schnyder, U., Buck, A., & Fehr, E. (2004). The neural basis of altruistic punishment. *Science, 305*, 1254–1258.

Diamond, J. (2005). *Collapse: How Societies Choose to Fail or Succeed*. New York: Viking.

Diekmann, A. (1985). Volunteer's Dilemma. *The Journal of Conflict Resolution, 29*, 605–610.

Doebeli, M., & Hauert, C. (2005). Models of cooperation based on the Prisoner's Dilemma and the Snowdrift game. *Ecology Letters, 8*, 748–766.

dos Santos, M., Rankin, D. J., & Wedekind, C. (2011). The evolution of punishment through reputation. *Proceedings of the Royal Society of London Series B, 278*, 371–377.

Dreber, A., Rand, D. G., Fudenberg, D., & Nowak, M. (2008). Winners don't punish. *Nature, 452*, 348–351.

Ernest-Jones, M., Nettle, D., & Bateson, M. (2011). Effects of eye images on everyday cooperative behavior: a field experiment. *Evolution and Human Behavior, 32*(3), 172–178.

Fehr, E., & Gächter, S. (2002). Altruistic punishment in humans. *Nature, 415*, 137–140.

Forsyth, P. A. I., & Hauert, C. (2011). Public goods games with reward in finite populations. *Journal of Mathematical Biology, 63*(1), 109–123.

Fowler, J. H. (2005). Altruistic punishment and the origin of cooperation. *Proceedings of the National Academy of Science of the USA, 102*, 7047–7049.

Gächter, S., Renner, E., & Sefton, M. (2008). The long-run benefits of punishment. *Science, 322*, 1510.

Gerber, A. S., Green, D. P., & Larimer, C. W. (2008). Social pressures and voter turnout: evidence from a large-scale field experiment. *American Political Science Review, 102*(1), 33–48.

Guala, F. (2012). Reciprocity: weak or strong? What punishment experiments do (and do not) show. *Behavioral and Brain Sciences, 35*, 1–59.

Gürerk, O., Irlenbusch, B., & Rockenbach, B. (2006). The competitive advantage of sanctioning institutions. *Science, 312*, 108–111.

Hardin, G. (1968). The tragedy of the commons. *Science, 162*, 1243–1248.

Hauert, C., Haiden, N., & Sigmund, K. (2004). The dynamics of public goods. *Discrete and Continuous Dynamical Systems B, 4*, 575–587.

Henrich, J. (2004). Cultural group selection, coevolutionary processes and large-scale cooperation. *Journal of Economic Behavior and Organization, 53*, 3–35.

Henrich, J., & Boyd, R. (2001). Why people punish defectors—Weak conformist transmission can stabilize costly enforcement of norms in cooperative dilemmas. *Journal of Theoretical Biology, 208*, 79–89.

Hilbe, C., & Sigmund, K. (2010). Incentives and opportunism: from the carrot to the stick. *Proceedings of the Royal Society of London Series B, 277*, 2427–2433.

Holekamp, K. E., & Sherman, P. W. (1989). Why male ground squirrels disperse: a multilevel analysis explains why only males leave home. *American Scientist, 77*(3), 232–239.

Hopfensitz, A., & Reuben, E. (2009). The importance of emotions for the effectiveness of social punishment. *The Economic Journal, 119*, 1534–1559.

Horita, Y. (2010). Punishers may be chosen as providers but not as recipients. *Letters on Evolutionary Behavioral Science, 1*, 6–9.

Janssen, M. A., & Bushman, C. (2008). Evolution of cooperation and altruistic punishment when retaliation is possible. *Journal of Theoretical Biology, 254*, 541–545.

Kiyonari, T., & Barclay, P. (2008). Cooperation in social dilemmas: free-riding may be thwarted by second-order rewards rather than punishment. *Journal of Personality and Social Psychology, 95*(4), 826–842.

Kiyonari, T., Declerck, C. H., Boone, C., & Pollet, T. (2008). Does intention matter? A comparison between Public Good and Common Resource Dilemma Games with positive and negative sanctions in one-shot interactions. Paper presentation at the 20th annual meeting of the Human Behavior and Evolution Society, June, 2008, Kyoto University, Kyoto, Japan.

Kiyonari, T., Shimoma, E., & Yamagishi, T. (2004). Second-order punishment in one-shot social dilemma. *International journal of psychology, 39*, 329.

Kümmerli, R., Colliard, C., Fietcher, N., Petitpierre, B., Russier, F., & Keller, L. (2007). Human cooperation in social dilemmas: comparing the Snowdrift game with the Prisoner's Dilemma. *Proceedings of the Royal Society of London Series B, 274,* 2965–2970.

Kurzban, R., DeScioli, P., & O'Brien, E. (2007). Audience effects on moralistic punishment. *Evolution and Human Behavior, 28,* 75–84.

Ledyard, J. O. (1995). Public goods: a survey of experimental research. In J. H. Kagel & A. E. Roth (Eds.), *The Handbook of Experimental Economics* (pp. 111–194). Princeton, NJ: Princeton University Press.

Masclet, D., Noussair, C., Tucker, S., & Villeval, M. C. (2003). Monetary and non-monetary punishment in the Voluntary Contributions Mechanism. *The American Economic Review, 93*(1), 366–380.

McCusker, C., & Carnevale, P. J. (1995). Framing in resource dilemmas: loss aversion and the moderating effects of sanctions. *Organizational Behavior and Human Decision Processes, 61,* 190–201.

Milinski, M. Semmann, D., & Krambeck, H. J. (2002). Reputation helps solve the 'tragedy of the commons'. *Nature, 415,* 424–426.

Milinski, M., Semman, D., Krambeck, H. J., & Marotzke, J. (2006). Stabilizing the earth's climate is not a losing game: supporting evidence from public goods experiments. *Proceedings of the National Academy of Science of the USA, 103,* 3994–3998.

Mulder, L. (2008). The difference between punishment and rewards in fostering moral concerns in social decision making. *Journal of Experimental Social Psychology, 44,* 1436–1443.

Murnighan, J. K., Kim, J. W., & Metzger, A. R. (1993). The volunteer dilemma. *Administrative Science Quarterly, 38,* 515–538.

Nelissen, R. (2008). The price you pay: cost-dependent reputation effects of altruistic punishment. *Evolution & Human Behavior, 29*(4), 242–248.

Nelissen, R., & Zeelenberg, M. (2009). Moral emotions as determinants of third-party punishment: anger, guilt, and the functions of altruistic sanctions. *Judgment and Decision-Making, 4*(7), 543–553.

Nikiforakis, N. (2008). Punishment and counter-punishment in public goods games: can we really govern ourselves? *Journal of Public Economics, 92,* 91–112.

Nikiforakis, N., & Normann, H. T. (2008). A comparative analysis of punishment in public-good experiments. *Experimental Economics, 11*(4), 358–369.

Nowak, M. A., & Sigmund, K. (2005). Evolution of indirect reciprocity. *Nature, 437,* 1291–1298.

O'Gorman, R., Henrich, J., & Van Vugt, M. (2009). Constraining free-riding in public goods games: designated solitary punishers can sustain human cooperation. *Proceedings of the Royal Society of London Series B, 276,* 323–329.

Oliver, P. (1980). Rewards and punishment as selective incentives for collective action: theoretical investigations. *American Journal of Sociology, 85,* 1356–1375.

Ostrom, E. (1990). *Governing the commons.* New York: Cambridge University Press.

Ostrom, E. J., Walker, J., & Gardner, R. (1992). Covenants with and without a sword: self-governance is possible. *American Political Science Review, 86,* 404–417.

Panchanathan, K., & Boyd, R. (2004). Indirect reciprocity can stabilize cooperation without the second-order free rider problem. *Nature, 432,* 499–502.

Piazza, J., & Bering, J. M. (2008). The effects of perceived anonymity on altruistic punishment. *Evolutionary Psychology, 6*(3), 487–501.

Raihani, N. J., Grutter, A. S., & Bshary, R. (2010). Punishers benefit from third-party punishment in fish. *Science, 327*, 171.

Raihani, N. J., & Bshary, R. (2011). The evolution of punishment in n-player public goods games: a volunteer's dilemma. *Evolution, 65*(10), 2725–2728.

Rand, D. G., Dreber, A., Ellingsen, T., Fudenberg, D., & Nowak, M. A. (2009). Positive interactions promote cooperation. *Science, 325*, 1272–1275.

Rankin, D. J., dos Santos, M., & Wedekind, C. (2009). The evolutionary significance of costly punishment is still to be demonstrated. *Proceedings of the National Academy of Science of the USA, 106*(50), E135.

Rockenbach, B., & Milinski, M. (2006). The efficient interaction of indirect reciprocity and costly punishment. *Nature, 444*, 718–723.

Rockenbach, B., & Milinski, M. (2011). To qualify as a social partner, humans hide severe punishment, although their observed cooperativeness is decisive. *Proceedings of the National Academy of Science of the USA, 108*(45), 18307–18312.

Sefton, M., Shupp, R., & Walker, J. M. (2007). The effects of rewards and sanctions in provision of public goods. *Economic Inquiry, 45*(4), 671–690.

Semmann, D., Krambeck, H.-J., & Milinski, M. (2004). Strategic investment in reputation. *Behavioral Ecology and Sociobiology, 56*, 248–252.

Sigmund, K., Hauert, C., & Nowak, M. A. (2001). Reward and punishment. *Proceedings of the National Academy of Science of the USA, 98*, 10757–10762.

Skinner, B. F. (1971). *Beyond Freedom and Dignity*. New York, NY: Knopf.

Sober, E., & Wilson, D. S. (1999). *Unto Others: The Evolution and Psychology of Unselfish Behavior*. Cambridge, MA: Harvard University Press.

Tinbergen, N. (1968). On war and peace in animals and man. *Science, 160*, 1411–1418.

Trivers, R. L. (1971). The evolution of reciprocal altruism. *Quarterly Review of Biology, 46*, 35–57.

United States Department of State International Information Programs (n.d.) *Cuban Liberty and Democratic Solidarity (Libertad) Act of 1996*. Retrieved December 13, 2007, from http://usinfo.state.gov/regional/ar/us-cuba/libertad.htm

Vyrastekova, J., & van Soest, D. (2008). On the (in)effectiveness of rewards in sustaining cooperation. *Experimental Economics, 11*, 53–65.

de Weerd, H., & Verbrugge, R. (2011). Evolution of altruistic punishment in heterogenous populations. *Journal of Theoretical Biology, 290*, 88–103.

West, S. A., Gardner, A., Shuker, D. M., Reynolds, T., Burton-Chellow, M., Sykes, E. M., Guinnee, M. A., & Griffin, A. S. (2006). Cooperation and the scale of competition in humans. *Current Biology, 16*, 1103–1106.

West, S. A., Griffin, A. S., & Gardner, A. (2007). Social semantics: altruism, cooperation, mutualism, strong reciprocity and group selection. *Journal of Evolutionary Biology, 20*, 415–432.

Wu, J.-J., Zhang, B.-Y., Zhou, Z. X., He, Q. Q., Zheng, X. D., Cressman, R., & Tao, Y. (2009). Costly punishment does not always increase cooperation. *Proceedings of the National Academy of Science of the USA, 106*(41), 17448–17551.

Yamagishi, T. (1986). The provision of a sanctioning system as a public good. *Journal of Personality and Social Psychology, 51*, 110–116.

11 Self-governance Through Altruistic Punishment?

■ NIKOS NIKIFORAKIS

Abstract
Evidence from laboratory experiments indicates that many individuals are willing to incur a cost to punish free riders in social dilemmas even when they cannot anticipate a material benefit from their action. This type of behavior which has been termed "altruistic punishment" has attracted considerable attention across social sciences as it suggests a simple way for promoting cooperation. Despite numerous experiments, however, important questions still remain unanswered such as whether altruistic punishment actually makes individuals better off, or whether altruistic punishment can account for some of the cooperation observed in daily life. This chapter reviews some of the research on altruistic punishment focusing on findings which appear to be robust and important questions that are as yet unanswered. I argue that while there can be little doubt that many individuals are willing to enforce cooperation at a personal cost, the conditions required for altruistic punishment to promote efficiency by itself appear to be rare in daily life. The chapter concludes with a claim that the extensive focus on altruistic punishment as a mechanism for promoting cooperation is misplaced and with a discussion of topics for future research.

■ **INTRODUCTION**

Few phenomena have attracted as much interdisciplinary attention in the last decade as the willingness of individuals to punish free riders at a personal cost. Economists, social psychologists, biologists, anthropologists and neuroscientists have produced hundreds of articles (Balliet et al., 2011) examining what has come to be known as "altruistic punishment" (Fehr & Gaechter, 2002). This interest stems partly from the fact that altruistic punishment can serve as a simple mechanism for increasing cooperation when there is a tension between private and group interest (e.g., Masclet et al., 2003; Rockenbach & Milinski, 2006), but also from a desire to understand how the propensity to punish at a cost could have evolved (e.g., Boyd et al., 2010; Dreber et al., 2008).

The research program that has emerged is impressive in its diversity. Novel laboratory experiments, field experiments, game-theoretic and evolutionary models have all helped to sharpen our understanding of the issues related to altruistic punishment, as well as shed light on the human propensity to cooperate with others. Some findings seem now undisputed, such as the fact that the willingness to engage in altruistic punishment is a real phenomenon and not merely a lab artifact (e.g., Balafoutas & Nikiforakis, 2012; Guala, 2012) or that the threat of altruistic punishment can help promote cooperation under certain circumstances. However, despite the numerous studies on the topic, some important questions remain unanswered: Can altruistic punishment make individuals better off or do the costs of punishment exceed the benefits of cooperation? Is altruistic punishment observed and can it account for some of the cooperation observed in daily life?

This chapter reviews some of the research on altruistic punishment, focusing on evidence related to the two open questions mentioned previously. I will argue that *efficiency* and not cooperation levels are the important metric by which to judge the efficacy of altruistic punishment—a point which is sometimes forgotten. I will also argue that altruistic punishment is unlikely to improve efficiency *by itself* in most instances in daily life, and that the focus in future research should shift from altruistic punishment to its underlying cause: negative emotions.

The chapter begins by briefly discussing some of the early studies documenting the human propensity to punish at a cost. I then offer a summary of what appear to be robust findings in the altruistic punishment literature, at this point in time. Throughout, I focus mainly on empirical evidence, although theoretical studies are also discussed at different points. I proceed to discuss two important questions that either remain unanswered or in which the evidence appears to be mixed. The final section concludes by summarizing what we have learned so far and questions for future research.

DEFINITION AND EARLY STUDIES

One can find many characterizations of punishment in the literature. There is *costly* punishment, *peer* punishment, *prosocial* punishment, *moralistic* punishment and *altruistic* punishment. Before we proceed further, therefore, it is useful to define exactly what we mean by the term altruistic punishment. In the words of Fehr and Gaechter (2002) who coined the term:

> "*Altruistic punishment means that individuals punish, although the punishment is costly for them and yields no material gain.*" (p. 137)

This implies that altruistic punishment is *costly*.[1] However, as the following passage suggests, not all costly punishment is altruistic.

> "*Punishment may well benefit the future group members of a punished subject, if that subject responds to the punishment by raising investments in the following periods. In this sense, punishment is altruistic.*" (p. 137)

Therefore, for punishment to be altruistic it must have the potential to benefit others. This is the key feature of altruistic punishment and the difference between the willingness to reject low offers in the ultimatum game and altruistic punishment. Altruistic punishment constitutes a second-order public good; individuals have an incentive to let others punish free riders.

---

1. In a recent article, Gintis and Fehr (2012) allowed for the possibility that altruistic punishment could be costless. This is a point that warrants some attention in the future. For the purpose of this chapter, however, I maintain that altruistic punishment is costly for the punisher.

The first evidence of altruistic punishment was published in Yamagishi (1986), who showed that participants in a laboratory experiment were willing to *voluntarily* contribute to a punishment mechanism that sanctioned the lowest contributor in their group (see also Yamagishi (1988a, 1988b)). Ostrom, Gardner and Walker (1992) were the first to study the willingness to punish themselves in a common pool resource, and found that individuals punished frequently and punishment was mostly aimed towards group members who over-extracted from the pool. Related to Ostrom et al. (1992), Fehr and Gaechter (2000, 2002) studied the willingness to punish free riders in a linear public-good game and found that most people in their experiment used the option to punish, and that punishment was proportional to one's contribution below the average of their group.

The two studies by Fehr and Gaechter were important as, unlike in the previous studies, subjects were assigned into new groups in every round in some experimental treatments. This implied that the authors could rule out the possibility that altruistic punishment was driven by strategic considerations. As the design of Fehr and Gaechter (2002) has become the most widely used environment to examine altruistic punishment (see Balliet et al., 2011), it is worth briefly discussing it. Individuals were placed in groups of typically four individuals. In the first stage of the game, each group member was given the same endowment that they had to divide between a private and a public account. Contributions to the public account increased monotonically (and by the same amount) the earnings of other group members, but reduced the earnings of the individual. In the second stage, individuals were informed about how much each of their peers contributed to the public account and were given the opportunity to reduce the earnings of any group member at a personal cost. In particular, each punishment point the individual assigns to another group member costs one token, and reduces the earnings of the recipient by three tokens. To avoid the possibility of counter-punishment or other meta-strategies, subjects were only informed about the total number of punishment they received and were assigned new identification numbers in each period.

ROBUST FINDINGS ABOUT ALTRUISTIC PUNISHMENT

In order to determine whether a finding is robust, I adopted the (somewhat arbitrary and rather strict) following criteria: (*i*) A finding must have been replicated in *at least* five studies, and (*ii*) no contrary evidence was found in any study. Throughout the vast experimental literature on altruistic punishment, four findings appear to be robust.

(1) *Individuals are willing to use costly punishment to promote cooperation or avenge free-riding, even in one-shot interactions.* This first finding is hardly in need of an extensive discussion. All studies I am aware of find that the majority of individuals are willing to punish group members with above-average earnings (either due to free-riding on the provision of the public good or due to over-extracting from a common pool resource). Similarly, the extent of punishment increases as the earnings of the individual increase relative to the group average. Some people also use the opportunity to punish high contributors, but they are typically

a minority amongst punishers (Cinyabuguma et al., 2006; Hermann et al., 2008; Nikiforakis, 2008; Ostrom et al., 1992).

(2) *Altruistic punishment is an ordinary and inferior good.* Economists define a good as "ordinary" if an increase in its price leads to a reduction of the demand for it. A good is said to be "inferior" when its demand decreases when the income of an individual increases (Varian, 1999). Several researchers have investigated whether punishment is sensitive to changes in its cost and in the potential punisher's income. Punishment here refers to the *income reduction caused* by the punisher to the target. Ambrus and Greiner (2012), Anderson and Putterman (2006), Carpenter (2007), Egas and Riedl (2008) and Nikiforakis and Normann (2008) all found evidence that altruistic punishment is an ordinary and inferior good. This means that as the cost of punishment and the income of the punisher increase, the amount of punishment meted out decreases. The fact that punishment is an inferior good can be easily explained by the fact that individuals with low earnings are typically those who cooperate with others. The fact that punishment is an ordinary good indicates that punishment is sensitive to its cost.

(3) *The threat of altruistic punishment helps sustain cooperation in lab experiments, if the fee-to-fine ratio is sufficiently low.* As mentioned previously, most studies on altruistic punishment use the design of Fehr and Gaechter (2002). In all (but one) experiments, the evidence indicates that the opportunity to punish helps sustain or even increase the *average* level of cooperation in laboratory experiments relative to a treatment in which altruistic punishment is not possible. However, the efficacy of punishment in sustaining cooperation has been shown to be a function of the fee-to-fine ratio (i.e., the cost of purchasing a punishment point relative to the income reduction this point causes to the target). This ratio (which is usually 1/3) reflects the relative cost of punishment: the lower the ratio is, the cheaper it is to punish. Egas and Riedl (2008) and Nikiforakis and Normann (2008) showed that as the fee-to-fine ratio increases, so does the levels of cooperation. If the fee-to-fine ratio is higher than 1/2, cooperation does not deteriorate over time and is significantly higher than the treatment without punishment (see Figure 11.1a).[2] A similar finding is reported in Yamagishi (1986).[3]

There is an exception to finding (3) which should be mentioned as, if I were to apply my criterion for selecting robust findings strictly, it would exclude finding (3) from the list.[4] The evidence regards a framing effect, which I reported in Nikiforakis (2010).[5] In this study, I used the same design as Fehr and Gaechter (2002) with the only difference being the format used to provide subjects with feedback at

---

2. In many instances, the threat of punishment suffices to sustain cooperation (Denant-Boemont et al., 2007; Engelmann and Nikiforakis, 2012; Masclet et al., 2013; Nikiforakis and Engelmann, 2011).
3. Interestingly, in a recent meta-study, Balliet et al. (2011) find that costless punishment appears to be less effective than costly punishment.
4. I decided to make an exception, as I think this result has been widely replicated and is generally believed to be true. For this reason, I chose to use the evidence from Nikiforakis (2010) simply as a cautionary note about institutional design.
5. A framing effect is said to occur if changes in the experiment, which do not affect incentives in the game, alter decisions.

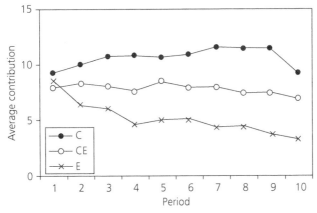

Figure 11.1 Average contribution over time in Nikiforakis (2010). The experiment uses the Fehr and Gaechter (2002) design varying only the format in which individuals receive feedback about the actions of others.

the start of the second stage. Similar to Fehr and Gaechter (2002), in a treatment in which subjects are informed about the contributions of their peers (treatment C in Figure 11.1), contributions appear to increase over time. When subjects are informed about both the contributions and the *earnings* of their peers (treatment CE), cooperation is sustained at the starting level. When subjects are informed instead only about the *earnings* of their peers (treatment E), although this information affects neither incentives nor punishment behavior, cooperation breaks down over time.

How can we explain the sensitivity of cooperation to changes in the feedback format? One explanation is that altruistic punishment has the potential to transform the public-good game from a social dilemma to a coordination game. Contributing more than others lowers one's earnings; contributing less than others triggers punishment. If punishment is sufficiently strong, individuals may be better off contributing as much as their peers. The question then that each group member must answer is, how much will the others contribute? The feedback about individual contributions makes salient who is cooperating, who is not, and, ultimately, the collective benefit from contributing to the public account; the feedback about individual earnings emphasizes the private benefit from free-riding. Since players choose their contributions simultaneously, they have to form expectations about the contributions of their peers. Their expectations and, as a result, contributions can be affected by the feedback format which acts as a coordination device.[6] These results suggest the importance of testing the impact of altruistic punishment in different environments and institutions.[7]

(4) *The threat of counter-punishment is an important determinant of the willingness to engage in altruistic punishment.* Counter-punishment refers to the

---

6. This explanation is supported by the fact that when feedback is given in one of two formats (i.e., in treatments C and E) the variance in contributions decreases significantly over time, but not when both formats are used simultaneously (i.e., in treatment CE).
7. For more on this point, see also Cason and Gangadharan (2012).

willingness of an individual to avenge punishment. In decentralized interactions (especially in one-shot), when individuals have the opportunity to punish, their targets typically have the opportunity to counter-punish. Nikiforakis (2008) found that about a quarter of all sanctions were retaliated at a personal cost, even in the last period of the game. In anticipation of counter-punishment, individuals were less willing to engage in altruistic punishment. This, in turn, reduced both cooperation levels and efficiency. Similar results are reported in the laboratory experiments of Denant-Boemont et al. (2007), Engelmann and Nikiforakis (2012), Nikiforakis and Engelmann (2011), and Nikiforakis, Noussair and Wilkening (2012).

In Balafoutas and Nikiforakis (2012), we report the first evidence of altruistic punishment in a one-shot, natural field experiment. The overall rates of punishment were low relative to those observed in the lab. Survey respondents stated that the main reason for their unwillingness to punish was the fear of counter-punishment. In light of this evidence, an interesting topic for future research is to explain how the willingness for counter-punishment may have evolved.

■ TWO OPEN QUESTIONS REGARDING ALTRUISTIC PUNISHMENT

Despite the hundreds of experiments on altruistic punishment, some key questions remain unanswered. In this section, I discuss two of the most important. The impact of altruistic punishment on efficiency and whether altruistic punishment can explain some of the cooperation observed in daily life.

(1) Does Altruistic Punishment Improve Efficiency?

A lot of the attention on the impact of altruistic punishment literature has been placed on whether it helps improve cooperation prospects (see, e.g., Fehr & Gaechter, 2002; Balliet et al., 2011), but this attention is misplaced. In a typical social dilemma, higher levels of cooperation imply higher earnings for the players. However, this is not necessarily the case when altruistic punishment is permitted, as it is costly both for the punisher and the target. In other words, higher cooperation rates do not necessarily imply that the group as a whole is better off. Another metric to evaluate the efficacy of altruistic punishment is efficiency.

The term efficiency in this literature typically refers to the sum of individual earnings.[8] Why should we care about efficiency over cooperation?, one may ask. There are at least two good reasons. First, if we are interested in designing

---

8. Some may view this approach is paternalistic. The fact that people *are* willing to use costly punishment, they may argue, is evidence that they enjoy the act of punishing. However, this does not imply that individuals as a group are overall better off when they can punish. First, we do not know how the target of punishment feels and whether his disutility exceeds the utility of the punisher. Second, we do not know how large the (potential) disutility of a target of counter-punishment is. Third, we do not know whether individuals would rather be governed by an institution that is solely in charge of punishing or punish themselves and risk getting caught in a feud. Until we have answers to these questions, ignoring non-monetary benefits and costs provides us with a reasonable approximation of welfare.

institutions and policies that improve social welfare, the relevant metric is efficiency and not the level of cooperation. Second, the evolution of the willingness to punish at a cost relies often on group selection (Boyd et al., 2003; Bowles et al., 2003). If punishment is costly, then punishers suffer a disadvantage relative to free-riders or cooperators that do not punish (e.g., Dreber et al., 2008).[9] These costs, however, can be compensated if the group as a whole does better, as it improves the group's chances of winning inter-group contests.

The Fee-to-fine Ratio and Efficiency

With few exceptions, one finds two regularities in the early experimental studies: (*i*) group earnings are increasing over time relative to a baseline treatment without punishment opportunities; (*ii*) on average, altruistic punishment either does not improve efficiency or reduces it.[10] The failure of altruistic punishment to increase efficiency had been noted already in the early studies of Yamagishi (1986) and Ostrom et al. (1992). This appears to be an especially robust result when the fee-to-fine ratio of punishment is high (Yamagishi, 1986; Egas & Riedl, 2008; and Nikiforakis & Normann, 2008). As Yamagishi (1986, p. 114) noted: "The results...suggest that an ineffective sanctioning system is not only useless but could actually be harmful to the total welfare of the group."

Figure 11.2 illustrates this point clearly by presenting group earnings in an experiment I ran with Hans Normann (Nikiforakis & Normann, 2008). In this study, the cost to the punisher of purchasing a punishment point was kept constant (1 token), but we varied the punishment effectiveness (i.e., the amount by which each punishment point reduces the earnings of the target). We ran four treatments that differ in the effectiveness of punishment: "1", "2", "3", and "4". This implies that the fee-to-fine ratio, respectively, was 1:1, 1:2, 1:3 and 1:4. We also ran a treatment without punishment opportunities (treatment "0") to evaluate whether punishment effectiveness affects the success of altruistic punishment in improving group earnings relative to the baseline. Note that the impact of the fee-to-fine ratio is not easy to predict. On the one hand, higher effectiveness is likely to increase cooperation levels. On the other hand, the act of punishment reduces earnings by a larger amount.

Figure 11.2 presents the Cumulative Relative Earnings (CRE) in each treatment of Nikiforakis and Normann (2008) relative to the baseline treatment without

---

9. Note that evolutionary models like Boyd et al. (2003) and Bowles et al. (2003) show that altruistic punishment can be profitable for groups. However, these models allow only for a very limited set of punishment strategies. More recent models allowing for a richer set of punishment strategies show that the conditions for altruistic punishment to evolve are more strict (e.g., Boyd et al., 2010; Janssen & Bushman, 2008; Rand et al., 2010; Rand & Nowak, 2011).

10. As an example, Gaechter et al. (2008, p. 1510) write regarding this point: "For instance, a recent study (Hermann et al., 2008) reported cooperation experiments with and without punishment conducted in 16 participant pools around the world. With the exception of three participant pools, the average payoff in experiments with punishment opportunities was lower than the average without punishment; and in those three participant pools with higher payoffs the increase was very small."

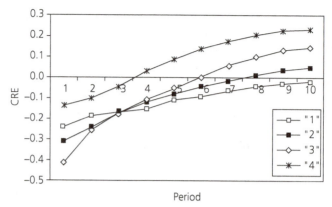

Figure 11.2 Cumulative relative earnings as a function of the effectiveness of punishment (taken from Nikiforakis and Normann, 2008).

punishment opportunities. When CRE = x (or $-x$) in period t, it means that the *sum* of group earnings over all periods up to period t in that treatment, were x percent higher (or lower) than in the baseline treatment. Figure 11.2 illustrates clearly the two regularities mentioned previously. In the first period, all treatments with punishment opportunities have CRE < 0 as contribution rates are similar to those in the baseline treatment and individuals incur the punishment-associated costs. Throughout the experiment, CRE increases in all treatments. However, as can be seen in Figure 11.2, the increase in "1" is not sufficient to offset the losses that occurred in the first periods. Altruistic punishment increases total earnings significantly only when its effectiveness is 3 and 4.

The Long-run Benefits and Costs of Altruistic Punishment

In a widely-cited study, Gaechter et al. (2008) acknowledge the absence of a positive effect of costly punishment in most laboratory experiments. In addition, they noted that most of these experiments employed a short time horizon (10 repetitions). The authors argued that given the increasing trend in group earnings, if groups interact for a sufficiently long time horizon, the sum of the benefits from altruistic punishment over all periods (i.e., the higher levels of cooperation) would ultimately outweigh the punishment. Gaechter et al. considered treatments with and without punishment using the design of Fehr and Gaechter (2002). In line with their hypothesis, they found that while punishment reduces efficiency in 10-period experiments, it improves it in a 50-period time horizon. The explanation they provide is that once cooperation is established, the costs of punishment are low because punishment is rarely used.

An important feature in Gaechter et al. (2008) is that altruistic punishment cannot be retaliated. However, in daily life, and especially in interactions that occur over a long time, horizon punishment can lead to long cycles of revenge, i.e., feuds. This implies that even if the threat of altruistic punishment can establish cooperation, the costs of the feuds can be substantial enough so that they outweigh

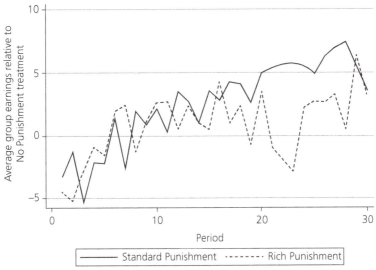

Figure 11.3 Average group earnings relative to a treatment without punishment (taken from Engelmann and Nikiforakis, 2012).

the benefits of higher levels of cooperation, even if punishment is rare. That is precisely what the evidence from a new experiment indicates.

In Engelmann and Nikiforakis (2012) we use a design that allows for complex punishment strategies by imposing minimal restrictions of who can punish whom and when. The experiment consists of (*i*) a no-punishment treatment (NP), (*ii*) a treatment with a single-punishment stage (the SP treatment) that is similar to that in Gaechter et al. (2008), and (*iii*) a rich-punishment treatment (the RP treatment) that is similar to one of the treatments in Nikiforakis and Engelmann (2011). The number of punishment stages in the RP treatment is endogenously determined by the actions of participants. Therefore, this treatment in a way includes the NP and SP treatments as special cases. The experiment lasted for 30 periods, as feuds could increase considerably the duration of the experiment.

The data indicates that while the extent of punishment is lower in RP than SP, cooperation levels are similar across these two treatments, and higher than in NP. What is most important, however, is that while the benefits of higher cooperation eventually outweigh the costs of punishment in SP, group earnings show *no tendency* to increase over time in RP relative to the treatment without punishment *significant* (see Figure 11.3). The reason is that in some groups the threat of altruistic punishment is not sufficiently strong to maintain cooperation while in others some group members get caught into very costly feuds.

Another important feature in Gaechter et al. (2008) is that individual contributions are perfectly observed. Ambrus and Greiner (2012) show that if others' contributions are misrepresented with 10-percent probability—depending on the fee-to-fine ratio of punishment—group earnings are either lower or not significantly different from a treatment without punishment opportunities, despite a 50-period time horizon. I will discuss this study in a bit more detail below.

Normative Conflict and Efficiency

An unexplored feature of the design of Fehr and Gaechter (2002) is that individuals are *symmetric*; they receive the same endowment and enjoy the same benefit from the public good. The symmetry allows individuals to determine more easily what constitutes "fair" behavior (we all contribute the same, we all earn the same) and what constitutes "unfair" behavior (someone contributes less than others and earns more). However, outside the lab, individuals often differ in at least one of the previously-mentioned dimensions. Two recent studies showed that this asymmetry could give rise to *normative conflict* (Nikiforakis et al., 2012; Reuben & Riedl, 2013).

A normative conflict arises when there coexist multiple plausible normative rules about how one ought to behave in a given situation. A normative rule, in turn, is a behavioral rule with properties that are likely to appeal to a large group of individuals (e.g., equal contribution by all individuals or contributing so that all parties receive equal earnings), and hence likely to satisfy the conditions required for it to be adopted as a social norm (Nikiforakis et al., 2012). In Nikiforakis et al. (2012) and Reuben and Riedl (2013) there are at least two such rules: equal contributions for all (which implies unequal earnings) or equal earnings for all (which implies unequal contributions). The use of punishment to enforce one of the normative rules could provoke counter-punishment and lead to a feud if the individuals concerned disagree about which rule is appropriate

Both studies provide evidence that the asymmetric benefits from the public account generate normative conflict.[11] Reuben and Riedl (2013) find that asymmetric endowments do not generate normative conflict. Nikiforakis et al. (2012) show that the introduction of normative conflict increases the likelihood that altruistic punishment triggers counter-punishment by a factor of nearly three: 37% of instances of punishment trigger counter-punishment when there is normative conflict, compared to 14% when group members derive the same benefit from the public good. As a result, group earnings are lower in the presence of normative conflict relative to a treatment with punishment and feuding opportunities in which there is no such conflict.

In another recent study, Xiao and Kunreuther (2012) investigate the impact of altruistic punishment in stochastic social dilemmas. In the game, a player must decide whether to incur a cost to reduce the risk of a negative outcome, knowing that she may experience this outcome nevertheless if her partner has chosen not to do the same. Normative conflict may exist in this game. On the one hand, not incurring the cost increases the probability of the negative outcome occurring. On the other hand, the willingness to invest depends on an individual's risk attitudes, while group earnings are the highest when everyone decides not to invest (as long as the negative outcome does not occur). The results indicate that group earnings

---

11. See also Reuben and Riedl (2009) for the impact of punishment on efficiency in privileged groups in which some (but not all) group members have a private incentive to contribute to the public good. The authors find that altruistic punishment does not increase efficiency when groups are asymmetric.

in the presence of normative conflict and punishment opportunities are not significantly different to those in a treatment without punishment opportunities.

Punishment under Uncertainty and Efficiency

Another feature of most social-dilemma experiments is that there is no uncertainty about the level of cooperation of other group members. However, in daily life, there is often uncertainty about others' contributions. Ambrus and Greiner (2012) and Grechenig et al. (2010) investigate the impact of altruistic punishment in such a setting.

The setup of Grechenig et al. (2010) follows the design of Fehr and Gaechter (2002) with an interesting twist. Rather than observe the actual contributions of others in their group, group member i receives a signal about the contribution of player j. The signal is accurate with probability λ. With probability $1-\lambda$, the signal is a random draw between $\{0, 1, \ldots 20\}$ with each number being equally likely. The experiment consists of three treatments. In the first treatment, $\lambda = 1$ (there is no uncertainty about j's contribution). Behavior in this treatment is compared to two treatments with $\lambda = 0.90$ (little uncertainty) and $\lambda = 0.50$ (high level of uncertainty). The authors also collect data from a treatment without punishment opportunities and $\lambda = 0.50$.

The results of Grechenig et al. (2010) indicate that the greater the uncertainty is, the greater the extent of punishment. Cooperation levels are similar in the punishment treatments with $\lambda = 1$ and $\lambda = 0.90$, but when $\lambda = 0.5$, the threat of punishment does not significantly increase contributions relative to the treatment without punishment. Consequently, when $\lambda = 0.90$, group earnings are substantially lower compared to the baseline treatment with $\lambda = 1$, and similar to the treatment in which there are no punishment opportunities. When uncertainty increases further, i.e., when $\lambda = 0.50$, group earnings are *lower* than that obtained in the game without punishment.

A similar experiment is that of Ambrus and Greiner (2012), which was discussed briefly previously. The three main differences in the two experiments are the following. First, the experiment in Ambrus and Greiner (2012) lasts 50 periods. Second, an individual can only choose whether to cooperate or not. Third, the noise structure is different, as with 10-percent probability someone who cooperated will appear as if they defected. As mentioned, the opportunity to punish reduces group earnings when there is uncertainty about the cooperation of others.

(2) Can Altruistic Punishment Account for Some of the Cooperation Observed in Daily Life?

The propensity to engage in altruistic punishment has been repeatedly documented in laboratory experiments, as has its positive impact on cooperation rates. The obvious question to ask next is whether altruistic punishment has a similar effect in the field. It is far from obvious that individuals will be willing to punish free riders in the field as they do in the lab, for a number of reasons. For example, the potential damage a punished free rider can cause to the punisher is not limited to his experimental earnings, but may be much larger (see cases discussed later in this chapter), making individuals reluctant to bare that cost. Therefore, before we can answer whether altruistic punishment can explain cooperation in the field, we need to first ask whether altruistic punishment is actually observed in daily life.

To answer this question, it is important to remind ourselves what exactly we mean by altruistic punishment. Following the definition in section 2, for punishment to be classified as altruistic, it must satisfy three criteria: (1) it must be *costly for the punisher*; (2) the punisher must derive *no material benefit* from his actions; and (3) punishment must have the *potential to provide a social benefit*. Since in repeated interactions we cannot rule out the possibility that the punisher derives material benefits from his actions (criterion *ii*), we need to consider one-shot interactions.[12]

The only evidence from one-shot interactions in the field so far comes from a recent natural field experiment we conducted in the main subway station in Athens, Greece (Balafoutas & Nikiforakis, 2012). Since the station is used daily by hundreds of thousands of passengers, it implies that interactions are one-shot and strategic motives for punishing are minimized (criterion 2). Survey evidence we collected also suggests that most individuals were concerned about being counter-punished, which implies that punishment was costly (criterion 1). Further, since we considered the violations of efficiency-enhancing social norms, punishment also satisfied the third criterion and could thus be defined as *altruistic*. Finally, costly punishment was the only way to enforce the norm, and only one person at a time could punish the violator, thus, ruling out the second-order public good problem.

The results indicate that norm violations trigger strong negative emotions. In line with laboratory evidence, observers of the violation engage in altruistic punishment, although these individuals are a minority. Interestingly, we find that violations of the better known of the two norms we studied (non-littering) are substantially *less* likely to trigger punishment (4 vs. 19 percent), although they trigger stronger negative emotions. The survey evidence suggests that the reason for this is the beliefs that violators of well-known norms are more likely to

---

12. In an excellent review of the punishment literature, Guala (2012) surveyed existing evidence regarding the use of punishment in anthropological studies. He concluded that there is *no* evidence that costly punishment is used in acephalous groups. Individuals instead appear to be using strategies that avoid counter-punishment and feuds from breaking out (e.g., gossip, ostracism, coordinated punishment). Since interactions in these groups are repeated and there is a small risk of counter-punishment (if any), this type of punishment appears to be fairly *costless* and thus cannot be classified as altruistic. However, this evidence is important as it suggests that, given the option, people will opt for costless punishment—a point to which I will return to in the next section. See also Krueger and Mas (2004) and Mas (2008) for evidence of punishment in labor relations. In these two studies, interactions are repeated, punishment appears to be coordinated by workers' unions, and punishment was "practically undetectable" (Mas, 2008), which implies that there is no risk of (targeted) counter-punishment. It is also worth noting that punishment in Krueger and Mas (2004) and Mas (2008) was likely to be inefficient. Punishment was *very* costly for the target but also reduced the welfare of third parties.

counter-punish—the fear of counter-punishment was the main reason individuals stated for not punishing. Men were more likely than women to punish violators, while the decision to punish is unaffected by the violator's height and gender.

So, in summary, altruistic punishment *is* observed in the field, even if in only a small minority of cases. Does it improve cooperation rates? The experiment of Balafoutas and Nikiforakis (2012) was not meant to answer this question, as violations were exogenous. However, it must be noted that both norms we studied (non-littering, standing on the right side of escalators) were widely adhered to.[13] This provides some indirect evidence that altruistic punishment may serve to promote cooperation in the field. Of course, other factors could also explain norm adherence in our experiment, such as internalization of norms. Noussair et al. (2011) find that punishment does not improve cooperation rates in a framed-field experiment with recreational fishermen. Therefore, this question remains open.

The question of whether altruistic punishment improves efficiency also remains. Recently, there have been a number of high-profile cases in Europe where punishers of norm violators were either severely beaten or killed. In one case in Germany, for example, a pensioner was severely beaten for asking two teenagers to stop smoking in a Munich subway station (Spiegel, 2008; see also Edwards, 2011; Fresco, 2008; and Spiegel, 2010). While running the experiment reported in Balafoutas and Nikiforakis (2012), we also witnessed a serious fight between a punisher and a violator of the escalators norm; luckily, the violator was not a member of our research team! This evidence raises questions whether altruistic punishment can increase efficiency outside the laboratory and may explain why inflicting physical harm onto others is outlawed in most developed countries.[14] However, additional studies on the willingness to punish norm violations of different norms and in different populations are required in order to improve our understanding of the impact of altruistic punishment on cooperation and, most importantly, efficiency.

DISCUSSION

It has been argued that "the altruistic punishment of defectors is a key motive for the explanation of cooperation" (Fehr & Gaechter, 2002; p. 137). Accordingly, hundreds of subsequent studies have explored the willingness of individuals to punish free riders at a cost, and the efficacy of peer punishment in promoting cooperation and efficiency. The evidence that has been reviewed in this chapter raises questions about the correct interpretation of this claim. Costly, uncoordinated punishment among peers certainly does not appear able to explain

---

13. This was also one of the reasons we opted to exogenously violate norms. The other reason was that we wanted to control the features of the violators.

14. Related to this is the evidence from societies in which individuals had an obligation to avenge perceived injustice towards them or their families. The threat of a feud was meant to discourage anti-social behavior. However, punishment in many instances led to feuds. As Boehm (Boehm, 1984, p. 183) writes: "[t]he question remains whether feuds created more disruption than they controlled."

most of the cooperation amongst humans. For one, costly peer punishment is often illegal in developed countries. Further, as seen in this chapter, the conditions required for altruistic punishment to improve efficiency are special (e.g., absence of counter-punishment opportunities, absence of normative conflict, perfect monitoring) and unlikely to be common outside the lab (which raises the issue of how a preference for altruistic punishment may have evolved). In line with this, costly punishment of free riders appears to be rare in anthropological studies (Guala, 2012).[15] In contrast, from ancient times, societies have invested in costly institutions in charge of tackling free-riding. If costly, uncoordinated punishment was sufficient (and efficient), why do societies make this investment?

How should we interpret this claim then? It seems undisputed that some individuals are willing to engage in costly punishment to promote cooperation, both in the lab and in the field, when costly punishment is the *only* option available to them (Balafoutas & Nikiforakis, 2012). However, perhaps unsurprisingly, people will choose to use a costless way to communicate their feelings towards defectors, such as withholding reward or help (Nikiforakis & Mitchell, 2013; Rockenbach and Milinski, 2006), talking to their target (Xiao & Houser, 2005), or spreading gossip (Henrich & Henrich, 2007) when possible. Individuals, therefore, do not appear to have a preference to use costly punishment. *They have a preference for expressing negative emotions toward the free rider.* These emotions are the "key motive" for explaining cooperation. The role of emotions was also mentioned by Fehr and Gaechter (2002, p. 137), who wrote that "negative emotions toward defectors are the proximate mechanism behind altruistic punishment." However, with very few exceptions (e.g., Hopfensitz & Reuben, 2009; Nikiforakis & Mitchell, 2013; Xiao & Houser, 2005), the role of emotions in promoting cooperation and efficiency in social dilemmas has been overlooked in favor of costly punishment.

In light of this evidence, I believe that the emphasis in future research should move away from altruistic punishment as a mechanism for promoting cooperation and efficiency. Instead, the focus may be better placed on how individuals express their emotions under different circumstances and how we can design institutions that harness these emotions in the best possible way to promote the well-being of individuals. Another interesting topic for future research is how different environmental conditions affect the design/selection of institutions. Some studies have already started investigating this topic (e.g., Ertan et al., 2009; Gürerk et al., 2006; Putterman et al., 2011; Noussair & Tan, 2011). Finally, future research could also explore how negative emotions may have evolved over time. These models will allow us to better understand the evolution of institutions and, ultimately, human cooperation.

---

15. Similar to humans, non-humans also have a preference for using costless over costly punishment. A recent study suggests that costly punishment among non-humans is rare (Raihani et al., 2012).

REFERENCES

Ambrus, A., & Greiner, B. (2012). Imperfect Public Monitoring with Costly Punishment—An Experimental Study. *American Economic Review, 102,* 3317–3332.

Anderson, C., & Putterman, L. (2006). Do Non-Strategic Sanctions Obey the Law of Demand? The Demand for Punishment in the Voluntary Contribution Mechanism. *Games and Economic Behavior, 54*(1), 1–24.

Balafoutas, L., & Nikiforakis, N. (2012). Norm Enforcement in the City: A Natural Field Experiment. *European Economic Review, 56,* 1773–1785.

Balliet, D., Mulder, L. B., & Van Lange, P. A. M. (2011). Reward, Punishment, and Cooperation: A Meta-Analysis. *Psychological Bulletin, 137*(4), 594–615.

Bowles, S., Choi, J.-K., & Hopfensitz, A. (2003). The Co-evolution of Individual Behaviors and Social Institutions. *Journal of Theoretical Biology, 223,* 135–147.

Boyd, R., Gintis, H., Bowles, S., & Richerson, P. J. (2003). The Evolution of Altruistic Punishment. *Proceedings of the National Academy of Sciences, 100,* 3531–3535.

Boyd, R., Gintis, H., & Bowles S. (2010). Coordinated Contingent Punishment is Group-Beneficial and Can Proliferate When Rare. *Science, 328,* 617–620.

Carpenter, J. (2007). The Demand for Punishment. *Journal of Economic Behavior & Organization, 62*(4), 522–542.

Cason, T. N., & Gangadharan, L. (2012). Promoting Cooperation in Nonlinear Social Dilemmas through Peer-punishment. Working paper, Purdue University.

Cinyabuguma, M., Page, T., & Putterman L. (2006). Can Second-Order Punishment Deter Perverse Punishment? *Experimental Economics, 9,* 265–279.

Denant-Boemont, L., Masclet, D., & Noussair, C. (2007). Punishment, Counterpunishment and Sanction Enforcement in a Social Dilemma Experiment. *Economic Theory, 33,* 145–167.

Dreber, A., Rand, D. G., Fudenberg, D., & Nowak, M. A. (2008). Winners Don't Punish. *Nature, 452,* 348–351.

Edwards, R. (2011). Police Officers Beaten by Mob after Asking Girl to Pick up Litter. *The Telegraph,* September 6. Available at: http://www.telegraph.co.uk/news/uknews/2433514/Police-officers-beaten-by-mob-after-asking-girl-to-pick-up-litter.html

Egas, M., & Riedl, A. (2008). The Economics of Altruistic Punishment and the Maintenance of Cooperation. *Proceedings of the Royal Society B, 275,* 871–878.

Engelmann, D., & Nikiforakis, N. (2012). In the Long Run we are all Dead: On the Benefits of Peer Punishment in Rich Environments. University of Mannheim, Department of Economics, Working Paper ECON 12-22.

Ertan, A., Page, T., & Putterman, L. (2009). Who to Punish? Individual Decisions and Majority Rule in Mitigating the Free-Rider Problem. *European Economic Review, 53,* 495–511.

Fehr, E., & Gächter, S. (2000). Cooperation and Punishment in Public Goods Experiments. *American Economic Review, 90,* 980–994.

Fehr, E., & Gächter, S. (2002). Altruistic Punishment in Humans. *Nature, 415,* 137–140.

Fresco, A. (2008). Four Years for Teenagers who Killed Evren Anil. *The Times,* April 5. Available at: http://www.timesonline.co.uk/tol/news/uk/crime/article3684893.ece

Gächter, S., Renner, E., & Sefton, M. (2008). The Long-Run Benefits of Punishment. *Science, 322,* 1510.

Gintis, H., & Fehr, E. (2012). The Social Structure of Cooperation and Punishment. *Behavioral and Brain Sciences, 35,* 28–29.

Grechenig, K., Nicklisch, A., & Thöni, C. (2010). Punishment Despite Reasonable Doubt—A Public Goods Experiment with Sanctions under Uncertainty. *Journal of Empirical Legal Studies*, 7, 847–867.

Guala, F. (2012). Reciprocity: Weak or Strong? What Punishment Experiments Do (and Do Not) Demonstrate. *Behavioral and Brain Sciences*, 35, 1–15.

Gürerk, O., Irlendbusch, B., & Rockenbach, B. (2006). The Competitive Advantage of Sanctioning Institutions, *Science*, 312, 108–111.

Henrich, N., & Henrich, J. (2007). *Why humans cooperate*. Oxford: Oxford University Press.

Herrmann, B., Thöni, C., & Gächter, S. (2008). Antisocial Punishment Across Societies. *Science*, 319, 1362–1367.

Hopfensitz, A., & Reuben, E. (2009). The Importance of Emotions for the Effectiveness of Social Punishment. *The Economic Journal*, 119(540): 1534–1559.

Janssen, M. A., & Bushman, C. (2008). Evolution of Cooperation and Altruistic Punishment When Retaliation is Possible. *Journal of Theoretical Biology*, 254, 541–545.

Krueger, A., & Mas, A. (2004). Strikes, Scabs, and Tread Separations: Labor Strife and the Production of Defective Bridgestone/Firestone Tires. *Journal of Political Economy*, 112, 253–289.

Mas, A. (2008). Labor Unrest and the Quality of Production: Evidence from the Construction Equipment Resale Market. *Review of Economic Studies*, 75, 229–258.

Masclet, D., Noussair, C., Tucker, S., & Villeval, M.-C. (2003). Monetary and Non-Monetary Punishment in the Voluntary Contribution Mechanism. *American Economic Review*, 93, 366–380.

Masclet, D., Noussair, C., & Villeval, M.-C. (2013). Threat and Punishment in Public Good Experiments. forthcoming *Economic Inquiry*.

Nikiforakis, N. (2008). Punishment and Counter-punishment in Public Good Games: Can we Really Govern Ourselves? *Journal of Public Economics*, 92, 91–112.

Nikiforakis, N. (2010). Feedback, Punishment and Cooperation in Public Good Experiments. *Games and Economic Behavior*, 68, 689–702.

Nikiforakis, N., & Engelmann, D. (2011). Altruistic Punishment and the Threat of Feuds. *Journal of Economic Behavior and Organization*, 78, 319–332.

Nikiforakis, N., & Mitchell, H. (2013). Mixing the Carrots with the Sticks: Third Party Punishment and Reward. Forthcoming *Experimental Economics*.

Nikiforakis, N., & Normann, H. T. (2008). A Comparative Statics Analysis of Punishment in Public-good Experiments. *Experimental Economics*, 11, 358–369.

Nikiforakis, N., Noussair, C. N., & Wilkening, T. (2012). Normative Conflict & Feuds: The Limits of Self-Enforcement. *Journal of Public Economics*, 96, 797–807.

Noussair, C. N., van Soest, D., & Stoop, J., (2011). Punishment, Reward, and Cooperation in a Framed Field Experiment. MPRA Paper No. 34067.

Noussair, C. N., & Tan, F. (2011). Voting on punishment systems within a heterogeneous group. *Journal of Public Economic Theory*, 13(5), 661–693.

Ostrom, E., Walker, J., & Gardner, R. (1992). Covenants with and without a Sword: Self Governance is Possible. *American Political Science Review*, 86, 404–417.

Putterman, L., Tyran, J.-R., & Kamei, K. (2011). Public Goods and Voting on Formal Sanction Schemes: An Experiment. *Journal of Public Economics*, 95(9–10), 1213–1222.

Raihani, N. J., Thornton, A., & Bshary, R. (2012). Punishment and Cooooperation in Nature. *Trends in Ecology and Evolution*, 27(5), 288–295.

Rand, D. G., & Nowak, M. A. (2011). The Evolution of Antisocial Punishment in Optional Public Goods Games. *Nature Communications*, 2, 434.

Rand, D. G., Armao, J., Nakamaru, M., & Ohtsuki, H. (2010). Anti-Social Punishment Can Prevent the Co-Evolution of Punishment and Cooperation. *Journal of Theoretical Biology*, 265, 624–632.

Reuben, E., & Riedl, A. (2013). Enforcement of Contribution Norms in Public Good Games with Heterogeneous Populations. *Games and Economic Behavior*, 77, 122–137.

Rockenbach, B., & Milinski, M. (2006). The Efficient Interaction of Indirect Reciprocity and Costly Punishment. *Nature*, 444, 718–723.

Spiegel, Der. (2008). Immigrants Get Long Sentences For Attacking German Pensioner. *Der Spiegel*, August 7. Available at: http://www.spiegel.de/international/germany/0,1518,564651,00.html l

Spiegel, Der. (2010). Murder on a Station Platform: German Teenagers Jailed for Killing 'Hero'. *Der Spiegel*, June 9. Available at: http://www.spiegel.de/international/germany/0,1518,715963,00.html

Varian, H. R. (1999). *Intermediate Microeconomics (5th ed.)*. New York and London: Norton.

Xiao, E., & Houser, D. (2005). Emotion Expression in Human Punishment Behavior. *Proceedings of National Academy of Science*, 102(20), 7398–7401.

Xiao, E., & Kunreuther, H. (2012). *Punishment and Cooperation in Stochastic Prisoner's Dilemma Game*. NBER Working Paper 28458.

Yamagishi, T. (1986). The Provision of a Sanctioning System as a Public Good. *Journal of Personality and Social Psychology*, 51(1), 110–116.

Yamagishi, T. (1988a). Seriousness of Social Dilemmas and the Provision of a Sanctioning System. *Social Psychology Quarterly*, 51(1), 32–42.

Yamagishi, T. (1988b). The Provision of a Sanctioning System in the United States and Japan. *Social Psychology Quarterly*, 51(3), 265–271.

12 Beyond Kin: Cooperation in a Tribal Society

■ PIERRE LIENARD

Abstract

How can extensive cooperation be stabilized in a tribal society without central institutions at an affordable cost to its members? The argument presented here is based on data gathered among Turkana pastoralist groups of northwest Kenya. These traditional herder communities provide a natural setting to study cooperation and social order maintenance in a decentralized society. The present study focuses on a regional cooperation and defense apparatus involving several local units. Although the regional coalitional network is grounded in kin and matrimonial relations, friendship bonds, and clientelism, the extensive cooperation supporting that network would be unsustainable if not for the institution of generation- and age-sets system. The Turkana age-set system facilitates the mobilization and coordination of autonomous groups while motivating the mutual monitoring of agents' commitment and behavior without the cost of supplying third-party sanctioning institutions.

■ INTRODUCTION

Human cooperation presents a major challenge: When to invest in cooperation when the potential for defection exists? In order to keep naturally self-interested individuals committed to a cooperative strategy, specific problems need to be addressed. Monitoring for potential cheaters must be maintained, free-riding sanctioned and the cost of both monitoring and sanctioning should be shared by the collectivity of cooperators. The puzzle of human cooperation has stimulated an impressive amount of original research in various disciplines (e.g., Olson, 1965; Hardin, 1968; Yamagishi, 1986, 1988; Ostrom, 1990; Boyd & Richerson, 1992; Gintis, 2000; Patton, 2000; Fehr et al., 2002; Price et al., 2002; Cosmides & Tooby, 2005; Marlowe, 2009 Shinada & Yamagishi, 2010). The present research contributes to the debate by providing a case study based on data gathered in a traditionally decentralized and acephalous pastoral society, the Turkana of Kenya. The contribution addresses the question of the implementation of supra-local cooperation in a social context where stable third-party institutions are not available.

The traditional pastoral Turkana society is an interesting case study exactly because it combines these two features: [a] extensive supra-familial and -local cooperation and [b] absence of third-party institutions. The society does not have any traditional central institution wielding any form of permanent political control over the public domain. Some individuals, at times, reach enough notoriety and power allowing them to muster enough allies to exert greater political influence.

However, the nature of the Turkana society and its ecological setting render such a divisive, cliquish form of political control highly unstable as a long-term strategy and limited in scope.

The study population lives in arid and semi-arid rangelands in northwest Kenya at the border with Uganda and South Sudan. The ecology of the area explains in part the atomization of the society into discrete, autonomous and self-reliant economic units, groups of polygynous households, exploiting specific ranges. When rainfall is sustained and temporary pastures, green, the groups of polygynous households settle far apart in the arid plain of the Turkana homeland so that pressures on the pastoral resources are reduced. Given the extreme ecological constraints, these are ideal conditions. Competition for pastoral resources is low. Herdsmen autonomously organize their pastoral movements and residences, loosely coordinate with friends exploiting adjacent areas and decide on the degree of socialization they wish to entertain.

When rainfall is insufficient to keep pastures inviting, households need to move to dry-season rangelands located on higher ground in the foothills and plateaus at the perimeter of the arid plain, in areas typically closer to homelands of other tribes. The Turkana have been engaged in cycles of hostility with surrounding tribes. Hostilities involve cattle rustlings, fights for access to strategic rangelands and preemptive aggressions and retaliatory raids. Occupying zones near enemies thus requires the coordination of local economic units into larger cooperative and defense ensembles. Pastoral settlements need to be larger in order to provide safety in numbers.

The organization of large pastoral camps brings about significant costs to their members. A higher population density means resource competition. It forces the community to migrate at a faster rate given the greater speed of exhaustion of local resources. The camp must be fortified with perimeters of thorny bushes. Members of households are diverted from their pastoral routines for safety patrols or reconnaissance of potential sites. Everyone feels the emotional burden of living in close proximity to a great number of people and relying strongly on others for one's safety. There is a greater likelihood of being repeatedly asked to share resources. Herdsmen are pressed to pay for the fulfillment of collective services. Scouts and warriors must be thanked and compensated for their risky investment. Cooperation networks must be re-ignited. Norm enforcement calls for retribution. Camp membership begs for commitment signals. All acknowledgements, compensations and expression of commitment and friendship typically involve the sacrifice of livestock to feed collectivities of individuals. Thus in order for the large agglomeration of households to get organized efficiently, members must pay their dues and take on their share of the collective burden. Such are the conditions of large temporary gatherings of households that they provide social agents with many opportunities of skirting responsibilities or downright free-riding.

A complex process builds camps for extended periods of time from the building blocks of basic self-reliant polygynous units without third-party institutions. Large camp communities regularly vary in size given the repeated defections of families willing to embrace the consequences of falling back on poorer rangelands in less exposed areas while not enduring the harsh conditions of collective camp life and the risk of overexposure to the enemy. Separating from the camp in areas closer to enemy territories is hardly an option for richer households in need of pastoral resources in greater abundance for their large herds. Too many defections have dire consequences for the remaining population, as the camp size might not provide enough safety anymore. Reaching a certain threshold of households to organize a resilient community while avoiding the burden of too many profiteers is a fragile balance that needs to be struck. As we will see, wealthy herdsmen attempt to counter some of the forces of fission by transferring resources to less affluent heads of households. Those sustained transfers are prime means for wealthy males to build a reputation and to buy political favors by organizing clienteles. But once again, such politics cannot alone account for the maintenance of large cooperative units such as the large pastoral camps occupying the perimeter of the Turkana central plain. What institutional construct could facilitate that?

The institutions of generation- and age-set systems seem to be a good candidate. Age-sets are mobilization devices that coordinate groups of male coevals by giving them mutual rights, duties and individual and collective responsibilities. As we will see, the institution does not resolve the cooperation puzzle by creating costly third-party sanctioning institutions. The generation- and age-set institution provides what Shinada & Yamagishi (2010) identify as a structural solution to the cooperation dilemma. It does so by altering the individuals' incentive structure, broadening the pool of social agents having an inherent and direct interest in the monitoring and policing of other agents' behavior given its collective consequences. The institution enables a generalized and cheaper second-party sanctioning system, even among socially distant agents.

■ THE STUDY POPULATION ~ THE TURKANA PASTORALIST *NGILUKUMONG*

The data presented here were gathered in pastoralist communities belonging to the *Ngilukumong* territorial section of the Kenyan Turkana tribe. The *Ngilukumong* section dwells in the Turkana West district of Turkana County. The study population, close to 1,250 people, flanked by five smaller groups, exploits around 3,000 km² of rangelands in the northwest of the county close to the border with northeastern Uganda near its northern border with South Sudan (Figure 12.1, around yellow dot).

The traditional communities of the county still depend on livestock production (sheep, goats, cattle, and camels) for meat, milk and other derivatives as subsistence staple foodstuff and as transportation means (donkeys).

■ TERRITORIAL SECTIONS AND GRAZING UNITS

The tribal-wide polity consists of fourteen major territorial sections (*ekitela*)[1]. Each of the sections is attached to a territory providing the resources required

---

1. Personal data. There are debates about the exact number. See Muller (1989) for a discussion.

Beyond Kin: Cooperation in a Tribal Society ■ 217

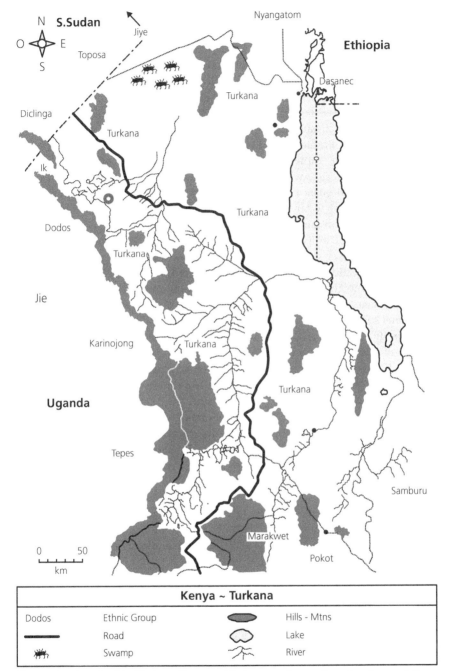

Figure 12.1 A map of the Turkana County with the area of research centered around the yellow dot. The map is not a perfect or complete depiction of every road, elevation, and topographical feature.

by human and animal populations for the whole of an ordinary year. The section is the unit within which essential matters such as region-wide defense or far-ranging migrations in extended drought are organized. The Turkana County where the sections reside for most ordinary years is a hill-dotted plain, carved by seasonal river channels, hemmed in by escarpments under the control of other tribes (west and south) and Lake Turkana (eastern flank). The central plain does not have lasting water resources[2]. Significant rains, falling anytime between March and August, provide short-lived grasslands in the plain (Turkana District Profile—Arid Lands Resource Management Project). When the grass dries out, cattle herds need to migrate to the foothills adjacent to other tribes' territories, where pastoral resources last longer. The less choosy camels, sheep and goats reside in the plain for longer given their reliance on browsing and lesser water needs. The county's geographic features, and consequent constraints on land uses, account for the division in economically independent territorial units. A self-sufficient territory includes portions of river basins for wells, wet-season rangelands and dry-season refuge zones.

Territorial section membership is open. A herd owner may leave a section by permanently moving his operation to a new community. The new membership is not automatically recognized; time does the assimilation work by testing the newcomer's loyalty to his new community. Sections are economic units attached to naturally disjoint territories. They are made of nested structures. Small local groups of families, pastoral partners and clients associate with other similar groups sharing the same ecological area to form an *adakar*, or grazing unit, with a strong corporate identity. Several of those communities that regionally coordinate their movements create an *arigan*, a unit that aggregates for safety reasons in a large camp when close to enemy territories. Across adjacent regions, several *arigan* can coordinate their long-distance migration patterns and defense strategies when moving closer to enemy territories. The corporate identity of a group of *arigan* is weaker, as interactions are hard to sustain given the distance separating the communities' respective home ranges and the difficulty of aggregating all units in one location for any period of time. The complex bottom-up system of coalitions maintaining the corporate identity of the sections (and eventually all the way to the tribal level) can best be understood as Russian-doll like, with independent entities of equal status selectively and temporarily organized in larger special-purpose corporate groups.

The pastoral communities of the research area have been engaged in hostilities involving casualties, cattle rustlings, and preemptive and retaliatory raids with surrounding tribes. When dwelling near enemy territories, those communities assemble in large camps. It affords safety but also more conflicts, competition for pastoral resources, mobility, begging for and theft of animals, and duties toward fellow *arigan* members. Our large study community (*arigan*) comprises 1,254 individuals split among 80 households unevenly distributed between 6 grazing

---

2. The water of Lake Turkana cannot be sustainably consumed given its high alkalinity and elevated salt content.

units (*adakar*). The biggest of those units, the core of the *arigan*, comprises 522 individuals in 38 households. All other units began as offshoots of the large unit.

An *adakar* is a stable social environment within which social agents interact regularly, allowing for the fostering of personal ties and loyalty among its members (Gulliver, 1951). Its members acknowledge belonging to a unit with a corporate identity entailing responsibility for the unit's reputation, commitment to its maintenance (as costs are incurred), rights of all members to access basic needs in times of want (e.g., no one goes hungry while others enjoy a plenty), privilege to use the common pool of resources (i.e., if one puts his share of effort, one is entitled to the benefit)[3], and mutual duties of defense and succor. That identification and the consequent loyalty trump affiliations to larger units.

The denizens of the *adakar* ideally conceived of their community as a *mutualist* society. Residents associate freely. A strong egalitarian norm shapes interactions among coevals. Social agents and, more particularly so, males are expected to be self-reliant and individualistic. Opportunistic behaviors are readily anticipated, which give their particular competitive nature to many Turkana social affairs. In such a world, self-realization demands from agents that they be fast to address challenges and to engage in agonistic interactions. In such conditions too, one's reputation is of utter importance and needs to be supported by appropriate actions.

In spite of the strong individualistic and agonistic tendencies at work in the *adakar* pastoral communities, those units are surprisingly stable. The *adakar* affords a year-round protection against the enemy. Furthermore, the systematic association between households allows families to rely on each other for minimizing the inherent risks of a highly specialized pastoral economy. Herdsmen exchange surplus animals, rely on partners to replenish their stock, or acquire studs from others to diversify the genetics of their herds. Families associate to dig wells and water the animals or to take care of each other's herds when need arises.

In order to be able to benefit from their association to the camp community, social agents have to balance generosity, hence advertising their quality as cooperators, with enough selfishness to avoid becoming the systematic target of exploitative behaviors. Such a balancing act required great social skills, given the fundamental norm regulating social interactions within the *adakar*: members have a mutual obligation to cooperate when a request for support is addressed. Belonging to an *adakar* community implies the tacit acceptance of that norm. (Lienard & Anselmo, 2004).

Many everyday ordinary social interactions involve requests, from begging for tobacco to chew to the more significant request of an animal to eat. To refuse flatly is unwelcome. When a significant request is made, an abrupt refusal is bound to lead to a rapid escalation into an abusive and aggressive interaction. There is indeed an expectation that any request made be addressed appropriately, that is, that either the object of the request or a substitute be given, a promise of providing

---

3. Digging wells is a good illustration. No one is prohibited to use a source of water but one has to put the effort in the scouting that was necessary to find it and the digging of wells.

the good later be made, or a reasonable justification for the refusal be offered. When no agreement is reached or a breach of the norm requiring addressing a request occurs, onlookers typically intervene and offer suggestions in order for a consensus to emerge. (Lienard & Anselmo, 2004).

In such social interactions it is interesting to note that very rarely is the legitimacy of making the request, and to have it addressed, put into question. Furthermore the audience seems to typically side with the requester and not the requestee. Not addressing one's request is evidence of one's extreme selfishness, implying the rejection of a fundamental principle supporting the whole edification of the pastoral community: the expectation of mutual assistance and consequent circulations of goods and possessions among the members of the community. Agents systematically behaving selfishly threaten the proper functioning of the whole system. They are the subject of gossip and abusive mockery. Given the high reputational cost of being accused of selfishness in the closed environment of the *adakar*, the targets of such low-cost sanctioning strategies, such as gossip, go to great length to change the collective perception.

■ FAMILIAL NEPOTISM, MATRIMONIAL ALLIANCES AND CLIENTELES

The 38 households of the main unit of the study *arigan* vary in sizes: from compound households composed of a herd owner, his wives, his mother, younger brothers and wives, unmarried sisters with offspring, and aunts to small households comprising very few people. In the core we find one large compound household of 62 persons, two of 30 or more people, five of 20 or more people, fourteen of 10 or more people, and the rest, close to 10.

Not everyone has an equal voice in the core. Members of the community readily acknowledge an existing hierarchy. Twelve of those 38 households are considered essential to the existence of the camp. Those essential households are divided into three groups, from very influential to moderately so. Five households compose the camp's head. Six are influential but have less political power because they are smaller and not as rich as the influential five. The third group comprises one wealthy household, influential but less involved in political decision-making. All other households are considered followers.

Wealthy households have at least 80 heads of cattle. There are eight such households in the core. The numbers of head of cattle they own greatly vary from eighty to several hundred. Middle-range households have 30 to 80 heads of cattle. There are 26 of those in the core. Four poor households have less than 30 heads of cattle. Of the very influential five, four belong to the wealthy and one to the middle-range group. The two most influential households combine the two largest numbers of members (36 and 62) with great livestock resources (among the four richest households). Of the last six rich households, five are ranked in either one of the three influential groups. The last wealthy household is not ranked or considered influential. Of the twenty-six middle-range households, five households are ranked among the influential 12. Those households have a decent number of people with two units of 20 people or above, two 10 people and above and two close to 10 people. The four poor households have small numbers of people (maximum 11, minimum seven).

The Turkana patrilineal society practices polygyny with a strong rule of virilocality. Allied groups of related males typically constitute the backbone of larger social units. The study *arigan* comprises approximately 250 males in their twenties or older. In order to appraise the degree of relatedness between those men, we inquired about the relations each of 106 males had with one another. Two categories of relations were investigated: (1) primary relations such as first-degree kin relationships (parent/offspring, brothers, uncle/nephew, and cousins) and marriage/concubinage[4] relations, and (2) easily traced relations involving more distant kin relationships. Those categories of relations were chosen, as they have the great potential to give rise to sustained and normative circulations of animals (gift, exchange, bride price) and provisioning of succor between individuals thus related.

Six hundred and eighty-seven primary relations (6.48 relations/individual) and 174 secondary relations (1.64 relations/individual) were identified, giving a total of 8.12 relations per individual. Although the number of relations per male individual ascertains the high degree of relatedness between the *arigan's* men, the figure hides an essential aspect of the social structure. A few families dominate the camp. Affluent families entertain complex networks of relations with one another based on shared ancestry but also on alliances through marriage and concubinage. Members of those dominant groups pull within their sphere of influence other herdsmen and their households through numerous stock associations, which are elective relationships linking two herdsmen having the goal to satisfy animal husbandry requirements (e.g., exchange of animals).

Wealthy families seem to be partly responsible for some form of integration of the basic social units supporting the *arigan's* general structure by establishing strategic marriage alliances and organizing clientele relations thanks to systematic transfers of resources. However, the type of organization described here is likely to be systematically affected by the fission of larger social units into smaller cliques with, at their core, influential families and their clients. Indeed, wealthy herdsmen with large families can afford to grow their herd, as they have the necessary labor within their households. They can in turn divert animals for new bride-price payments and for supporting more concubines. Being more attractive, they easily establish stock associations with others. They are able to support many clients by transferring animals to less wealthy households, securing for themselves a greater political say. The risks of systematic fission between powerful families and their associates, desertion of disgruntled social groups and split into contrasted units are real given the potential for enhanced rivalry, favoritism and unfair treatment afforded by such an organization based on familial segments and cliques.

---

4. *Apese a ngabwes*, "girl of the skirt (worn by married women)." Concubines are women for whom the bride-price of animals has not been paid. The offspring of a concubine belong to her father's lineage. Fathering children with a concubine involves duties such as the payment of animals for each birth. Males use concubinage to cement their relations. Well-off 50 and up males typically have several such relationships on top of regular marriages.

The problem of fragmentation is compounded by the inherent competition among males of the same families for access to the family herd animals[5]. Given the practice of polygyny, fathers intent on marrying again compete with their sons over access to animals for bride-price. Brothers or uncles and nephews do, too, as one kin's withholding of animals to promote his personal advancement cost others the use of the resource for future aims. The basic Turkana social unit, with its feature of shallow genealogical memory, reflects that intra-family competition. The history of the partitioning of the *arigan*'s community into smaller autonomous grazing units provides evidence of such dissolving forces at work within familial units and larger social groups.

LOCAL CLIQUES MODULATE THE SIZE OF COOPERATIVE UNITS

Why is the population not more atomized given the powerful dissolutive forces? Recent historical events account for the emergence of a Turkana tribal sentiment (Lamphear, 1988, 1992, 1993; Müller, 1989). During the 19th century, an original group expanded from the foothills of west central Turkana into adjacent plains, where it progressively split into regional social units. Early in the 20th century, the colonial conquest interrupted the repeated fission into new territorial groups. A tribal identity emerged in the common opposition to the invader. (Gulliver, 1951; Lamphear, 1976, 1992) After independence, ethnic clashes flared up once again (Mkutu, 2008). Thanks to the previous phase of population growth and integration, communication between distant groups was easier, explaining the regional-level coordination of raiding activities and the conflict escalation between tribes starting in the mid 70s (Lamphear, 1992; Mukutu, 2008). As tribal integration has affected all regional groups, the risk of being exposed to sizeable enemy forces is greater under modern conditions. Reaching a critical mass of people is required to withstand enemy onslaughts, thus the incentive to maintain larger cooperative regional units. Both the historical demographic and strategic considerations provide some rationale for the greater integration of the Turkana. What might have been the institutional mechanisms that helped local autonomous groups to counter their fissiparous tendencies and to sustain larger groups and regional alliances?

The regular transfers of resources taking place at sacrificial feasts, involving the killing of large animals for male collectivities, play a role in the broadening of the social base supporting larger social units. Such sacrifices are performed regularly

---

5. The basic social unit is the *awi*, a polygynous family with, at its core, a *pater*, his wives and offspring. The *awi* comprises *ekol*, matrifocal groups (mothers and offspring) having some economic autonomy. Each wife is allocated animals for her use. The pater's ownership of the herd stays undivided. A man can take control of his deceased full brother's *awi*. If the *awi* is not "repossessed," inheritance is transmitted to sons along the lines of the division in *ekol*. Full brothers subsist on their *ekol*'s part of the original herd, until further growth and split. In such systems, competition over animals occurs. Beyond a certain genealogical depth, males attempt to shed their duties toward kin.

at rain or apotropaic rituals, as payment to a group for reconnaissance and raiding activities or as gifts to particular age groups. The practice involves transfers of large quantities of meat. The overall picture is one of wealthier herdsmen compensating less affluent members of the community in exchange for some form of enhanced status, greater political say and social clout.

At such sacrifices, mature animals are killed and the meat consumed by groups of males. The gift of a large animal for a sacrifice may involve the back-payment of an immature female animal to the sacrificial victim's owner. The individual killing the sacrificial victim makes the payment. It is understood that the immature female will produce offspring that will replace the sacrificial animal. The victim's owner and killer share the sacrificial cost: by letting go of a long-cared-for neutered animal (7 years to maturity) or by relinquishing the fertility potential of a young animal. Both take a risk—to see the young animal die before reproduction while relinquishing a sure asset or to miss out on the young animal's future contribution. An individual who is both giver and killer is particularly praiseworthy. The head of the study *arigan*'s most influential household did so more often than anybody else.

Between 2007 and 2011 most of the large sacrificial victims in our pastoral community (*arigan*) were Turkana zebu oxen. The mature body weight of a male zebu of such breed reaches a minimum of 320 kg (706 lbs) (Rege et al., 2001). An estimated 55.83 oxen were sacrificed annually, giving a figure of 11,111 kg (24, 496 lbs) (hanging weight) of sacrificial meat per year for the camp. Most animals were sacrificed at the onset, during or at the end of the dry season. In an ordinary year, for four months the population dwells in the plains away from the enemy. It is a time of plenty. Less sacrifices for male collectivities take place. Excluding those months, we reach the number of 1,490 kg (3,285 lbs) of sacrificial meat per dry-season month for our community or an average of 133 grams (.3 lbs) of deboned meat per day per adult male. Although lacking refinement, this figure illustrates that the resource transfers are quite large, particularly so given that the transfers are made during the harshest period of the year.

Most large animals sacrificed in the five-year interval came from the wealthier households. In the *arigan*'s core, eight herdsmen gave fifty-seven percent of the sacrificial animals. Of those eight, seven belong to the groups of wealthy or middle-range households. Two of the greatest providers belong to the same compound household, ranked first in political influence and among the four richest households of the core. They gave 22 animals in the last five years. The second largest contributor gave 10 animals, the third, nine, the fourth and fifth, eight, and the sixth biggest contributor, seven. All those individuals belong to the group of the 12 most influential households of the *arigan*'s core.

If the picture is one of wealthier individuals supporting less affluent community members, it does not mean that less well-off herdsmen can altogether escape contributing some animals, at the very least occasionally. If they cannot donate animals for large festive gatherings, according to their capacity, from time to time they'll offer goats or sheep to sacrifice for smaller groups of males. Wealthy community members test the commitment of other poorer individuals by regularly requesting animals to organize such sacrificial feats. Herdsmen must participate in that community-wide reciprocal gift giving linking men to one another. Individuals contribute proportionally to their resources; there is no expectation of strict equivalence between numbers and size of animals given. There is, though, an expectation to commit resources regularly to the system of mutual exchange and offering. Failing to do so exposes oneself to a suspicion of unreliability and extreme selfishness, which deter potential cooperators.

A herdsman not contributing sufficiently in proportion to his standard of living takes the risk of being forcefully asked to sacrifice animals as expressions of commitment to the grazing unit. When systematically failing to contribute, an individual is quickly identified as stingy. The unfair behavior is appraised as evidence of the individual's lack of commitment and disloyalty, fundamentally equivalent to a breach of the norm of mutual benevolence unifying the members of the pastoral unit. There are several forms of adequate responses to such a breach. They all involve an element of factional politics.

Groups of men performing a collective duty such as patrolling and reconnaissance may request animals from the stingy herdsman in retribution for their service, instead of asking other men with good reputation. A band of warriors (*ajore*) upon returning from a raid might seize animals in the corral of the selfish individual to organize a collective sacrifice. Through various oracular practices, a soothsayer might identify for a special-purpose sacrifice an animal with a specific coat color pattern that can only be found in the herd of the stingy herdsman. When the time comes to organize a collective feast, the community of the *adakar* might specifically target the disloyal herdsman to get animals on which to feast.

The collective pressure can be applied with more or less violence. The seizing of animals in the herdsman's corral can display features of a highly ritualized aggression where episodes of request alternate with energetic rebuttals until progressively the owner of the requested animals is won over, abandons the opposition and gets publically praised for his good deed. But the seizing can be conducted much more forcefully and approximate what could be seen as real retaliation against the uncooperative herdsman. There are other instances of deviance involving sanctioning by cliques and factions. The systematic non-respects of collective pastoral decisions by rogue families are among the most common violations. Behaviors such as the grazing of pastures left to rest by the pastoral community for later use or the systematic and unauthorized use of other people's wells typically evoke angry reactions from the parties impacted by the wrongdoing.

There are thus rewards, costs and challenges associated with camp membership. The wealthy herdsmen accept to share their wealth with less affluent members in exchange for an enhanced status and a greater political clout, thus achieving greater authority in the process of collective decision-making in factional, pastoral and war affairs. In the meantime, they secure safety for their households through the increase in camp membership. The poorer herdsmen get paid for relinquishing some autonomy and staying in the large pastoral community. Less affluent herdsmen make as good a bet for success when putting affluent members of the camp in charge. As the latter's wealth suggests, rich herdsmen have been successful so far and have much to lose.

The strategy of subsidizing the less affluent members of the large pastoral community partially reaches its objective of integrating autonomous units into larger ensembles. At the very same time, though, it helps to concentrate power in the hands of individuals backed by personal cliques, bringing back the potential for divisive politics to reverse the achievement of the redistribution system. The consequence of such factional politics was witnessed in the study community by the successive defections of prominent members of dominated social units that were unable to alter the balance of power in their favor.

The system of redistribution allows for the increase of the social base supporting broader cooperative units but, given its inherent limitations, it does not suffice to stabilize the large coalitions necessary for an *arigan* community to thrive. What could support such extensive cooperation? When presenting the practice of sacrificial feast, we mentioned an essential aspect of that form of resource transfer. It is performed in favor of *specific male groups*. We see later in this chapter that the Turkana age ranking and the organizational principle of seniority structuring the interaction of male groups explains how, despite the presence of strong dissolutive forces, large cooperative units are implemented and maintained when need arises.

GENERATION- AND AGE-SET SYSTEM

The Dualistic Reciprocal Nature of the Modern *Ngilukumong* System

The Paranilote classificatory generational system comprises two dimensions: generational rank and age distinction. The age and generational criteria are of great relevance for males' socio-political identity but much less so for females'. The generational ranking specifies where a given generation finds itself in the succession of classificatory generations since an original generation. The age distinction creates groups of male coevals ranked according to the criterion of seniority (junior vs. senior groups). The generations are divided into informal male age-sets until initiation. Upon initiation, a set has a name, a recognized corporate identity and acts as a constituted socio-political group.

Generational systems are complex dynamic classificatory systems that must adapt to demographic realities. A high fertility rate and fast population growth lead to under- and over-aging, that is, situations in which responsibilities associated to an individual's physiological age do not match the ones attached to that of his classificatory rank (i.e., his structural age). The Turkana system went through demographic changes leading to a progressive reinforcement of the age criterion and a disappearance of the generational ranking (for the transformation and the phenomenon of under- and over-aging, see Gulliver, 1958; Baxter and Almagor, 1978; Lamphear, 1989; Müller, 1989; Tornay, 1989). There are two names used alternately to designate the Turkana generations (*anaket*): Mountains and Leopards. A male child is born in the alternate classificatory generation to his biological father's[6]. Mountains engender Leopards and conversely. In the *Ngilukumong* territorial section there is no more

---

6. The generational distinction is relevant for men only, as females at their marriage join their husband's generation.

ranking of the generations. It is now a system of alternations more so than a succession of generations proper.

Each alternate generation has its uninterrupted list of names for the age-sets that constitute it. Age-mates can thus belong to competing age-sets simultaneously opened to recruitment (either Mountains or Leopards). By joining their respective alternation at birth, males enter a system organizing relations between senior and juniors and between classificatory "fathers" (the respective elders of one's alternation) and "sons" (all elders' juniors in that alternation). The distinction between biological and classificatory fatherhood introduced by the dual generational organization plays a role in facilitating the integration of the society beyond the limits of the familial groups and cliques.

Ideationally the classificatory fatherhood is important in public affairs: religious, ritual and political ones. Mountains or Leopards classificatory "sons" rely respectively on Mountains or Leopards classificatory "fathers" in ritual endeavors. "Sons" have to sacrifice and to serve their "fathers." "Fathers" bless their sons and intervene on their behalf (ritually, politically, and in public disputes). "Sons" owe political ritual obedience and support to their "fathers" and rely on their respective age-set apparatus to express themselves politically.

In such a dualistic system, biological fathers engage in reciprocal coaching of each other's sons. Beyond the strict realm of family affairs, for public purposes, fathers thus rely on external agents for controlling their biological sons. Such cross-cutting kin ties opens up the nepotistic familial cell to gains through the increasing size of cooperation networks. Furthermore, in a social world based on the fulfillment of such reciprocal services, extreme forms of behavior are less likely. Spite against, favoritism towards, or neglect of, youths is dampened. A father is too lax with his unruly biological son. The latter's classificatory "fathers" may sanction the disruption of public order. A group of classificatory "fathers" neglects their responsibility toward their "sons"; they invite retaliation in kind against their biological sons by the latter's classificatory "fathers."

The Age-set as a Self-policing and Socializing Unit

At a young age, Turkana boys start organizing informal groups while playing. Those social units regroup youths of similar age. The process of internal organization at work within those informal groups goes hand in hand with attempts by those units as bodies in constitution at achieving public recognition. The members of such groups use different means to that end: specific identifiers (names, adornments) and resounding feats (challenges, audacious actions, going to raid with older age-sets). With time, those units acquire for themselves various emblematic "character traits" or stereotypes: e.g., "the mischievous ones," "the ones of the brown gun (seized from the enemy)." Those nicknames are used interchangeably until initiation, when the original informal groups are properly split according to the Mountains-Leopards generational divide. The groups receive an initiation name that usually refers to characteristics of one of the sacrificial victims ("(Those of) the bull without horn" [*Ngilemaniko*]). From then on a favored appellation is used as main designator. Age-sets are then corporate groups with a collective identity that has been sanctioned through a set of regional initiations. The regional contingent of an age-set is typically dispersed wide apart in the various communities of a section. There are correspondences between the names of age-sets belonging to different sections that are known of members belonging to sections living close by, less so otherwise.

The types of solidarity born out of the age-set membership is orthogonal to the one fostered by family ties and cliques. Age-sets act as units in numerous life situations: in rituals, festive social gatherings, political or factional strife, and warfare. Individuals consistently rely on members of their age-sets for the enhancement of their social status, the recognition of their rights and their survival when engaged in hostilities. Age-mates expect help from each other to acquire animals for marriage payments. Local groups of fellow age-set members endeavor to woo girls in other camps. Those groups mutually challenge each other in collective dances lasting the whole night. Age-mates of uninitiated age groups and younger initiated age-sets are in charge of spying, reconnaissance and patrolling buffering areas between enemy territories and *arigan*. When enemy presence is detected, local warrior units (*ajore*), made of age set-based coherent sub-units, cordon off areas where herds graze to prevent any surprise attack. Local members of age-sets engage in raiding activities, the vast majority of which are of very small scale involving one or two dozen youngsters in search of animals to steal. Larger-scale raids involve regional groups of local members of age-sets led by members of older age-sets. Regional warrior units occasionally join other such units from different territorial sections in loose confederations of warriors when region-wide raids are launched against other tribes.

As individual reputation is closely tied to the reputation of his age-set, there is a strong incentive for age-mates to monitor each other's behavior to avoid harsh conflict, defection, betrayal, treachery and other forms of gross misbehavior that could impact everyone's reputation and the *esprit de corps*. Self-policing takes various forms: direct retaliation (i.e., fight) against the faulty member, temporary shunning, request for compensation, for sacrificial animals or other forms of commitment signals (e.g., gifts, money...). An age-set system indeed creates a reputation marketplace with very specific features. Groups of coevals, loyal and responsible toward one another, acquire a corporate identity. Each member is a standard-bearer of his age-set's collective identity. The reliance on other group members' behavior for one's reputation constitutes a strong incentive for mutual monitoring. Hence, investing in internal policing and detection of rule breakers, traitors and defectors holds it own reward for any member: avoiding public disgrace, reprobation or disapproval, which in turn could impact one's reputation and credibility.

In a system of corporate group interactions, external agents infer an individual's value based on the perceived "behavior" or "character" of the group to which that agent pertains (Dubreuil, 2010). Belonging to a group of people systematically misbehaving (and publically exposed!) while not engaging in any counterbalancing collective prowess deserving of public praise is inevitably costly even for its best-behaved members. However, self-policing does not fully guarantee that the age-set, as a unit, systematically adopts prosocial behaviors benefiting society.

Self-policing is primarily targeted at maintaining loyalty within the group. Local members of young age-sets engage regularly in reprehensible behaviors such as stealing small livestock in the herds of members of their camp. To understand how social order and extensive cooperation can be maintained in such conditions, the nature of the age-set system and its organizational principle, seniority, need to be investigated further.

The Age-set System as the Division of Power

The Turkana age-set system is seen to control and to limit power in social groups larger than families or cliques without requiring any costly third-party apparatus. It resolves in a very elegant way some of the typical problems of organization of sustained cooperation in collective actions: the cost of supplying and maintaining compliance institutions and the problem of committing agents to the maintenance of that compliance system (Ostrom, 1990). The seniority organizational principle allows for the ranking of groups of coevals in a hierarchical order. The information need for maintaining the whole system is minimal (information about age and age-set membership). It is easily generalizable and implementable in situations where collectivities of individuals not entirely acquainted interact (ease of scaling up or down). It is firmly grounded in a set of human intuitions and expectations. We suspect that older people have more experience, as they have lived longer. They usually have wider social networks and typically have access to greater resources than younger people, hence have more political clout.

The structure of the age-set system helps to maintain social order. A situation observed in the field will make us understand how it is so. Consider a pastoral unit located in rangelands near the Uganda border. Enemy settlements are nearby on the other side of a very steep escarpment (3 km/1.86 miles on a directional line). Small clashes with the enemy, constant back-and-forth stealing and stealthy incursions have lasted for some time now. The agglomeration of households is quite large. Despite the dangers, members of the camp are lulled into a false sense of security. With other young sets, an age group soon to be initiated is supposed to be in charge of daily monitoring areas of possible enemy penetration. But members of that uninitiated group have taken the habit of ditching their pastoral responsibilities to trek all the way to a location where they can buy locally distilled alcohol.

At first, besides the usual gossip and complaints, the matter does not reach a critical point until an infuriated older herdsman, father of one of the misbehaving youths, decides to ask for the help of members of an age-set (in their mid 30s). For securing their cooperation, the father invites the age-set to some sacrificial meat. A sanction is agreed upon: all members of the offending age-set will be lavishly whipped upon their return from the range the next day. After their ordeal, the age-mates are made to sacrifice an animal to the punishers as payback for the latter intercession. They will also "feed" the elders (of both alternations) of the camp as a way to express their contrition and for the reestablishment of ordinary peaceful relations. They will be assigned to supervised reconnaissance duties for some time.

On several occasions, the author witnessed similar sanctioning that took place when members of young age–sets were caught in the act of stealing livestock in herds of their own camp. Once again in all those occurrences of punishment, an individual or a group of herdsmen complain about disappearing animals. The age-set as a whole is harshly punished, must pay back animals as compensation, and feed their punishers and the elders. The process of sanctioning defectors, cheaters, thieves and other wrongdoers follows a typical sequence: First inflicting harm as a form of retaliation against wrongdoers, followed by indemnification of the wronged individual(s) or collectivity, then compensation offered to the set that took upon itself to inflict the punishment and, in most critical situations, eventually the offering of sacrificial meat to elders for making overall amends.

There are many other situations in which local members of age-sets mobilize to enforce collective decisions or norms and to extract collective benefits. As we have already mentioned, when a herdsman systematically dodges his collective responsibilities and duties (e.g., systematically failing to participate in the camp-wide system of sacrificial animal offering or feeding a group of raiders on the go or upon their return), a warrior party may decide to seize some of the herdsman's animals to sacrifice for themselves. When a collective decision is taken to send men to perform a dangerous mission (a retaliatory raid, for instance), the deputed age-sets in unison may decide to beg animals from herdsmen to feed on before leaving. They'll do the same upon their return. Alternatively an age-set may also request animals from some of their members or from other herdsmen to offer sacrificial meat to their elders to be blessed in return.

As those examples illustrate, the age-set system broadens the pool of motivations and incentives for enforcing collective decisions and norms, and maintaining some form of social order. By systematically altering the payoff structure of social dilemma situations, the system assures that there are always large contingents of agents having a direct interest in seeing the norm being followed and willing to incur the cost of monitoring and sanctioning, if need be. The seniority principle helps in the organization of groups beyond the local level by providing a ready-made structure of enforcement based on the major criterion of age. Furthermore, the systematic payment of compensation to all parties eliminates the risk of ever being in situations of second-order social dilemma, as the incentive to punish wrongdoers is kept strong (Shinada & Yamagishi, 2010). Motivation to punish never gets expended. The way the sanctioning is decided upon and implemented by coalitions of age-sets reduces the risk of division into small factions. The process of reparation through collective feats and public amends make the community whole once again instead of alienating social groups.

Given how the male social political system is structured, it is not difficult to find people eager to invest in its maintenance. Older individuals have a direct stake in seeing the younger ones behaving appropriately in the system (as that behavior supports their present-day position). Any individual infraction is a direct threat to anybody above him (as much as to his coevals, see previously), as it threatens the whole system in which individuals' privileges and social base are grounded. Indeed, in situations where norm infractions take place, the age-set system transforms all males into potential second-parties. It is thus easy for older groups of coevals to muster enough support to enforce the norms. Furthermore, as we have seen, the Turkana age-set system has refined its capacity to incentivize all agents present into monitoring and sanctioning rule- and norm-breakers through a policy of systematic reparation payments.

In such conditions we might expect abuse to be the norm, creating an *absolutist* gerontocracy. Younger men entering the age-set systems would suffer years of abuse. In a certain sense, age-set systems *are* inherently biased toward older people and younger people *do* have to suffer some exploitation until they are old enough to resist more forcefully their elders' demand. As seen previously, in the Turkana system, that inherent bias is countered by two organizational principles: the dualistic generational division implying a distinction between biological and classificatory fathers, and the splitting of the male population into *many* distinct corporate groups. The fact that the male population is divided into many distinct groups having reciprocal duties and rights makes it necessary to reach some form of consensus when important decisions have to be made. As older age-sets can coalesce to sanction younger ones, younger age-sets can also, to a point, coalesce to resist the pressures from above. Such a situation is more likely to happen when a limited number of people attempt to enforce extreme and abusive decisions. Unfair decisions to punish an age-set for a crime none of its members has committed can be systematically resisted by adopting a common front and pleading collectively that the decision be reconsidered.

Social Retaliation and Punishment in Turkana Society

In light of the recent debates evoked by Guala (2012), we may wonder how widespread punishment is beyond the familial sphere in the Turkana society. Furthermore, we should also wonder if some of the most common sanctions we observe in the Turkana social world can be considered as real punishment, involving aspects of both retributive and restorative justices.

Occasional and unexceptional breaches of collective norms do not ever seem to evoke strong reactions. There is indeed a great general tolerance for irregular uncouthness, pettiness and other forms of selfish or uncooperative behaviors of small to moderate magnitude (e.g., refusing to acknowledge a request for help, neglecting one's duty to the pastoral community, not sharing a resource when being begged). One might retaliate in gossiping about how selfish or careless such an individual has been in such an instance, decide to divert for a time one's social investment away from the misbehaving agents, or express one's frustration directly to the wrongdoer. Most of the time, however, those occasional uncooperative or selfish behaviors are appraised for what they are: unavoidable awkward moments and frustrations of ordinary, at times claustrophobic, camp life.

In order to raise some form of significant discontent and to trigger a reaction, the behavior needs to be repetitive, hence reaching a certain threshold of unacceptability. In extreme situations, the conflict can escalate into actual fighting and dueling. In most cases, gossip, mockery and public obloquy are the typical slow-pace, low-cost strategies relied upon to build a consensus and muster enough support to eventually retaliate against the systematic wrongdoers. The retaliation is just that, a social retaliation involving cliques, clienteles, and factions. The strike is a show of power and an attempt to reassert dominance and control. The objective is to threaten, to inflict a cost in relation to how dire the harm inflicted is perceived to be and eventually to deter an agent from misbehaving again. The aggression is not conceived of as punishment and it does not involve parties unlikely to extract some form of benefit from the participation. Engaging in retaliation without appropriate backing and sufficient reasons can be costly in terms of social interaction and reputation within the restricted social world of a camp. If not directly affected by the wrongdoing or belonging to a coalition party to the conflict, people typically abstain from intervening. This does not expose them to retaliation on the part of the factions in conflict. That absence of sanction of social agents who do not participate in such factional sanctions is striking in the Turkana social world. Even in situations where low-cost strategies such as shunning, opprobrium or scorn are adopted by members of the community against someone, people who would breach the social blockade to interact with the discredited individual do not seem to expose themselves to an automatic retaliation (using the same low-cost strategies).

The concept of punishment can more meaningfully be applied to the model of collective sanctioning occurring in the context of the generation- and age-set system. The sanctions are focused on the fact that norms were breached. In its most dramatic expression, the punishment involves flogging. It is more likely to be a collective (i.e., a group of coevals) than an individual sanction, even if sometimes it means that innocents are punished along with wrongdoers. The punished ones must endure the harrowing experience without retaliating. The punishers get compensated for their intervention. Integral parts of the sanctions, such as additional payments to a collectivity of individuals, such as elders, are aimed at reasserting the proper ordering of the generation- and age-set institution. Corrective actions and making public amends are essential aspects of the whole process.

If in the context of the age-set system the punishment is institutionalized, it does not mean that it is widespread. Who is in charge of deciding that a punishment needs to be applied? Age-sets can belong to one of four main age categories: (1) unmarried youngsters typically in charge of protecting herds, reconnaissance and raiding activities (in their late teens and 20s), (2) family men increasingly focusing on pastoral duties (30s and 40s), (3) established middle-age men controlling the political decision-making power (50s and 60s) and (4) elders, in charge of the politico-religious activities, and maintenance of collective values. The group of elders is the keystone of the whole age-set system, with ultimate decisional power in a situation of irredeemable conflict. They have the capacity to order, to sanction, or to oppose punishment. Elders typically participate in the negotiations aimed at establishing the amount of the compensations to be paid to the prejudiced parties.

To whom and when is the punishment more likely to be administered? In more than a decade of acquaintance with the Turkana society, the author has only heard of or directly witnessed punishments administered to groups of unmarried youngsters or young males in their early 30s. The Turkana generation-and age-set system indeed seems to be in existence primarily to contain the unruly young males, most of them unmarried yet not fully socialized and periodically engaged in violent raiding activities against enemy communities. The typical reasons for the punishment to occur were linked to a lack of care in the performance of the ordinary duties of that age category such as, among other things, protecting the grazing herds, cordoning off the rangelands, patrolling areas bordering enemy territories, providing succor when a raid occurs, or scouting for fresh grass and water.

CONCLUSIONS

Given the extreme environmental, economic and social constraints prevailing in the study area, the organization of extensive cooperation in the traditional Turkana tribal society presents significant challenges. The society is highly fragmented into small regional groups of autonomous social units. The large agglomeration of households is naturally made complex, given how the scarce pastoral resources are distributed in the environment. Fast adaptation is key to success, making it hard for very large groups to be as responsive as smaller highly mobile and fissile units. However, despite the inherent problems of resource competition and depletion that large agglomerations of people create in the Turkana ecology, households must assemble in large, safer social units when moving closer to the perimeter of the homeland, in the proximity of enemy territories.

In this contribution, I presented the institutional mechanisms supporting a large cooperative ensemble built from basic independent units without reliance on a system of third-party institutions. I have shown how larger supra-local units could be created from the building blocks of corporate groups of progressively increasing magnitudes. The complex process involved tradeoffs (e.g., power for resource, status for payment, independence for safety) that individual and corporate groups had to weigh carefully at every level of increased nesting into larger units. Several institutional mechanisms facilitated different forms of coalitional principles (clientele, seniority), allowing for the increase in size of the basic cooperative units. At times those mechanisms pulled the coalitional forces in orthogonal or opposite ways. In the Turkana social system, the age-sets are mobilization devices coordinating groups of coevals. By altering the individuals' incentive structure, the seniority principle supporting the age ranking systematically broadens the pool of social agents directly interested in monitoring and policing others, enabling the creation of a cheap generalized second-party sanctioning system, eventually allowing for greater social ensemble to be maintained periodically when need arises.

Acephalous tribal societies present interesting situations for investigating the emergence of complex systems of cooperation without easy norm enforcement based on third-party institutions, as we find them in nation-states. Decentralized tribal ensembles, although typically composed of smaller economically autonomous entities, are not just collections of smaller band-like units. They have moved away from a strictly egalitarian social world but do not rely on hierarchies of permanent political offices to maintain social order. Their social world is populated by competing agents freely associating and cooperating with one another while social control is still diffuse and not systematically organized. The cost of monitoring and sanctioning deviance is kept low thanks to particular strategies and institutions. The general structuration of such decentralized tribes rests on the nesting of corporate groups with different interests and objectives—at times converging, and eventually leading to the periodic creation of larger purpose-built groups. In our case study, the institutional buildup grounded in strong intuitions about seniority and coevality seem to be sufficient to sustain the creation of a very complex and extended social system.

ACKNOWLEDGEMENTS

The author wishes to thank Paul Lomosingo for his assistance in the field and the National Museums of Kenya, Nairobi, Kenya, for facilitating the research.

REFERENCES

Baxter, P. T. W., & Almagor, U. E. (1978). *Age, generation, and time: some features of East African age organisations*. New York: St. Martin's Press.

Boyd, R., & Richerson, P. (1992). Punishment allows the evolution of cooperation (or anything else) in sizeable groups. *Ethology and Sociobiology*, 13, 171–195.

Cosmides, L., & Tooby, J. (2005). Neurocognitive adaptations designed for social exchange. In D. M. Buss (Ed.), *Handbook of evolutionary psychology* (pp. 584–627). Hoboken, NJ: Wiley.

Dubreuil, B. (2010). *Human Evolution and the Origins of Hierarchies: The State of Nature*. New York, NY: Cambridge University Press.

Fehr, E., Fischbacher, U., & Gächter, S. (2002). Strong Reciprocity, Human Cooperation and the Enforcement of Social Norms. *Human Nature*, 13, 1–25.

Gintis, H. (2000). Strong reciprocity and human sociality. *Journal of Theoretical Biology*, 2006, 169–179.

Guala, F. (2012). Reciprocity: Weak or strong? What punishment experiments do (and do not) demonstrate. *Behavioral and Brain Sciences*, 35(1), 1–15.

Gulliver, P. H. (1951). *A Preliminary Survey of the Turkana* (New Series, no. 26). Cape Town: Commonwealth School of African Studies.

Gulliver, P. H. (1958). "The Turkana Age Organisation." *American Anthropologist*, 60(5), 900–922.

Lamphear, J. (1976). *The Traditional History of the Jie of Uganda*, Oxford: Clarendon Press.

Lamphear, J. (1988). "The People of the Grey Bull: the Origin and Expansion of the Turkana." in *Journal of African History*, 29, 27–39.

Lamphear, J. (1989). Historical Dimensions of Dual Organization: The Generation-Class System of the Jie and the Turkana. In D. Maybury-Lewis & U. Almagor (Eds.), *The Attraction of Opposites: Thought and Society in the Dualistic Mode* (pp. 235–254). Ann Arbor, MI: University of Michigan Press.

Lamphear, J. (1992). *The Scattering Time: Turkana Responses to Colonial Rule*. (Oxford Studies in African Affairs, XXIII, 308pp.). Oxford: Clarendon Press.

Lamphear, J. (1993). Aspects of 'Becoming Turkana': Interactions & Assimilation Between Maa- & Ateker-Speaker. In T. T. Spear & R. Waller (Eds.), *Being Maasai: Ethnicity & Identity in East Africa* (pp. 87–104). London: J. Currey; Dar es Salaam: Mkuki na Nyota; Nairobi: EAEP; Athens: Ohio University Press.

Lienard, P., & Anselmo, F. (2004). The social construction of emotions: gratification and gratitude among the Turkana and Nyangatom of East Africa. In S. Van Wolputte & G. Verswijver (Eds.), *At the Fringes of Modernity. People, Cattle, Transitions*. (African Pastoralists Studies 2, pp. 150–198, photographs). Tervuren: RMCA.

Marlowe, F. (2009). Hadza Cooperation: Second-Party Punishment, Yes; Third-Party Punishment, No. *Human Nature, 20*, 417–430.

Müller, H. K. (1989). *Changing Generations: Dynamics of Generation and Age-Sets in Southeastern Sudan (Toposa) and Northwestern Kenya (Turkana)*. Saarbrücken, Fort Lauderdale: Verlag Breitenbach Publishers.

Mkutu, K. A. (2008). *Guns and Governance in the Rift Valley; Pastoralist Conflict and Small Arms*. Oxford: James Currey; Bloomington & Indianapolis: Indiana University Press.

Olson, M. (1965). *The Logic of Collective Action: Public Goods and the Theory of Groups*. Cambridge University Press.

Ostrom, E. (1990). *Governing the Commons: The Evolution of Institutions for Collective Action*. Cambridge University Press.

Patton, J. Q. (2000). Reciprocal altruism and warfare: a case from the Ecuadorian Amazon. In L. Cronk, N. A. Chagnon & W. Irons, (Eds.), *Adaptation and human behavior: an anthropological perspective* (pp. 417–436). Aldine de Gruyter.

Price, M. E., Cosmides, L., & Tooby, J. (2002). Punitive sentiment as an anti-free rider psychological device. *Evolution and Human Behavior, 23*, 203–231.

Rege J. E. O., Kahi A. K., Okomo-Adhiambo, M., Mwacharo, J., & Hanotte, O. (2001). *Zebu cattle of Kenya: Uses, performance, farmer preferences, measures of genetic diversity and options for improved use* (Animal Genetic Resources Research 1, 103 pp.). Nairobi, Kenya: ILRI (International Livestock Research Institute).

Shinada, M., & Yamagishi, T. (2010). Bringing back Leviathan into Social Dilemmas. In A. Biel, D. Eek, T. Garling & M. Gustafsson (Eds.), *New Issues and Paradigms in Research on Social Dilemmas*. NY: Springer Science.

Tornay, S. (1989). *Un système générationnel: les Nyangatom de l'Éthiopie du sud-ouest et les peuples apparentés*, thèse présentée en vue du grade de *docteur ès letters*.

Yamagishi, T. (1986). The provision of a sanctioning system as a public goods problem. *Journal of Personality and Social Psychology, 50*, 67–73.

Yamagishi, T. (1988). The provision of a sanctioning system in the United States and Japan. *Social Psychology Quaterly, 51*, 265–271.

INDEX

adakar (grazing unit), 218–219
adolescence
    bargaining and, 172
    brain development, 163–164
    cognitive and social development of, 161–163
    cognitive control, 166, 176
    decision-making studies, 176
    developmental phase, 161
    dictator game and, 165
    fairness considerations, development of, 164–168
    hidden ultimatum game, 167–168
    Mini-UG (ultimatum game), 166–167
    perspective-taking, 162
    punishment behavior, 173–175
    risk-taking, 162
    social exclusion and, 174
    social rejection and, 162
    standard ultimatum game, 165–166
    trust, learning to, 173
affective node, 164
age, effects on cooperation, 78
age distinction, 225
age-set system
    bias toward older people in, 230
    as division of power, 228–230
    membership, 227
    motivations and incentives, 229
    reputation in, 227
    sanctioning in, 228–229
    self-policing, 226–228
    structure of, 228
aggression, 44, 231
altruism, 37, 44
altruistic punishment. *See also* counter-punishment
    cost/benefit of, 204–205
    in daily life, 207–209
    definition, 198, 208
    early studies of, 199
    efficiency of, 202–203
    to increase cooperation, 197
    inferior good and, 200
    noncooperators and, 76, 128–129
    robust findings about, 199–202
    sanctions and, 121
    in stochastic social dilemmas, 206
anger, 78, 121
anti-social punishment, 23, 37, 91, 99–100
apese a ngabwes (girl of the skirt), 221
awi (social unit), 222

bad reputation. *See* reputation
bargaining, 172
biased inequity aversion model, 20
brain development in adolescents, 163–164
Brave Leader game, 189

centralized incentive systems
    central monitors and, 92
    decentralized incentives vs., 94–103
    disadvantages of, 92–93
    peer-to-peer punishment, 91
    second-order punishment, 91–92
    with team leader, 93
centralized sanctions, 71, 75
central monitors, 92, 104
cheating, 55
cognitive-regulatory node, 164
collective control, 5–6
collectively managed punishment, 61–62, 65, 191
collective sanctions, 125–126, 128, 231–232
communication as tool for cooperation, 40
concubines, 221
cooperation
    age and effects on, 78
    altruistic punishment to promote, 76, 121, 128–129, 189–190, 197
    changes in, 78
    communication as tool for, 40
    costs of, 190–191
    direct effect on, 117

235

cooperation (*Cont.*)
 effectiveness of incentives, 42
 effects of age on, 78
 efficiency vs., 202–203
 emotions as motive to, 210
 fee-to-fine ratio, 200–201
 functions of, 183
 higher-order punishment and, 25
 human, 214
 incentives to promote, 88–95
 index of, 3
 indirect effect on, 117
 motivational approach to, 116
 promoting, 4
 psychology of, 72–73
 punishment effects on, 20–21
 ruptured, 173
 sanctions and, 75–80, 116–119, 122–127
 self-interest and, 42
 structural approach to, 116
 sustainable, 122–127, 200–201
costly punishment, 6–8, 40, 46, 208. *See also* altruistic punishment
counter-punishment, 24, 201–202, 206
Cuban Liberty and Democratic Solidarity Act of 1996, 186–187
Cyberball (game), 174

Dawes, Robyn, 1
decentralized incentives
 centralized incentives vs., 94–103
 peer-to-peer punishment, 89–91
decentralized sanctions, 71, 123
detection node, 164
dictator game, 55, 121, 165
disgust, 168
DLPFC (dorsolateral prefrontal cortex), 168
"do-no-harm" principle, 76, 79, 80
dorsolateral prefrontal cortex (DLPFC), 168
Dragon-Slayer game, 189

economics, 118–119
efficiency
 cooperation vs., 202–203
 definition, 202
 fee-to-fine ratio and, 203–204
 measuring, 142
 normative conflict and, 206–207
 uncertainty and, 207
egalitarianism, 38
emotion-inducing system, 163
emotion-regulating system, 163
emotions
 anger, 78, 121
 disgust, 168
 to injustice, 121
 "levels of analysis" and, 184
 moral, 72
 negative, 7
 norm violations and, 208–209
 rewards driven by, 78–79
 role of, 210
 to trigger punishment, 188–189
endogenous leadership, 135–136
evolutionary theory, 34, 35

fairness considerations
 development of, 164–168
 neural substrates of, 168–169
fee-to-fine ratio, 200–201, 203–204
financial sanctions, 71–72
formal sanctions, 28–29
free-riders, 7, 39

generational systems, 225–226
Goal/Expectation Theory, 117, 124, 125
gossip, 230
groups
 causes and consequences of members in, 142–145
 cooperation and, 9, 88–95

Hardin, Gerret, 5–6
Helms-Burton Act (1996), 186–187
Hero game, 189
hidden ultimatum game, 167–168
higher-order punishment, 24–25
horizon punishment, 204–205
human cooperation, 214

incentives
 in age-set system, 229
 centralized systems to administer, 92–93

Index

decentralized systems, 87, 89–91
  of defecting, 117
  effectiveness of, 36
  to promote cooperation, 88–95
  public good games study, 88–89
  self-interest vs. collective interest, 36
  as solution to social dilemmas, 34–35
"incentive to discipline," 103–104
Index of Cooperation, 3
indirect reciprocity, 127
inefficient equilibrium, 1–2
inequity aversion, 22
informal sanctions, 27, 28–29
insula, 168
interdependence theory
  conflicting interests and, 41–43
  definition, 35–36
  given matrix thesis, 36–37
  information availability, 45–46
  lab/field discrepancy in, 45–46
  perceived transformation of motivation, 39–41, 44
  self-interest vs. collective interest, 37–38
  symmetrical dependency, 46
  temporal structure and, 43–44, 45
  transformation of motivation thesis, 37–38
  trust and, 37
interpersonal trust, 72–73

just desserts perspective, 120–121, 127, 128–129

leadership
  definition, 133–134
  in economic terms, 134
  effects of, in public good games experiment, 149–150
  endogenous, 135–136
  rewards vs. punishment, 135
  sequential contributions in, 134, 136
  voluntary, in public good games experiment, 146–149, 151–152
legitimacy, 56
long-term sanctioning system, 126–127

maximizing difference game, 42
McCarthy, Joseph, 186–187

medial PFC, 170
Mini-UG (ultimatum game), 166–167
monetary sanctions, 117–119
moral emotions, 72, 122, 128–129
motivations
  in age-set system, 229
  altruistic punishment perspective, 121
  direct, 72
  in economic terms, 118–119
  egalitarianism, 38
  indirect, 72–73
  interdependence theory and, 37–38
  joint gain, 38
  just desserts perspective, 120–121
  long-term, 119–122
  moral emotion perspective, 122
  of pro-social punisher, 19–20, 47
  for punishment, 18
  sanctions and, 81
  self-interest, 119
  short-term cooperation and, 118
  towards cooperation, 8
"mutual coercion mutually agreed-upon," 123
mutualist society, 219

negative reciprocity, 20, 22. *See also* reciprocity
neuroscience perspective, 121, 163–164, 168–169, 176–177
Ngilukumong system, 225–226
normative conflict, 206–207
normative rule, 206
norms. *See* social norms

one-shot dilemmas, 43
outcomes
  collective, 38
  reward and punishment as part of, 3–4

Paranilote classificatory generational system, 225
pastoral camps, 215–216
payoff structure, 4
peer pressure, 27–28
peer punishment, 6, 39, 89, 91, 174, 185, 210
peer-to-peer incentives, 89–91

peer-to-peer sanctions, 30
penalty sanctions, 117
perceived legitimacy, 56
perspective-taking, 162
perverse punishment, 23, 91
polygyny, 221
positive reciprocity, 20, 170. *See also* reciprocity
power and leadership, 9–10
prisoner's dilemma, 2, 3, 189
prisoner's dilemma game, 42, 125–126, 168
privatization, 5
Producer-Scrounger game, 189
proselfs, 78
prosocials, 78
puberty, 161
public good
  challenges to, 4–5
  contributing to, 183
  definition, 183
public good dilemma, 7, 47
public good games
  centralized vs. decentralized incentives and, 95–103
  decentralized incentives, 89–91
  experiment (*see* public good games experiment)
  incentives to promote cooperation in, 88–95
  sequential contributions in, 134, 136
  voluntary contribution mechanism and, 18–20
public good games experiment
  basics of, 136
  effects of, 139–150
  experimental treatments, 137–138
  procedures, 138–139
  results of, 151–152
public recognition, 124
punishing behavior, 173–175
punishment. *See also* reward and punishment
  after social exclusion, 173–175
  altruistic, 76
  among group members, 6–8
  anti-social, 23, 91, 99–100
  cheating and, 55
  collective, 61–62, 65, 191, 231–232
  compensation and, 173

  costly, 6–8, 40
  as a costly signal, 188–189
  counter, 24
  counter-punish, 186
  cross-societal variations, 23–24
  developmental differences in, 173–175
  dictator game, 55, 121
  effectiveness of, 7–8, 21–22
  fee-to-fine ratio, 200–201, 203
  free-riders and, 7
  higher-order, 24–25
  horizon, 204–205
  incentive structure to, 189–190
  and its effects on cooperation, 20–21
  laws about, 64
  misdirected, 23
  motivations for, 18
  in noisy settings, 80
  non-monetary, 123–125
  non-strategic, 22
  peer, 6, 89
  perverse, 23, 91
  in political domains, 186–187
  prescriptive rules around, 53–55
  in a public goods game, 54–55
  reciprocity and, 20
  reluctance to, 79–80
  restrictive rules and, 55–56, 58–60
  sanction-free vs. sanction-permitting environment, 26–27
  second order, 24–25, 53, 91–92, 185–186
  self organization through, 6
  social retaliation and, 230–232
  third party, 55, 121
  triggered by emotions, 188–189
  trust and, 7–8
  uncertainty and, 207
  voluntary punishers and, 54, 60–61, 65
  as a Volunteer's Dilemma, 189–190
punishment incentives
  centralized, 91–95
  decentralized, 89–91
punishment rights, 56, 57–58

random income game, 38
rational choice theory, 34
received economic theory, 19

reciprocity, 20, 35, 127, 169–170, 183, 187–188
reinforcement-based learning, 190
rejection, 168
reputation, 8, 124, 126–127, 192, 227
resource dilemma, 7
retaliation, 24, 42–43, 230–232
retribution, 77
reward and punishment. *See also* punishment
  centralized, 91–95
  as collective sanctioning systems, 4–6
  costs of, 190–191
  decentralized incentives, 89–91
  effect on behavior, 36
  emotions and, 78–79
  meaning of, 2
  and motives in social dilemma decision making, 8–9
  non-monetary sanctions and, 123–125
  outcomes of, 3–4
  psychological response to, 37
  reciprocity and, 187–188
  reinforcement-based learning, 190
  sanction-free vs. sanction-permitting environment, 26–27
  sanctioning systems and, 2–3, 123–125
reward sanctions, 117
rights, punishment, 56

sanctioning systems
  decentralized, 9–10
  long-term, 126
  reward and punishment as, 4–6
sanctions
  in age-set system, 228–229
  alternative type of, 28
  altruistic punishment and, 76
  altruistic punishment perspective, 121
  centralized, 71, 75
  collective, 125–126, 231–232
  consequences of, 71–75
  cooperation and, 75–80, 116–119, 122–127
  decentralized, 71, 123
  drawbacks of, 73–74
  effects of, 80–81
  emotional basis of, 77–78
  evasion of, 73–74
  financial, 71–72
  ineffective, 70
  influence on cooperation, 72–73
  informal, 27, 56–62
  informal vs. formal, 28–29
  just desserts perspective, 120–121
  long-term motivations and, 119–122
  long-term outcomes, 126–127
  monetary, 117–119, 127–128
  moral emotions and, 72, 122
  non-monetary, 123–125
  peer-to-peer behaviors in, 185–190
  penalty, 117
  retribution and, 77
  reward, 117
  role of, 116–117
  size of, 74–75
  social, 27
  structural approach to, 127–128
  in the workplace, 71–72
second order public good, 5
second order punishment, 24–25, 91–92, 185–186, 191
second order rewards, 187–188
second-order social dilemma, 5
self-control, 5
self-governance, 87
self-interest
  vs. collective interest, 36, 37–38, 47
  in hidden ultimatum game, 167–168
  sanctions and, 119
  social interdependence and, 41–42
self-organization through punishment, 6
self-policing, 226–228
"shadow of the future" phenomenon, 126
shared resources, 5
Snowdrift game, 189
social dilemmas
  challenges to, 4–5
  definition, 1–2, 53, 151
  with distinguishable roles, 63–64
  incentives as solution to, 34–35
  informal sanctions in, 56–62
  with no distinguishable roles, 64–65
  punishment rights, 56, 57–58
  second-order, 5, 53
  use of rewards, limitations to, 90

social exclusion, 174
social information processing network (SIPN) model, 163–164
social interactions
    lab/field discrepancy of, 45–46
    one-shot, 172
    repeated, 172, 175–176
    variations in, 43
social justice, 120–121
social norms
    breaking, 64
    definition, 52
    with distinguishable roles, 63–64
    informal sanctions and, 56–62
    prescriptive rules and, 53–55
    punishment for violations, 64
    restrictive rules, 55–56, 58–60
    violations, 208–209
social rejection, 162
social retaliation. *See* retaliation
social sanctions, 27
social value orientations, 78
standard economic theory, 19, 87
standard ultimatum game (UG), 165–166
Stop Signal Task, 166
strong reciprocity, 9

Tang Code, 64
third party punishment, 55, 121, 174
trust
    in adolescents, 173
    in authorities, 75
    development of, 37
    effectiveness of punishment and, 7–8
    interpersonal, 72–73
    learning to, 173
    neuroscientific studies and, 170–172
    reciprocity and, 169–170
Trust Game (TG), 169–170
Turkana County
    age distinction, 225
    age-set system (*see* age-set system)
    camp memberships, 224
    collective duty of men in, 224
    cooperative units, size of, 222–225
    ecology of, 214–216
    familial units in, 220–222
    generational systems, 225–226
    geography of, 218
    grazing unit, 218–219
    households, 220–221
    intra-family competition, 221–222
    matrimonial alliances, 221
    pastoral camps, 215–216
    polygyny, 221
    sacrificial feasts, 222–223
    social interactions in, 219–220
    territorial sections of, 216–220
    tribal integration, 222

verbal rewards, 188
voluntary contribution mechanism, 18–20, 21–22, 28–29
voluntary leadership, 151–152, 153
voluntary punishers, 54, 60–61, 65
Volunteer's Dilemma, 182, 189–190
voting, 27, 30

workplace sanctions, 71–72